The *Philosophy* of *Josiah Royce*

ISBN 0–915145–41–3

Previously published by
T. Y. Crowell Company as ISBN 0–690–61839–5

THE

PHILOSOPHY

OF

Josiah Royce

Edited and with an Introduction by *John K. Roth*

HACKETT PUBLISHING COMPANY

Indianapolis / Cambridge

JOSIAH ROYCE: 1855–1916

Printed in the United States of America
First printing

Cover design by Richard L. Listenberger

For further information, please address
Hackett Publishing Company, Inc.
P.O. Box 55573
Indianapolis, IN 46205

Library of Congress Cataloging in Publication Data
Royce, Josiah, 1855–1916.
The Philosophy of Josiah Royce.

Reprint. Originally published: New York: Crowell,
1971.
Bibliography: p.
Includes index.
1. Philosophy — Addresses, essays, lectures.
2. Religion — Philosophy — Addresses, essays, lectures.
3. Ethics — Addresses, essays, lectures. I. Roth, John K.
II. Title.
B945.R61   1982   191   82-2932
ISBN 0–915145–42–1   AACR2
ISBN 0–915145–41–3 (pbk.)

PREFACE

One of Josiah Royce's most important ideas is that the positive achievements of any individual depend largely on help and support received from others. This insight came to life with new vitality as I prepared this book for publication. Many people and institutions have aided my work, and the following deserve special thanks.

First, I am grateful to my students at Claremont Men's College. Their response to my teaching of Royce convinced me that it would be useful to bring a cross section of his major writings together in a single volume that would be easily available to undergraduates. Mr. Leslie Rowe of the Thomas Y. Crowell Company and Apollo Editions supported my suggestion, and his efforts made publication possible.

Financial support and time to work on the project were provided by (1) an Arnold L. Graves and Lois S. Graves Award in the Humanities, administered by Pomona College under auspices of the American Council of Learned Societies, (2) a summer grant from The Henry Salvatori Center for the Study of Individual Freedom in the Modern World, and (3) a research grant and a leave of absence from Claremont Men's College. This generosity enabled me to spend the 1970–71 academic year at Harvard University. Royce's papers are there, and I am grateful for the cooperation I received from the staff of the Widener and Houghton Libraries, especially that of Mr. Charles Montalbano, Supervisor of the Widener Stack.

Thanks are also due to Professor Herbert W. Schneider and his son Edward, who were kind enough to invite me and my family to spend a month on their picturesque farm at Peacham, Vermont, during the summer of 1970. Most of the introduction to this book was written there. Finally my wife and son, Lynn and Andy, gave me the love and encouragement that only a family can provide. Without them, life would lose much of its richness.

Claremont Men's College
Claremont, California

CONTENTS

vii

PART IV

SELECTIONS FROM *The Problem of Christianity*
AND *The Hope of the Great Community*

INTRODUCTION

by John K. Roth

The Relation of Josiah Royce to Current American Problems and Contemporary Philosophy

The name of Josiah Royce is hardly a household word in America today. Apart from a small circle of teachers and students with special interests in the intellectual history of our country, few contemporary Americans will have heard of Royce, let alone understand his importance in our past and his relevance for the present and the future. It is not difficult to see why this is the case. First, there is little in an account of Royce's life that will prompt widespread interest. His biography has its unusual aspects, but in many ways it is a typical American story. Born in Grass Valley, California, on November 20, 1855, to parents who had been lured west by gold, Royce's early years were spent in the atmosphere of a mining town. His first schooling came from his mother and older sisters. In addition to being timid, Royce describes himself as a boy who was "redheaded, freckled, countrified, quaint, and unable to play boys' games." [1] These factors made it difficult for him to adjust to life in a large grammar school when his family moved to San Francisco in 1866.

In 1871, Royce entered the University of California at Berkeley. His record was distinguished, and after his graduation in 1875, a group of local businessmen provided funds which enabled him to study in Germany for a year. Although Royce notes that there was no formal philosophy course at the University of California during his student years, he had read philosophy on his own, especially the works of Spencer and Mill, and had developed deep philosophical interests while an undergraduate. Thus, Royce used his year in Germany to further his philosophical studies, concentrating on Schopenhauer and Schelling in addition to following closely the lectures given by Lotze at Göttingen.

[1] Josiah Royce, "Words of Professor Royce at the Walton Hotel at Philadelphia, December 29, 1915," *The Hope of the Great Community* (New York: The Macmillan Company, 1916), p. 126.

Returning to the United States in 1876, Royce enrolled as a graduate student at Johns Hopkins University. During that year he became acquainted with William James, who came to Johns Hopkins as a visiting professor from Harvard University. The friendship started at Johns Hopkins deepened and lasted for many years. Moreover, the relationship between these two long-time colleagues is one of the most interesting aspects of American intellectual history. Although Royce and James had profound philosophical differences, they were always loyal and helpful to each other. One of the early instances of the latter fact occurred in 1882 when, largely because of James's influence, Royce received an invitation to come to Harvard as an instructor. Since receiving his Ph.D. at Johns Hopkins, Royce had been teaching at the University of California, but his appointment mainly entailed teaching freshman English, and he longed for the chance to work in an environment that would provide more opportunity to teach philosophy. Thus, although the initial Harvard offer was for one year only, Royce moved his family to Cambridge.

Once at Harvard, his work was well received, and arrangements were made for him to stay on. In 1885 he published his first major book, *The Religious Aspect of Philosophy*, and was made Assistant Professor of Philosophy. Royce remained at Harvard for the rest of his life, becoming Professor of the History of Philosophy in 1892. When he died at Cambridge on September 14, 1916, Royce left behind a reputation as an outstanding teacher and a prolific writer. In addition to *The Religious Aspect of Philosophy*, his most important works include *The Spirit of Modern Philosophy* (1892), *Studies of Good and Evil* (1898), *The World and the Individual* (1899, 1901), which consists of Royce's Gifford Lectures, *The Philosophy of Loyalty* (1908), *The Sources of Religious Insight* (1912), *The Problem of Christianity* (1913), and *The Hope of the Great Community* (1916).

These facts add up to a life and career of great distinction, but they are hardly sufficient in themselves to keep Royce at the center of our attention. Moreover, when it is noted that his philosophy, *absolute idealism*, is not much in vogue today, there may seem to be few reasons for not allowing the dead—both the man and his philosophy—to rest in peace. There is, however, solid justification for attempting to win a new hearing for Royce. We may begin to see why this is true by considering some characteristics of our present situation and the relation they bear to his philosophy.

Although our age may be characterized less by the traditional philosophical virtues of quiet reflection, dispassionate debate, and rigorous logical analysis than by social and political activism, emotionally charged protest, and appeals to gut-level feelings and intuitions, there is still a sense in which our times are profoundly philosophical. We live in an age of crisis, and our precarious circumstances raise important philosophical issues. Our ecological problems, our deep divisions over foreign involvements and race relations, our turmoil over the role and responsibility of educational institutions in our land, and the general uncertainty that we reveal concerning our pursuit of moral values and religious ideals are in themselves forms of philosophical questioning and searching. In fact, we need not push our investigation of these contemporary problems very far before we find that we raise the most basic philosophical questions: What is the nature of existence, and what meaning can or should we find in life.

It is precisely at this point that we can first begin to see Royce's relevance, for no philosopher in America or elsewhere has ever been more direct or persistent in focusing and attempting to answer these fundamental questions. Because we find ourselves confronted at every turn, either directly or indirectly, by the problem of the nature and meaning of existence, we will do well to learn what Royce's life-long study of these issues led him to conclude.

At this point, an additional factor about our contemporary life can be brought out with illuminating results. If our times are philosophical in the sense described above, we also find ourselves rebelling against the past. In particular, we are rarely satisfied with either the analyses or the conclusions that previous philosophers have developed. If we could simply agree on some past philosophical view, the divisions among us might be less radical. But we are not inclined in this direction. Not only do we lack a common philosophical framework, but we are also little disposed to believe that the past can give us the inspiration and unity that we need. How, then, do these facts fit with the suggestion that Royce has something important to give us?

First, it must be acknowledged that our rebellion against the philosophical past is not altogether out of place. Philosophers are finite and fallible. They make mistakes—factual, logical, and speculative. Moreover, the needs and circumstances of men change so as to accentuate new problems and provide novel insights that cry out for fresh philosophical illumination. Still further, and perhaps hardest to deal with adequately, the moods and feelings of individuals and communities are not always the same, and a philosophy that does not speak to these conditions directly, sympathetically, and critically neither should nor will strike a sensitive audience as either believable or adequate. Where philosophy is concerned, the passage of time and experience is always creating gaps of believability and adequacy, and it is largely for this reason that men continue to ask philosophical questions and that new statements and formulations are called for and produced.

On the other hand, it is important to understand that we can learn from the past even while we rebel against it. By studying previous thought with the aim of discovering its inadequacies and the reasons for them, we can often get genuine insights into our own frame of mind. In addition, if we are critical not only of previous philosophy but also of our own assumptions and dispositions, we may find that the past contains positive insights of its own which can come to life for us.

With particular reference to Royce, there is yet another important point about our relation to past philosophy: Our reaction to past philosophy is neither uniform nor unchanging. Even rebellion manifests itself in degrees, and its chief targets shift as life moves on. This means that the assessment of a philosopher's contributions can change, and although no previous thinker will have the last word for the present generation, his position can move from one of sharp attack, or mere neglect, to one of critical, but positive, appreciation. A brief sketch of Royce's place in the history of philosophy may help to illustrate these generalizations.

As already noted, Royce represents a philosophical position—absolute idealism—which is presently out of style. The precise nature of his idealism is a difficult issue that can be handled adequately only by studying his writings. For now, however, suffice it to say that his basic philosophical stance is characterized by at least the following qualities: (1) the view that man can know the basic structures of reality and that it is possible to develop a philosophical system that will describe, clarify, and prove these structures for us; (2) the conviction that reality is an Eternal and Absolute Mind and Will, (a) which manifests itself in, but is not exhausted by, a vastly rich temporal universe of real individual beings who are organically and socially related, and (b) whose awareness unifies and knows all of these manifestations as a fully good and meaningful totality; and (3) the belief, in particular, that human life is a manifestation of the Absolute and that every man is ultimately assured of fulfilling, positive significance for his life by virtue of his being an essential component in the universal community known and willed by the Absolute.[2]

Keeping these characteristics in mind, it is of further importance to note that this idealism of Royce's was not an isolated perspective in the philosophical world of his time. Rather, it was a version of one of the dominant intellectual trends in much of Western Europe and the United States in the last half of the nineteenth century and into the early years of the twentieth century. Idealism was part of the philosophical mainstream during those years, and Royce was its most articulate and influential American spokesman.

Philosophies, however, wax and wane, and if Royce represented part of the mainstream, he also lived during a period when philosophical currents were shifting. In the late nineteenth century and with an ever increasing voice in the early decades of the twentieth, strong reactions against idealism were heard. They were prompted largely by the view that the absolutism of the idealists—in terms of both the content and the strength of their claims—was not grounded empirically to a sufficient degree and that it tended to swallow up the individual in an Eternal perspective which robbed men of freedom and which failed to do justice to the implications and significance of our moral striving and search for truth.

If these basic objections to idealism are combined and emphasized in various ways, they can be found at the roots of the philosophical movements that have dominated the twentieth century thus far: logical positivism, analytic philosophy, existentialism, phenomenology, and pragmatism.[3] All of these recent developments have idealism in their backgrounds. They have many points of disagreement, but if they also share some insights, as

[2] It is well to note that Royce frequently uses the concepts of the Absolute and God interchangeably. His practice will be followed in this introduction.

[3] One other contemporary trend,"process philosophy," which is grounded in the work of Whitehead and Hartshorne, is worth mentioning in this context. Its influence has been less than that of the perspectives already named, but it is increasing. Moreover, although its methods are not those of idealism, the broad metaphysical concerns of "process philosophy" and many of the views it develops put it closer to Royce's thought than the other movements noted here.

numerous commentators are now suggesting, this may be partly due to the fact that they are all in some way reactions against a common idealistic heritage.

In any case, as far as Royce in particular was concerned, the chief criticism of his views came from men who were instrumental in the development of pragmatism and especially from his friend and colleague William James. James and Royce shared many ideas, but they were fundamentally at odds over at least three points. First, they differed in their basic convictions about the power of human reason. Royce was inclined to believe that men could know the basic nature of reality with certainty. A rational analysis could produce clear and final conclusions about the structures of existence which are necessary to produce, explain, and fulfill human experience. James, on the other hand, emphasized the tentativeness of every philosophical claim and was forever leery of arguments that claimed to prove the ultimate structures of reality. To put the contrast another way: Royce believed that reality must be structured in one basic way and that men could really know at least the general outlines of that structure, while James, acknowledging that reality must be some way or other, maintained that error might pervade any philosophical conclusion and that our philosophical theories were primarily options for belief, not propositions whose truth or falsity could be conclusively known.

James's stance, however, did not mean that he held no firm convictions about the nature of reality. In fact, two of his central views conflicted directly with Royce's philosophy and constituted James's major objections to idealism as Royce developed it. As we shall see in more detail below, Royce believed that our experience of declaring beliefs or propositions to be true or false was intelligible only if an Absolute Knower existed whose awareness constituted the ultimate standard required to make these declarations meaningful. James's famous pragmatic theory of truth was formed in the face of this idealistic thesis. In place of the idealistic theory of truth, James offered what he took to be a more empirically grounded analysis of our ascription of truth or falsity to beliefs or propositions. Instead of claiming that the truth or falsity of our beliefs or propositions is determined by their agreement or disagreement with the awareness of an Absolute Knower, James argued that if a belief or proposition is true, it is sufficient to say that this means that it leads us to have particular expectations which, upon critical testing, get fulfilled in experience. By the same token, if a belief or proposition is false, it is sufficient to say that this means that the belief or proposition leads us to have particular expectations which, upon critical testing, do not get fulfilled. Of course, many of our beliefs and propositions lead us to have particular expectations which we have not checked or are not yet in a position to check for fulfillment or the lack thereof. In James's account, these beliefs or propositions *become* true or false as proper testing occurs. This means that, Royce to the contrary notwithstanding, truth is not something fixed and complete in an Eternal Mind, but a property that a belief or proposition comes to have as it is tested and verified in experience.

True to his philosophic temperament, James did not offer his theory as an absolutely final position, nor did he claim to have shown that Royce's view was totally impossible. He acknowledged that Royce's Absolute Knower might exist, but he failed to see the necessity of this Being's existence, a point about which Royce seemed firmly convinced. In fact, and this constitutes the final basic difference between Royce and James that we need to note, James took the existence of Royce's Absolute not only to be unnecessary but also to be a strong roadblock to an adequate and believable understanding of man's moral striving and freedom. Royce argued that there was no conflict between the all-encompassing knowledge and will of the Absolute and the existence of genuinely free human individuals. He also asserted that a man's quest for meaning could be fulfilled only if his existence comprised a vital component of the Absolute's life. Far from assuring us of positive meaning, James took Royce's Absolute to rob us of meaning and integrity. It seemed to James that the Absolute turned human existence into a theological determinism in which our lives were eternally complete no matter how open-ended and free they might seem to us in time. Coupling this apparent rejection of freedom with the view that Royce's supposedly perfect Absolute also seemed to be responsible for the production of evil and suffering, James concluded that Royce's idealism was unsound, not only because of its speculative excesses and epistemological weaknesses, but also because of its ultimately debilitating effect on man's will and moral sensitivity.

Royce defended himself by arguing that his critics had misunderstood his philosophy, by examining the positions from which the criticisms were launched with an eye out to show that they were themselves indefensible, and by refining his own positive views. One result was that he emerged as one of the most penetrating critics of pragmatism, especially where its theory of truth was concerned. Royce's defense of idealism, however, was not entirely successful. Philosophical trends were changing, and pragmatism became more and more influential. In Europe, a similar pattern emerged. The influence of idealism was declining, and in its place philosophical concerns that were to be shaped into the movements of logical positivism, analytic philosophy, existentialism, and phenomenology began to emerge with more and more strength. Although these new movements contained more idealism than they usually cared to admit, by the middle decades of this century little emphasis was placed on idealism except as a point of view to criticize while stating the case for new perspectives.

Now we must ask our basic question once again: If idealism has been committed to the flames, why should we concern ourselves with Royce's thought? Earlier we mentioned that Royce's place in the history of philosophy is important in answering this question, and now we are in a position to make the point clear. The influence of philosophies changes as time passes. This pattern will continue. Thus, if idealism and Royce in particular were criticized, rejected, and then largely ignored, although not before leaving a lasting positive impact, who will be the next candidates for this process? The answer is clear: As new concerns develop, movements that presently form the mainstream of philosophical interest will themselves pass into eclipse.

There is evidence that this has already happened with some of the twentieth-century movements we have noted. Few philosophers today would describe themselves as logical positivists, although, as was the case with idealism, the influence of this perspective is lasting. The situation is similar with pragmatism. Considerable attention is presently directed toward the work of Peirce, James, and Dewey, but this phenomenon often has more of the flavor of rediscovery and revival of interest in the pragmatic tradition than of simple continuation of a dominant trend.

With analytic philosophy, existentialism, and phenomenology, the circumstances are a little different. These perspectives remain vigorous and influential, but they all have their roots in the thought of earlier generations. It should not be surprising, therefore, if we find that they no longer speak so strongly and clearly as we approach a new century. Already there are some indications that a shift of interest is forthcoming. Students are often ahead of their teachers, and today's student generation does not seem satisfied with the mainstream trends. The analytic philosopher's overriding concern with language and its uses seems narrow to young men and women living in a world where language may cease to exist altogether. The existentialist's concern with the individual man and the phenomenologist's plea for pure and unbiased description of experience can still capture the interest and concern of today's students, but at the same time there is a feeling that these are also incomplete perspectives in a world where a revitalized sense of community is desperately needed and where men require more than descriptions of experience to make their existence intelligible and meaningful.

The basic point can be put this way: If idealism erred by claiming to understand the whole of reality too well, the philosophies that have dominated our century thus far have erred by restricting their attention too much. In our time of crisis, one of our greatest needs is to find a vision of the whole of reality which can help us to understand what is happening and which might give us guidance for our actions. Logical positivism, pragmatism, and analytic philosophy have helped us to understand the significance of language, both in general and in relation to specific concepts. The descriptions of human experience produced in phenomenology, existentialism, and pragmatism have made us keenly aware both of the desirability of describing experience as it is lived and felt and of our position as finite, fallible beings whose freedom places us in the responsible and risk-filled positions of determining the character of a changing and ambiguous world. Yet, in the midst of analysis and description, even in the face of the claim that our existence is ultimately opaque, the human spirit needs and should long for more. Especially in times of crisis such as ours, there is a need to try to see things whole, to hope and strive for a way to affirm the basic intelligibility, meaningfulness, and goodness of our lives, both individually and communally. Without such effort, man's future is not very bright.

Put another way, we need to become constructive metaphysical thinkers. Moreover, if this is the case, we may gain valuable instruction by studying philosophers who have tried to carry out this task before. Royce is such a figure. If one thing shines through his writings, it is the desire to see things whole and the courage to strive for an interpretation of existence that affirms the fundamental intelligibility, meaningfulness, and goodness of human life and that gives guidance for our moral striving.

Royce worked long and hard at his chosen task, and he may be able to help us to a new view of things. The latter point is worth underscoring, for we cannot simply reinstate Royce's philosophy as the one that we need now. Too much has happened to allow that. In addition, to try to do so would be contrary to Royce's spirit, for he was convinced that each age must think and interpret reality for itself. On the other hand, Royce's philosophy raises many vital questions for us in a striking manner, and his treatment of them can provide important insights as we try to clarify our vision. We can begin to illustrate these last claims by considering in greater detail the content of Royce's thought as it is exemplified in the selections contained in this volume.

Royce's Basic Philosophical Themes

With two short exceptions, the selections in this book are from four of Royce's most substantial works: *The Religious Aspect of Philosophy* (1885), *The World and the Individual* (1899, 1901), *The Philosophy of Loyalty* (1908), and *The Problem of Christianity* (1913). All of the selections are arranged in chronological order which helps to reveal the development of his thought. A brief commentary on four areas of Royce's thought, corresponding in a general way to the major books mentioned above, should help to orient the reader.

I   ERROR, TRUTH, AND REALITY

Royce wrote many books, but most of his basic ideas can be found, at least in germinal form, in *The Religious Aspect of Philosophy*. One of the first questions he raises in the book is, What is religion? His answer contains three basic components. Wherever religion is found, it involves (1) a moral code, (2) elements such as ritual, myth, or literature which inspire enthusiasm and dedication toward the moral code, and (3) a theoretical factor, namely, a view about the nature of reality as a whole. Royce concentrates on the fact that religion entails claims about what ought to be done and about the structure of reality, for it is precisely this fact that establishes an interesting and inextricable relation between philosophy and religion.

Philosophy's relation to religion has at least two dimensions. On the one hand, philosophy has a critical and an analytic function. It comes to life whenever it finds claims being made about morality and reality. It submits such claims to examination, checking to see what warrants their assertion and whether these warrants are sound. On the other hand, Royce believes that philosophy is more than a critical discipline. Built into it is the human concern of trying to get positive answers to questions such as: What ought I to do? For what can I hope? In this respect, it has a thrust similar to that of religion, and it is proper to say that there is a religious aspect of philosophy.

Royce does not, however, intend to imply that philosophy can take the place of religion. Religious expression and practice are not identical to philosophical understanding, and the former has its place as well as the latter. Religion and philosophy are different but complementary dimensions of human life. Religion needs philosophy because the philosopher can engage in the critical and analytic task that is needed to ground religion firmly. On the other hand, as philosophy discovers that religion is an important expression of human hopes and feelings, it can also receive important insights and suggestions from religion that will help to further the philosophical attempt to uncover positive answers to life's fundamental questions.

Having laid out these general relationships between philosophy and religion, Royce proceeds to the two major tasks he sets for himself. The first is to search for a moral ideal that can stand in the face of philosophical criticism. The chapters that constitute his quest for such an ideal do not appear in this collection of his writings. Briefly summarized, however, Royce finds that virtually every ethical perspective that philosophy has developed heretofore is subject to some criticism which will leave a person skeptical about its ultimate validity. Either the moral ideal rests on the fallacy of confusing *what is* with *what ought to be,* or the ideal rests on some appeal to authority, intuition, or conscience that will not stand up under critical scrutiny. Skeptism, however, is not the final outcome for Royce, for out of the skepticism produced by the seemingly endless warfare of ideals, a firmly grounded ethical perspective emerges.

To show that this is true, Royce suggests that we think about the phenomenon of genuine moral skepticism. He argues that such skepticism occurs only when one understands a number of views, tries to hold them together, and yet sees that no view is saved from being undercut by some other. He suggests that this situation is analogous to a conflict of wills: Each component is real; each seeks to assert itself; but an impasse is reached. The components cannot stand together successfully, and none seems capable of dominating the field. The point that most interests Royce about this genuine skepticism, however, is that in its pure form the position itself entails the holding of a higher ideal. The genuine skeptic tries to hold a variety of perspectives together. If he never tried to do this, there would be no skepticism but rather allegiance to some particular ideal or other. The genuine skeptic then, seeks for *unity* or *harmony* of perspectives, but his problem is that this is not actualized because the perspectives conflict too radically.

It is Royce's thesis, therefore, that the ideal of holding together a plurality of views in unity or harmony is one that can stand secure. No matter how extensive skepticism may be, this ideal emerges out of the phenomenon itself. All that is required to turn this idea into our fundamental moral ideal is to interpret the conflicting views as human wills. When this is done, the ideal to be aimed at is a harmony of wills. This ideal enjoins every man to eliminate narrow, selfish interests and to avoid arbitrary limitations on human activity. Instead, every man should strive for a genuine community of wills where the full reality and integrity of one's fellows are recognized and where a maximum of self-expression is coupled with a minimum of destructive conflict.

Royce reworked the ideas of harmony and community again and again, but it is not for the initial sounding of this moral theme that *The Religious Aspect of Philosophy* is best known. The most significant part of the book is found in the concluding chapters where he turns to the task of determining whether a theory of reality can be found that fits and supports the moral perspective already stated. The form of inquiry is similar to that used in arriving at his moral ideal. Royce examines various theories about reality, including the common-sense notion that the world is made up of a variety of independently existing objects and persons besides oneself, and submits them to criticism with the result that doubt remains about their ultimate grounding. At best it seems that these various convictions about reality are only postulates which seem true and upon which we operate but which are not finally demonstrated. One must rest content with postulates if nothing better can be found, but Royce pushes on and argues that a firmer position is available.

This claim rests on an analysis of the conditions which Royce believes must exist if our ordinary claims concerning the truth and falsity of propositions are to be intelligible. In particular, he concentrates on the phenomenon of error. Unless he is talking nonsense, even the most radical skeptic must admit that error is possible. That is, there is a real difference between true and false propositions. One cannot deny this without affirming the very point in question. Denial of the claim produces self-contradiction and removes sense from the denial. But, then, what precisely is the nature of error, and what are the conditions that make it possible? Error cannot exist in a vacuum, and by clarifying both its nature and the conditions that ground its possibility, Royce believes that reliable insights into the structure of reality itself can be obtained.

In analyzing the nature of error, Royce first points out that truth and falsity or error are concepts that apply to *judgments.* Moreover, judgments cannot exist apart from a mind that picks out or focuses on an object. For example, in order for a statement (e.g., the boat is blue) to be either true or false, there must be an intention behind the statement which directs it toward some object. A thought or statement which does not intend to refer to anything can be neither true nor false. Thus, one fundamental condition for the existence of error is that our thoughts or statements have a purpose or intention to refer to some object. Moreover, for an error to exist, a judgment must fail to refer correctly to the object toward which it intends to point. For example, we would say that the judgment "Josiah Royce was born in Canada" does not refer to its object (Josiah Royce) correctly, and this fact constitutes the erroneous quality of the judgment.

Having stated these basic conditions for error, the central issue now becomes: How can our judgments ever really be erroneous, and how is it possible for us to know, as we often rightfully claim to do, that some of our judgments are erroneous? First, Royce argues, the conditions suggested by common sense are inadequate. This view maintains that the objects we judge are essentially independent of or external to the judgments made about them. Such a view, however, cannot explain the possibility or knowledge of error, because it fails to make clear how there can be any intentional or referential relationship between a judgment and an object external to it sufficient to constitute an error.

Royce's analysis concludes that we can only make sense of our claims that error exists and that we can and do know that some particular judgments are erroneous if there exists a higher thought or judgment which does, in fact, achieve the unique purpose which an erroneous judgment fails to fulfill and which also correctly judges that erroneous thought as having failed to fulfill that purpose. A perspective that includes both the object judged and the judgment is required. This perspective knows the object as it is and at the same time knows the judgment of the object and in such a way as to see that it is mistaken.

What, then, is an error? An error, we reply, is an incomplete thought, that to a higher thought, which includes it and its intended object, is known as having failed in the purpose that it more or less clearly had, and that is fully realized in this higher thought. And without such higher inclusive thought, an assertion has no external object, and is no error.[4]

To put Royce's central point in still another way, for the existence and knowledge of error to be possible, a perspective that grasps the truth completely and wholly must exist. Apart from such a perspective, incompleteness and indeterminateness dominate reality in a way that reduces the concept of error to unintelligibility.

It is important to note two other conclusions that Royce draws out of his analysis. First, for an object and a judgment of it to be known by the higher thought Royce has mentioned, neither can be external to or independent of the higher thought. If this is not the case, then insurmountable problems arise concerning how external or independent objects can be genuinely referred to and known. Ultimately, then, the contents of the higher thought must be self-understood manifestations of that higher thought itself. Second, because it does not seem possible for us to place any limit on the number of possible errors or degrees of error, we not only require a higher or more inclusive thought to account for error, but also we require an absolute or infinitely extensive thought. In short, the overarching perspective that is necessary to make error intelligible turns out to be a complete awareness of all truth and all possible error, and, in addition, the comprehensive knowledge of this Absolute Knower or God entails that the contents of its knowledge are actually the results of its own self-awareness, not external or independent objects as common sense might suppose.

Royce's view does not mean that our common experience of objects, persons, and events in space and time is illusory, although it does suggest that reality is not always as it appears at first glance. The world of objects, persons, and events which we experience is fully real, but the outcome of Royce's analysis is that the reality of these things rests in their being manifestations of a fully self-conscious Absolute Thought or God, and not in their independence of

---

[4] Josiah Royce, *The Religious Aspect of Philosophy* (Boston: Houghton Mifflin Company, 1885), p. 425.

or externality to thought. In fact, as Royce understands the outcome of his exploration into the possibility of error, reality turns out to be one infinite thought which grasps time completely from a perspective of eternity.

In the final chapter of *The Religious Aspect of Philosophy*, Royce assesses the significance of his findings as they relate to the task of seeing whether the moral perspective sketched earlier is grounded and supported by reality itself. He denies that his discovery about the Absolute can enable us to have a priori knowledge about the details of life or that it assures that all our personal ambitions will be fulfilled. On the other hand, he does claim that the clarity and completeness of the Absolute's perspective entail its having moral knowledge.

Royce's world is one where things are finally and accurately judged as to their value and moral worth. Moreover, the life of the Absolute is itself a manifestation of the moral ideal of unity, for the Absolute holds together a vastly rich set of experiences and wills. Still further, since the knowledge of the Absolute is perfect, it follows that the totality of existence is known by the Absolute as fully good. For the Absolute, knowing and being actual go together. If the Absolute's knowledge is perfect, it knows fully what is desirable, and, hence, what is desirable exists fully. Thus, according to Royce, the world as a whole is and must be absolutely good. The moral ideal is supported, and philosophy turns out to have a religious aspect that is positive in its content. Men can be assured that they live in a meaningful and moral universe, and that as they strive for the actualization of harmony and unity in human life they are moving in the direction of a closer realization of the life of God.

One sticky problem remains. In a world of absolute goodness, why is there evil and suffering? Royce grappled with this issue all of his life, and he tried to defend the view that evil and suffering have a place in a world of absolute goodness without glossing over the negativity that evil and suffering bring into the world. Royce makes a start in developing this position at the close of *The Religious Aspect of Philosophy*. A more penetrating discussion, however, is to be found in his essay "The Problem of Job," which is included in this volume in place of the sketch found at the end of *The Religious Aspect of Philosophy*.

In "The Problem of Job," Royce argues that the perfection of the universe is incompatible with the presence of evil and suffering if one maintains that the evil and suffering we experience are simply

produced by our freedom or inflicted upon us by any force, divine
or otherwise, external to our universe. But this incompatibility can
be overcome if one holds that our experiences of evil and suffering
are themselves fully experienced by God as the necessary conditions
for his own perfection and, hence, for the perfection of reality as
a whole. This is precisely what Royce's idealism maintains. On
this view,

The answer to Job is: God is not in ultimate essence another being than
yourself. He is the Absolute Being. You truly are one with God, part
of his life. He is the very soul of your soul. And so, here is the first
truth: When you suffer, *your sufferings are God's sufferings,* not his
external work, not his external penalty, not the fruit of his neglect,
but identically his own personal woe. In you God himself suffers, precisely as you do, and has all your concern in overcoming this grief.[5]

But why does God suffer? Royce's answer is that such experience
is necessary for the perfection of the Absolute's life. Full goodness entails the presence and overcoming of evil.

Royce's idealism assures us that God overcomes evil. His knowledge is absolute and, hence, of the desirable; and what God knows
is the case. But the greatest goodness does not exist where evil is
absent altogether. Our world, then, which is the best of all possible
worlds, *must* contain evil. Royce emphasizes that this does not
mean that evil is illusory or simply good in disguise. Evil is just as
real as it can be, and perfection consists in the overcoming of evil.
In fact, if men do evil and suffer in the world, they can also be
agents for overcoming these negativities. Through atoning action
and through the realization that every human life is a component of
the perfection of the Absolute, a sense of meaning and joy is possible even in the face of tragedy, wrongdoing, and sorrow.

To this point, our discussion has concentrated on Royce's conception of and argument for the Absolute. Many questions remain,
however, and some of these have to do with issues concerning the
nature of human selfhood. What more can be said about the relation of the individual man and the Absolute or about the relation of
the individual man to his fellows and nature? Some discussion of
The World and the Individual will help to shed light on such
problems.

---

[5] Josiah Royce, "The Problem of Job." *Studies of Good and Evil* (New
York: D. Appleton and Company, 1898), p. 14.

2   IDEAS, PURPOSE, AND SELFHOOD

Our selections from *The World and the Individual* concentrate on Royce's understanding of the nature of man. Although it is not possible to summarize the entire work here, a few comments about *The World and the Individual* as a whole can provide a foundation for understanding his theory of the human self. At the outset, Royce states that his purpose in the two volumes of the work is "to show what we mean by Being in general, and by the special sorts of Reality that we attribute to God, to the World, and to the Human Individual." [6] The nature and meaning of being is his topic, and in the first volume, subtitled "The Four Historical Conceptions of Being," Royce mainly argues for his own idealistic metaphysics. His method has two thrusts. On the one hand, he develops a positive argument for idealism from epistemological considerations, utilizing and supplementing ideas sketched already in *The Religious Aspect of Philosophy*. On the other hand, he criticizes other theories of being and, finding them wanting, argues that idealism remains as the only viable option.

One important aspect of Royce's positive argument for idealism revolves around his analysis of the nature of an idea. For Royce, an idea is an expression of purpose. He defines the concept in the following terms: "By the word 'Idea,' . . . I shall mean in the end any state of consciousness, whether simple or complex, which, when present, is then and there viewed as at least the partial expression or embodiment of a single conscious purpose." [7] Ideas do not exist in a vacuum. They require intentions, purposes at their core. But now the analysis pushes deeper by clarifying the fact that ideas have *meaning*.

Royce suggests that there are two senses in which an idea has meaning. On the one hand, it has an *internal* meaning. That is, in so far as an idea is the expression of a purpose, the idea is a partial embodiment of that purpose. Thus, if I have an idea of Mount Baldy, my idea expresses some purpose or intention on my part. This is the idea's internal meaning. On the other hand, to have an idea is to have an idea *of something*; it is to refer to something that seems to stand apart from the idea itself. For example, my idea of

---

[6] Josiah Royce, *The World and the Individual* (New York: The Macmillan Company, 1899, 1901), Vol. I, p. 11.

[7] *Ibid,* Vol. I, p. 22.

Mount Baldy says something about an object different from myself and my idea. Royce calls this relation between the idea and its
referent the *external* meaning of the idea.

In some ways, these two kinds of meaning appear to be very different, because we can have intentions that get embodied in ideas
and yet the ideas that we have may not refer correctly to their intended objects. Royce accepts this fact, but he is struck by a point
that affirms the close relation between internal and external meaning, namely, that external meanings could not exist if there were
no intentions, purposes, or selectivity of consciousness at the outset.
An idea cannot represent something external, either falsely or
truly, without an intention that brings the idea and its representative function into existence. In fact, Royce suggests, we can
best understand the external meaning of an idea as an aspect of its
internal meaning. The external meaning of an idea is, then, a
dimension of the completion of an intention or a purpose.

Coupling this interpretation with his convictions that we never
find a world independent of ideas and that our experiences and
claims concerning truth and error are intelligible only if there is an
Absolute Knower, Royce goes on to claim that reality itself is
thought and that the universe is the manifestation of the purpose
and will of the Absolute Knower. Royce puts it this way: "In brief,
by considerations of this type, we propose to answer the question:
What is to be? by the assertion that: To be means simply to express, to embody the complete internal meaning of a certain absolute system of ideas,—a system, moreover, which is genuinely implied in the true internal meaning or purpose of every finite idea,
however fragmentary." [8]

As Royce works toward the idealistic position summarized in the
passage above, he criticizes three other theories of being: realism,
mysticism, and critical rationalism. The general structure of his analysis is as follows: None of the three is an adequate theory primarily because of internal breakdowns. Each view, however, contains insights that can be put to good use and which are utilized in
idealism. Realism holds that there is no essential relation between .
things and thoughts or experiences of them, even though it is
through thoughts and experiences that things are known. The common-sense notion that objects exist apart from us is a form of realism. This theory is sound in placing great stress on the individuality
of the things that exist and on the factors of resistance that we find

---

[8] *Ibid*, Vol. I, p. 36.

in our encounters with objects and persons. But its fatal difficulty is that it never makes really clear how beings can be independent of thought and yet be genuinely known. Thought seems to permeate reality more extensively than the realist is willing to admit, and in the end it is not possible to get thought out of the picture sufficiently to allow realism to stand as an adequate metaphysical theory.

As Royce understands it, mysticism, which stresses the unity of being, is one result of frustrations over the inadequacies of realism. The mystic senses the deep problems in the realistic position and concludes both that reality is One and that the distinctions produced by human experience and reason are illusory. Mysticism has a valuable insight in pointing out the unity of being, but it pushes this emphasis too far. By stressing unity to such a degree that individual human experience and ideas are illusory, the mystic strips the One of content and, hence, makes it indistinguishable from nonbeing. Moreover, the mystic is left without any grounds to support the truth of his view. In fact, if human experiences and ideas are illusory, it is simply not intelligible for the mystic to affirm that being is One, because the mystical view can have meaning only in contrast to the finite and pluralistic dimensions of reality. These facts cut to the core of mysticism, since the point of the mystical quest is to achieve awareness about the true nature of reality.

Critical rationalism asserts that to say that something is real is to point to certain experiences that one could have. This position, which Royce takes to be Kantian and to have some close affinities with pragmatism, is not fully adequate either. It makes reality dependent on what is yet to be, namely, the experiences that would make a claim or a proposition valid. Royce's point is that the reality in question must be in existence for validating experiences to be possible in the first place, and, thus, it is misleading to make experiences yet to come the fundamental criterion for reality. Critical rationalism is headed in the right direction by keeping reality and experience close together, but it falls short by failing to accentuate the fact that the validity of our propositions depends on what is real rather than vice versa.

The inadequacies of these three conceptions of being, coupled with his own positive development of idealism from epistemological considerations, occupy most of Royce's attention in the first volume of *The World and the Individual*. In the second volume, "Nature, Man, and the Moral Order," he shows in greater detail how idealism can illuminate problems that stand closer to the more practical interests of men. It is in this context that he concentrates on certain interesting issues about human.selfhood.

We can begin to clarify Royce's conception of the human self and some of the most important relations of this self to the Absolute, other men, and the natural environment by unpacking the following theme: *The human self is a center of purpose and striving.* Royce's concept of the self has moral content. He rejects the notion that the human self is a static substance or thing. It is instead a temporal process of experiencing, willing, and choosing, which is both an active aspect of the moral order willed by the Absolute and a questing for unity, understanding, and fulfillment of its own. As temporal beings, we are always trying to find ourselves, but Royce believes that we never fully grasp or understand ourselves at any single instant of time. We are in a process of becoming ourselves, and we are self-determining, free beings who do not know in advance what the detailed outcomes of our searching and striving will be. As long as we live in time, we experience an essential incompleteness with respect to who we are.

This essential incompleteness is not, however, the final word. If it were, Royce would agree with those who affirm that existence is ultimately absurd and without final positive meaning. Royce's idealistic metaphysics, however, allows him to hold that there is a perspective which knows us as complete, fulfilled beings. We are, after all, manifestations of the Absolute, and from its eternal perspective all being is comprehended as complete and fulfilling.

When faced by the objection that this theory amounts to a theological determinism which makes one's life complete before he lives it and which makes inescapable the evil that men do and the suffering that they experience, Royce replies as follows: The Absolute's eternal knowledge is not a temporal foreknowing. Instead, it is a grasp of the entire temporal order which comprehends our freedom in all its aspects, but which does not eliminate our freedom or makes it illusory. From eternity God knows our free acts as free, but his knowledge does not exhaustively determine or cause them. As for the evil that men do and the suffering that they experience, Royce continues to argue that evil and suffering are necessary conditions for the absolute goodness and perfection of being as a whole. The finitude, incompleteness, and conflict of our temporal lives produce frustration. Thus, human life, as we experience it now, involves suffering and a struggle with evil. But in facing these obstacles courageously, in achieving success wherever we can, and in recognizing that our relation to the Absolute entails the overcoming of every evil, we can experience positive meaning and joy in time.

Evil and suffering are necessary for perfection, but evidently the particular instances of evildoing and suffering that result from man's freedom are not themselves necessary. To assert this would undercut Royce's doctrine of freedom, and he does not wish to move in this direction. God experiences such events and knows them fully in all of their pathos from his eternal perspective, but he does not determine our evil deeds and their particular consequences for us. What he does do, on Royce's theory, is to overcome every instance of evil and suffering so that the perfection of all being is secured. In the final analysis, Royce asserts, this means that even the negativity of death will be overcome. Royce believes that idealism entails human immortality, and some of his arguments to this effect are to be found in "The Union of God and Man," which is the concluding chapter of *The World and the Individual*. No attempt will be made here to summarize these complex arguments. It can be pointed out, however, that apart from a positive doctrine of immortality, reality is shot full of incompleteness and negativity. Such an outcome would conflict deeply with Royce's understanding of the Absolute as an Eternal Will and Mind which is a completely fulfilled and positively meaningful totality. Royce concludes, therefore, that our existence as meaningful components in the Absolute's awareness entails that we live beyond death and that we ultimately comprehend fully the nature, significance, and fulfillment of our own lives.

Having elaborated some details of the relationship between the human self and the Absolute, who is in the end the highest instance of Selfhood, consider some of Royce's insights about the inextricable relations of a man to his fellows and to his natural environment. One of Royce's basic views is that our very concept of selfhood, our thinking of ourselves as individuals, is a social product.

. . . the distinction between Self and not-Self has a predominantly *Social origin,* and implies a more or less obviously present contrast between what we at any moment view as the life of another person, a fellow-being, or, as you may for short in general call him, an Alter, and the life, which, by contrast with that of the Alter, is just then viewed as the life of the present Ego. . . . I affirm that our empirical self-consciousness, from moment to moment, depends upon a series of contrast-effects, whose psychological origin lies in our literal social life, and whose continuance in our present conscious life, whenever we are alone, is due to habit, to our memory of literal social relations, and to an imaginative idealization of these relations.[9]

Moreover, it is clear that our lives and well-being are essentially related to the natural order and to our understanding and care of it. All of the purposes and goals we pursue, which are the very core of our selfhood, thrust us into interaction with other men and with nature. In fact, if we begin stripping away these relationships, we find very quickly that the self that remains is a bare abstraction and not anything that can be identified with a living person.

Any doctrine, therefore, which understands the individual as being related to other men and to nature in only accidental ways is dangerously mistaken. Human selfhood can exist only in a world community, and it is clear that if any substantial self-fulfillment and positive meaning in time are to be experienced, full recognition of the mutual dependencies that figure in our lives will have to be present. No action or event occurs in a vacuum. The actions of one affect the many. My well-being is vitally linked to the well-being of others and to nature. This means not only that my actions may do harm to others, but that I can act in such a way as to make the world better and, in particular, to help atone for evil that may occur. In such service, Royce believes, we will find that our temporal search for fulfillment most achieves success.

These latter considerations leave us in the area of moral philosophy. But it is in *The Philosophy of Loyalty* that we find Royce's most forceful attempt to develop an ethical position that is consistent with his view of the self and with his idealism as a whole.

3   LOYALTY AND THE MORAL LIFE

Royce's analysis of human life in *The Philosophy of Loyalty* leads him to assert the following principle to help us establish a pattern of life that will bring maximum fulfillment to the individual and to the community as a whole: "*In choosing and in serving the cause to which you are to be loyal, be, in any case, loyal to loyalty.*" [10] What are we to make of such an assertion?

We can begin to unpack Royce's idea by recalling and extending

---

[9] *Ibid,* Vol. II, p. 260.

[10] Josiah Royce, *The Philosophy of Loyalty* (New York: The Macmillan Company, 1908), p. 121.

some of the basic features of his theory of selfhood and by seeing how his understanding of loyalty fits with them. Royce's understanding is that human selfhood is a temporal process whose existence is grounded in the ultimate purpose of the Absolute, but whose concrete actualization depends on the willing and choosing of the individual within a social and natural context. The human self has a structure, an essence, from the outset by virtue of its being a part of a meaningful totality, but its becoming concrete and specific is, in Royce's view, the result of self-determination. For human beings this process of self-determination ultimately entails the giving of oneself to goals and causes. We become persons by acting, by pursuing interests, by striving for the achievement of ends. By the same token, the self will either be fragmented or unified in direct proportion to one's success in finding and actualizing a life pattern that can be consistently and harmoniously pursued through time. Such a pattern will entail, among other things, a chance for the discovery, expression, and cultivation of talents and abilities and a recognition of the fact that one is a member of a world community in which the well-being of one member is bound up with the well-being of every other member.

The most crucial point for Royce at this juncture, however, is the fact that the meaningfulness of human life in time depends on dedication to causes. In short, meaningfulness depends on loyalty, which Royce defines at the outset as: *"The willing and practical and thoroughgoing devotion of a person to a cause."* [11] As the definition makes clear, loyalty depends on freedom. A person's life will not be very fulfilling unless he has the power and opportunity to make free choices. But the bare possession of such power and opportunity is not sufficient for a meaningful life. Only when one uses his freedom to *commit* himself to something is fulfilling meaning actually experienced. Without loyalty, then, life is empty and hollow, but wherever loyalty is present some positive meaning will be experienced.

At this point, however, a serious problem appears. Granted that loyalty is a necessary condition for a meaningful life, how are we to cope with the fact that the causes to which one can be loyal are not uniformly good? In fact, it would have to be admitted that some causes are simply destructive of the sense of community that Royce wants us to appreciate and actualize. Royce is fully aware of these factors, and it is precisely for this reason that his ultimate ethical principle speaks in terms of *loyalty to loyalty*. Some causes

[11] *Ibid*, p. 16.

to which one can devote himself are divisive and destructive for both the individual and the community, but the fact remains that the act of being loyal, of devoting oneself, is a positive good wherever it occurs. Even in cases where we disagree strongly with the cause for which a man works, we may appreciate and recognize the value of his being dedicated. Furthermore, if we ask what constitutes the negativity of causes which, upon honest critical evaluation, we regard as wrong, Royce believes that this negativity consists primarily in the fact that such causes are incomplete instances of loyalty. Such causes arbitrarily or selfishly limit or destroy other forms of loyalty.

Royce further observes that loyalty to *any specific cause* may conflict arbitrarily with some other cause to which men are loyal. For this reason, loyalty to any specific cause is not suitable to define the *basic* principle of morality. Royce concludes, therefore, that the most fundamental principle of the moral life can best be articulated in terms of the general cause of *loyalty to loyalty*. Our fundamental moral responsibility ought to be that of being loyal to loyalty.

Is this idea, however, anything more than a formal principle which is essentially devoid of concrete content? Royce's answer is positive. He does not believe that this basic ethical principle gives us quick and ready-made solutions to moral dilemmas, but he is convinced that the principle of loyalty to loyalty provides a genuine ideal that can help to unite us as a true community. Loyalty to loyalty points toward a community where all individuals are free, where they use and develop their particular talents and abilities and cultivate personal interests, but where all of these persons and factors exist together in maximum harmony and mutual support and with a minimum of destructive conflict. The concept of loyalty to loyalty keeps us oriented in such a direction, for it urges us to be dedicated to the cause of extending human well-being in all of its dimensions. In Royce's view, the community and individual life and freedom will grow and prosper just to the degree that men pursue the end of loyalty to loyalty.

But how does a concrete individual pursue and cultivate the end of loyalty to loyalty? Royce's answer is that one does this by discovering and developing his particular talents and abilities with an eye out to find and implement the ways in which these gifts can best be used for the well-being of the human community. Royce's philosophy of loyalty strives to remove any ultimate opposition between authentic individuality and genuine community. He constantly urges the individual to develop himself as far as possible, but argues at the same time that such development is possible only in a social context and is fulfilled only in the giving of oneself for others.

The concrete choices about the best ways in which to be loyal to loyalty will always be finite and fallible, but even if a particular project fails, the man who strives to be fully loyal will be a worthy example to his fellows. Often, in fact, the most vibrant instances of loyalty to loyalty appear in human lives that are marked by defeat, tragedy, and great suffering. These instances radiate an integrity and significance that cannot be missed altogether, and others will be inspired by them. Here is a further inkling of a basic facet of Royce's theory of good and evil, namely, that the greatest good is vitally linked to devotion to ideals in the face of evil and to acts that overcome evil by creative action which sets right the wreckage that is left behind.

At the end of *The Philosophy of Loyalty*, Royce suggests that there is an essential relation between a life of loyalty and religion. Briefly stated, this relation hinges on the fact that the religious life seeks to find and experience a basic communal dimension in all existence. In this community of being, the lives of individuals are to be unified, harmonized, and fulfilled in an altogether meaningful totality. In Royce's view, therefore, the genuinely religious life will be one of loyalty, because the religious man will recognize that he himself has a vital role to play in the establishment of such a community and that loyalty to loyalty is crucial for its actualization. On the other hand, although the genuinely loyal man may not be overtly or self-consciously religious, his life pattern has an essentially religious aspect. He, too, seeks to find himself in the reality of true community. Moreover, implicit in this devotion is the understanding that unless such community is ultimately real, the self is left in a fragmented condition, and negativity and death have the final words in life's drama.

The religious man lives in the faith (which in Royce's view, is justified by idealistic metaphysics) that a fulfilling community of being is a reality. Such faith, expressed through ritual, myth, and sacred writings, can help to foster a life of loyalty. On the other hand, the ultimate meaningfulness of the life of loyalty rests on the hope that a fundamentally religious vision of reality is true. The life of loyalty, then, both pushes toward and can be sustained by a religious life style.

4 CHRISTIANITY AND COMMUNITY

Royce continued to reflect on the relations between loyalty, community, and religion, and these themes are at the heart of his last major work, *The Problem of Christianity.* The basic issue that motivates the book is this: "In what sense can the modern man consistently be, in creed, a Christian?" [12] His question suggests an attempt to demythologize Christianity so as to let its fundamental claims about reality stand out clearly. His goal is to see what claims are essential to the Christian faith and whether this core of meaning can speak to men of an increasingly scientific and secular outlook. Royce finds the essence of the Christian faith neither exclusively in the moral teachings of Jesus nor in particular beliefs as to who Jesus was. Factors of this kind are important components in articulating the essence of Christianity, but of themselves they are insufficient for understanding it.

For Royce, the essence of the Christian faith revolves around the rich, but often neglected, concept of the Holy Spirit. He believes that this concept points toward the fundamental claim that all being and human life in particular both are and are intended to be a community of love and loyalty. In spite of the fragmentation, sin, and guilt that mar our existence, this Christian perspective affirms that the universe and its human inhabitants are manifestations of God's will, which is characterized by active and continuing concern and care for all that exists and which restores us and urges us toward a responsible, loyal, and loving use of freedom. This conviction—that in spite of sin we are both in and called to extend a community of love and loyalty—stands at the core of Christianity in Royce's interpretation.

Two other tasks are combined with Royce's goal of laying bare the fundamental claims of the Christian faith. First, as was the case with loyalty itself, he argues that the essence of the Christian faith speaks directly to human needs that are both contemporary and perennial. A reflective man can readily understand that his own well-being and that of the community are inextricably tied together and that, in particular, love and loyalty are indispensable ingredients for bringing out the best that is within us. In addition, a thoughtful man can recognize that if his own existence is

[12] Josiah Royce, *The Problem of Christianity* (New York: The Macmillan Company, 1913), Vol. I, p. 14.

to have ultimate significance and not to be swallowed up in negation and death, there must be a communal dimension to reality
which transcends these qualities and which allows for a more extensive degree of self-understanding than is ever afforded us in our
present temporal existence. Thus, Royce affirms that in all dimensions of life, "We are saved through and in the community." [13]

Royce believes that when we peel off the extraneous aspects of
the Christian faith we are left with claims about reality that can
speak to us with meaning and power. These claims can provide a
framework for comprehending our past, and they can give us a
goal and a hope for the future that can transform our present
existence from that of a conflict of individual wills to that of a
harmonious and mutually sustaining community. But is it possible
to develop a philosophical analysis that will help us to see that
reality is, in fact, structured along the lines that the Christian
faith suggests? This is the final issue that Royce pursues. Perhaps it
seems strange that after all his previous work, which was directed
in part toward demonstration of this very point, Royce would still
be trying to formulate an answer to such a question. This is only
testimony, however, to the fact that Royce was continually trying to
refine his basic view and to set it forth so that it would be more
striking and conclusive.

How does Royce pursue this final issue in *The Problem of
Christianity*? He is struck by the fact that our experience is full
of acts of *interpretation*. That is, our experience, either individually or socially, has the structure of our being confronted by
things, persons, and events, all of which have some meaning or
other and which require reflective thought in order for their meaning to be brought out. This suggests that reality itself has a communal structure. Everywhere we turn there are phenomena that
elicit and receive interpretation, and wherever there is interpretation of phenomena there is a triadic relationship of factors. First,
the interpretation of things, persons, or events entails the reality
of a valid meaning which we attempt to discover and which is the
expression of and does not exist apart from mind. According to
Royce this ultimately implies that anything capable of being interpreted is itself the intelligible manifestation of mind. Second,
an act of interpretation requires an interpreter, and, third, someone
to whom the interpretation is directed. The latter person, of course,
may be the interpreter himself.

Now consider the fact that being itself can be an object for

[13] *Ibid*, Vol. II, p. 390.

interpretation. That is, we can ask what it means to be or exist. We may not be able to interpret being with total accuracy, but because being can confront us as an object for interpretation, we can be sure that it is a manifestation of mind and that it does have some overall interpretation which is true. Thus, Royce's conclusion is that reality is a community of interpretation and that ultimately there is a totally valid interpretation of being and an Absolute Interpreter. To this extent, at least, reality bears out the communal structure toward which the Christian faith points.

Moreover, Royce implies that the overall outcome of the interpretive process is something fully positive. Every tragedy, every instance of suffering, evil, and negation, finds its interpretation in Royce's world. That is, all of these events are transcended by being interpreted, which gives them meaning that extends beyond their bare negativity. In the final analysis, the fact that there is interpretation implies full positive significance for all existence. Negation is not totally eliminated from existence, but it is overcome, put in a broader perspective that is completely fulfilling. In short, the concept of the community of interpretation and the essential Christian idea of a universal community of love and loyalty point toward the same reality.

Some Problems and Useful Insights in Royce's Philosophy

It will be well to conclude this introduction by answering a rephrased version of Royce's question about the Christian faith: What is there in Royce's thought that contemporary men can utilize? First, it is unlikely that many of us will be totally convinced by the dialectical arguments that Royce puts forth to demonstrate the truth of absolute idealism. The current mood is skeptical about proofs or demonstrations wherever they occur. Even for those of us who are willing to study Royce's analysis of error and his theory of interpretation with seriousness, the outcome is likely to be uncertainty about his conclusions, if not outright rejection. Nevertheless, in the face of these reactions, Royce still has a vital lesson for us. He is right in emphasizing that being must have some structure or other and that unless we can get some insight about it our lives are left fragmented and perhaps even swallowed up in meaninglessness.

If we do not find Royce's theories about error, truth, and reality to be acceptable, what interpretation will we offer? Will our interpretation be one that can stand rational analysis, including the penetrating questions that he asks of philosophical views that differ from his own idealism? Royce helps us to see an important fact about ourselves, namely, that to be fully human and to make our temporal existence as meaningful as possible, we must learn to think about metaphysical questions. Life cries out for philosophical interpretation. We may not share Royce's conviction that the quest for this interpretation will produce fulfilling results such as he claims for his idealism. But we can appreciate his belief that apart from such attempts we will always fall short of the degree of self-understanding that is available to us.

There is a second dimension of Royce's thought that is worth noting in an assessment of the continuing relevance of his thought. Royce tried to develop a viable philosophical view that would assure us that we live in a world that is totally meaningful and fully good. This is illustrated over and over again in his claim that although we presently have only a fragmentary vision of the whole of being, there is an overarching perspective of which we are vital components, and this perspective grasps the totality and sees it as meaningful and good in a way that is also significant and fulfilling for us.

Royce's view is that this perspective is eternal. It grasps the entire temporal process as a completed whole. Contemporary men will have difficulty with this position when it is put into contact with our experience of freedom. We will ask the same question that Royce's critics put to him: Is it not the case that the knowledge of the Absolute determines our existence by making our lives complete before we have actualized them in time? Moreover, we are unlikely to be satisfied with Royce's replies that his theory does not compromise our freedom. Our experience of freedom, with its pervasive elements of risk and uncertainty, leaves us impressed with the open-endedness, incompleteness, and indeterminateness of existence. If existence is known as complete from any perspective, either temporal or eternal, our experience of freedom loses its full validity and integrity. But our mood is such that we are more likely to affirm the full validity and integrity of our experience of freedom than to assent to a theory involving Royce's Absolute Knower. Royce's defense to the contrary notwithstanding, the Absolute Knower smacks too much of determinism for our freedom-oriented perspective.

Once more, however, Royce's philosophy has a lesson for us even as we rebel against it. He was convinced that without an eternally complete knowledge of reality in which we ultimately participate there could never be a full extension of positive meaning for human beings. Without this eternal dimension to existence, life might be free but it could never be totally fulfilled. Recognizing that men long for meaning as well as for freedom, his idealism sought the completion of temporal existence in the eternal and overarching perspective of the Absolute. Royce, therefore, puts a hard question to us: Given our contemporary mood about freedom, what kind of meaning is available to us? Does our experience, especially that of freedom, entail ultimate opacity or absurdity in existence, or is there some metaphysical or theological option which can give us hope for full and lasting positive significance without at the same time conflicting with the radical open-endedness which our experience of freedom entails? Royce's philosophy forces us to ask the right questions about freedom and meaning, and we must clarify these issues if self-understanding is to occur.

A third point relates closely to the preceding comments about freedom and meaning. Royce's metaphysics offers an intriguing thesis about the place of evil and suffering in our existence. In his attempt to keep freedom alive, Royce seems to deny that every instance of evil and suffering is necessary, but he does assert that some instances of this kind are necessary for the perfection of existence. The best world is not one in which there is no evil and suffering, but rather one in which these negativities are present and overcome—which, in Royce's view, is ultimately the case. This position is not unintelligible to us, but Royce's provocative suggestion is insufficiently developed. He leaves us with a basic perplexity which can be developed as follows.

The key issue has to do with the degree of evil and suffering that we find in existence. First, if as Royce believes, this is the best of all possible worlds, and evil and suffering are necessary for the goodness of existence, how is the conclusion to be avoided that just the particular instances of suffering and evil that do exist are themselves necessary? In spite of Royce's attempt to maintain the reality of freedom, his theory of evil and suffering throws it into jeopardy. In addition, he does not make very clear just why the evil and suffering that exist are precisely the right amounts to help make this the best of all possible worlds. In his view that evil and suffering are required for the good to be actualized, why would not a higher degree of these negative qualities be desirable in our present existence? Or why could there not be a little less evil and suffering without threatening the perfection of existence? To say that from the all-encompassing perspective of the Absolute the amounts are just right and that in the end things are perfectly balanced will not be likely to assuage our doubts completely.

Again, we may find that Royce's position either strikes us as unworkable or leaves us with an incomplete insight. But at the same time, he continues to raise the right questions for us. What is the place of evil and suffering in our experience and in reality as a whole? Does it make any sense to say that we live in the best of all possible worlds? If not, what can we say about the ultimate power, if any, that grounds our universe? Does the presence of evil and suffering in our existence force us to deny God, or is it possible to develop a viable theology that goes further than Royce's in making the evil and suffering in our world intelligible? Royce gives us a valuable clue to the latter question in arguing for the inextricable connection between good and evil, but contemporary thinkers will need to develop the suggestion with a greater emphasis on the relations among good, evil, and freedom than Royce provides.

Finally, we may not share Royce's conviction that the universe is ultimately a community of loyalty and love, but we can appreciate and utilize his insights about the essential relationships that an individual person bears to his fellows and his natural environment. His basic thesis—that we are not isolated individuals but fundamentally related to other men and nature so that one man's fulfillment is linked with that of all other beings and is dependent on properly focused human loyalty in particular—is an insight whose validity is being driven home daily and with a vengeance. One has only to reflect on our ecological, racial, and international crises to see that this is the case.

With these latter aspects of Royce's philosophy we can and ought to have little quarrel. But even in these points of agreement, we must remember that he continues to offer a great challenge to us. He argues that our concern must extend beyond man and nature to an attempt to discover our relation to the fundamental power that grounds all that we experience. To fail to do this is to fall short of full humanity and to give up the quest for meaning too soon. It is perhaps Royce's greatest gift to us that he extolled this ideal and that he was bold enough to try to fulfill it. By so doing, his life exhibited the highest level of loyalty. In our time of crisis, his efforts can inspire us to strive anew for self-understanding, community, and lasting meaning.

PART I

---

*The Religious Aspect
of Philosophy*
AND
*Studies of Good
and Evil*

1 ❧ INTRODUCTION; RELIGION AS A MORAL CODE AND AS A THEORY [1]

Auch bezweifl' ich, dass du glaubest,
　Was so rechter Glaube heisst,
Glaubst wohl nicht an Gott den Vater,
　An den Sohn und heil'gen Geist.

—HEINE

Intending in the following pages to sketch certain philosophic opinions that seem to him to have a religious bearing, the author must begin by stating what he understands to be the nature of religion, and how he conceives philosophy to be related to religion.

We speak commonly of religious feelings and of religious beliefs; but we find difficulty in agreeing about what makes either beliefs or feelings religious. A feeling is not religious merely because it is strong, nor yet because it is also morally valuable, nor yet because it is elevated. If the strength and the moral value of a feeling made it religious, patriotism would be religion. If elevation of feeling were enough, all higher artistic emotion would be religious. But such views would seem to most persons very inadequate. As for belief, it is not religious merely because it is a belief in the supernatural. Not merely is superstition as such very different from religion, but even a belief in God as the highest of beings need not be a religious belief. If La Place had needed what he called "that hypothesis," the Deity, when introduced into his celestial mechanics, would have been but a mathematical symbol, or a formula like Taylor's theorem, —no true object of religious veneration. On the other hand, Spi-

[1] Josiah Royce, *The Religious Aspect of Philosophy* (Boston: Houghton Mifflin Company, 1885), Chap. I, pp. 1–14. The chapter is reprinted in its entirety.—Editor's note.

noza s impersonal Substance, or the Nirvâna of the Buddhists, or any one of many like notions, may have, either as doctrines about the world or as ideals of human conduct, immense religious value. Very much that we associate with religion is therefore non-essential to religion. Yet religion is something unique in human belief and emotion, and must not be dissolved into any lower or more commonplace elements. What then is religion?

I

So much at all events seems sure about religion. It has to do with action. It is impossible without some appearance of moral purpose. A totally immoral religion may exist; but it is like a totally unseaworthy ship at sea, or like a rotten bank, or like a wild-cat mine. It deceives its followers. It pretends to guide them into morality of some sort. If it is blind or wicked, not its error makes it religious, but the faith of its followers in its worth. A religion may teach the men of one tribe to torture and kill men of another tribe. But even such a religion would pretend to teach right conduct. Religion, however, gives us more than a moral code. A moral code alone, with its "Thou shalt," would be no more religious than is the civil code. A religion adds something to the moral code. And what it adds is, first, enthusiasm. Somehow it makes the faithful regard the moral law with devotion, reverence, love. By history, by parable, by myth, by ceremony, by song, by whatever means you will, the religion gives to the mere code life and warmth. A religion not only commands the faithful, but gives them something that they are glad to live for, and if need be to die for.

But not yet have we mentioned the element of religion that makes it especially interesting to a student of theoretical philosophy. So far as we have gone, ethical philosophy would criticise the codes of various religions, while theoretical philosophy would have no part in the work. But, in fact, religion always adds another element. Not only does religion teach devotion to a moral code, but the means that it uses to this end include a more or less complete theory of things. Religion says not merely *do and feel,* but also *believe.* A religion tells us about the things that it declares to exist, and most especially it tells us about their relations to the moral code and to the religious feeling. There may be a religion without a supernatural, but there cannot be a religion

without a theoretical element, without a statement of some supposed matter of fact, as part of the religious doctrine.

These three elements, then, go to constitute any religion. A
religion must teach some moral code, must in some way inspire
a strong feeling of devotion to that code, and in so doing must
show something in the nature of things that answers to the code
or that serves to reinforce the feeling. A religion is therefore practical, emotional, and theoretical; it teaches us to do, to feel, and to
believe, and it teaches the belief as a means to its teaching of the
action and of the feeling.

II

We may now see how philosophy is related to religion. Philosophy is not directly concerned with feeling, but both action and
belief are direct objects of philosophical criticism. And on the
other hand, in so far as philosophy suggests general rules for
conduct, or discusses the theories about the world, philosophy
must have a religious aspect. Religion invites the scrutiny of
philosophy, and philosophy may not neglect the problems of religion. Kant's fundamental problems: *What do I know?* and
What ought I to do? are of religious interest no less than of
philosophic interest. They ask how the highest thought of man
stands related to his highest needs, and what in things answers
to our best ideals. Surely no one ought to fear such questions, nor
ought any philosophic student to hesitate to suggest in answer to
them whatever after due reflection he honestly can suggest, poor
and tentative though it may be. In fact there is no defense for one
as sincere thinker if, undertaking to pay attention to philosophy
as such, he willfully or thoughtlessly neglects such problems on
the ground that he has no time for them. Surely he has time to be
not merely a student of philosophy, but also a man, and these
things are among the essentials of humanity, which the non-
philosophic treat in their way, and which philosophic students
must treat in theirs.

When, however, we say that the thinker must study and revere
these questions, we must not fancy that because of their importance he may prejudge them. Assumptions, postulates, *a priori*
demands, these indeed are in all thinking, and no thinker is
without such. But prejudice, *i.e.*, foregone conclusions in ques-
tionable matters, deliberate unwillingness to let the light shine

upon our beliefs, all this is foreign to true thought. Thinking is
for us just the clarifying of our minds, and because clearness is
necessary to the unity of thought, necessary to lessen the strife
of sects and the bitterness of doubt, necessary to save our minds
from hopeless, everlasting wandering, therefore to resist the
clarifying process, even while we undertake it, is to sin against
what is best in us, and is also to sin against humanity. Deliberately insincere, dishonest thinking is downright blasphemy. And
so, if we take interest in these things, our duty is plain. Here
are questions of tremendous importance to us and to the world.
We are sluggards or cowards if, pretending to be philosophic
students and genuine seekers of truth, we do not attempt to do
something with these questions. We are worse than cowards if,
attempting to consider them, we do otherwise than reverently,
fearlessly, and honestly.

I I I

The religious thought of our time has reached a position that
arouses the anxiety of all serious thinkers, and the interest of many
who are not serious. We are not content with what we learned
from our fathers; we want to correct their dogmas, to prove what
they held fast without proof, to work out our own salvation by
our own efforts. But we know not yet what form our coming
faith will take. We are not yet agreed even about the kind of
question that we shall put to ourselves when we begin any specific
religious inquiry. People suggest very various facts or aspects of
facts in the world as having a religious value. The variety of the
suggestions shows the vagueness of the questions that people
have in mind when they talk of religion. One man wants to
worship Natural Law, or even Nature in general. Another finds
Humanity to be his ideal object of religious veneration. Yet
another gravely insists that the Unknowable satisfies his religious
longings. Now it is something to be plain in expressing a question,
even if you cannot give an answer. We shall do something if we
only find out what it is that we ought to seek. And the foregoing
considerations may help us in this way, even if what follows
should be wholly ineffective. For we have tried to give a definition
that shall express, not merely what a Buddhist or a Catholic or a
Comtist or an Hegelian means by his religion, but what all men
everywhere mean by religion. They all want religion to define

for them their duty, to give them the heart to do it, and to point out to them such things in the real world as shall help them to be steadfast in their devotion to duty. When people pray that they may be made happy, they still desire to learn what they are to do in order to become happy. When saints of any creed look up to their God as their only good, they are seeking for guidance in the right way. The savages of whom we hear so much nowadays have indeed low forms of religion, but these religions of theirs still require them to do something, and tell them why it is worth while to do this, and make them more or less enthusiastic in doing it. Among ourselves, the poor and the lonely, the desolate and the afflicted, when they demand religious comfort, want something that shall tell them what to do with life, and how to take up once more the burdens of their broken existence. And the religious philosophers must submit to the same test that humanity everywhere proposes to its religions. If one tries to regulate our diet by his theories, he must have the one object, whatever his theory, since he wants to tell us what is healthful for us. If he tells us to eat nothing but snow, that is his fault. The true object of the theory of diet remains the same. And so if men have expressed all sorts of one-sided, disheartening, inadequate views of religion, that does not make the object of religious theory less catholic, less comprehensive, less definitely human. A man who propounds a religious system must have a moral code, an emotional life, and some theory of things to offer us. With less we cannot be content. He need not, indeed, know or pretend to know very much about our wonderful world, but he must know something, and that something must be of definite value.

To state the whole otherwise. Purely theoretic philosophy tries to find out what it can about the real world. When it makes this effort, it has to be perfectly indifferent to consequences. It may not shudder or murmur if it comes upon unspeakably dreadful truths. If it finds nothing in the world but evil, it must still accept the truth, and must calmly state it without praise and without condemnation. Theoretic philosophy knows no passion save the passion for truth, has no fear save the fear of error, cherishes no hope save the hope of theoretic success. But religious philosophy has other objects in addition to these. Religious philosophy is indeed neither the foe nor the mistress of theoretic philosophy. Religious philosophy dare not be in opposition to the truths that theory may have established. But over and above these truths it seeks something else. It seeks to know their value. It comes to the world with other interests, in addition to the purely theoretic ones. It wants to know what in the world is worthy of worship as the good. It seeks not merely the truth, but the inspiring truth. It defines for itself goodness, moral worth, and then it asks, *What in this world is worth anything?* Its demands in this regard are boundless. It will be content only with the best it can find. Having formulated for itself its ideal of worth, it asks at the outset: *Is there then, anywhere in the universe, any real thing of Infinite Worth?* If this cannot be found, then and then only will religious philosophy be content with less. Then it will still ask: *What in this world is worth most?* It cannot make realities, but it is determined to judge them. It cannot be content with blind faith, and demands the actual truth as much as theoretic philosophy demands it; but religious philosophy treats this truth only as the material for its ideal judgments. It seeks the ideal among the realities.

Upon such a quest as this, we ask the reader to accompany us in the following pages. We have not space to be exhaustive, nor in fact to offer much more than suggestions; but we want the suggestions to be explicit, and we hope that they may stimulate some reader, and may perhaps help him in completing his own trains of thought.

IV

People come to such questions as these with certain prejudices about the method and spirit of inquiry; and all their work may be hampered by these prejudices. Let us say yet a little more of what we think as to this matter. There are two extremes to fear in religious philosophy: indifference that arises from a dogmatic disposition to deny, and timidity that arises from an excessive show of reverence for the objects of religious faith. Both of these extreme moods have their defective methods in dealing with religious philosophy. The over-skeptical man looks with impatience on all lengthy discussions of these topics. There can be nothing in it all, he says: nothing but what Hume, in an eloquent passage, called sophistry and delusion. Why spend time to puzzle over these insoluble mysteries? Hence his method is: swift work, clear statement of known difficulties, keen ridicule of hasty assumptions, and then a burning of the old deserted Moscow of theology, and a bewildering flight into the inaccessible wintry wastes, where no army of religious philosophers shall follow him. Now for our part we want to be as skeptical as anybody; and we personally always admire the freedom of motion that pure skepticism gives. Our trouble with it all, however, is that, after we have enjoyed the freedom and the frosty air of pure philosophic skepticism for a while, we find ourselves unexpectedly in the midst of philosophic truth that needs closer examination. The short and easy agnostic method is not enough. You must supplement skepticism by philosophy; and when you do so, you find yourself forced to accept, not indeed the old theology of your childhood, but something that satisfies, oddly enough, certain religious longings, that, as skeptic, you had carefully tried to forget. Then you find yourself with what you may have to call a religious doctrine; and then you may have to state it as we are here going to do, not in an easy or fascinating way, such as the pure skeptic can so well follow, but at all events with some approach to a serious and sustained effort to consider hard questions from many sides. The skeptical method is not only a good, but also a necessary beginning of religious philosophy. But we are bound to go deeper than mere superficial agnosticism. If, however, any reader is already sure that we cannot go deeper, and that modern popular agnosticism has exhausted all that can be said on religious questions, then we bid him an immediate and joyous farewell. If we had not something to say in this book that seems to us both foreign to the popular modern agnostic range of discussion, and deeper than the insight of popular modern skepticism, we should say nothing. The undertaking of this book is not to wrangle in the old way over the well-known ordinary debates of to-day, but to turn the flank of the common popular thought on these topics altogether, by going back to a type of philosophic investigation, that is nowadays familiar indeed to a certain school of specialists, but forgotten by the general public. In this type of investigation, we have furthermore something to offer that seems to us no mere repetition of the views of other thinkers, but an effort to make at least one little step in advance of the thoughts that the great masters of philosophy have given to us. Yet we know indeed that the range of any useful independent thought in philosophy must be, in case of any one individual, very narrow.

The other mood and its method remain. It is the mood of excessive reverence. It wastes capital letters on all the pronouns and adjectives that have to do with the objects of religious faith; but it fears to do these objects the honor to get clear ideas about them. Now we respect this mood when it appears in men who do well their life-work, who need their religious faith for their work, and who do not feel any calling as truth-seekers. No man has any business to set up his vocation as the highest one; and the man for whom truth is useful in his actual life-work as an inspiration, revealed to him only in feeling, is welcome to his feelings, is worthy of all regard from those whose vocation is philosophy, and shall not be tormented by our speculations. He is careful and troubled about many things; the world needs him, and philosophy does not. We only lay claim to our own rights, and do not want to interfere with his. Our right to clear thought, we must insist upon. For looked at philosophically, and apart from the necessary limitations of the hard worker, all this dumb reverence, this vague use of vague names, has its serious dangers. You are reverent, we may say to the man who regards philosophic criticism as a dangerous trifling with stupendous truths; you are reverent, but what do you reverence? Have a care lest what you reverence shall turn out to be your own vague and confused notions, and not the real divine Truth at all. Take heed lest your object of worship be only your own little pet infinite, that is sublime to you mainly because it is yours, and that is in truth about as divine and infinite as your hat. For this is the danger that besets these vague and lofty sentiments. Unreflected upon, uncriticized, dumbly experienced, dumbly dreaded, these, your religious objects, may become mere feelings, mere visceral sensations of yours, that you have on Sunday mornings, or when you pray. Of course, if you are a worker, you may actually realize these vague ideas, in so far as they inspire you to work. If they do, they shall be judged by their fruits. Otherwise, do not trust too confidently their religious value. You, individually regarded, are but a mass of thought and feeling. What is only yours and in you, is not divine at all. Unless you lift it up into the light of thought and examine it often, how do you know into what your cherished religious ideal may not have rotted in the darkness of your emotions? Once in a while, there does come to a man some terrible revelation of himself in a great sorrow. Then in the tumult of anguish he looks for his religious faith to clothe his nakedness against the tempest; and he finds perhaps some moth-eaten old garment that profits him nothing, so that his soul miserably perishes in the frost of doubt. Such a man has expected God to come to his help in every time of need; but the only god he has actually and consciously had, has been his own little contemptible, private notion and dim feeling of a god, which he has never dared fairly to look at. Any respectable wooden idol would have done him better service; for then a man could know where and what his idol is. Such is only too apt to be the real state of the man who regards it as profanity to think clearly and sensibly on religious topics.

We claim, then, the right to criticise as fearlessly, as thoroughly, and as skeptically as may be, the foundations of conduct and faith. For what we criticise are, at the outset, our own notions, which we want to have conform to the truth, if so be that there is any truth. As for doubt on religious questions, that is for a truth-seeker not only a privilege but a duty; and, as we shall experience all through this study, doubt has a curious and very valuable place in philosophy. Philosophic truth, as such, comes to us first under the form of doubt; and we never can be very near it in our search unless, for a longer or shorter time, we have come to despair of it altogether. First, then, the despair of a thorough-going doubt, and then the discovery that this doubt contains in its bosom the truth that we are sworn to discover, however we can,—this is the typical philosophic experience. May the memory of this suggestion support the failing patience of the kindly disposed reader through some of the longer and more wearisome stretches of dry skeptical analysis over which we must try to journey together. Whatever may be the truth, it must lie beyond those deserts.

2 ❧ THE POSSIBILITY OF ERROR [1]

On ne sert dignement la philosophie qu'avec le même
feu qu'on sent pour une maîtresse.
—ROUSSEAU, *Nouvelle Heloïse*

We have before us our theorem, and an outline of its proof. We
are here to expand this argument. We have some notion of the
magnitude of the issues that are at stake. We had found ourselves baffled in our search for a certainty by numerous difficulties. We had found only one way remaining so far quite clear.
That was the way of postulating what the moral consciousness
seems to demand about the world beyond experience. For many
thinkers since Kant, that way has seemed in fact the only one.
They live in a world of action. "Doubt," they say, "clouds all
theory. One must *act as if* the world were the supporter of our
moral demands. One must have faith. One must make the grand
effort, one must risk all for the sake of the great prize. If the
world is against us, still we will not admit the fact until we are
crushed. If the cold reality cares naught for our moral efforts, so
be it when we come to know the fact, but meanwhile we will act
as if legions of angels were ready to support our demand for
whatever not our selfish interest, but the great interest of the
Good, requires." Such is the view of the men whose religion is
founded upon a Postulate.

We, too, felt that such faith is religious. We were willing to
accept it, if nothing better could be found. But we were not content with it. Life has its unheroic days, when mere postulates
fail us. At such times we grow weary of toiling, evil seems
actually triumphant, and, worse than all, the sense that there really
is any perfect goodness yet unattained, that there is any worth or
reason in our fight for goodness, seems to desert us. And then

---

[1] Josiah Royce, *The Religious Aspect of Philosophy* (Boston: Houghton Mifflin Company, 1885), Chap. XI, pp. 384–435. The chapter is
reprinted in its entirety.—Editor's note.

it will indeed be well if. we can get for ourselves something more and better than mere postulates. If we cannot, we shall not seek to hide the fact. Better eternal despondency than a deliberate lie about our deepest thoughts and their meaning. If we are not honest, at least in our philosophy, then are we wholly base. To try once more is not dishonest.

So we did make the effort, and, in the last chapter, we sketched a result that seemed nearly within our reach. An unexpected result this, because it springs from the very heart of skepticism itself. We doubted to the last extremity. We let everything go, and then all of a sudden we seemed to find that we could not lose one priceless treasure, try as we would. Our wildest doubt assumed this, namely, that error is possible. And so our wildest doubt assumed the actual existence of those conditions that make error possible. *The conditions that determine the logical possiblity of error must themselves be absolute truth,* that was the treasure that remained to us amid all our doubts. And how rich that treasure is, we dimly saw in the last discussion. That dim insight we must now try to make clearer. Perhaps our previous discussion has shown us that the effort is worth making.

Yet of one thing the reader shall be warned. The path that we travel is hereabouts very thorny and stony. It is a path of difficult philosophical investigation. Nobody ought to follow it who does not desire to. We hope that the reader will skip the whole of this chapter unless he wants to find even more of dullness than the rest of this sleepy book has discovered to him. For us, too, the arid way would seem hard, were it not for the precious prize at the end of it.

I

The story of the following investigation shall first be very briefly told. The author had long sought, especially in the discussions of Kant's "Kritik," and in the books of the post-Kantians, for help in seeing the ultimate principles that lie at the basis of knowledge. He had found the old and well-known troubles. Experience of itself can give no certainty about general principles. We must therefore, said Kant, bring our own principles with us to experience. We know then of causation, because causation is a fundamental principle of our thought, whereby we set our experience to rights. And so long as we think, we shall think into experience the connection of cause and effect, which otherwise would not be there. But hereupon the questions arose that have so often been asked of Kant and the Kantians. Why just these principles and no others? "That is inexplicable," replies Kant. Very well, then, suppose we give up applying to experience those arbitrary principles of ours. Suppose we choose to stop thinking of experience as causally connected. What then? "But you cannot stop," says Kant. "Your thought, being what it is, must follow this one fashion forever." Nay, we reply, how knowest thou that, Master? Why may not our thought get a new fashion some day? And then what is now a necessary principle, for example, that every event has a cause, would become unnecessary or even nonsensical. Do we then know *a priori* that our *a priori* principles must always remain such? If so, how come we by this new knowledge?

So Kant leaves us still uncertain about any fundamental principles upon which a sure knowledge of the world can be founded.

Let us, then, examine a little deeper. Are there any certain judgments possible at all? If one is skeptical in a thorough-going way, as the author tried to be, he is apt to reach, through an effort to revise Kant's view, a position something like the following,—a provisional position of course, but one that results from the effort to accept nothing without criticism: "Kant's result is that our judgments about the real world are founded on an union of thought and sense, thought giving the appearance of necessity to our judgment, sense giving the material. The necessity of any judgment amounts then only to what may be summed up in the words: *So the present union of thought and sense makes things appear.* If either thought or sense altered its character, truth would alter. Hence every sincere judgment is indeed true for the moment in which it is made, but not necessarily true for other moments. We only postulate that it is true for other moments." "And so," to continue this view, "it is only by means of postulates that our thought even seems to have any unity from moment to moment. We live in the present. If our thought has other truth or falsity than this, we do not know it. Past and future exist not for this present. They are only postulated. Save as postulated, they have no present meaning."

When he held and expressed this view, the author is free to admit that he was not always clear whether he ought to call it the doctrine of the relativity of truth or not. It might have avoided the absurdities of total relativity by taking form as a doctrine that the present moment's judgment is really true or false, for a real past and future, but that we, being limited to present moments, can never compare our judgments with reality to find whether our judgments are true or false. But although this interpretation is possible, this view often did express itself for the author as the doctrine of the total relativity of truth. The latter doctrine to be sure has no real meaning, but the author used with many others to fancy that it had.

To apply the view to the case of causal relations. "We continually postulate," the author used to point out, "we demand, without being able to prove it, that nature in future shall be uniform." So, carrying out this thought, the author used to say: "In fact future nature is not given to us, just as the past is not given to us. Sense-data and thought unite at every instant afresh to form a new judgment and a new postulate. Only in the present has any judgment evident validity. And our postulate of causal relation is just a way of looking at this world of conceived past and future *data*. Such postulates avoid being absurd efforts to regulate independent facts of sense, because, and only because, we have in experience no complete series of facts of sense at all, only from moment to moment single facts, about which we make single judgments. All the rest we *must* postulate or else do without them." Thus one reaches a skepticism as nearly complete as is possible to any one with earnest activity of thought in him. From moment to moment one can be sure of each moment. All else is postulate.

From the depths of this imperfectly defined skepticism, which seemed to him provisionally the only view he could adopt, the author escaped only by asking the one question more: "If everything beyond the present is doubtful, then how can even that doubt be possible?" With this question that bare relativity of the present moment is given up. What are the conditions that make doubt logically intelligible? These conditions really transcend the present moment. Plainly doubt implies that the statement doubted may be false. So here we have at least one supposed general truth, namely, "All but the immediate content of the present moment's judgment, being doubtful, we may be in error about it." But *what then is an error?* This becomes at once a problem of exciting interest. Attacking it, the author was led through the wilderness of the following argument.

II

Yet before we undertake this special examination of the nature of error, the reader must pardon us for adding yet another explanatory word. The difficulty of the whole discussion will lie in the fact that we shall be studying the possibility of the plainest and most familiar of commonplaces. Common sense hates to do such things, because common sense thinks that the whole matter is sure from the outset. Common sense is willing to ask whether God exists, but unwilling to inquire how it is possible that there can exist an error about anything. But foreseeing that something is to follow from all this, we must beg common sense to be patient. We have not the shadow of doubt ourselves about the possibility of error. That is the steadfast rock on which we build. Our inquiry, ultra-skeptical as it may at moments seem, is into the question: *How* is the error possible? Or, in other words: *What is an error?* Now there can be little doubt that common sense is not ready with any general answer to such a question. Error is a word with many senses. By error we often mean just a statement that arouses our antipathy. Yet we all admit upon reflection, that our antipathy can neither make nor be used to define real error. Adam Smith declares, with common sense on his side, in his "Theory of the Moral Sentiments," [2] that: "To approve or disapprove of the opinions of others is acknowledged, by everybody, to mean no more than to observe their agreement or disagreement with our own." Yet no one would accept as a definition of error the statement that: *Error is any opinion that I personally do not like.* Error has thus a very puzzling character. For common sense will readily admit that if a statement is erroneous, it must appear erroneous to every "right mind" that is in possession of the facts. Hence the personal taste of one man is not enough to define it. Else there might be as many sorts of error as there are minds. It is only the "right mind" whose personal taste shall decide what is an error in any particular case. But what then is a normal mind? Who is the right-minded judge? There seems to be danger that common sense shall run at this point into an infinite regress. I say: *That opinion is an error.* What do I mean? Do I mean that I do not like that opinion? Nay, I mean more. I mean

[2] Part I, Sec. I, Chap. III, near the beginning.

that *I ought not to like or to accept it.* Why ought I not? *Because the ideally right-minded person would not,* seeing the given facts, hold that opinion about them. But who is the ideally right-minded person? Well, common sense may answer, *It is my ideal person, the right-minded man as I conceive him.* But why is my ideal the true ideal? *Because I like it?*—Nay, *because, to the ideal judge, that kind of mind would seem the ideal.* But who is the ideal judge? And so common sense is driven from point to point, unable to get to anything definite.

So much, then, to show in general that common sense does not know what an error is, and needs more light upon the subject. Let common sense not disturb us, then, in our further search, by the constant and indignant protest that error must somehow exist, and that doubt on that subject is nonsense. Nobody has any doubts on that subject. We ask only *how* error exists and how it can exist.

For the rest, what follows is not any effort to demonstrate in fair and orderly array, from any one principle or axiom, what must be the nature of error, but to use every and any device that may offer itself, general analysis, special example, comparison and contrast of cases,—anything that shall lead us to the insight into what an error is and implies. For at last, immediate insight must decide.

We shall study our problem thus. We shall take either some accepted definition of error, or some special class of cases, and we shall ask: How is error in that case, or in accordance with that definition, possible? Since error plainly is possible in some way, we shall have only to inquire: *What are the logical conditions* that make it possible? We shall take up the ordinary suppositions that common sense seems to make about what here determines the possibility of error. We shall show that these suppositions are inadequate. Then the result will be that, on the ordinary suppositions, error would be impossible. But that result would be absurd, if these were the only possible suppositions. Hence the ordinary suppositions must somehow be supplemented. When, therefore, we seem to say in the following that error is impossible, we shall mean only, impossible under the ordinary suppositions of common sense. What supplement we need to these suppositions, our argument will show us. In sum we shall find the state of the case to be this: Common sense regards an assertion as true or as false apart from any other assertion or thought, and solely in reference to its own object. For common sense each judgment, as a separate creation, stands out alone, looking at its object, and trying to agree with it. If it succeeds, we have truth. If the judgment fails, we have error. But, as we shall find, this view of common sense is unintelligible. A judgment cannot have an object and fail to agree therewith, unless this judgment is part of an organism of thought. Alone, as a separate fact, a judgment has no intelligible object beyond itself. And therefore the presuppositions of common sense must be supplemented or else abandoned. Either then there is no error, or else judgments are true or false only in reference to a higher inclusive thought, which they presuppose, and which must, in the last analysis, be assumed as Infinite and all-inclusive. This result we shall reach by no mystical insight, by no revelation, nor yet by any mere postulate such as we used in former discussions, but by a simple, dry analysis of the meaning of our own thought.

The most formidable opponent of our argument will be, after all, however, not common sense, but that thought mentioned in the last chapter,—the thought that may try to content itself with somewhat plausible jargon, and to say that: *"There is no real difference between truth and error at all, only a kind of opinion or consensus of men about a conventional distinction between what they choose to call truth and what they choose to call error."* This view, as the author has confessed, he once tried to hold. Still this meaningless doctrine of relativity is not the same as the view that contents itself with the postulates before discussed. That view might take, and for the author at one time did take, the possible and intelligible form thus expressible: *"Truth and error, though really distinguishable, are for us distinguished only through our postulates, in so far as relates to past and future time."* Such views, while not denying that there is real truth, despair of the attainability for us of more than momentary truth. But the doctrine of Total Relativity, this view above expressed, differs from genuine skepticism. It tries to put even skepticism to rest, by declaring the opinion, *that there is error,* to be itself an error. This is not merely a moderate expression of human limitations, but jargon, and therefore formidable, because jargon is always unanswerable. When the famous Cretan declared all statements made by Cretans to be in all cases lies, his declaration was hard to refute, because it was such honest-seeming nonsense. Even so with the statement that declares the very existence of error to be an erroneously believed fancy. No *consensus* of men can make an error erroneous. We can only find or commit an error, not create it. When we commit an error, we say what was an error already. If our skeptical view in previous chapters seemed to regard truth and error as mere objects of our postulates, that was only because, to our skepticism, the real truth, the real error, about any real past and future, seemed beyond our reach, so that we had to content ourselves with postulates. But that real error exists is absolutely indubitable.

This being the case, it is evident that even the most thorough-going skepticism is full of assumptions. If I say, "There may be no money in that purse yonder," I assume the existence of the purse yonder in order to make just that particular doubt possible. Of course, however, just that doubt may be rendered meaningless by the discovery of the actual non-existence of that particular purse. If there is no purse yonder, then it is nonsensical either to affirm or to deny that it contains money. And so if the purse of which I speak is an hallucination of mine, then the doubt about whether, as an actually existent purse, it has money in it, is deprived of sense. My real error in that case would lie in supposing the purse itself to exist. If, however, I abandon the first doubt, and go on to doubt the real existence of the purse, I equally assume a room, or some other environment, or at all events the universe, as existent, in order to give sense to my question whether the purse has any being in this environment or in this universe. But if I go yet further, and doubt whether there is any universe at all outside of my thought, what does my doubt yet mean? If it is to be a doubt with any real sense, it must be a doubt still with an object before it. It seems then to imply an assumed order of being, in which there are at least two elements, my lonely thought about an universe, and an empty environment of this thought, in which there is, in fact, no universe. But this empty environment, whose nature is such that my thought does wrong to suppose it to be an universe, what is that? Surely if the doubt is to have meaning, this idea needs further examination. The absolute skepticism is thus full of assumptions.

The first European thinker who seems to have discussed our present problem was Plato, in a too-much-neglected passage of the "Theætetus," [3] where Socrates, replying to the second definition of knowledge given by Theætetus, namely, *knowledge is True Opinion,* answers that his great difficulty has often been to see how any opinion can possibly be false. The conclusion reached by Plato is no very definite one, but the discussion is deeply

[3] Plato, *Th.,* p. 187 *sqq.*

suggestive. And we cannot do better here than to pray that the shade of the mighty Greek may deign to save us now in our distress, and to show us that true nature of error.

III

Logicians are agreed that single ideas, thoughts viewed apart from judgments, are neither true nor false. Only a judgment can be false. And if a reasoning process is said to be false, the real error lies still in an actual or suppressed assertion. A fallacy is a false assertion that a certain conclusion follows from certain premises. Error is therefore generally defined as a judgment that does not agree with its object. In the erroneous judgment, subject and predicate are so combined as, in the object, the corresponding elements are not combined. And thus the judgment comes to be false. Now, in this definition, nothing is doubtful or obscure save the one thing, namely, the *assumed relation between the judgment and its object.* The definition assumes as quite clear that a judgment has an object, wherewith it can agree or not agree. And what is meant by the agreement would not be obscure, if we could see what is meant by the object, and by the possession of this object implied in the pronoun *its.* What then is meant by *its object?* The difficulties involved in this phrase begin to appear as soon as you look closer. First then the object of the assertion is as such supposed to be neither the subject nor the predicate thereof. It is external to the judgment. It has a nature of its own. Furthermore, not all judgments have the same object, so that objects are very numerous. But from the infinity of real or of possible objects the judgment somehow picks out its own. Thus then for a judgment to have an object, there must be something about the judgment that shows what one of the external objects that are beyond itself this judgment does pick out as its own. But this something that gives the judgment its object can only be the intention wherewith the judgment is accompanied. A judgment has as object only what it intends to have as object. It has to conform only to that to which it wants to conform. But the essence of an intention is the knowledge of what one intends. One can, for instance, intend a deed or any of its consequences only in so far as he foresees them. I cannot be said to intend the accidental or the remote or even the immediate consequences of anything that I do, unless I foresaw that they would follow; and this is true however much the lawyers and judges may find it practically necessary to hold me responsible for these consequences. Even so we all find it practically useful to regard one of our fellows as in error in case his assertions, as we understand them, seem to us to lead to consequences that we do not approve. But our criticisms of his opinions, just like legal judgments of his acts, are not intended to be exact. Common sense will admit that, unless a man is thinking of the object of which I suppose him to be thinking, he makes no real error by merely failing to agree with the object that I have in mind. If the knights in the fable judge each other to be wrong, that is because each knight takes the other's shield to be identical with the shield as he himself has it in mind. In fact neither of them is in error, unless his assertion is false for the shield as he intended to make it his object.

So then judgments err only by disagreeing with their intended objects, and they can intend an object only in so far forth as this object is known to the thought that makes the judgment. Such, it would seem, is the consequence of the common-sense view. But in this case a judgment can be in error only if it is knowingly in error. That also, as it seems, follows from the common-sense suppositions. Or, if we will have it in syllogistic form:—

Everything intended is something known. The object even of an erroneous judgment is intended. ∴ The object even of an error is something known.

Or: Only what is known can be erred about. Nor can we yet be content with what common sense will at once reply, namely, that our syllogism uses *known* ambiguously, and that the object of an erroneous judgment is known enough to constitute it the object, and not enough to prevent the error about it. This must no doubt be the fact, but it is not of itself clear; on the contrary, just here is the problem. As common sense conceives the matter, the object of a judgment is not as such the whole outside world of common sense, with all its intimate interdependence of facts, with all its unity in the midst of diversity. On the contrary, the object of any judgment is just that portion of the then conceived world, just that fragment, that aspect, that element of a supposed reality, which is seized upon for the purposes of just this judgment. Only such a momentarily grasped fragment of the truth can possibly be present in any one moment of thought as the object of a single assertion. Now it is hard to say how within this arbitrarily chosen fragment itself there can still be room for

the partial knowledge that is sufficient to give to the judgment its object, but insufficient to secure to the judgment its accuracy. If I aim at a mark with my gun, I can fail to hit it, because choosing and hitting a mark are totally distinct acts. But, in the judgment, choosing and knowing the object seem inseparable. No doubt somehow our difficulty is soluble, but we are here trying first to show that it is a difficulty.

To illustrate here by a familiar case, when we speak of things that are solely matters of personal preference, such as the pleasure of a sleigh-ride, the taste of olives, or the comfort of a given room, and when we only try to tell how these things appear to us, then plainly our judgments, if sincere, cannot be in error. As these things are to us, so they are. We are their measure. To doubt our truthfulness in these cases is to doubt after the fashion of the student who wondered whether the star that the astronomers call Uranus may not be something else after all, and not really Uranus. Surely science does not progress very far or run into great danger of error so long as it employs itself in discovering such occult mysteries as the names of the stars. But our present question is, How do judgments that can be and that are erroneous differ in nature from these that cannot be erroneous? If astronomers would be equally right in case they should agree to call Uranus Humpty Dumpty, why are not all judgments equally favored? Since the judgment chooses its own object, and has it only in so far as it chooses it, how can it be in that partial relation to its object which is implied in the supposition of an erroneous assertion?

Yet again, to illustrate the difficulty in another aspect, we can note that not only is error impossible about the perfectly well-known, but that error is equally impossible, save in the form of direct self-contradiction, about what is absolutely unknown. Spite of the religious awe of some people in presence of the Unknowable, it is safe to say, somewhat irreverently, that about a really Unknowable nobody could make any sincere and self-consistent assertions that could be errors. For self-consistent assertions about the Unknowable would of necessity be meaningless. And being meaningless, they could not well be false. For instance, one could indeed not say that the Unknowable contemplates war with France, or makes sunspots, or will be the next Presidential candidate, because that would be contradicting one's self. For if the Unknowable did any of these things, it would no longer be the Unknowable, but would become either the known or the discoverable. But avoid such self-contradiction, and you cannot err about the Unknowable. For the Unknowable is simply our old friend *Abracadabra*, a word that has no meaning, and by hypothesis never can get any. So if I say that the Unknowable dines *in vacuo* with the chimera, or is Humpty Dumpty, I talk nonsense, and am therefore unable to make a mistake. Nonsense is error only when it involves self-contradiction. Avoid that, and nonsense cannot blunder, having no object outside of itself with which it must agree. But all this illustrates from the other side our difficulty. Is not the object of a judgment, in so far as it is unknown to that judgment, like the Unknowable for that judgment? To be in error about the application of a symbol, you must have a symbol that symbolizes something. But in so far as the thing symbolized is not known through the symbol, how is it symbolized by that symbol? Is it not, like the Unknowable, once for all out of the thought, so that one cannot just then be thinking about it at all, and so cannot, in this thought at least, be making blunders about it? But in so far as the thing symbolized is, through the symbol, in one's thought, why is it not known, and so correctly judged? All this involves that old question of the nature of symbols. They are to mean for us more than we know that they mean. How can that be? No doubt all that is really possible, but how?

IV

We follow our difficulty into another department. Let us attempt a sort of provisional psychological description of a judgment as a state of mind. So regarded, a judgment is simply a fact that occurs in somebody's thought. If we try to describe it as an occurrence, without asking whence it came, we shall perhaps find in it three elements,—elements which are in some fashion described in Ueberweg's well-known definition of a judgment as the "Consciousness about the objective validity of a subjective union of ideas." Our interpretation of them shall be this: The elements are: The *Subject*, with the accompanying shade of curiosity about it; the *Predicate*, with the accompanying sense of its worth in satisfying a part of our curiosity about the subject; and the *Sense of Dependence*, whereby we feel the value of this act to lie, not in itself, but in its agreement with a vaguely felt Beyond, that stands out there as Object.

Now this analysis of the elements of a judgment is no explanation of our difficulties; and in fact for the moment only embarrasses us more. But the nature of the difficulty may come home to us somewhat more clearly, if we try to follow the thread of this analysis a little further. Even if it is a very imperfect account, it may serve to lead us up to the true insight that we seek into the nature of error. Let us make the analysis a little more detailed.

In its typical form then, the judgment as a mental state seems to us to begin with a relatively incomplete or unstable or disconnected mass of consciousness, which we have called the Subject, as it first begins to be present to us. This subject-idea is attended by some degree of effort, namely, of attention, whose tendency is to complete this incomplete subject by bringing it into closer connection with more familiar mental life. This more familiar life is represented by the predicate-idea. If the effort is successful, the subject has new elements united to it, assumes in consciousness a definiteness, a coherency with other states, a familiarity, which it lacked at the outset of the act of judgment; and this coherency it gets through its union with the predicate. All this is accompanied further by what one for short may call a sense of dependence. The judgment feels itself not alone, but looks to a somewhat indefinite object as the model after which the present union of ideas is to be fashioned. And in this way we explain how the judgment is, in those words of Ueberweg's definition, "the consciousness about the objective validity of a subjective union of ideas."

Now as a mere completion of subject-idea through the addition of a predicate-idea, the judgment is simply a mental phenomenon, having interest only to the person that experiences it, and to a psychologist. But as true or as false the judgment must be viewed in respect to the indefinite object of what we have called the sense of dependence, whereby the judgment is accompanied. Seldom in any ordinary judgment does this object become perfectly full and clear; for to make it so would often require many, perhaps an infinite, series of judgments. Yet, for the one judgment, the object, whether full and clear or not, exists as object only in so far forth as the sense of dependence has defined it. And the judgment is true or false only with reference to this undefined object. The intention to agree with the object is contained in the sense of dependence upon the object, and remains for this judgment incomplete, like the object itself. Somewhat vaguely this single act intends to agree with this vague object.

Such being the case, how can the judgment, as thus described, fairly be called false? As mere psychological combination of ideas it is neither true nor false. As accompanied by the sense of dependence upon an object, it would be false if it disagreed with its imperfectly defined object. But, as described, the only object that the judgment has is this imperfectly defined one. With this, in so far as it is for the moment defined, the judgment must needs agree. In so far as it is not defined, it is however not object for this judgment at all, but for some other one. What the imperfect sense of dependence would further imply if it existed in a complete instead of in an incomplete state, nobody can tell, any more than one can tell what towns would grow up by a given rain-pool, if it were no pool, but a great lake. The object of a single judgment, being what it is, namely, a vaguely defined object, present to this judgment, is just what it is for this judgment, and the judgment seems once for all to be true, in case it is sincere.

Some one may here at once answer that we neglect in this description the close interdependence of various judgments. Thought, some one may say, is an organic unity. Separated from all else but its own incompletely defined object, a single judgment cannot be erroneous. Only in the organic unity of a series of judgments, having a common object, is the error of one of them possible. We reply that all this will turn out to be just our result. But the usual supposition at the outset is that any judgment has by itself its own object, so that thereby alone, apart from other judgments, it stands or falls. And thus far we have tried to show that this natural supposition leads us into difficulty. We cannot see how a single sincere judgment should possibly fail to agree with its own chosen object. But enough of our problem in general. We must consider certain classes of errors more in detail. Let us see how, in these special classes of cases, we shall succeed in verifying the natural presupposition of common sense, which regards error as possible only when our object is not wholly present to mind, and which assumes that a judgment can have an object that is yet only partially present to mind. In choosing the classes of cases, we shall first follow common sense as to their definition. We shall take just the assumptions of daily life, and shall show that they lead us into difficulty. We are not for the first bound to explain why these assumptions are made. That common sense makes them is enough.

But let the reader remember: The whole value of our argument lies in its perfect generality. However much we dwell on particular classes of errors, we care nothing for the proof that just those errors are inexplicable, but only for the fact that they illustrate how, without some entirely new hypothesis, absolutely all error becomes impossible. This or that class of judgments may be one in which all the judgments are relative, but the total relativity of our thought implies an incomprehensible and contradictory state of things. Any hypothesis about error that makes total relativity the only admissible view, must therefore give place to some new hypothesis. And our illustrations in the following are intended to show that just what constitutes the difficulty in respect of these illustrations, makes the existence of any error inexplicable without some new hypothesis.

V

The class of errors that we shall first take seems, to common sense, common enough. It is the class known as errors about our neighbor's states of mind. Let us then, for argument's sake, assume without proof that our neighbors do exist. For we are not here concerned to answer Solipsism, but merely to exemplify the difficulties about the nature of error. If our neighbors did not exist, then the nature of the error that would lie in saying that they do exist would present almost exactly the same difficulties. We prefer, however, to begin with the common-sense assumption about ourselves and our neighbors as separate individuals, and to ask how error can then arise in judging of our neighbors' minds.

In the first place then: Who is my neighbor? Surely, on the assumptions that we all make, and that we made all through the ethical part of our discussion, he is no one of my thoughts, nor is any part of him ever any part of my thought. He is not my object, but, in Professor Clifford's phrase, an "eject," wholly outside of my ideas. He is no "thing in my dream," just as I am not in his dream.

Yet I make judgments about him, and he makes them about me. And when I make judgments about him, I do so by having in my thought some set of my own ideas that, although not himself, do yet, as I say, represent him. A kind of dummy, a symbol, a graven image of my own thought's creation, a phantom of mine, stands there in me as the representative of his mind;

and all I say about my neighbor's inner life refers directly to this representative. The Scottish philosophy has had much to say to the world about what it calls direct or presentative, as opposed to representative, knowledge of objects. But surely the most obstinate Scottish philosopher that ever ate oatmeal cannot hold so tenaciously by his national doctrine as to say that I have, according to common sense, anything but a representative knowledge of my neighbor's thoughts and feelings. That is the only sort of knowledge that common sense will regard as possible to me, if so much as that is possible. But how I can know about this outside being is not now our concern. We notice only that our difficulty about error comes back to us in a new form. For how can I err about my neighbor, since, for this common-sense view, he is not even partly in my thoughts? How can I intend that as the object of my thought which never can be object for me at all?

But not everybody will at once feel the force of this question. We must be more explicit. Let us take the now so familiar suggestion of our great humorist about the six people that take part in every conversation between two persons. If John and Thomas are talking together, then the real John and Thomas, their respective ideas of themselves, and their ideas of each other, are all parties to the conversation. Let us consider four of these persons, namely, the real John, the real Thomas, John as Thomas conceives him, and Thomas as John conceives him. When John judges, of whom does he think? Plainly of that which can be an object to his thoughts, namely, of *his* Thomas. About whom then can he err? About *his* Thomas? No, for he knowns him too well. His conception of Thomas is his conception, and what he asserts it to be, that it is for him. About the real Thomas? No, for it should seem, according to common sense, that he has nothing to do with the real Thomas in his thought, since that Thomas never becomes any part of his thought at all. "But," says one, "there must be some fallacy here, since we are sure that John *can* err about the real Thomas." Indeed he can, say we; but ours is not this fallacy. Common sense has made it. Common sense has said: "Thomas never is in John's thought, and yet John can blunder about Thomas." How shall we unravel the knot?

One way suggests itself. Mayhap we have been too narrow in our definition of *object*. Common sense surely insists that objects are outside of our thought. If, then, I have a judgment, and another being sees both my judgment and some outside object that was not in my thought, and sees how that thought is unlike the object in some critical respect, this being could say that my assertion was an error. So then with John and Thomas. *If Thomas could know John's thoughts about him,* then Thomas could possibly see John's error. That is what is meant by the error in John's thought.

But mere disagreement of a thought with any random object does not make the thought erroneous. The judgment must disagree with *its chosen* object. If John never has Thomas in thought at all, how *can* John choose the real Thomas as his object? If I judge about a penholder that is in this room, and if the next room is in all respects like this, save for a penholder in it, with which my assertion does not agree, who, looking at that penholder in that other room, can say that my judgment is false? For I meant not that penholder when I spoke, but this one. I knew perhaps nothing about that one, had it not in mind, and so could not err about it. Even so, suppose that outside of John there is a real Thomas, similar, as it happens, to John's ideal Thomas, but lacking some thought or affection that John attributes to his ideal Thomas. Does that make John's notion an error? No, for he spoke and could speak only of his ideal Thomas. The real Thomas was the other room, that he knew not of, the other side of the shield, that he never could conceive. His Thomas was his phantom Thomas. This phantom it is that he judges and thinks about, and his thoughts may have their own consistency or inconsistency. But with the real other person they have nothing to do. The real other is not his object, and how can he err about what is not object for him?

Absurd, indeed, some one will reply to us. John and Thomas have to deal with representative phantoms of each other, to be sure; but that only makes each more apt to err about the real other. And the test that they can err is a very simple one. Suppose a spectator, a third person, to whom John and Thomas were both somehow directly present, so that he as it were included both of them. Then John's judgment of his phantom Thomas would be by this spectator at once compared with the real Thomas, and even so would Thomas's judgment of John be treated. If now John's phantom Thomas agreed with the real Thomas, then John's ideas would be declared in so far truthful; otherwise they would be erroneous. And this explains what is meant by John's power to err about Thomas.

The explanation is fair enough for its own purpose, and we

shall need it again before long. But just now we cannot be content with it. For what we want to know is not what the judgment of a third thinker would be in case these two were somehow not independent beings at all, but things in this third being's thought. For we have started out with the supposition of common sense that John and Thomas are not dreams or thoughts of some higher third being, but that they are independent beings by themselves. Our supposition may have to be given up hereafter, but for the present we want to hold fast to it. And so John's judgment, which we had supposed to be about the independently existing Thomas, has now turned out to be only a judgment about John's idea of Thomas. But judgments are false only in case they disagree with their intended objects. What, however, is the object of John's judgment when he thinks about Thomas? Not the real Thomas, who could not possibly be an object in another man's thoughts. John's real object being an ideal Thomas, he cannot, if sincere, and if fully conscious of what he means by Thomas, fail to agree in his statements with his own ideal. In short, on this our original supposition, John and Thomas are independent entities, each of which cannot possibly enter in real person into the thoughts of the other. Each may be somehow represented in the other's thoughts by a phantom, and only this phantom can be intended by the other when he judges about the first. For unless one talks nonsense, it should seem as if one could mean only what one has in mind.

Thus, like the characters in a certain Bab ballad, real John, real Thomas, the people in this simple tale, are total strangers to each other. You might as well ask a blind man to make true or false judgments about the real effects of certain combinations of colors, as to ask either John or Thomas, defined as common sense defines them, to make any judgments about each other. Common sense will assert that a blind man can learn and repeat verbally correct statements about color, or verbally false statements about color, but, according to the common-sense view, in no case can he err about color-ideas as such, which are never present to him. You will be quite ready to say that a dog can make mistakes about the odors of the numberless tracks on the highway. You will assure us, however, that you cannot make mistakes about them because these odors do not exist for you. According to the common-sense view, a mathematician can make blunders in demonstrating the properties of equations. A Bushman cannot, for he can have no ideas corresponding to equations. But how then can John or Thomas make errors about each other, when neither is more present to the other than is color to the blind man, the odor of the tracks on the highway to the dog's master, or the idea of an equation to a Bushman? Here common sense forsakes us, assuring us that there is such error, but refusing to define it.

The inconsistency involved in all this common-sense view, and the consequences of the inconsistency, will appear yet better with yet further illustration. A dream is false in so far as it contains the judgment that such and such things exist apart from us; but at least in so far as we merely assert in our dreams about the objects as we conceive them, we make true assertions. But is not our actual life of assertions about actual fellow-beings much like a dream to which there should happen to correspond some real scene or event in the world? Such correspondence would not make the dream really "true," nor yet false. It would be a co-incidence, remarkable for an outside observer, but none the less would the dreamer be thinking in his dream not about external objects, but about the things in his dream. But is not our sup-posed Thomas so and only so in the thought of John as he would be if John chanced to dream of a Thomas that was, to an external spectator, like the real one? Is not then the phantom Thomas, John's only direct object, actually a thing in John's thought? Is then the independent Thomas an object for John in any sense?

Yet again. Let us suppose that two men are shut up, each in a closed room by himself, and for his whole life; and let us sup-pose that by a lantern contrivance each of them is able at times to produce on the wall of the other's room a series of pictures. But neither of them can ever know what pictures he produces in the other's room, and neither can know anything of the other's room, as such, but only of the pictures. Let the two remain for-ever in this relation. One of them, A, sees on his wall pictures, which resemble more or less what he has seen in his own room at other times. Yet he perceives these to be only pictures, and he supposes them to represent what goes on in another room, which he conceives as like his own. He is interested, he examines the phenomena, he predicts their future changes, he passes judgment upon them. He may, if you like to continue the hypothesis, find some way of affecting them, by himself acting in a way mys-terious to himself so as to produce changes in B's actual room, which again affect the pictures that the real B produces in A's

room. Thus A might hold what he would call communication
with his phantom room. Even so, B lives with pictures before
him that are produced from A's room. Now one more supposition, namely, that A and B have absolutely no other means of
communication, that both are shut up altogether and always
have been, that neither has any objects before him but his own
thoughts and the changing pictures on the wall of his room. In
this case what difference does it make whether or no the pictures
in A's room are actually like the things that could be seen in B's
room? Will that make A's judgments either true or false? Even
if A, acting by means that he himself cannot understand, is able
to control the pictures on his wall by some alteration that he unconsciously produces in B's room and its pictures, still A cannot
be said to have any knowledge of the real B and his room at all.
And, for the same reason, A cannot make mistakes about the
real room of B, for he will never even think of that real room.
He will, like a man in a dream, think and be able to think
only of the pictures on his wall. And when he refers them to an
outside cause, he does not mean by this cause the real B and his
real room, for he has never dreamed of the real B, but only of
the pictures and of his own interpretation of them. He can therefore make no false judgments about B's room, any more than a
Bushman can make false judgments about the integral calculus.

If to our present world there does correspond a second world
somewhere off in space, a world exactly like this, where just the
same events at every instant do actually take place, still the
judgments that we make about our world are not actually true
or false with reference to that world, for we *mean* this world,
not that one, when we judge. Why are not John's Thomas and
the real Thomas related like this world and that second world
in distant space? Why are not both like the relation of A's conceived phantom room and B's real room? Nothing of either real
room is ever present to the other. Each prisoner can make true
or false judgments if at all, then, only about the pictures on his
wall; but neither has even the suggestion that could lead him to
make a blunder about the other's real room, of which he has and
can have not the faintest idea.

One reason why we fail to see at once this fact lies in the
constant tendency to regard the matter from the point of view
of a third person, instead of from the point of view that we still
implicitly attribute to A and B themselves. If A could get outside
of his room once and see B's room, then he could say: "My

picture was a good one," or the reverse. But, in the supposed case, he not only never sees B's room, but he never sees anything but his own pictures, never gets out of his room at all for any purpose. Hence, his sole objects of assertion being his pictures, he is innocent of any power to err about B's room as it is in itself, even as the man born blind is innocent of any power to err about the relations of colors.

Now this relation of A and B, as they were supposed to dwell in their perpetual imprisonment, is essentially like the relation that we previously postulated between two independent subjects. If I cannot have you in my thought at all, but only a picture produced by you, I am in respect to you like A confined to the pictures produced from B's room. However much I may fancy that I am talking of you, I am really talking about my idea of you, which for me can have no relation whatever to the real you. And so John and Thomas remain shut up in their prisons. Each thinks of his phantom of the other. Only a third person, who included them both, who in fact treated them as, in the Faust-Epilogue, the *Pater Seraphicus* treats the *selige Knaben* (*Er nimmt sie in sich,* says the stage direction)—only such an inclusive thought could compare the phantoms with the real, and only in him, not in themselves, would John and Thomas have any ideas of each other at all, true or false.

This result is foreign to our every-day thought, because this every-day thought really makes innocent use of two contradictory views of the relations of conscious beings. On the one hand we regard them as utterly remote from one another, as what Professor Clifford called ejects; and then we speak of them as if the thoughts of one could as such become thoughts of the other, or even as if one of them could as an independent being still become object in the thought of the other. No wonder that, with such contradictory assumptions as to the nature of our relations to our neighbors, we find it very easy to make absurd statements about the meaning of error. The contradiction of common sense has in fact just here much to do with the ethical illusion that we called the illusion of selfishness. To clear up this point will be useful to us, therefore, in more ways than one.

V I

Dissappointed once more in our efforts to understand how error is possible, we turn to another class of cases, which lie in a direction where, at least for this once, all will surely be plain. Errors about matters of fact or experience are certainly clear enough in nature. And as this class of errors is practically most important, the subtleties of our previous investigation may be dismissed with light heart so soon as we have gotten rid of the few little questions that will now beset us. It is to be noted that all errors about material objects, about the laws of nature, about history, and about the future, are alike errors about our actual or possible experiences. We expect or postulate an experience that at the given time, or under the given conditions, turns out to be other than it was postulated or expected to be. Now since our experiences not now present are objective facts, and capable of clear definition, it would seem clear that error concerning them is an easily comprehensible thing.

But alas! again we are disappointed. That errors in matters of experience are common enough is indubitable, but equally evident becomes the difficulty of defining what they are and how they are possible. Take the case of error about an expected future. What do we mean by a future time? How do we identify a particular time? Both these questions plunge us into the sea of problems about the nature of time itself. When I say, *Thus and so will it be at such and such a future moment,* I postulate certain realities not now given to my consciousness. And singular realities they are. For they have now no existence at all. Yet I postulate that I can err about them. Thus their non-existence is a peculiar kind of non-existence, and requires me to make just such and such affirmations about it. If I fail to correspond to the true nature of this non-existent reality, I make an error; and it is postulated not merely that my present statement will in that case hereafter turn out false or become false, but also that it is now false, is at this moment an error, even though the reality with which it is to agree is centuries off in the future. But this is not all the difficulty. I postulate also that an error in prediction can be discovered when the time comes by the failure of the prediction to verify itself. I postulate then that I can look back and say: Thus and thus I predicted about this moment, and thus and thus it has come to pass, and this event contradicts that expectation. But can I in fact ever accomplish this comparison at all? And is the comparison very easily intelligible? For when the event comes to pass, the expectation no longer exists. The two thoughts, namely, expectation and actual experience, are separate thoughts, far apart in time. How can I bring them together to compare them, so as to see if they have the same object? It will not do to appeal to memory for the purpose; for the same question would recur about the memory in its relation to the original thought. How can a past thought, being past, be compared to a present thought to see whether they stand related? The past thought lived in itself, had its own ideas of what it then called future, and its own interpretation thereof. How can you show, or intelligently affirm, that the conception which the past expectation had of its future moment is so identical with the conception which this present thought has of this present moment, as to make these two conceived moments one and the same? Here in short we have supposed two different ideas, one of an expected future, the other of an experienced present, and we have supposed the two ideas to be widely separated in time, and by hypothesis they are not together in one consciousness at all. Now how can one say that in fact they relate to the same moment at all? How is it intelligible to say that they do? How, in fine, can a not-given future be a real object of any thought; and how, when it is once the object thereof, can any subsequent moment be identified with this object?

A present thought and a past thought are in fact separate, even as were John and Thomas. Each one means the object that it thinks. How can they have a common object? Are they not once for all different thoughts, each with its own intent? But in order to render intelligible the existence of error about matters of fact, we must make the unintelligible assumption, so it would seem, that these two different thoughts have the same intent, and are but one. And such is the difficulty that we find in our second great class of cases.

VII

So much for the problem, both in general and in some particular instances. But now may not the reader insist, after all, that there can be in this wise no errors whatever? Contradictory as it seems, have we not, after all, put our judgments into a position whence escape for us is impossible? If every judgment is thus by its nature bound up in a closed circle of thought, with no outlook, can any one come afterwards and give it an external object? Perhaps, then, there is a way out of our difficulty by frankly saying that our thoughts may be neither truths nor errors beyond themselves, but just occurrences, with a meaning wholly subjective.

We desire the reader to try to realize this view of total relativity once more in the form in which, with all its inherent absurdities, it now comes back to us for the last time. It says, "Every judgment, *A is B,* in fact does agree and can agree only with its own object, which is present in mind when it is made. With no external object can it agree or fail to agree. It stands alone, with its own object. It has neither truth nor error beyond itself. It fulfills all its intentions, and is true, if it agrees with what was present to it when it was thought. Only in this sense is there any truth or falsity possible for our thought."

But once more, this inviting way out of the difficulty needs only to be tried to reveal its own contradictions. The thought that says, "No judgment is true beyond itself," is that thought true beyond itself or not? If it is true beyond itself, then we have the possibility of other truth than the merely subjective or relative truth. If it is false, then equally we have objective falsity. If it is neither true nor false, then the doctrine of relativity has not been affirmed at all as a truth. One sets up an idea of a world of separate, disorganized thoughts, and then says, "Each of them deals only with its own object, and they have no unity that could make them true or false." But still this world that one thus sets up must be the true world. Else is there no meaning in the doctrine of relativity. Twist as one will, one gets not out of the whirlpool of thought. Error must be real, and yet, as common sense arranges these judgments and their relations to one another, error cannot be real. There is so far no escape.

The perfectly general character of the argument must be understood. One might escape it if it applied to any one class of errors only. Then one would say: "In fact, the class of cases in question may be cases that exclude the possibility of both truth and error." But no, that cannot be urged against us, for our argument applies equally to all possible errors. In short, either no error at all is possible, or else there must be possible an infinite mass of error. For the possibilities of thought being infinite, either all thought is excluded once for all from the possibility of error, or else to every possible truth there can be opposed an infinite mass of error. All this infinite mass is at stake upon the issue of our investigation. Total relativity, or else an infinite possibility of truth and error; that is the alternative before us. And total relativity of thought involves self-contradiction.

Every way but one has been tried to lead us out of our difficulty. Shall we now give up the whole matter, and say that error
plainly exists, but baffles definition? This way may please most
people, but the critical philosophy knows of no unanswerable
problem affecting the work of thought in itself considered. Here
we need only patience and reflection, and we are sure to be some
day rewarded. And indeed our solution is not far off, but very
nigh us. We have indicated it all along. To explain how one
could be in error about his neighbor's thoughts, we suggested
the case where John and Thomas should be present to a third
thinker whose thought should include them both. We objected
to this suggestion that thus the natural presupposition that John
and Thomas are separate self-existent beings would be contra-
dicted. But on this natural presupposition neither of these two
subjects could become object to the other at all, and error would
here be impossible. Suppose then that we drop the natural presupposition, and say that John and Thomas are both actually
present to and included in a third and higher thought. To explain
the possibility of error about matters of fact seemed hard, because of the natural postulate that time is a pure succession of
separate moments, so that the future is now as future non-existent,
and so that judgments about the future lack real objects, capable
of identification. Let us then drop this natural postulate, and
declare time once for all present in all its moments to an universal all-inclusive thought. And to sum up, let us overcome all
our difficulties by declaring that all the many Beyonds, which
single significant judgments seem vaguely and separately to postulate, are present as fully realized intended objects to the unity
of an all-inclusive, absolutely clear, universal, and conscious
thought, of which all judgments, true or false, are but fragments,
the whole being at once Absolute Truth and Absolute Knowledge. Then all our puzzles will disappear at a stroke, and error
will be possible, because any one finite thought, viewed in relation to its own intent, may or may not be seen by this higher
thought as successful and adequate in this intent.

How this absolute thought is to be related to individual
thoughts, we can in general very simply define. When one says:
"This color now before me is red, and to say that it is blue would
be to make a blunder," one represents an including consciousness.
One includes in one's present thought three distinct elements,
and has them present in the unity of a single moment of insight.

These elements are, first, the perception of red; secondly, the reflective judgment whose object is this perception, and whose agreement with the object constitutes its own truth; and, thirdly, the erroneous reflection, *This is blue,* which is in the same thought compared with the perception and rejected as error. Now, viewed as separate acts of thought, apart from the unity of an including thought, these three elements would give rise to the same puzzles that we have been considering. It is their presence in a higher and inclusive thought that makes their relations plain. Even so we must conceive the relation of John's thought to the united total of thought that includes him and Thomas. Real John and his phantom Thomas, real Thomas and his phantom John, are all present as elements in the including consciousness, which completes the incomplete intentions of both the individuals, constitutes their true relations, and gives the thought of each about the other whatever of truth or of error it possesses. In short, error becomes possible as one moment or element in a higher truth, that is, in a consciousness that makes the error a part of itself, while recognizing it as error.

So far then we propose this as a possible solution for our puzzles. But now we may insist upon it as the only possible solution. *Either there is no such thing as error, which statement is a flat self-contradiction, or else there is an infinite unity of conscious thought to which is present all possible truth.* For suppose that there is error. Then there must be an infinite mass of error possible. If error is possible at all, then as many errors are possible as you please, since, to every truth, an indefinite mass of error may be opposed. Nor is this mere possibility enough. An error is possible for us when we are able to make a false judgment. But in order that the judgment should be false when made, it must have been false before it was made. An error is possible only when the judgment in which the error is to be expressed always was false. Error, if possible, is then eternally actual. Each error so possible implies a judgment whose intended object is beyond itself, and is also the object of the corresponding true judgment. But two judgments cannot have the same object save as they are both present to one thought. For as separate thoughts they would have separate subjects, predicates, intentions, and objects, even as we have previously seen in detail. So that every error implies a thought that includes it and the corresponding truth in the unity of one thought with the object of both of them. Only as present to an including thought are they either true or false. Thus then we are driven to assume an infinite thought, judging truth and error. But that this infinite thought must also be a rational unity, not a mere aggregate of truths, is evident from the fact that error is possible not only as to objects, but as to the relations of objects, so that all the possible relations of all the objects in space, in time, or in the world of the barely possible, must also be present to the all-including thought. And to know all relations at once is to know them in absolute rational unity, as forming in their wholeness one single thought.

What, then, is an error? An error, we reply, is an incomplete thought, that to a higher thought, which includes it and its intended object, is known as having failed in the purpose that it more or less clearly had, and that is fully realized in this higher thought. And without such higher inclusive thought, an assertion has no external object, and is no error.

VIII

If our argument were a Platonic dialogue, there would be hereabouts an interruption from some impatient Thrasymachus or Callicles or Polus, who would have been watching us, threatening and muttering, during all of the latter part of our discussion. At last, perhaps, συστρέψας ἑαυτὸν ὥσπερ θηρίον, he would spring upon us, and would say: "Why, you nonsense-mongers, have you not bethought you of the alternative that represents the reality in this question of yours? Namely, an error is an error, neither to the thought that thinks it, nor of necessity to any higher inclusive thought, but only to a *possible* critical thought that should undertake afterwards to compare it with its object. An error is a thought such that *if* a critical thought *did* come and compare it with its object, it *would be* seen to be false. And it has an object for such a critical thought. This critical thought need not be real and actually include it, but may be only a *possible* judge of its truth. Hence your Infinite all-knower is no reality, only a logical possibility; and your insight amounts to this, that if all *were* known to an all-knower, he *would judge* error to be mistaken. And so error is what he would perceive to be error. What does all that amount to but worthless tautology?"

This argument of our Thrasymachus is the only outwardly

plausible objection that we fear to the foregoing analysis, because it is the only objection that fully expresses the old-established view of common sense about such problems. Though common sense never formulates our present difficulty, common sense still dimly feels that to some possible (not actual) judge of truth, appeal is made when we say that a thing is false not merely for us, but in very truth. And this possible judge of common sense we have now unhesitatingly declared to be an Infinite Actuality, absolutely necessary to *constitute* the relation of truth and error. Without it there is for our view no truth or error conceivable. The words, *This is true*, or *This is false*, mean nothing, we declare, unless there is the inclusive thought for which the truth is true, the falsehood false. No barely possible judge, who *would* see the error *if* he were there, will do for us. He must be there, this judge, to constitute the error. Without him nothing but total subjectivity would be possible; and thought would then become purely a pathological phenomenon, an occurrence without truthfulness or falsity, an occurrence that would interest anybody if it could be observed; but that, unfortunately, being only a momentary phantom, could not be observed at all from without, but must be dimly felt from within. Our thought needs the Infinite Thought in order that it may get, through this Infinite judge, the privilege of being so much as even an error.

This, it will be said, is but reassertion. But how do we maintain this view against our Thrasymachus? Our answer is only a repetition of things that we have already had to say, in the argument for what we here reassert. If the judgment existed alone, without the inclusive thought to judge it, then, as it existed alone, it either had an object, or had none. But if it had none, it was no error. If it had one, then either it knew what its object actually was, or it did not know what its object was, or it partially knew and partially did not know what its object actually was. In the first case the judgment must have been an identical one, like the judgment *A pain is a pain*. Such a judgment knows its own object, therefore cannot fail to agree with it, and cannot be an error. If the judgment knew not its own object at all, then it had no meaning, and so could not have failed to agree with the object that it had not. If, however, this separate judgment knew its object enough to intend just that object, but not enough to insure agreement with it, all our difficulties return. The possible judge cannot give the judgment its complete object until he becomes its actual judge. Yet as fair judge he must then give it the object that it already had without him. Meanwhile, however, the judgment remains in the unintelligible attitude previously studied at length. It is somehow possessed of just the object it intends, but yet does not know in reality what it does intend, else it would avoid error. Its object, in so far as unknown to it, is no object for it; and yet only in so far as the object is thus unknown can it be erred about. What helps in all this the barely possible judge? The actual judge must be there; and for him the incomplete intention must be complete. He knows what is really this judgment's object, for he knows what is imperfectly meant in it. He knows the dream, and the interpretation thereof. He knows both the goal and the way thither. But all this is, to the separate judgment as such, a mystery.

In fact, the separate judgments, waiting for the possible judge to test them, are like a foolish man wandering in a wood, who is asked whether he has lost his way. "I may have lost it," he answers. "But whither are you going?" "That I cannot tell." "Have you no goal?" "I may have, but I have no notion what it is." "What then do you mean by saying that you may have lost the way to this place that you are not seeking? For you seem to be seeking no place; how then can you have lost the way thither?" "I mean that some possible other man, who was wise enough to find whither I am trying to go, might possibly, in his wisdom, also perceive that I am not on the way to that place. So I may be going away from my chosen goal, although I am unaware what goal it is that I have chosen." Such a demented man as this would fairly represent the meaningless claim of the separate judgment, either to truthfulness, or to the chance of error.

In short, though the partial thought may be, as such, unconscious of its own aim, it can be so unconscious only in case it is contained in a total thought as one moment thereof.

It will be seen that wherever we have dealt in the previous argument with the possibility of error as a mere possibility, we have had to use the result of the previous chapter concerning the nature of possibility itself. The idea of the barely possible, in which there is no actuality, is an empty idea. If anything is possible, then, when we say so, we postulate something as actually existent in order to constitute this possibility. The conditions of possible error must be actual. Bare possibility is blank nothingness. If the nature of error necessarily and with perfect generality demands certain conditions, then these conditions are as external as the erroneousness of error itself is eternal. And thus the inclusive thought, which constitutes the error, must be postulated as existent.

So, finally, let one try to affirm that the infinite content of the all-including mind does not exist, and that the foregoing idealism is a mere illusion of ours. He will find that he is involved in a circle from which there is no escape. For let him return to the position of total relativity and so say: "The infinite thought is unreal for me, and hence you are wrong." But then also he admits that we are right, for in affirming this infinite we affirm, according to this doctrine of total relativity itself, something that is just as true as it seems to us to be true. The opposing argument is thus at each moment of its progress involved in a contradiction. Or again, let him insist that our doctrine is not only relatively, but really false. Then however he will fail to show us what this real falsity is. In fact he says what all our previous examination shows to mean, this, namely, that an infinite thought does exist, and does experience the truth, and compares our thought with the truth, and then observes this thought of ours to be false, that is, it discovers that itself is non-existent. Whoever likes this result may hold it if he can.

IX

Now that our argument is completed as an investigation, let us review it in another way. We started from the fact of Error. That there is error is indubitable. What is, however, an error? The substance of our whole reasoning about the nature of error amounted to the result that in and of itself alone, no single judgment is or can be an error. Only as actually included in a higher thought, that gives to the first its completed object, and compares it therewith, is the first thought an error. It remains otherwise a mere mental fragment, a torso, a piece of driftwood, neither true nor false, objectless, no complete act of thought at all. But the higher thought must include the opposed truth, to which the error is compared in that higher thought. The higher thought is the whole truth, of which the error is by itself an incomplete fragment.

Now, as we saw with this as a starting-point, there is no stopping-place short of an Infinite Thought. The possibilities of error are infinite. Infinite then must be the inclusive thought. Here is this stick, this brickbat, this snow-flake: there is an infinite mass of error possible about any one of them, and notice, not merely possible is it, but actual. All the infinite series of blunders that you could make about them not only would be blunders, but in very truth now are blunders, though you personally could never commit them all. You cannot in fact *make* a truth or a falsehood by your thought. You only *find* one. From all eternity that truth was true, that falsehood false. Very well then, that infinite thought must somehow have had all that in it from the beginning. If a man doubts it, let him answer our previous difficulties. Let him show us how he can make an error save through the presence of an actual inclusive thought for which the error always was error and never became such at all. If he can do that, let him try. We should willingly accept the result if he could show it to us. But he cannot. We have rambled over those barren hills already too long. Save for Thought there is no truth, no error. Save for inclusive Thought, there is no truth, no error, in separate thoughts. Separate thoughts as such cannot then know or have the distinction between their own truth and their own falsity in themselves, and apart from the inclusive thought. There is then nothing of truth or of error to be found in the world of separate thoughts as such. All the thoughts are therefore in the last analysis actually true or false, only for the all-including Thought, the Infinite.

We could have reached the same result had we set out from the problem, *What is Truth?* We chose not to do so because our skepticism had the placid answer ready: "No matter *what* truth is, for very likely there is little or no truth at all to be had. Why trouble one's mind to define what a fairy or a brownie is?" "Very well, then," we said to our skepticism, "if that is thy play, we know a move that thou thinkest not of. We will not ask thee of truth, if thou thinkest there is none. We will ask thee of error, wherein thou revelest." And our skepticism very cheerfully, if somewhat incoherently, answers, that, "if there be little or no truth here below, there is at least any amount of error, which as skeptics we have all been detecting ever since we first went to school." "We thank thee for that word, oh friend, but now, what is an error?" Blessed be Socrates for that question. Upon that rock philosophy can, if it wants, build we know not yet how much.

It is enough for the moment to sum up the truth that we

have found. It is this: *"All reality must be present to the Unity of the Infinite Thought."* There is no chance of escape. For all reality is reality because true judgments can be made about it. And all reality, for the same reason, can be the object of false judgments. Therefore, since the false and the true judgments are all true or false as present to the infinite thought, along with their objects, no reality can escape. You and I and all of us, all good, all evil, all truth, all falsehood, all things actual and possible, exist as they exist, and are known for what they are, in and to the absolute thought; are therefore all judged as to their real character at this everlasting throne of judgment.

This we have found to be true, because we tried to doubt everything. We shall try to expound in the coming chapter the religious value of the conception. We can however at once see this in it: The Infinite Thought must, knowing all truth, include also a knowledge of all wills, and of their conflict. For him all this conflict, and all the other facts of the moral world, take place. He then must know the outcome of the conflict, that Moral Insight of our first book. In him then we have the Judge of our ideals, and the Judge of our conduct. He must know the exact value of the Good Will, which for him, like all other possible truth, must be an actually realized Fact. And so we cannot pause with a simply theoretical idealism. Our doctrine is practical too. We have found not only an infinite Seer of physical facts, but an infinite Seer of the Good as well as of the Evil. He knows what we have and what we lack. In looking for goodness we are in no wise looking for what the real world does not contain.

This, we say, we have found as a truth, because we tried to doubt everything. We have taken the wings of the morning, and we have fled; but behold, we are in the midst of the Spirit. Truly the words that some people have thought so fantastic ought henceforth to be put in the text-books as commonplaces of logical analysis:—

> They reckon ill that leave me out;
> When me they fly, I am the wings,
> I am the doubter and the doubt.

Everything finite we can doubt, but not the Infinite. That eludes even our skepticism. The world-builders, and the theodicies that were to justify them, we could well doubt. The apologetic devices wearied us. All the ontologies of the realistic schools were just pictures, that we could accept or reject as we chose by means of postulates. We tried to escape them all. We forsook all those gods that were yet no gods; but here we have found something that abides, and waxes not old, something in which there is no variableness, neither shadow of turning. No power it is to be resisted, no plan-maker to be foiled by fallen angels, nothing finite, nothing striving, seeking, losing, altering, growing weary; the All-Enfolder it is, and we know its name. Not Heart, nor Love, though these also are in it and of it; Thought it is, and all things are for Thought, and in it we live and move.

3 ❧ THE RELIGIOUS INSIGHT [1]

> If thou betake thyself to the ever-living and abiding Truth, the desertion or death of a friend shall not make thee sad.—*Imitation of Christ*
>
> Cum contra sapiens, quatenus ut talis consideratur, vix animo movetur, sed sui et Dei et rerum aeterna quadam necessitate conscius, nunquam esse desinit, sed semper vera animi acquiescentia potitur.
>
> —SPINOZA, *Ethica*

We are in a new world of Divine Life. The dark world of the powers has passed away from our thought. Here is the Eternal, for which all these powers exist, in which they dwell. Here we are in the presence of the Ideal Judge who knows all Good and Evil. From the other side the world as we approached it had seemed so restless, so disheartening, so deaf. The world of our postulates was a brighter one only because we determined to make it so. But there was something lonesome in the thought that the postulates got, as answer from the real world, only their own echo, and not always that. Their world was rather their own creation than an external something that gave them independent support. Sometimes there seemed to be nothing solid that could echo back anything at all. Now we seem to look upon a truth that satisfies indeed no selfish longings of ours, no whims of theological tradition, no demands of our personal narrow lives. We shall not learn in this way who is first in the kingdom of heaven, nor how the dead are raised, nor any answer to any other special demand of any set of men. We learn, however, this at least: *All truth is known to One Thought, and that Infinite.* What does that imply? Let us see.

I

Our argument is somewhat near to the thought that partially satisfied St. Augustine when he found it in his Plato. That there

[1] Josiah Royce, *The Religious Aspect of Philosophy* (Boston: Houghton Mifflin Company, 1885), Chap. XII, pp. 436–446.—Editor's note.

should be a truth at all implies, we have seen, that there should be an Infinite Truth, known to an Infinite Thought; or, in other words, that all is for thought, and without thought is nothing that is. We also are a part of this infinite thought. We know not yet more of the nature of this thought, save that it must be eternal, all-embracing, and One. What then shall we be able further to say about it?

To answer would be to expound a system of philosophy. But we must limit ourselves here to the necessary. And so, for the first, we shall try to point out what this ideal and infinite life of thought that we have found as the eternal truth of things *cannot* be expected to accomplish for the purposes of our religion, and then to consider what we may nevertheless dare to hope from it.

It cannot be expected to furnish us an *a priori* knowledge of any fact of experience, of any particular law of nature, of the destiny of any one finite being. All that remains just as dark as it was before. We neither rejoice in this result, nor lament it. Nobody who wanders into the ideal world may expect to find it ordered for his individual advantage; nor need he try to find there good investments for his money. The Infinite does not wait for his individual approval; although morally speaking he may do well to get the approval of the Infinite. The Infinite was not elected to office by his vote, and he may not impeach it for disregard of his humble petitions for good things, nor threaten it with want of confidence because it does not secure passage for his private bills. In so far as to say this is to condemn the Real, we unhesitatingly do so. But then, as we saw in our ethical discussion, the moral insight is not so much concerned with private bills, as with certain greater matters. If the moral insight wants religious support, possibly the failure of all these personal concerns of ours to find any hint of response from the Absolute, may not render impossible the ethical undertakings of the human spirit. If as individuals we must hear the dreadful words from the spirit of nature: *Du gleichst dem Geist den du begreifst, nicht mir;* still it is possible that with a higher insight, looking upon this same spirit in its eternal and inmost nature, we may yet come with full reason at last to say: *Erhabner Geist, du gabst mir, gabst mir alles, warum ich bat.* For there are demands and demands. Man, as lover, demands success in love, and the course of the world may thwart him; as toiler, he demands for himself personal immortality, and the course of the world may care naught for his individual life; as bereaved, as mourner over his dead, he may demand for his loved ones also this immortality, and the course of the world may leave the fate of all his loved ones mysterious forever; as lover of mankind, he may demand an infinite future of blessed progress for his race, and the law of the dissipation of energy may give him the only discoverable physical answer to his demand; as just man, he may cry aloud that evil shall cease from among men, and the wicked may still laugh in triumph unpunished. And yet for all this he may find some higher compensation. Agnostic as he will remain about all the powers of this world, about the outcome of all finite processes, he will take comfort in the assurance that an Infinite Reason is above all and through all, embracing everything, judging everything, infallible, perfect. To this Thought he may look up, saying: "Thou All-Knowing One seest us, what we are, and how we strive. Thou knowest our frame, and rememberest that we are as dust. In thy perfection is our Ideal. That thou art, is enough for our moral comfort. That thou knowest our evil and our good, that gives us our support in our little striving for the good. Not worthless would we be in thy sight; not of the vile, the base, the devilish party in the warfare of this world. Thou that judgest shalt say that we, even in our poor individual lives, are better than naught. Thou shalt know that in our weakness and blindness, in our pain and sorrow, in our little days, in our dark world, ignorant as to the future, confused with many doubts, beset with endless temptations, full of dread, of hesitation, of sloth, we yet sought, such as we were, to be in our own fashion like thee; to know the truth as thou knowest it, to be full of higher life as thou art full, to be above strife as thou art above it, to be of one Spirit as thou art One, to be perfect as thou art perfect. This thou shalt see in us, and this record shall be eternal, like our knowledge. In thee what we vaguely aim to conceive is clear light. In thee the peace that we strive to find is experienced. And when we try to do right, we know that thou seest both our striving and our successes and our failures. And herein we have comfort. We perish, but thou endurest. Ours is not thy eternity. But in thy eternity we would be remembered, not as rebels against the good, but as doers of the good; not as blots on the face of this part of thy infinite reality, but as healthy leaves that flourished for a time on the branches of the eternal tree of life, and that have fallen, though not into forgetfulness. For to thee nothing is forgotten."

This thought, of the Judge that never ceases to think of us and of all things, never changes, never mistakes, and that knows the Good simply because that Good is an element of the Truth —perhaps this can sustain us when all else fails. Nothing but this may be certain; but this, if it be not all that some people have sought, may be a help to us. This Religion may have no such hot little fires on its altars as we at first longed for; but then it is a very old objection to the stars to say that they bake us no bread, and only glitter up there in the dark to be looked at. Yet even the stars are worth something to us.

II

But if we leave these limitations of our view, and pass to its positive religious value, our first sense is one of joy and freedom to find that our long sought ideal of a perfect unity of life is here attained. Let us look away for a moment from our finite existence, with its doubts and its problems, to the conception of that infinite life. In that life is all truth, fully present in the unity of one eternal moment. The world is no mass of separate facts, stuck one to another in an external way, but, for the infinite, each fact is what it is only by reason of its place in the infinite unity. The world of life is then what we desired it to be, an organic total; and the individual selves are drops in this ocean of the absolute truth.

Thus then, seen in the light of this our result, the human tasks that we sketched in our ethical discussion find their place in the objective world. Now, and in fact for the first time, we can see what we were really trying to accomplish through our ideal. We were trying in a practical way to realize what we now perceive to be the fullness of the life of God. So that the one highest activity, in which all human activities were to join, is known to us now as the *progressive realization by men of the eternal life of an Infinite Spirit.* So whereas we formerly had to say to men: Devote yourselves to art, to science, to the state, or to any like work that does tend to organize your lives into one life, we may now substitute one absolute expression for all those accidental expressions, and may say: *Devote yourselves to losing your lives in the divine life.* For all these special aims that we have mentioned are but means of accomplishing the knowledge of the fullness of the truth. And Truth is God.

Now this precept is no barren abstraction. It means to take hold of every act of life, however humble and simple. "Where art thou, O man?" our ideal says to us. "Art thou not in God? To whom dost thou speak? With whom dost thou walk? What life is this in whose midst thou livest? What are all these things that thou seemest to touch? Whose is all this beauty that thou enjoyest in art, this unity that thou seekest to produce in thy state, this truth that thou pursuest in thy thought? All this is in God and of God. Thou hast never seen, or heard, or touched, or handled, or loved anything but God. Know this truth, and thy life must be transformed to thee in all its significance. Serve the whole God, not the irrationally separate part that thy delusions have made thee suppose to be an independent thing. Live out thy life in its full meaning; for behold, it is God's life."

So, as it seems, the best that we could have wished from the purely moral side is attained. The Divine Thought it is that actually accomplishes what we imperfectly sought to attain, when we defined for ourselves Duty. In the Divine Thought is perfectly and finally realized the Moral Insight and the Universal Will of our ethical discussion. And this insight and will are not realized as by some Power, that then should set about to accomplish their fulfillment externally. But in the infinite, where all is eternally complete, the insight is both present and fulfilled; the universal will gets what it seeks. There is no lack there, nor hesitation, nor striving, nor doubt, nor weariness; but all is eternally perfect triumph.

Now this, though it sounds mystical enough to our untrained common sense, is no mere poetry of thought. It is the direct philosophical outcome of what we have found by a purely logical process. The driest thought, the simplest fragment of rationality, involves this absolute, infinite, and perfect thought. And this it involves because it involves the possibility of error, and because, as separate from the infinite, this possibility of error in a single thought becomes unintelligible and contradictory. We did all that we could to escape this conclusion. We wandered in the thickets of confusion and contradiction, until there was no chance of finding there a further pathway. And then we turned to see, and behold, God was in this place, though we had known it not.

The genuine God that we thus found was no incomplete, struggling God, whom we might pity in his conflict with evil, but the all-embracing thought, in which the truth is eternally finished. And this God it is that we now see as the complete realization of our own ideal, as of all worthy ideals.

For consider if you will this element in our conception of this Thought. Can this infinite know itself as imperfect, or as not possessing some object that it knows to be good? This is impossible, and doubly so. Not only does the conception of an Infinite, in which and for which are all things, wholly exclude the possibility of any good thing beyond the Infinite itself, but also in still another way does the same truth appear. For if you suppose that this infinite thought desires some perfection G, that it has not, then either it is right in supposing this perfection to be truly desirable, or it is wrong. In either case the previous argument of Chapter XI shows us that the truth or the falsity of this judgment of desire about G must exist as known truth or falsity for a higher thought, which, including the thought that desires, and itself actually having this desired good thing, compares the desired object with the conception of the thought that desires it, and judges of them both. Above the desire, then, must in every case exist the satisfaction of the desire in a higher thought. So that for the Infinite there can be no unsatisfied desire. Unsatisfied desire exists only in the finite beings, not in the inclusive Infinite.

The world then, as a whole, is and must be absolutely good, since the infinite thought must know what is desirable, and knowing it, must have present in itself the true objects of desire. The existence of any amount of pain or of other evil, of crime or of baseness in the world as we see it, is, thus viewed, no evidence against the absolute goodness of things, rather a guaranty thereof. For all evil viewed externally is just an evidence to us finite beings that there exists something desirable, which we have not, and which we just now cannot get. However stubborn this evil is for us, that has naught to do with the perfection of the Infinite. For the infinite did not make this evil, but the evil, *together with the making of it,* which indeed was also in its separateness evil,—all this is a phenomenon for the infinite thought, which, in knowing this evil, merely knows the absolute desirableness of that which it also possesses, namely, the absolutely good.

We have used here an argument that could not be used in our

study of the "World of Doubt." When we there thought evil to be possible for the world as a whole, we conceived that a being who knew all the world would yet desire something better. But what would this imply? It implies that this being would desire a state of things different from the existing one, and would do so believing that state to be better than the existing one. But would he truly know this desired state to be better, or would he only hope so? Who truly knows the value of a state save the one that possesses it? Knowledge is of the present. Therefore this being would not really know the better state, unless it were already actual for him. But in that case he would include not only the present world, but the perfect world, and his total state could not be one of discontent. So the other alternative remains. Our supposed being would only hope the desired state to be better than what was real already for him. But would his hope be a true one? If so, then it could only be true in case this perfection is already realized in a higher thought. For the Infinite then the question, "Is there anything better than what exists?" must be nonsense. For him the actual and the possible fall together in one truth; and this one truth cannot be evil.

On another side, our conception gives us religious support. The imperfection of the purely moral view lay in part in the fact that there was an inner incompleteness about the very definition of our ideal, as well as a doubt about its attainability. This inner incompleteness must however be removed in and for the Infinite Mind. In dealing with the work of life, we came to a point where we said, thus far we can see our way, but beyond that our ideal remains incomplete. We must have faith, so we implied, that if we attained so much of the ideal social condition, the way from that point onward would become clear. But now we see why the way would of necessity become clear to one whose knowledge of life were broad enough and deep enough. For in the Infinite that includes all life, that rests above all finite strife in the absolute attainment of the ideal, there can be no incompleteness, no torso of an ideal, but a perfect knowledge of what is most excellent. Those faint foreshadowings of a perfect life that art and science and social work show to us, must be for the Infinite no faint forshadowings, but absolute certainty and perfect clearness. Hence by our religious doctrine we get not merely the assurance that such ideals as we have are realized for the Infinite; but, better than this, we get our first full assurance that our incomplete ideals have an actual completion as ideals. For we thus get our first full assurance that there is in the highest sense any definite ideal at all. Pessimism, as we have seen, implies either doubt about what the ideal state is, or unavoidable lack of that state. And the Infinite can be no Pessimist in either sense. . . .

4 🌿 THE PROBLEM OF JOB [1]

In speaking of the problem of Job, the present writer comes to the subject as a layman in theology, and as one ignorant of Hebrew scholarship. In referring to the original core of the Book of Job he follows, in a general way, the advice of Professor C. H. Toy; and concerning the text of the poem he is guided by the translation of Dr. Gilbert. What this paper has to attempt is neither criticism of the book, nor philological exposition of its obscurities, but a brief study of the central problem of the poem from the point of view of a student of philosophy.

The problem of our book is the personal problem of its hero, Job himself. Discarding, for the first, as of possibly separate authorship, the Prologue, the Epilogue and the addresses of Elihu and of the Lord, one may as well come at once to the point of view of Job, as expressed in his speeches to his friends. Here is stated the problem of which none of the later additions in our poem offer any intelligible solution. In the exposition of this problem the original author develops all his poetical skill, and records thoughts that can never grow old. This is the portion of our book which is most frequently quoted and which best expresses the genuine experience of suffering humanity. Here, then, the philosophical as well as the human interest of our poem centres.

I

Job's world, as he sees it, is organized in a fashion extremely familiar to us all. The main ideas of this cosmology are easy to be reviewed. The very simplicity of the scheme of the universe here involved serves to bring into clearer view the mystery and horror of the problem that besets Job himself. The world, for Job, is the work of a being who, in the very nature of the

[1] Josiah Royce, *Studies of Good and Evil* (New York: D. Appleton and Company, 1898), pp. 1–28. The essay is reprinted in its entirety. It was first published in the *New World*, Vol. VI (1897), pp. 261–281.—Editor's note.

case, ought to be intelligible (since he is wise), and friendly to the righteous, since, according to tradition, and by virtue of his divine wisdom itself, this God must know the value of a righteous man. But—here is the mystery—this God, as his works get known through our human experiences of evil, appears to us not friendly, but hopelessly foreign and hostile in his plans and his doings. The more, too, we study his ways with man, the less intelligible seems his nature. Tradition has dwelt upon his righteousness, has called him merciful, has magnified his love towards his servants, has described his justice in bringing to naught the wicked. One has learned to trust all these things, to conceive God in these terms, and to expect all this righteous government from him. Moreover, tradition joins with the pious observation of nature in assuring us of the omnipotence of God. Job himself pathetically insists that he never doubts, for an instant, God's power to do whatever in heaven or earth he may please to do. Nothing hinders God. No blind faith thwarts him. Sheol is naked before him. The abyss has no covering. The earth hangs over chaos because he orders it to do so. His power shatters the monsters and pierces the dragons. He can, then, do with evil precisely what he does with Rahab or with the shades, with the clouds or with the light or with the sea, namely, exactly what he chooses. Moreover, since he knows everything, and since the actual value of a righteous man is, for Job, an unquestionable and objective fact, God cannot fail to know this real worth of righteousness in his servants, as well as the real hatefulness and mischief of the wicked. God knows worth, and cannot be blind to it, since it is as real a fact as heaven and earth themselves.

Yet despite all these unquestioned facts, this God, who can do just what he chooses, "deprives of right" the righteous man, in Job's own case, and "vexes his soul," becomes towards him as a "tyrant," "persecutes" him "with strong hand," "dissolves" him "into storm," makes him a "byword" for outcasts, "casts" him "into the mire," renders him "a brother to jackals," deprives him of the poor joy of his "one day as a hireling," of the little delight that might come to him as a man before he descends hopelessly to the dark world of the shades, "watches over" him by day to oppress, by night to "terrify" him "with dreams and with visions"——in brief, acts as his enemy, "tears" him "in anger," "gnashes upon" him "with his teeth." All these are the expressions of Job himself. On the other hand, as, with equal wonder and horror the righteous Job reports, God on occasion does just the reverse of all this to the notoriously and deliberately wicked, who "grow old," "wax mighty in power," "see their offspring established," and their homes "secure from fear." If one turns from this view of God's especially unjust dealings with righteous and with wicked individuals to a general survey of his providential government of the world, one sees vast processes going on, as ingenious as they are merciless, as full of hints of a majestic wisdom as they are of indifference to every individual right.

> A mountain that falleth is shattered,
> And a rock is removed from its place;
> The waters do wear away stones,
> Its floods sweep the earth's dust away;
> And the hope of frail man thou destroyest.
> Thou subdu'st him for aye, and he goes;
> Marring his face thou rejectest him.

Here is a mere outline of the divine government as Job sees it. To express himself thus is for Job no momentary outburst of passion. Long days and nights he has brooded over these bitter facts of experience, before he has spoken at all. Unweariedly, in presence of his friends' objections, he reiterates his charges. He has the right of the sufferer to speak, and he uses it. He reports the facts that he sees. Of the paradox involved in all this he can make nothing. What is clear to him, however, is that this paradox is a matter for reasoning, not for blind authority. God ought to meet him face to face, and have the matter out in plain words. Job fears not to face his judge, or to demand his answer from God. God knows that Job has done nothing to deserve this fury. The question at issue between maker and creature is therefore one that demands a direct statement and a clear decision. "Why, since you can do precisely as you choose, and since you know, as all-knower, the value of a righteous servant, do you choose, as enemy, to persecute the righteous with this fury and persistence of hate?" Here is the problem.

The human interest of the issue thus so clearly stated by Job lies, of course, in the universality of just such experiences of undeserved ill here upon earth. What Job saw of evil we can see ourselves to-day whenever we choose. Witness Armenia. Witness the tornadoes and the earthquakes. Less interesting to us is the thesis mentioned by Job's friends, in the antiquated form in

which they state it, although to be sure, a similar thesis, in altered forms, is prevalent among us still. And of dramatic significance only is the earnestness with which Job defends his own
personal righteousness. So naïve a self-assurance as is his is not
in accordance with our modern conscience, and it is seldom indeed that our day would see any man sincerely using this phraseology of Job regarding his own consciousness of rectitude. But
what is to-day as fresh and real to us as it was to our poet is
the fact that all about us, say in every child born with an unearned heredity of misery, or in every pang of the oppressed,
or in every arbitrary coming of ill fortune, some form of innocence is beset with an evil that the sufferer has not deserved.
Job wins dramatic sympathy as an extreme, but for the purpose
all the more typical, case of this universal experience of unearned
ill fortune. In every such case we therefore still have the interest
that Job had in demanding the solution of this central problem
of evil. Herein, I need not say, lies the permanent significance
of the problem of Job,—a problem that wholly outlasts any
ancient Jewish controversy as to the question whether the divine
justice always does or does not act as Job's friends, in their devotion to tradition, declare that it acts. Here, then, is the point
where our poem touches a question, not merely of an older religion, but of philosophy, and of all time.

II

The general problem of evil has received, as is well known,
a great deal of attention from the philosophers. Few of them, at
least in European thought, have been as fearless in stating the
issue as was the original author of Job. The solutions offered
have, however, been very numerous. For our purposes they may
be reduced to a few.

First, then, one may escape Job's paradox by declining altogether to view the world in teleological terms. Evils, such as
death, disease, tempests, enemies, fires, are not, so one may declare, the works of God or of Satan, but are natural phenomena.
Natural, too, are the phenomena of our desires, of our pains,
sorrows and failures. No divine purpose rules or overrules any
of these things. That happens to us, at any time, which must
happen, in view of our natural limitations and of our ig-

norance. The way to better things is to understand nature better than we now do. For this view—a view often maintained in our day—there is no problem of evil, in Job's sense, at all. Evil there indeed is, but the only rational problems are those of natural laws. I need not here further consider this method, not of solving but of abolishing the problem before us, since my intent is, in this paper, to suggest the possibility of some genuinely teleological answer to Job's question. I mention this first view only to recognize, historically, its existence.

In the second place, one may deal with our problem by attempting any one, or a number, of those familiar and popular compromises between the belief in a world of natural law and the belief in teleological order, which are all, as compromises, reducible to the assertion that the presence of evil in the creation is a relatively insignificant, and an inevitable, incident of a plan that produces sentient creatures subject to law. Writers who expound such compromises have to point out that, since a burnt child dreads the fire, pain is, on the whole, useful as a warning. Evil is a transient discipline, whereby finite creatures learn their place in the system of things. Again, a sentient world cannot get on without some experience of suffering, since sentience means tenderness. Take away pain (so one still again often insists), take away pain, and we should not learn our share of natural truth. Pain is the pedagogue to teach us natural science. The contagious diseases, for instance, are useful in so far as they lead us in the end to study Bacteriology, and thus to get an insight into the life of certain beautiful creatures of God whose presence in the world we should otherwise blindly overlook! Moreover (to pass to still another variation of this sort of explanation), created beings obviously grow from less to more. First the lower, then the higher. Otherwise there could be no Evolution. And were there no evolution, how much of edifying natural science we should miss! But if one is evolved, if one grows from less to more, there must be something to mark the stages of growth. Now evil is useful to mark the lower stages of evolution. If you are to be, first an infant, then a man, or first a savage, then a civilized being, there must be evils attendant upon the earlier stages of your life—evils that make growth welcome and conscious. Thus, were there no colic and croup, were there no tumbles and crying-spells in infancy, there would be no sufficient incentives to loving parents to hasten the growing robustness of their children, and no motives to impel the children to long to grow big! Just so, cannibalism is valuable as a mark of a lower grade of evolution. Had there been no cannibalism we should realize less joyously than we do what a respectable thing it is to have become civilized! In brief, evil is, as it were, the dirt of the natural order, whose value is that, when you wash it off, you thereby learn the charm of the bath of evolution.

The foregoing are mere hints of familiar methods of playing about the edges of our problem, as children play barefoot in the shallowest reaches of the foam of the sea. In our poem, as Professor Toy expounds it, the speeches ascribed to Elihu contain the most hints of some such way of defining evil, as a merely transient incident of the discipline of the individual. With many writers explanations of this sort fill much space. They are even not without their proper place in popular discussion. But they have no interest for whoever has once come into the presence of Job's problem as it is in itself. A moment's thought reminds us of their superficiality. Pain is useful as a warning of danger. If we did not suffer, we should burn our hands off. Yes, but this explanation of one evil presupposes another, and a still unexplained and greater evil, namely, the existence of the danger of which we need to be thus warned. No doubt it is well that the past sufferings of the Armenians should teach the survivors, say the defenseless women and children, to have a wholesome fear in future of Turks. Does that explain, however, the need for the existence, or for the murderous doings of the Turks? If I can only reach a given goal by passing over a given road, say of evolution, it may be well for me to consent to the toilsome journey. Does that explain why I was created so far from my goal? Discipline, toil, penalty, surgery, are all explicable as means to ends, if only it be presupposed that there exists, and that there is quite otherwise explicable, the necessity for the situations which involve such fearful expenses. One justifies the surgery, but not the disease; the toil, but not the existence of the need for the toil; the penalty, but not the situation which has made the penalty necessary, when one points out that evil is in so many cases medicinal or disciplinary or prophylactic—an incident of imperfect stages of evolution, or the price of a distant good attained through misery. All such explanations, I insist, trade upon borrowed capital. But God, by hypothesis, is no borrower. He produces his own capital of ends and means. Every evil is explained on the foregoing plan only by presupposing at least an equal, and often a greater and preëxistent evil, namely, the very state of things which renders the first evil the only physically possible way of reaching a given goal. But what Job wants his judge to explain is not that evil *A* is a physical means of warding off some other greater evil *B*, in this cruel world where the waters wear away even the stones, and where hopes of man are so much frailer than the stones; but why a God who can do whatever he wishes chooses situations where such a heaped-up mass of evil means become what we should call physical necessities to the ends now physically possible.

No real explanation of the presence of evil can succeed which declares evil to be a merely physical necessity for one who desires, in this present world, to reach a given goal. Job's business is not with physical accidents, but with the God who chose to make this present nature; and an answer to Job must show that evil is not a physical but a logical necessity—something whose non-existence would simply contradict the very essence, the very perfection of God's own nature and power. This talk of medicinal and disciplinary evil, perfectly fair when applied to our poor fate-bound human surgeons, judges, jailors, or teachers, becomes cruelly, even cynically trivial when applied to explain the ways of a God who is to choose, not only the physical means to an end, but the very *Physis* itself in which path and goal are to exist together. I confess, as a layman, that whenever, at a funeral, in the company of mourners who are immediately facing Job's own personal problem, and who are sometimes, to say the least, wide enough awake to desire not to be stayed with relative comforts, but to ask that terrible and uttermost question of God himself, and to require the direct answer—that whenever, I say, in such company I have to listen to these half-way answers, to these superficial plashes in the wavelets at the water's edge of sorrow, while the black, unfathomed ocean of finite evil spreads out before our wide-opened eyes—well, at such times this trivial speech about useful burns and salutary medicines makes me, and I fancy others, simply and wearily heartsick. Some words are due to children at school, to peevish patients in the sickroom who need a little temporary quieting. But quite other speech is due to men and women when they are wakened to the higher reason of Job by the fierce anguish of our mortal life's ultimate facts. They deserve either our simple silence, or, if we are ready to speak, the speech of people who ourselves inquire as Job inquired.

III

A third method of dealing with our problem is in essence identical with the course which, in a very antiquated form, the friends of Job adopt. This method takes its best known expression in the doctrine that the presence of evil in the world is explained by the fact that the value of free will in moral agents logically involves, and so explains and justifies, the divine permission of the evil deeds of those finite beings who freely choose to sin, as well as the inevitable fruits of the sins. God creates agents with free will. He does so because the existence of such agents has of itself an infinite worth. Were there no free agents, the highest good could not be. But such agents, because they are free, can offend. The divine justice of necessity pursues such offenses with attendant evils. These evils, the result of sin, must, logically speaking, be permitted to exist, if God once creates the agents who have free will, and himself remains, as he must logically do, a just God. How much ill thus results depends upon the choice of the free agents, not upon God, who wills to have only good chosen, but of necessity must leave his free creatures to their own devices, so far as concerns their power to sin.

This view has the advantage of undertaking to regard evil as a logically necessary part of a perfect moral order, and not as a mere incident of an imperfectly adjusted physical mechanism. So dignified a doctrine, by virtue of its long history and its high theological reputation, needs here no extended exposition. I assume it as familiar, and pass at once to its difficulties. It has its share of truth. There is, I doubt not, moral free will in the universe. But the presence of evil in the world simply cannot be explained by free will alone. This is easy to show. One who maintains this view asserts, in substance, "All real evils are the results of the acts of free and finite moral agents." These agents may be angels or men. If there is evil in the city, the Lord has *not* done it, except in so far as his justice has acted in readjusting wrongs already done. Such ill is due to the deeds of his creatures. But hereupon one asks at once, in presence of any ill, "Who did this?" Job's friends answer: "The sufferer himself; his deed wrought his own undoing. God punishes only the sinner. Every one suffers for his own wrongdoing. Your will is the result of your crime."

But Job, and all his defenders of innocence, must at once reply: "Empirically speaking, this is obviously, in our visible world, simply not true. The sufferer may suffer innocently. The ill is often undeserved. The fathers sin; the child, diseased from birth, degraded, or a born wretch, may pay the penalty. The Turk or the active rebel sins. Armenia's helpless women and babes cry in vain unto God for help."

Hereupon the reply comes, although not indeed from Job's friends: "Alas! it is so. Sin means suffering; but the innocent may suffer *for* the guilty. This, to be sure, is God's way. One cannot help it. It is so." But therewith the whole effort to explain evil as a logically necessary result of free will and of divine justice alone is simply abandoned. The unearned ills are not justly due to the free will that indeed partly caused them, but to God who declines to protect the innocent. God owes the Turk and the rebel their due. He also owes to his innocent creatures, the babes and the women, his shelter. He owes to the sinning father his penalty, but to the son, born in our visible world a lost soul from the womb, God owes the shelter of his almighty wing, and no penalty. Thus Job's cry is once more in place. The ways of God are not thus justified.

But the partisan of free will as the true explanation of ill may reiterate his view in a new form. He may insist that we see but a fragment. Perhaps the soul born here as if lost, or the wretch doomed to pangs now unearned, sinned of old, in some previous state of existence. Perhaps Karma is to blame. You expiate to-day the sins of your own former existences. Thus the Hindoos varied the theme of our familiar doctrine. This is what Hindoo friends might have said to Job. Well, admit even that, if you like; and what then follows? Admit that here or in former ages the free deed of every present sufferer earned as its penalty every ill, physical or moral, that appears as besetting just this sufferer to-day. Admit that, and what logically follows? It follows, so I must insist, that the moral world itself, which this free-will theory of the source of evil, thus abstractly stated, was to save, is destroyed in its very heart and centre.

For consider. A suffers ill. B sees A suffering. Can B, the on-looker, help his suffering neighbor, A? Can he comfort him in any true way? No, a miserable comforter must B prove, like Job's friends, so long as B, believing in our present hypothesis, clings strictly to the logic of this abstract free-will explanation of the origin of evil. To A he says: "Well, you suffer for your own ill-doing. I therefore simply cannot relieve you. This is God's world of justice. If I tried to hinder God's justice from working in your case, I should at best only postpone your evil day. It would come, for God is just. You are hungry, thirsty, naked, sick, in prison. What can I do about it? All this is your own deed come back to you. God himself, although justly punishing, is not the author of evil. You are the sole originator of the ill." "Ah!" so A may cry out, "but can you not give me light, insight, instruction, sympathy? Can you not at least teach me to become good?" "No," B must reply, if he is a logical believer in the sole efficacy of the private free will of each finite agent as the one source, under the divine justice, of that agent's ill: "No, if you deserved light or any other comfort, God, being just, would enlighten you himself, even if I absolutely refused. But if you do not deserve light, I should preach to you in vain, for God's justice would harden your heart against any such good fortune as I could offer you from without, even if I spoke with the tongues of men and of angels. Your free will is yours. No deed of mine could give you a good free will, for what I gave you from without would not be *your* free will at all. Nor can any one but you cause your free will to be this or that. A great gulf is fixed between us. You and I, as sovereign free agents, live in God's holy world in sin-tight compartments and in evil-tight compartments too. I cannot hurt you, nor you me. You are damned for your own sins, while all that I can do is to look out for my own salvation." This, I say, is the logically inevitable result of asserting that every ill, physical or moral, that can happen to any agent, is solely the result of that agent's own free will acting under the government of the divine justice. The only possible consequence would indeed be that we live, every soul of us, in separate, as it were absolutely fire-proof, free-will compartments, so that real coöperation as to good and ill is excluded. What more cynical denial of the reality of any sort of moral world could be imagined than is involved in this horrible thesis, which no sane partisan of the abstract and traditional free-will explanation of the source of evil will to-day maintain, precisely because no such partisan really knows or can know what his doctrine logically means, while still continuing to maintain it.

Yet whenever one asserts with pious obscurity, that "No harm can come to the righteous," one in fact implies, with logical necessity, just this cynical consequence.

IV

There remains a fourth doctrine as to our problem. This doctrine is in essence the thesis of philosophical idealism, a thesis which I myself feel bound to maintain, and, so far as space here permits, to explain. The theoretical basis of this view, the philosophical reasons for the notion of the divine nature which it implies, I cannot here explain. That is another argument. But I desire to indicate how the view in question deals with Job's problem.

This view first frankly admits that Job's problem is, upon Job's presuppositions, simply and absolutely insoluble. Grant Job's own presupposition that God is a being other than this world, that he is its external creator and ruler, and then all solutions fail. God is then either cruel or helpless, as regards all real finite ill of the sort that Job endures. Job, moreover, is right in demanding a reasonable answer to his question. The only possible answer is, however, one that undertakes to develop what I hold to be the immortal soul of the doctrine of the divine atonement. The answer to Job is: God is not in ultimate essence another being than yourself. He is the Absolute Being. You truly are one with God, part of his life. He is the very soul of your soul. And so, here is the first truth: When you suffer, *your sufferings are God's sufferings,* not his external work, not his external penalty, not the fruit of his neglect, but identically his own personal woe. In you God himself suffers, precisely as you do, and has all your concern in overcoming this grief.

The true question then is: Why does God thus suffer? The sole possible, necessary, and sufficient answer is, Because without suffering, without ill, without woe, evil, tragedy, God's life could not be perfected. This grief is not a physical means to an external end. It is a logically necessary and eternal constituent of the divine life. It is logically necessary that the Captain of your salvation should be perfect through suffering. No outer nature compels him. He chooses this because he chooses his own perfect selfhood. He is perfect. His world is the best possible world. Yet all its finite regions know not only of joy but of defeat and sorrow, for thus alone, in the completeness of his eternity, can God in his wholeness be triumphantly perfect.

This, I say, is my thesis. In the absolute oneness of God with the sufferer, in the concept of the suffering and therefore triumphant God, lies the logical solution of the problem of evil. The doctrine of philosophical idealism is, as regards its purely theoretical aspects, a fairly familiar metaphysical theory at the present time. One may, then, presuppose here as known the fact that, for reasons which I have not now to expound, the idealist maintains that there is in the universe but one perfectly real being, namely, the Absolute, that the Absolute is self-conscious, and that his world is essentially in its wholeness the fulfillment *in actu* of an all-perfect ideal. We ourselves exist as fragments of the absolute life, or better, as partial functions in the unity of the absolute and conscious process of the world. On the other hand, our existence and our individuality are not illusory, but are what they are in an organic unity with the whole life of the Absolute Being. This doctrine once presupposed, our present task is to inquire what case idealism can make for the thesis just indicated as its answer to Job's problem.

In endeavoring to grapple with the theoretical problem of the place of evil in a world that, on the whole, is to be conceived, not only as good, but as perfect, there is happily one essentially decisive consideration concerning good and evil which falls directly within the scope of our own human experience, and which concerns matters at once familiar and momentous as well as too much neglected in philosophy. When we use such words as good, evil, perfect, we easily deceive ourselves by the merely abstract meanings which we associate with each of the terms taken apart from the other. We forget the experiences from which the words have been abstracted. To these experiences we must return whenever we want really to comprehend the words. If we take the mere words, in their abstraction, it is easy to say, for instance, that if life has any evil in it at all, it must needs not be so perfect as life would be were there no evil in it whatever. Just so, speaking abstractly, it is easy to say that, in estimating life, one has to set the good over against the evil, and to compare their respective sums. It is easy to declare that, since we hate evil, wherever and just so far as we recognize it, our sole human interest in the world must be furthered by the removal of evil from the world. And thus viewing the case, one readily comes to say that if God views as not only good but perfect a world in which we find so much evil, the divine point of view must be very foreign to ours, so that Job's rebellious pessimism seems well in order, and Prometheus appears to defy the world-ruler in a genuinely humane spirit. Shocked, however, by the apparent impiety of this result, some teachers, considering divine matters, still misled by the same one-sided use of words, have opposed one falsely abstract view by another, and have strangely asserted that the solution must be in proclaiming that since God's world, the real world, in order to be perfect, must be without evil, what we men call evil must be a mere illusion—a mirage of the human point of view—a dark vision which God, who sees all truth, sees not at all. To God, so this view asserts, the eternal world in its wholeness is not only perfect, but has merely the perfection of an utterly transparent crystal, unstained by any color of ill. Only mortal error imagines that there is any evil. There is no evil but only good in the real world, and that is why God finds the world perfect, whatever mortals dream.

Now neither of these abstract views is my view. I consider them both the result of a thoughtless trust in abstract words. I regard evil as a distinctly real fact, a fact just as real as the most helpless and hopeless sufferer finds it to be when he is in pain. Furthermore, I hold that God's point of view is not foreign to ours. I hold that God willingly, freely, and consciously suffers in us when we suffer, and that our grief is his. And despite all this I maintain that the world from God's point of view fulfills the divine ideal and is perfect. And I hold that when we abandon the one-sided abstract ideas which the words good, evil, and perfect suggest, and when we go back to the concrete experiences upon which these very words are founded, we can see, even within the limits of our own experience, facts which make these very paradoxes perfectly intelligible, and even commonplace.

As for that essentially pernicious view, nowadays somewhat current amongst a certain class of gentle but inconsequent people —the view that all evil is *merely* an illusion and that there is no such thing in God's world—I can say of it only in passing that it is often advanced as an idealistic view, but that, in my opinion, it is false idealism. Good idealism it is to regard all finite experience as an appearance, a hint, often a very poor hint, of deeper truth. Good idealism it is to admit that man can err about truth that lies beyond his finite range of experience. And very good idealism it is to assert that all truth, and so all finite experience, exists in and for the mind of God, and no-

where outside of or apart from God. But it is not good idealism
to assert that any facts which fall within the range of finite experience are, even while they are experienced, mere illusions.
God's truth is inclusive, not exclusive. What you experience
God experiences. The difference lies only in this, that God sees
in unity what you see in fragments. For the rest, if one said,
"The source and seat of evil is only the error of mortal mind,"
one would but have changed the name of one's problem. If the
evil were but the error, the error would still be the evil, and altering the name would not have diminished the horror of the evil
of this finite world.

V

But I hasten from the false idealism to the true; from the abstractions to the enlightening insights of our life. As a fact, idealism does not say: The finite world is, as such, a mere illusion. A
sound idealism says, whatever we experience is a fragment, and,
as far as it goes, a genuine fragment of the truth of the divine
mind. With this principle before us, let us consider directly our
own experiences of good and of evil, to see whether they are
abstractly opposed to each other as the mere words often suggest.
We must begin with the elementary and even trivial facts. We
shall soon come to something deeper.

By good, as we mortals experience it, we mean something that,
when it comes or is expected, we actively welcome, try to attain
or keep, and regard with content. By evil in general, as it is in
our experience, we mean whatever we find in any sense repugnant and intolerable. I use the words repugnant and intolerable
because I wish to indicate that words for evil frequently, like
the words for good, directly refer to our actions as such. Commonly and rightly, when we speak of evil, we make reference to
acts of resistance, of struggle, of shrinking, of flight, of removal
of ourselves from a source of mischief—acts which not only follow upon the experience of evil, but which serve to define in a
useful fashion what we mean by evil. The opposing acts of pursuit and of welcome define what we mean by good. By the evil
which we experience we mean precisely whatever we regard as
something to be gotten rid of, shrunken from, put out of sight,
of hearing, or of memory, eschewed, expelled, assailed, or otherwise directly or indirectly resisted. By good we mean whatever

we regard as something to be welcomed, pursued, won, grasped, held, persisted in, preserved. And we show all this in our acts in presence of any grade of good or evil, sensuous, æsthetic, ideal, moral. To shun, to flee, to resist, to destroy, these are our primary attitudes towards ill; the opposing acts are our primary attitudes towards the good; and whether you regard us as animals or as moralists, whether it is a sweet taste, a poem, a virtue, or God that we look to as good, and whether it is a burn or a temptation, an outward physical foe, or a stealthy, inward, ideal enemy, that we regard as evil. In all our organs of voluntary movement, in all our deeds, in a turn of the eye, in a sigh, a groan, in a hostile gesture, in an act of silent contempt, we can show in endlessly varied ways the same general attitude of repugnance.

But man is a very complex creature. He has many organs. He performs many acts at once, and he experiences his performance of these acts in one highly complex life of consciousness. As the next feature of his life we all observe that he can at the same time shun one object and grasp at another. In this way he can have at once present to him a consciousness of good and a consciousness of ill. But so far in our account these sorts of experience appear merely as facts side by side. Man loves, and he *also* hates, loves this, and hates that, assumes an attitude of repugnance towards one object, while he welcomes another. So far the usual theory follows man's life, and calls it an experience of good and ill as mingled but exclusively and abstractly opposed facts. For such a view the final question as to the worth of a man's life is merely the question whether there are more intense acts of satisfaction and of welcome than of repugnance and disdain in his conscious life.

But this is by no means an adequate notion of the complexity of man's life, even as an animal. If every conscious act of hindrance, of thwarting, of repugnance, means just in so far an awareness of some evil, it is noteworthy that men can have and can show just such tendencies, not only towards external experiences, but towards their own acts. That is, men can be seen trying to thwart and to hinder even their own acts themselves, at the very moment when they note the occurrence of these acts. One can consciously have an impulse to do something, and at that very moment a conscious disposition to hinder or to thwart as an evil that very impulse. If, on the other hand, every conscious act of attainment, of pursuit, of reinforcement, involves the awareness of some good, it is equally obvious that one can show by one's acts a disposition to reinforce or to emphasize or to increase, not only the externally present gifts of fortune, but also one's own deeds, in so far as one observes them. And in our complex lives it is common enough to find ourselves actually trying to reinforce and to insist upon a situation which involves for us, even at the moment of its occurrence, a great deal of repugnance. In such cases we often act as if we felt the very thwarting of our own primary impulses to be so much of a conscious good that we persist in pursuing and reinforcing the very situation in which this thwarting and hindering of our own impulses is sure to arise.

In brief, as phenomena of this kind show, man is a being who can to a very great extent find a sort of secondary satisfaction in the very act of thwarting his own desires, and thus of assuring for the time his own dissatisfactions. On the other hand, man can to an indefinite degree find himself dissatisfied with his satisfactions and disposed to thwart, not merely his external enemies, but his own inmost impulses themselves. But I now affirm that in all such cases you cannot simply say that man is preferring the less of two evils, or the greater of two goods, as if the good and the evil stood merely side by side in his experience. On the contrary, in such cases, man is not merely setting his acts or his estimates of good and evil side by side and taking the sum of each; but he is making his own relatively primary acts, impulses, desires, the objects of all sorts of secondary impulses, desires, and reflective observations. His whole inner state is one of tension; and he is either making a secondary experience of evil out of his estimate of a primary experience of good, as is the case when he at once finds himself disposed to pursue a given good and to thwart this pursuit as being an evil pursuit; or else he is making a secondary experience of good out of his primary experience of evil, as when he is primarily dissatisfied with his situation, but yet secondarily regards this very dissatisfaction as itself a desirable state. In this way man comes not only to love some things and also to hate other things, he comes to love his own hates and to hate his own loves in an endlessly complex hierarchy of superposed interests in his own interests.

Now it is easy to say that such states of inner tension, where our conscious lives are full of a warfare of the self with itself, are contradictory or absurd states. But it is easy to say this only when you dwell on the words and fail to observe the facts of experience. As a fact, not only our lowest but our highest states of activity are the ones which are fullest of this crossing, conflict, and complex interrelation of loves and hates, of attractions and repugnances. As a merely physiological fact, we begin no muscular act without at the same time initiating acts which involve the innervation of opposing sets of muscles, and these opposing sets of muscles hinder each other's freedom. Every sort of control of movement means the conflicting play of opposed muscular impulses. We do nothing simple, and we will no complex act without willing what involves a certain measure of opposition between the impulses or partial acts which go to make up the whole act. If one passes from single acts to long series of acts, one finds only the more obviously this interweaving of repugnance and of acceptance, of pursuit and of flight, upon which every complex type of conduct depends.

One could easily at this point spend time by dwelling upon numerous and relatively trivial instances of this interweaving of conflicting motives as it appears in all our life. I prefer to pass such instances over with a mere mention. There is, for instance, the whole marvelous consciousness of play, in its benign and in its evil forms. In any game that fascinates, one loves victory and shuns defeat, and yet as a loyal supporter of the game scorns anything that makes victory certain in advance; thus as a lover of fair play preferring to risk the defeat that he all the while shuns, and partly thwarting the very love of victory that from moment to moment fires his hopes. There are, again, the numerous cases in which we prefer to go to places where we are sure to be in a considerable measure dissatisfied; to engage, for instance, in social functions that absorbingly fascinate us despite or even in view of the very fact that, as long as they continue, they keep us in a state of tension which makes us, amongst other things, long to have the whole occasion over. Taking a wider view, one may observe that the greater part of the freest products of the activity of civilization, in ceremonies, in formalities, in the long social drama of flight, of pursuit, of repartee, of contest and of courtesy, involve an elaborate and systematic delaying and hindering of elemental human desires, which we continually outwit, postpone and thwart, even while we nourish them. When students of human nature assert that hunger and love rule the social world, they recognize that the elemental in human nature is trained by civilization into the service of the highest demands of the Spirit. But such students have to recognize that the elemental rules the higher world only in so far as the elemental is not only cultivated, but endlessly thwarted, delayed, outwitted, like a constitutional monarch, who is said to be a sovereign, but who, while he rules, must not govern.

But I pass from such instances, which in all their universality are still, I admit, philosophically speaking, trivial, because they depend upon the accidents of human nature. I pass from these instances to point out what must be the law, not only of human nature, but of every broader form of life as well. I maintain that this organization of life by virtue of the tension of manifold impulses and interests is not a mere accident of our imperfect human nature, but must be a type of the organization of every rational life. There are good and bad states of tension, there are conflicts that can only be justified when resolved into some higher form of harmony. But I insist that, in general, the only harmony that can exist in the realm of the spirit is the harmony that we possess when we thwart the present but more elemental impulse for the sake of the higher unity of experience; as when we rejoice in the endurance of the tragedies of life, because they show us the depth of life, or when we know that it is better to have loved and lost than never to have loved at all, or when we possess a virtue in the moment of victory over the tempter. And the reason why this is true lies in the fact that the more one's experience fulfills ideals, the more that experience presents to one, not of ignorance, but of triumphantly wealthy acquaintance with the facts of manifold, varied and tragic life, full of tension and thereby of unity. Now this is an universal and not merely human law. It is not those innocent of evil who are fullest of the life of God, but those who in their own case have experienced the triumph over evil. It is not those naturally ignorant of fear, or those who, like Siegfried, have never shivered, who possess the genuine experience of courage; but the brave are those who have fears, but control their fears. Such know the genuine virtues of the hero. Were it otherwise, only the stupid could be perfect heroes.

To be sure it is quite false to say, as the foolish do, that the object of life is merely that we may "know life" as an irrational chaos of experiences of good and of evil. But knowing the good in life is a matter which concerns the form, rather than the mere content of life. One who knows life wisely knows indeed much of the content of life; but he knows the good of life in so far as, in the unity of his experience, he finds the evil of his

experience not abolished, but subordinated, and in so far relatively thwarted by a control which annuls its triumph even while
experiencing its existence.

V I

Generalizing the lesson of experience we may then say: It is
logically impossible that a complete knower of truth should fail
to know, to experience, to have present to his insight, the fact
of actually existing evil. On the other hand, it is equally impossible for one to know a higher good than comes from the
subordination of evil to good in a total experience. When one
first loving, in an elemental way, whatever you please, himself
hinders, delays, thwarts his elemental interest in the interest of
some larger whole of experience, he not only knows more fact,
but he possesses a higher good than would or could be present
to one who was aware neither of the elemental impulse, nor
of the thwarting of it in the tension of a richer life. The knowing of the good, in the higher sense, depends upon contemplating the overcoming and subordination of a less significant impulse, which survives even in order that it should be subordinated.
Now this law, this form of the knowledge of the good, applies
as well to the existence of moral as to that of sensuous ill. If
moral evil were simply destroyed and wiped away from the
external world, the knowledge of moral goodness would also be
destroyed. For the love of moral good is the thwarting of lower
loves for the sake of the higher organization. What is needed,
then, for the definition of the divine knowledge of a world
that in its wholeness is perfect, is not a divine knowledge that
shall ignore, wipe out and utterly make naught the existence of
any ill, whether physical or moral, but a divine knowledge to
which shall be present that love of the world as a whole which
is fulfilled in the endurance of physical ill, in the subordination
of moral ill, in the thwarting of impulses which survive even
when subordinated, in the acceptance of repugnances which are
still eternal, in the triumph over an enemy that endures even
through its eternal defeat, and in the discovery that the endless
tension of the finite world is included in the contemplative consciousness of the repose and harmony of eternity. To view God's
nature thus is to view his nature as the whole idealistic theory
views him, not as the Infinite One beyond the finite imperfec-

tions, but as the being whose unity determines the very constitution, the lack, the tension, and relative disharmony of the
finite world.

The existence of evil, then, is not only consistent with the
perfection of the universe, but is necessary for the very existence
of that perfection. This is what we see when we no longer
permit ourselves to be deceived by the abstract meanings of the
words good and evil into thinking that these two opponents exist
merely as mutually exclusive facts side by side in experience,
but when we go back to the facts of life and perceive that all
relatively higher good, in the trivial as in the more truly spiritual
realm, is known only in so far as, from some higher reflective
point of view, we accept as good the thwarting of an existent
interest that is even thereby declared to be a relative ill, and love
a tension of various impulses which even thereby involves, as
the object of our love, the existence of what gives us aversion or
grief. Now if the love of God is more inclusive than the love of
man, even as the divine world of experience is richer than the
human world, we can simply set no human limit to the intensity
of conflict, to the tragedies of existence, to the pangs of finitude,
to the degree of moral ill, which in the end is included in the
life that God not only loves, but finds the fulfillment of the perfect ideal. If peace means satisfaction, acceptance of the whole
of an experience as good, and if even we, in our weakness, can
frequently find rest in the very presence of conflict and of tension, in the very endurance of ill in a good cause, in the hero's
triumph over temptation, or in the mourner's tearless refusal to
accept the lower comforts of forgetfulness, or to wish that the
lost one's preciousness had been less painfully revealed by death
—well, if even we know our little share of this harmony in
the midst of the wrecks and disorders of life, what limit shall
we set to the divine power to face this world of his own sorrows, and to find peace in the victory over all its ills.

But in this last expression I have pronounced the word that
serves to link this theory as to the place of evil in a good world
with the practical problem of every sufferer. Job's rebellion came
from the thought that God, as a sovereign, is far off, and that,
for his pleasure, his creature suffers. Our own theory comes to
the mourner with the assurance: "Your suffering, just as it is in
you, is God's suffering. No chasm divides you from God. He is
not remote from you even in his eternity. He is here. His eternity
means merely the completeness of his experience. But that com-

pleteness is inclusive. Your sorrow is one of the included facts."
I do not say: "God sympathizes with you from without, would
spare you if he could, pities you with helpless external pity
merely as a father pities his children." I say: "God here sorrows, not *with* but *in* your sorrow. Your grief is identically his
grief, and what you know as your loss, God knows as his loss,
just in and through the very moment when you grieve."

But hereupon the sufferer perchance responds: "If this is
God's loss, could he not have prevented it? To him are present
in unity all the worlds; and yet he must lack just this for which
I grieve." I respond: "He suffers here that he may triumph.
For the triumph of the wise is no easy thing. Their lives are
not light, but sorrowful. Yet they rejoice in their sorrow, not, to
be sure, because it is mere experience, but because, for them, it
becomes part of a strenuous whole of life. They wander and
find their home even in wandering. They long, and attain
through their very love of longing. Peace they find in triumphant warfare. Contentment they have most of all in endurance.
Sovereignty they win in endless service. The eternal world
contains Gethsemane."

Yet the mourner may still insist: "If my sorrow is God's,
his triumph is not mine. Mine is the woe. His is the peace."
But my theory is a philosophy. It proposes to be coherent. I must
persist: "It is your fault that you are thus sundered from God's
triumph. His experience in its wholeness cannot now be yours,
for you just as you—this individual—are now but a fragment,
and see his truth as through a glass darkly. But if you see his
truth at all, through even the dimmest light of a glimmering
reason, remember, that truth is in fact your own truth, your own
fulfillment, the whole from which your life cannot be divorced,
the reality that you mean even when you most doubt, the desire
of your heart even when you are most blind, the perfection that
you unconsciously strove for even when you were an infant, the
complete Self apart from whom you mean nothing, the very life
that gives your life the only value which it can have. In thought,
if not in the fulfillment of thought, in aim if not in attainment of aim, in aspiration if not in the presence of the revealed
fact, you can view God's triumph and peace as your triumph and
peace. Your defeat will be no less real than it is, nor will you
falsely call your evil a mere illusion. But you will see not only
the grief but the truth, your rescue, your triumph."

Well, to what ill-fortune does not just such reasoning apply?

I insist: our conclusion is essentially universal. It discounts any evil that experience may contain. All the horrors of the natural order, all the concealments of the divine plan by our natural ignorance, find their general relation to the unity of the divine experience indicated in advance by this account of the problem of evil.

"Yes," one may continue, "ill-fortune you have discovered, but how about moral evil? What if the sinner now triumphantly retorts: 'Aha! So my will is God's will. All then is well with me.'" I reply: What I have said disposes of moral ill precisely as definitely as of physical ill. What the evil will is to the good man, whose goodness depends upon its existence, but also upon the thwarting and the condemnation of its aim, just such is the sinner's will to the divine plan. God's will, we say to the sinner, is your will. Yes, but it is your will thwarted, scorned, overcome, defeated. In the eternal world you are seen, possessed, present, but your damnation is also seen including and thwarting you. Your apparent victory in this world stands simply for the vigor of your impulses. God wills you not to triumph. And that is the use of you in the world—the use of evil generally—to be hated but endured, to be triumphed over through the very fact of your presence, to be willed down even in the very life of which you are a part.

But to the serious moral agent we say: What you mean when you say that evil in this temporal world ought not to exist, and ought to be suppressed, is simply what God means by seeing that evil ought to be and is endlessly thwarted, endured, but subordinated. In the natural world you are the minister of God's triumph. Your deed is his. You can never clean the world of evil; but you can subordinate evil. The justification of the presence in the world of the morally evil becomes apparent to us mortals only in so far as this evil is overcome and condemned. It exists only that it may be cast down. Courage, then, for God works in you. In the order of time you embody in outer acts what is for him the truth of his eternity.

PART II

SELECTIONS FROM

*The World and
the Individual*

5 ❧ INTRODUCTION: THE RELIGIOUS PROBLEMS AND THE THEORY OF BEING [1]

In the literature of Natural Religion at least three different conceptions of the subject are represented. The first of these conceptions regards Natural Religion as a search for what a well-known phrase has called "the way through Nature to God." If we accept this conception, we begin by recognizing both the existence of the physical world and the validity of the ordinary methods and conceptions of the special sciences of nature. We undertake to investigate what light, if any, the broader generalizations of natural science, when once accepted as statements about external reality, throw upon the problems of religion. It belongs, for instance, to this sort of inquiry to ask: What countenance does the present state of science give to the traditional argument from Design?

The second of our three conceptions views Religion less as a doctrine to be proved or disproved through a study of the external world than as a kind of consciousness whose justification lies in its rank amongst the various inner manifestations of our human nature. Man, so this conception holds, is essentially a religious being. He has religion because his own inmost nature craves it. If you wish, then, to justify religion, or even to comprehend it, you must view it, not as a theory to be proved or disproved by an appeal to external reality, but rather as a faith to be estimated through reference to the inner consciousness of those who need, who create, and who enjoy religion. From this point of view the study of Natural Religion concerns itself less with proof than with confession, with a taxing of interior values, and with a description of the religious experience of man-

1 Josiah Royce, *The World and the Individual* (New York: The Macmillan Company, 1899, 1901), Vol. I, Lecture I, pp. 3–43. The lecture is reprinted in its entirety.—Editor's note.

kind. A somewhat extended interpretation of this point of view treats the purely historical study of the various religions of mankind as a contribution to our comprehension of Natural Religion.

But a third conception of the study of Natural Religion remains. This third view identifies the doctrine in question with the fundamental Philosophy of Religion. It is the Nature of Things, viewed in the light of the most critical examination of our reason, that is now the object of an inquiry into Natural Religion. The problems at issue are, for this view, those of Aristotle's *Metaphysics,* of Fichte's *Wissenschaftslehre,* of Hegel's *Logik,* —of all the undertakings that, in the history of thought, have most directly attempted the contemplation of Being as Being. For our first conception the student of Natural Religion, having accepted the natural knowledge of his time as valid, and not having attempted to delve beneath the foundations of that knowledge, seeks to interpret external nature in the light of religious interests. For our second conception Natural Religion is viewed simply as the voice of human nature itself, whose faith is to be expressed, whose ideals are to be recorded, whose will and whose needs are to be, above all, consulted and portrayed, since, for this view, the consciousness of those who believe in religious truth is, when once made articulate, its own apology. But, for our third conception, the office of the student of Natural Religion is to deal with the most fundamental metaphysical problems. He is for this view a thorough-going critic of the foundations of our faith, and of the means of our insight into the true nature of Reality.

All these three conceptions, however much they may differ, have in common what makes it proper enough to view them as conceptions of the study of Natural Religion. For they are all three concerned with religion; they can all alike be pursued without explicit dependence upon any creed as to a revealed religion; and finally, they are busied about some relation between the natural order of truth and the contents of religious doctrine. They differ in the sort of natural truth that forms their starting-point, or that limits the scope of the investigation which they propose. I suppose that no one of these various lines of inquiry will ever come to be wholly neglected. But their office is distinct. And I mention them here in order all the more clearly to say, at the outset, that our own business, in these lectures, is with the most neglected and arduous of the methods of studying the relations between religion and the ultimate problems of the Theory of Being. From the first, to be sure, we shall be concerned, in one sense, with human nature, as every philosophy has to be concerned. And in the latter half of this course the Philosophy of Nature will play a part in our investigation. But the central problem of our discussion will be the question: What is Reality?

I

In thus stating, in the opening words, the plan of these lectures, I do so with a full sense of the shadow that such a programme may, at the first glimpse, seem to cast upon the prospects of our whole undertaking. It is true that, in calling the fundamental problems of the Metaphysic of Religion relatively neglected, I do not fail to recognize that they are both ancient and celebrated, and that some of us may think them even hackneyed. It is certainly not uncommon to call them antiquated. But what I have meant by the phrase "relatively neglected" is that, compared with the more easily accessible fashions of dealing with Natural Religion, the strictly metaphysical treatment less frequently involves that sort of ardent hand-to-hand struggle with the genuine issues themselves that goes on when men are hopefully interested in a study for its own sake. It is one thing to expound, or even to assail, the theology of Hegel or of St. Thomas, or to report any of those various quaint opinions of philosophers in which even the popular mind often delights. It is another thing to grapple with the issues of life for one's self. The wiser religions have always told us that we cannot be saved through the piety of our neighbors, but have to work out our own salvation with fear and trembling. Well, just so the theoretical student of Natural Religion has to learn that he cannot comprehend ultimate philosophical truth merely by reading the reports of other people's reasonings, but must do his thinking for himself, not indeed without due instruction, but certainly without depending wholly upon his text-books. And if this be true, then the final issues of religious philosophy may be said to be relatively neglected, so long as students are not constantly afresh grappling with the ancient problems, and giving them renderings due to direct personal contact with their intricacies. It is not a question of any needed originality of opinion, but it is rather a matter of our individual intimacy with these issues.

And now, in recognizing the fact of the comparative neglect of the Theory of Being in the discussions of Natural Religion, I recognize also the motives that tend to make such an inquiry seem, at the first glimpse, unpromising. These motives may be expressed in the forms of three objections, namely, first, that such undertakings are pretentious, by reason of the dignity and the mystery of the topic; secondly, that they are dreary, by reason of the subtle distinctions and the airy abstractions involved in every such research; and thirdly, that they are opposed, in spirit, to the sort of study for which in our day the sciences of experience have given the only worthy model.

Such objections are as inevitable as they are, to lovers of philosophy, harmless. Philosophy necessarily involves a good deal of courage; but so does life in general. It is pretentious to wrestle with angels; but there are some blessings that you cannot win in any other way. Philosophy is an old affair in human history; but that does not make the effort at individuality in one's fashion of thinking a less worthy ideal for every new mind. As to the dreariness of metaphysics, it is always the case, both in religion, and in thinking about religion, that, just as the letter killeth, and the spirit giveth life, so the mere report of tradition is dreary, but the inward life of thinking for one's self the meaning within or behind the tradition constitutes the very coming of the Spirit of Truth himself into our own spirits; and that, coming of the Spirit, in so far as it occurs at all, never seems to any of us dreary. As for the fine-drawn distinctions and airy abstractions, no distinction is ever too subtle for you, at the moment when it occurs to you to make that distinction for yourself, and not merely to hear that somebody else has made it. And no abstraction seems to you too airy in the hour when you rise upon your own wings to the region where just that abstraction happens to be an element in the concrete fulness of your thoughtful life. Now it chances to be a truth of metaphysics, as it is an experience of religion, that just when you are most individual, most alone, as it were, in your personal thinking, about ultimate and divine matters, you are most completely one with that universal Spirit of Truth of which we just spoke. It is then your personal process of thinking that both gives interest to the subject and secures your relation to the Reality. Hence not the universality nor yet the ultimate character of the principles of which we think, but rather our own sluggishness in thinking, is responsible for the supposed dreariness of the

Theory of Being. As Aristotle observed, that Theory itself is what all men most desire. You may in these regions either think or not think the truth; but you cannot think the truth without loving it; and the dreariness which men often impute to Metaphysics, is merely the dreariness of not understanding the subject, —a sort of dreariness for which indeed there is no help except learning to understand. In fact, nobody can ever regret seeing ultimate truth. That we shall hereafter find to be, so to speak, one of the immediate implications of our very definition of Being. When people complain of philosophy as a dreary enterprise, they are then merely complaining of their own lack of philosophical insight. The lover of philosophy can only offer them his sincerest agreement, and sympathy, so far as concerns the ground of their own complaint. He too shares their complaint, for he is human, and finds his own unwisdom dreary. But he is at least looking lovingly toward yonder shining light, while they walk wearily with their backs to the Celestial City.

As to the supposed opposition between the methods of philosophy and those of the special sciences of experience,—it exists, but it does not mean any real opposition of spirit. Here are two ways of getting insight, not two opposed creeds. The very wealth and the growth of modern empirical research furnish especially strong reasons for supposing that the time is near when the central problems of the Theory of Being shall be ready for restatement. Our life does not grow long and healthily in one region, without being ready for new growth in other regions. The indirect influence of special science upon philosophy is sure, but does not always mean a logical dependence of philosophy upon the empirical results of science. Just so, pure mathematical science has no logical dependence upon physics. Yet we have all heard how largely physical science has influenced the lines of investigation followed by the modern mathematicians. Within the mathematical realm itself, pure Algebra, when once abstractly defined, is not logically dependent upon Geometry for its principles or for its theories, yet some theories of modern Algebra have actually developed largely under the spell, as it were, of ideas of an unquestionable geometrical origin. Now a similar relation, I think, will in future find the development of pure Philosophy, and in particular of Rational Theology, to the progress of the special sciences, both mathematical and empirical. I do not think it right to regard philosophy merely as a compendium of the results of special science. Philosophy has its own field. But on the other hand, to reflect upon the meaning of life and of science (and in such thorough-going Reflection philosophy consists), is a process whose seriousness and wealth must grow as our human life and science progress. And hence every great new advance of science demands a fresh consideration of philosophic issues, and will insure in the end a power to grasp, more critically and more deeply, the central problem of Being itself. Hence the more we possess of special science, the more hope we ought to have for pure Philosophy.

II

So much then for the most general definition and justification of the proposed scope of these lectures. I cannot forbear to point out the easily recognizable fact that, in thus defining the plan before us, I have merely tried to adhere, so far as I can, to the programme explicitly laid down by Lord Gifford. A study of religion is required of your lecturer, and Lord Gifford, as appears from the words of his Will, would himself have thought, above all, of studying religion not only as a matter of purely natural and rational knowledge, but primarily as a body of Ontological problems and opinions, in other words as, in its theory, a branch of the Theory of Being. It is of "God, the only Substance," that your lecturer, if his Ontology so far agrees with Lord Gifford's, will principally speak. Well then, I can best work in the spirit of Lord Gifford's requirements if I explicitly devote our principal attention to the ultimate problems of Ontology, laying due stress upon their relations to Religion.

And now let me venture to sketch, in outline, the particular discussions by which I propose to contribute my fragment towards a study of the inexhaustible problems propounded by Lord Gifford's Will. Programmes in philosophy, as Hegel used to say, mean far less than in other enterprises. But even here some sort of programme is needed to fix in advance our attention.

My precise undertaking then, in the following lectures, is to show what we mean by Being in general, and by the special sorts of Reality that we attribute to God, to the World, and to the Human Individual. These I regard as the problems of the ontology of religion. In every step of this undertaking I shall actually be, in a psychological and in an historical sense, dependent, both for my ideas and for their organization, upon this or that philosophical or theological tradition (well known to every student of philosophy); and therefore I must early introduce into my work a sketch of certain philosophical traditions in which we are to be especially interested. Here, of course, you might expect to find, as such an historical introduction to our later critical enterprises, either a summary of the history of the principal religious ideas, or some account of the technical history of the Philosophy of Religion itself. Yet for neither of these two very natural enterprises shall I have time. My very fragmentary historical discussions will be limited to an attempt to depict some of the principal conceptions concerning the ultimate nature of Being, in other words to sketch the history of what one might call the ontological predicate of the expression *to be*, or *to be real*, used as a means of asserting that something exists. I shall dwell upon the nature of Being, because to assert that God is, or that the World is, or even, with Descartes, that I am, implies that one knows what it is to be, or in other words, what the so-called existential predicate itself involves. Now it is true that the existential predicate, the word *is* used to assert the real Being of any object, is often viewed as something of an absolutely simple, ultimate, and indescribable meaning. Yet even if this view were sound, the ultimate and the simple are, in philosophy, as truly and as much topics for reflective study as are the most complex and derived ideas of our minds. Moreover, a great deal of popular religion seems to involve the notion that it is both easier and more important to know *that* God is, than to know, with any sort of articulation, *What* God is, so that if you express even a total ignorance of the Divine nature and attributes, there are some very traditionally minded people who will hardly dare to disagree with you, while if you express the least doubt of the assertion that God is, the same people will at once view you with horror as an atheist. Now this preference in much popular religious thinking for the ontological predicate in its purity is not an altogether rational preference. Yet we shall find that it is based upon very deep and even very worthy, if vague, instincts. It is true that if I pretend to know no attributes whatever, characterizing a given object X, I seem to have won very little by believing that X nevertheless exists. Yet the fondness for the Unknowable in theology has been to some extent supported by the dim feeling that even in asserting the bare existence of a being, and especially of God, I am already committed to extremely important attributes, whose definition, even if not yet overt, is already, however darkly, implied in my abstract statement. It is interesting, therefore, to study historically what men have supposed themselves to mean by the ontological predicate.

The basis having been thus laid in the history of the subject, our lectures, at various points in the historical summary, will have at some length to undertake a critical comparison and analysis of the various meanings of the ontological predicate. Such an analysis will constantly show us unexpected connections of these meanings with the concrete interests of religion. We shall find it with ontology, as it certainly is with ethics. People often regard moral philosophy as a topic very abstract and dry. And yet wherever two or three are gathered together indulging in gossip about the doings of their neighbors, their speech, even if it involves out-and-out scandal, is devoted to a more or less critical discussion, to an illustration, and even to a sort of analysis of what are really very deep ethical problems,—problems about what men ought to do, and about the intricate relations between law and passion in human life. Well, as even the most frivolous or scandalous gossip really manifests an intense, if rude concern, for the primal questions of moral philosophy, so our children and all our most simple and devout souls constantly talk ontology, discourse of being, face the central issues of reality, but know it not. Yet once face the true connection of abstract theory and daily life, and then one easily sees that life means theory, and that you deal constantly, and decisively, with the problems of the Theory of Being whenever you utter a serious word. This then is the reason why our ontological studies will bear directly upon the daily concerns of religion.

Our discussion of the general meaning and of the relative value of the various ontological predicates will, moreover, throw light, as we go, upon some of the best known of the special issues of the history of theology. We shall see, for instance, what has been the real motive that has made the doctrine of the speculative Mystics so important a factor in the life of the more complex religious faiths. We shall see too, in the great historical conflicts between the Realistic and the Mystical conceptions of the nature of Reality, the source of some of the most important controversies concerning the being and attributes of God, the existence of the physical world, and the nature of human individuality. Thus we shall gradually approach a position where we shall learn the inevitableness of a certain final conception of the meaning of our ontological predicates; and the result of our critical study will be a light that we may not wholly have anticipated, both upon the conception of God, and upon our notion of the relations between God, the World, and the Human Individual. With the development of these fundamental conceptions, the first of my two series of lectures will close. We shall herewith have stated the bases of religion.

The second series I intend first to devote to the application of our fundamental conceptions to the more special problems of the nature of the human Ego, the meaning of the finite realm called the Physical World, and the interpretation of Evolution. The vast extent of the discussions thus suggested will be limited, in our own case, by the very fact that we shall here be attempting merely the application of a single very general ontological idea to a few problems which we shall view rather as illustrations of our central thesis concerning Reality, than as matters to be exhaustively considered for their own sake. Having thus sketched our Cosmology, if I may call it such, we shall then conclude the whole undertaking by a summary discussion of the problems of Good and Evil, of Freedom, of Immortality, and of the destiny of the Individual, still reviewing our problems in the light of our general conception of Being. The title that I shall have given to the whole course of lectures, "The World and the Individual," will thus, I hope, prove to be justified by the scope of our discussion in the two divisions of this course.

III

The plan of the proposed investigation has now been set before you in outline. May I next undertake to indicate a little more precisely not merely what problems we are to attempt, but the sort of positive argument that we are to use, and the kind of result that we may hope to reach? A philosophy must indeed be judged not by its theses, but by its methods; and not upon the basis of mere summaries, but after a consideration of the details of its argument. Yet it helps to make clearer the way through an intricate realm of inquiry if one first surveys, as it were, from above, the country through which, in such an enterprise, the road is to pass. I propose then, to indicate at once, and in the rest of this lecture, where the central problem of the

Theory of Being lies, and by what method I think that this problem is, in a general sense, to be solved. To state the proposed solution, however, even in the most abstract and necessarily unconvincing fashion, is to arouse comments as to the meaning of this thesis, as to its consequences, and, above all, in a discussion like the present, as to its bearing upon the more practical interests of religion. I think that we may be helped to an understanding hereafter, if I attempt at once to call out, and, by anticipation, to answer, a few such comments.

I am one of those who hold that when you ask the question: What is an Idea? and: How can Ideas stand in any true relation to Reality? you attack the world-knot in the way that promises most for the untying of its meshes. This way is, of course, very ancient. It is the way of Plato, and, in a sense, already the way of his Master. It is, in a different sense, the way of Kant. If you view philosophy in this fashion, you subordinate the study of the World as Fact to a reflection upon the World as Idea. Begin by accepting, upon faith and tradition, the mere brute Reality of the World as Fact, and there you are, sunk deep in an ocean of mysteries. The further you then proceed in the study of that world, the longer seems the way to God or to clearness, unless you from the start carry with you some sort of faith, perhaps a very blind and immediate faith, that God reigns, or that the facts in themselves are somehow clear. The World as Fact surprises you with all sorts of strange contrasts. Now it reveals to you, in the mechanics and physics of the stars or in the processes of living beings, vast realms of marvellous reasonableness; now it bewilders you, in the endless diversities of natural facts, by a chaos of unintelligible fragments and of scattered events; now it lifts up your heart with wondrous glimpses of ineffable goodness; and now it arouses your wrath by frightful signs of cruelty and baseness. Conceive it as a realm for pure scientific theory; and, so far as your knowledge reaches, it is full at once of the show of a noble order, and of hints. of a vain chance. On the other hand, conceive it as a realm of values, attempt to estimate its worth, and it baffles you with caprices, like a charming and yet hopelessly wayward child, or like a bad fairy. That is the world of brute natural fact as you, with your present form of consciousness, are forced to observe it, if you try to get any total impression of its behavior. And so, this World of Fact daily announces itself to you as a defiant mystery—a mystery such as Job faced, and such as the latest agnostic summary of empirical results, in their bearing upon our largest human interests, or such as even the latest pessimistic novel will no doubt any day present afresh to you, in all the ancient unkindliness that belongs to human fortune.

The World as Fact, is, then, for all of us, persistently baffling, unless we find somewhere else the key to it. The philosophers of the Platonic type have, however, long ago told us that this defect of our world of fact is due, at bottom, simply to the fault of our human type of consciousness. And hence a whole realm of philosophical inquiry has been devoted, in the best ages of speculative thinking, to a criticism of this human type of consciousness itself. Upon such a criticism, Plato founded his conception of the Ideal World. By such criticism, Plotinus sought to find the way upwards, through Soul to the realm of the Intellect, and beyond the Intellect to his Absolute "One." Through a similar criticism, Scholastic doctrine attempted to purify our human type of consciousness, until it should reach the realm of genuine spirituality, and attain an insight but a little lower than that of the conceived angelic type of intelligence. For all such thinkers, the raising of our type of consciousness to some higher level meant not only the winning of insight into Reality, but also the attainment of an inner and distinctly religious ideal. To a later and less technically pious form of thinking, one sees the transition of Spinoza, who was at once, as we now know, a child of Scholasticism, and a student of the more modern physical conceptions of his day,—at once a mystic, a realist, and a partisan of nature. For Spinoza too, it is our type of finite consciousness that makes our daily world of fact, or, as he prefers to say, of imagination, seem chaotic; and the way to truth still is to be found through an inner and reflective purification of experience. A widely different interpretation is given to the same fundamental conception, by Kant. But in Kant's case also, remote from his interests as is anything savoring of mysticism, the end of philosophical insight is again the vindication of a higher form of consciousness. For Kant, however, this is the consciousness of the Moral Reason, which recognizes no facts as worthy of its form of assurance, except the facts implied by the Good Will, and by the Law of the good will. All these ways then of asserting the primacy of the World as Idea over the World as Fact, agree in dealing with the problem of Reality from the side of the means through which we are supposed to be able to attain reality, that is, from the side of the Ideas.

IV

But if this is to be the general nature of our own inquiry also, then everything for us will depend upon the fundamental questions, already stated, viz. first: What is an Idea? and second: How can an Idea be related to Reality? In the treatment of both these questions, however, various methods and theories at once come into sight. And, to begin with one of the favorite issues, namely the fundamental definition of the word "idea" itself, there is a well-known tendency in a good deal of philosophy, both ancient and modern, either to define an idea, as an Image, destined to picture facts external to the idea, or else, in some other way, to lay stress upon the *externally* cognitive or "representative" value of an idea as its immediately obvious and its most essential aspect. From this point of view, men have conceived that the power of ideas to know a Reality external to themselves, was indeed either something too obvious to excite inquiry, or else an ultimate and inexplicable power. "Ideas exist," says this view, "and they exist as knowing facts external to themselves. And this is their fundamental character." Now I myself shall, in these lectures, regard this power of ideas to cognize facts external to themselves not as a primal fact of existence but as an aspect of ideas which decidedly needs reflective consideration, and a very critical restatement. Hence I cannot here begin by saying: "Ideas are states of mind that image facts external to themselves." That would be useful enough as a definition of ideas in a Psychology of Cognition. For such a Psychology would presuppose what we are here critically to consider, namely, the very possibility of a cognition of Being. But, for the purpose of our present theory, the definition of the term "idea" must be made in such wise as not formally to presuppose the power of ideas to have cognitive relations to outer objects.

Moreover, in attempting a definition of the general term "idea," while I shall not be attempting a psychology of cognition, I shall myself be guided by certain psychological analyses of the mere contents of our consciousness,—analyses which have become prominent in recent discussion. What is often called the active and sometimes also the motor aspect of our mental life, has been much dwelt upon of late. This is no place, and at present we have no need, for a psychological theory of the origin or of the causes of what is called activity, but as a fact, you have in your mental life a sort of consciousness accompanying the processes by which, as the psychologists are accustomed to say, you adjust your organism to its environment; and this sort of consciousness differs, in some notable features, from what takes place in your mind in so far as the mere excitation of your sense organs by the outer world is regarded apart from the experiences that you have when you are said to react upon your impressions. The difference between merely seeing your friend, or hearing his voice, and consciously or actively regarding him as your friend, and behaving towards him in a friendly way, is a difference obvious to consciousness, whatever your theory of the sources of mental activity. Now this difference between outer sense impressions, or images derived from such impressions, and active responses to sense impressions, or ideas founded upon such responses, is not merely a difference between what is sometimes called the intellect, and what is called the will. For, as a fact, the intellectual life is as much bound up with our consciousness of our acts as is the will. There is no purely intellectual life, just as there is no purely voluntary life. The difference between knowledge and will, so far as it has a metaphysical meaning, will concern us much later. For the present, it is enough to note that your intelligent ideas of things never consist of mere images of the things, but always involve a consciousness of how you propose to act towards the things of which you have ideas. A sword is an object that you would propose to use, or to regard in one way, while a pen is to be used in another; your idea of the object involves the memory of the appropriate act. Your idea of your friend differs from your idea of your enemy by virtue of your consciousness of your different attitude and intended behaviour towards these objects. Complex scientific ideas, viewed as to their conscious significance, are, as Professor Stout [2] has well said, plans of action, ways of constructing the objects of your scientific consciousness. Intelligent ideas then, belong, so to speak, to the motor side of your life rather than to the merely sensory. This was what Kant meant by the spontaneity of the understanding. To be sure, a true scientific idea is a mental construction supposed to correspond with an outer object, or to imitate that object. But when we try to define the idea in itself, as a conscious fact, our best means is to lay stress upon the sort of will,

[2] Stout, *Analytic Psychology*, Vol. II, Chap. VIII, especially pp. 114, 124.

or active meaning, which any idea involves for the mind that
forms the idea.

By the word "Idea," then, as we shall use it when, after
having criticised opposing theories, we come to state, in these
lectures, our own thesis, I shall mean in the end any state of
consciousness, whether simple or complex, which, when present,
is then and there viewed as at least the partial expression or
embodiment of a single conscious purpose. I shall indeed say
nothing for the present as to what causes an idea. But I shall
assert that an idea appears in consciousness as having the significance of an act of will. I shall also dwell upon the inner purpose, and not upon the external relations, as the primary and
essential feature of an idea. For instance, you sing to yourself
a melody, you are then and there conscious that the melody as
you hear yourself singing it, partially fulfils and embodies a
purpose. Well, in this sense, your melody, at the moment when
you sing it, or even when you silently listen to its imagined
presence, constitutes a musical idea, and is often so called.
You may so regard the melody without yet explicitly dwelling
upon the externally cognitive value of the musical idea, as the
representative of a melody sung or composed by somebody else.
You may even suppose the melody original with yourself,
unique, and sung now for the first time. Even so, it would remain
just as truly a musical idea, however partial or fragmentary; for
it would then and there, when sung, or even when inwardly
heard, partly embody your own conscious purpose. In the same
sense, any conscious act, at the moment when you perform it,
not merely expresses, but is, in my present sense, an idea. To
count ten is thus also an idea, if the counting fulfils and embodies, in however incomplete and fragmentary a way, your
conscious purpose, and that quite apart from the fact that counting ten also may enable you to cognize the numerical character
of facts external to the conscious idea of ten itself. In brief, an
idea, in my present definition may, and, as a fact always does,
if you please, appear to be representative of a fact existent
beyond itself. But the primary character, which makes it an
idea, is not this its representative character, is not its vicarious
assumption of the responsibility of standing for a being beyond
itself, but is its inner character as relatively fulfilling the purpose
(that is, as presenting the partial fulfilment of the purpose),
which is in the consciousness of the moment wherein the idea
takes place. It is in this sense that we speak of any artistic idea,

as present in the creative mind of the artist. I propose, in stating my own view hereafter, to use the word "idea" in this general sense.

Well, this definition of the primary character of an idea, enables me at once to deal with a conception which will play no small part in our later discussions. I refer to the very conception of the Meaning of an idea. One very fair way to define an idea, had we chosen to use that way, might have been to say: An Idea is any state of mind that has a conscious meaning. Thus, according to my present usage of the word "idea," a color, when merely seen, is in so far, for consciousness, no idea. A brute noise, merely heard, is no idea. But a melody, when sung, a picture, when in its wholeness actively appreciated, or the inner memory of your friend now in your mind, is an idea. For each of these latter states means something to you at the instant when you get it present to consciousness. But now, what is this meaning of any idea? What does one mean by a meaning? To this question, I give, for the instant, an intentionally partial answer. I have just said that an idea is any state of mind, or complex of states, that, when present, is consciously viewed as the relatively completed embodiment, and therefore already as the partial fulfilment of a purpose. Now this purpose, just in so far as it gets a present conscious embodiment in the contents and in the form of the complex state called the idea, constitutes what I shall hereafter call the Internal Meaning of the Idea. Or, to repeat, the state or complex of states called the idea, presents to consciousness the expressed although in general the incomplete fulfilment of a purpose. In presence of this fulfilment, one could, as it were, consciously say: "That is what I want, and just in so far I have it. The purpose of singing or of imagining the melody is what I want fulfilled; and, in this musical idea, I have it at least partially fulfilled." Well, this purpose, when viewed as fulfilled through the state called the idea, is the internal meaning of the idea. Or yet once more,—to distinguish our terms a little more sharply,—in advance of the presence of the idea in consciousness, one could abstractly speak of the purpose as somewhat not yet fulfilled. Hereupon let there come the idea as the complex of conscious states, the so-called act wherein this purpose gets, as it were, embodied, and relatively speaking, accomplished. Then, finally, we shall have the internal meaning of the idea, and this internal meaning of the completed idea is the purpose viewed as so far embodied in the idea, the soul, as it were, which the idea gives body. Any idea then, viewed as a collection of states, must have its internal meaning, since, being an idea, it does in some degree embody its purpose. And our two terms, "purpose embodied in the idea," and "internal meaning of the idea," represent the same subject-matter viewed in two aspects. The purpose which the idea, when it comes, is to fulfil, may first be viewed apart from the fulfilment. Then it remains, so far, mere purpose. Or it may be viewed as expressed and so far partially accomplished by means of the complex state called the idea, and then it is termed "the present internal meaning of this state."

V

So now we have defined what we mean by an idea, and what we mean by the internal meaning of an idea. But ideas often seem to have a meaning, yes, as one must add, finite ideas always undertake or appear to have a meaning, that is not exhausted by this conscious internal meaning presented and relatively fulfilled at the moment when the idea is there for our finite view. The melody sung, the artist's idea, the thought of your absent friend—a thought on which you love to dwell: all these not merely have their obvious internal meaning, as meeting a conscious purpose by their very presence, but also they at least appear to have that other sort of meaning, that reference beyond themselves to objects, that cognitive relation to outer facts, that attempted correspondence with outer facts, which many accounts of our ideas regard as their primary, inexplicable, and ultimate character. I call this second, and, for me, still problematic and derived aspect of the nature of ideas, their apparently External Meaning. In this sense it is that I say, "The melody sung by me not only is an idea internally meaning the embodiment of my purpose at the instant when I sing it, but also is an idea that means, and that in this sense externally means, the object called, say, a certain theme which Beethoven composed." In this same sense, your idea of your absent friend, is, for my definition, an idea primarily, because you now fulfil some of your love for dwelling upon your inner affection for your friend by getting the idea present to mind. But you also regard it as an idea which, in the external sense, is said to mean the real being called your friend, in so far as the idea is said to refer to that real friend, and to resemble him. This external meaning, I say, appears to be very different from the internal meaning, and wholly to transcend the latter.

By thus first distinguishing sharply between the conscious internal meaning of an idea and its apparently external meaning, we get before us an important way of stating the problem of knowledge or, in other words, the problem of the whole relation between Idea and Being. We shall find this not only a very general, but a very fundamental, and, as I believe, despite numerous philosophical discussions, still a comparatively neglected way. And in problems of this kind so much turns upon the statement of the issue, that I must be excused for thus dwelling at length, at this early stage, upon the precise sense in which we are to employ our terms.

Plainly, then, whoever studies either a special science, or a problem of general metaphysics, is indeed concerned with what he then and there views as the external meaning of certain ideas. And an idea, when thus viewed, appears as if it were essentially a sort of imitation or image of a being, and this being, the external object of our thoughtful imitation, appears to be, in so far, quite separate from these our ideas that imitate its characters or that attempt to correspond to them. From such a point of view, our ideas seemed destined to perform a task which is externally set for them by the real world. I count, but I count, in ordinary life, what I take to be real objects, existent quite apart from my counting. Suppose that I count ships seen from the shore. There, says common sense, are the ships, sailing by themselves, and quite indifferent to whether anybody counts them or not. In advance of the counting, the ships, in so far as they are a real collection, have their number. This common sense also presupposes. Let there be seen, yonder, on the sea, nine ships or ten; this number of the real ships is in itself determinate. It does not result from my counting, but is the standard for the latter to follow. The numerical ideas of anybody who counts the ships must either repeat the preëxistent facts, or else fail to report those facts accurately. That alternative seems absolute and final. The question how anybody ever comes to count ships at all, is a question for psychology. But there remains for the seeker after metaphysical truth, just as much as for the man of common sense, the apparently sharp alternative: Either actual ships, whose multitude is just what it happens to be, whose number preëxists, in advance of any counting, are correctly represented by the ideas of one who happens to be able to count, or else these ships are incorrectly counted. In the latter case we seem to be forced to say that the counting process misses its external aim. In the former case we say that the ideas expressed by the one who counts are true. But in both cases alike the ideas in question thus appear to be true or false by virtue of their external meaning, by virtue of the fact that they either correspond or do not correspond to facts which are themselves no part of the ideas. This simple instance of the ships and of the ideas of a man who sits watching and counting the ships, is obviously typical of all instances of the familiar relation of ideas to Being, as the metaphysic of common sense views Being, or of the relation of ideas to what we have here called the objects of their external meaning. That ideas have such external meanings, that they do refer to facts existent wholly apart from themselves, that their relation to these facts is one of successful correspondence or of error-producing non-correspondence, that the ideas in so far aim, not merely to embody, like the musical ideas just exemplified, an internal purpose, but also to imitate, in the form of their conscious structure and in the relationship of their own elements, the structure and relationship of a world of independent facts,—what could possibly seem, from such a common-sense point of view, more obvious than all this? And if common sense presupposes that ideas have such external meanings, how much more does not natural science appear to involve the recognition of this essentially imitative function of ideas?

In any special natural science, a scientific description appears as an adjustment, express, conscious, exact, of the internal structure of a system of ideas to the external structure of a world of preëxistent facts; and the business of science has been repeatedly defined, of late years, as simply and wholly taken up with the exact description of the facts of nature. Now the world of Being, when viewed in this light, appears to mean simply the same as the fact world, the external object of our ideas, the object that ideas must imitate, whatever their internal purpose, unless they want to be false. But for this very reason, no study of the inner structure of ideas, of their conscious conformity to their internal purpose, can so far promise to throw any direct light upon their success in fulfilling their external purpose. Or, as people usually say, you cannot make out the truth about facts by studying your "mere ideas." And so, as people constantly insist, no devotion to the elaboration of the internal meaning of your own ideas can get you in presence of the truth about Being.

The world of Being is whatever it happens to be, as the collection of ships is what it is, before you count. Internal purposes cannot predetermine external conformity to truth. You cannot evolve facts out of your inner consciousness. Ideas about Being are not to be justified like melodies, by their internal conformity to the purpose of the moment when they consciously live. They must submit to standards that they themselves in no sense create. Such is the burden of common sense, and of special science, when they tell us about this aspect of the meaning of our ideas.

I state thus explicitly a very familiar view as to the whole externally cognitive function and value of ideas. I mean thus to emphasize the primary appearance of hopeless contrast between the internal purpose and the external validity of ideas. In fact, nothing could seem sharper than the contrast thus indicated between the melody on the one hand, the musical idea, as it comes to mind and is enjoyed for its beauty while it passes before consciousness, and the counting of the ships, on the other hand,—a process whose whole success depends upon its conformity to what seem to be absolutely indifferent and independent outer facts. In the one case we have the embodiment of a conscious inner purpose,—a purpose which is won through the very act of the moment, and by virture of the mere presence of a certain series of mental contents. In the other case we have a conformity to outer truth,—a conformity that no inner clearness, no well-wrought network of cunning ideal contrivance, can secure, unless the idea first submits to the authority of external existence.

And yet, sharp as is this apparent contrast, every student of philosophy knows how profound are also the motives that have led some philosophers to doubt whether such contrast can really be as ultimate as it seems. After all, the counting of the ships is valid or invalid *not* alone because of the supposed independent being of the ships, but also because of the conscious act whereby just this collection of ships was first consciously selected for counting. After all, then, no idea is true or is false except with reference to the object that this very idea first means to select as its own object. Apart from what the idea itself thus somehow assigns as its own task, even that independent being yonder, if you assume such being, cannot determine the success or failure of the idea. It is the idea then that first says: "I mean this or that object. That is for my object. Of that I am thinking. To that I want to conform." And apart from such conscious selection, apart from such ideal predetermination of the object on the part of the idea, apart from such free voluntary submission of the idea to its self-imposed task, the object itself, the fact world, in its independence, can do nothing either to confirm or refute the idea. Now in this extremely elementary consideration, namely, in the consideration that unless ideas first voluntarily bind themselves to a given task, and so, by their internal purpose, already commit themselves to a certain selection of its object, they are neither true nor false,—in this consideration, I say, there may be hidden consequences that we shall later find momentous for the whole theory of Being and of truth. This consideration, that despite the seemingly hopeless contrast between internal and external meaning, ideas really possess truth or falsity only by virtue of their own selection of their task as ideas, is essentially the same as the consideration that led Kant to regard the understanding as the creator of the phenomenal nature over which science gradually wins conscious control, and that led Hegel to call the world the embodied Idea. This consideration, then, is not novel, but I believe it to be fundamental and of inexhaustible importance. I believe also that some of its aspects are still far too much neglected. And I propose to devote these lectures to its elaboration, and to a study of its relations to the various conceptions of Reality which have determined the scientific and religious life of humanity.

In any case I say, then, at the outset, that the whole problem of the nature of Being will for us, in the end, reduce to the question: How is the internal meaning of ideas consistent with their apparently external meaning? Or again: How is it possible that an idea, which is an idea essentially and primarily because of the inner purpose that it consciously fulfils by its presence, also possesses a meaning that in any sense appears to go beyond this internal purpose? We shall, in dealing with this problem, first find, by a development of the consideration just barely indicated, that the external meaning must itself be interpreted, not primarily in the sense of mere dependence upon the brute facts, but in terms of the inner purpose of the idea itself. We shall, perhaps to our surprise, reach the seemingly paradoxical and essentially idealistic thesis that no being in heaven or in earth, or in the waters under the earth, has power to give to an idea any purpose unless, the idea itself, as idea, as a fragment of life, as a conscious thrill, so to speak, of inner meaning, first somehow truly learns so to develop its internal meaning as to assign to itself just that specific purpose. In other words, we shall find that while, for our purposes, we, the critics, must first sharply distinguish the apparently external purpose that, as it were, from without, we assign to the idea, from the internal meaning of the idea, as present to a passing conscious instant, still, this our assignment of the external purpose, this our assertion that the idea knows or resembles, or imitates, or corresponds to, fact wholly beyond itself, must in the end be justified, if at all, by appeal to the truth, *i.e.* to the adequate expression and development of the internal meaning of the idea itself. In other words, we shall find either that the external meaning is genuinely continuous with the internal meaning, and is inwardly involved in the latter, or else that the idea has no external meaning at all. In brief, our abstract sundering of the apparently external from the consciously internal meaning of the idea must be first made very sharp, as we have just deliberately made it, only in order that later, when we learn the true relations, we may come to see the genuine and final unity of internal and external meaning. Our first definition of the idea seems to make, yes, in its abstract statement deliberately tries to make, as you see, the external meaning something sharply contrasted with the internal meaning. Our final result will simply reabsorb the secondary aspect, the external meaning, into the completed primary aspect,—the completely embodied internal meaning of the idea. We shall assert, in the end, that the final meaning of every complete idea, when fully developed, must be viewed as wholly an internal meaning, and that all apparently external meanings become consistent with internal meanings only by virtue of thus coming to be viewed as aspects of the true internal meaning.

To illustrate this thesis by the cases already used: The melody sung or internally but voluntarily heard, in the moment of memory, is, for the singer's or hearer's consciousness, a musical idea. It has so far its internal meaning. And to say so much first means simply that to the singer, as he sings, or to the silent memory of a musical imagination, the present melody imperfectly and partially fulfils a conscious purpose, the purpose of the flying moment. On the other hand, the melody may be viewed by a critic as an idea corresponding to external facts. The singer or hearer too may himself say as he sings or remembers: "This is the song my beloved sang," or "This is the theme that Beethoven composed in his Fidelio." In such a case, the idea is said to have its apparently external meaning, and this, its reference to facts not now and here given, is the idea's general relation to what we call true Being. And such reference not only seems at first very sharply different from the internal meaning, but must, for our purposes, at first be sundered by definition from that internal meaning even more sharply then common sense distinguishes the two. For abstract sundering is, in us mortals, the necessary preliminary to grasping the unity of truth. The internal meaning is a purpose present in the passing moment, but here imperfectly embodied. Common sense calls it, as such, an expression of transient living intent, an affair of Will. Psychology explains the presence and the partial present efficacy of this purpose by the laws of motor processes, of Habit, or of what is often called association. Ethical doctrine finds in such winning of inner purposes the region where Conscience itself, and the pure moral Intention, are most concerned. On the other hand, the apparently external meaning of the idea is at first said to be an affair of the externally cognitive intellect, and of the hard facts of an independently real world. Not purpose, but the unchangeable laws of the Reality, not the inner life, but the Universe, thus at first seems from without to assign to the idea whatever external meaning it is to obtain. Subject and Object are here supposed to meet,—to meet in this fact that ideas have external meaning,—but to meet as foreign powers.

Now we are first to recognize, even more clearly, I say, than common sense, the sharpness of this apparent antithesis between the conscious internal and the seemingly external meaning. Here, as I have said, is indeed the world-knot. We are to recognize the problem, but we are, nevertheless, to answer it in the end (when we get behind the appearances, and supplement the abstractions), by the thesis that at bottom, the external meaning is only apparently external, and, in very truth, is but an aspect of the completely developed internal meaning. We are to assert that just what the internal meaning already imperfectly but consciously is, namely, purpose relatively fulfilled, just that, and nothing else, the apparently external meaning when truly comprehended also proves to be, namely, the entire expression of the very Will that is fragmentarily embodied in the life of the flying conscious idea,—the fulfilment of the very aim that is hinted in the instant. Or, in other words, we are to assert that, in the case mentioned, the artist who composed, the beloved who sang the melody, are in verity present, as truly implied aspects of meaning, and as fulfilling a purpose, in the completely de-

veloped internal meaning of the very idea that now, in its finitude, seems to view them merely as absent. I deliberately choose,
in this way, a paradoxical illustration. The argument must hereafter justify the thesis. I can here only indicate what we hereafter propose to develop as our theory of the true relation of
Idea and Being. It will also be a theory, as you see, of the unity
of the whole very World Life itself.

In brief, by considerations of this type, we propose to answer
the question: What is to be? by the assertion that: To be means
simply to express, to embody the complete internal meaning of
a certain absolute system of ideas,—a system, moreover, which is
genuinely implied in the true internal meaning or purpose of
every finite idea, however fragmentary.

VI

You may observe already, even in this wholly preliminary
sketch of the particular form of Idealism to be developed in these
lectures, two principal features. First, Our account of the nature
of Being, and of the relation between Idea and Being, is to be
founded explicitly upon a theory of the way in which ideas
possess their own meaning. Secondly, Our theory of the nature
of Meaning is to be founded upon a definition in terms of Will
and Purpose. We do not indeed say, Our will causes our ideas.
But we do say, Our ideas now imperfectly embody our will.
And the real world is just our whole will embodied.

I may add, at once, two further remarks concerning the more
technical aspects of the argument by which we shall develop
our thesis. The first remark is, that the process by which we
shall pass from a study of the first or fragmentary internal meaning of finite ideas to that conception of their completed internal
meaning in terms of which our theory of Being is to be defined,
is a process analogous to that by which modern mathematical
speculation has undertaken to deal with its own concepts of
the type called by the Germans *Grenzbegriffe,* or Limiting Concepts, or better, Concepts of Limits. As a fact, one of the first
things to be noted about our conception of Being is that, as a
matter of Logic, it is the concept of a limit, namely of that
limit to which the internal meaning or purpose of an idea tends
as it grows consciously determinate. Our Being resembles the
concept of the so-called irrational numbers. Somewhat as they

are related to the various so-called "fundamental series" of rational numbers, somewhat in that way is Being related to the various thinking processes that approach it, as it were, from without, and undertake to define it as at once their external meaning, and their unattainable goal. That which is, is for thought, at once the fulfilment and the limit of the thinking process. The thinking process itself is a process whereby at once meanings tend to become determinate, and external objects tend to become internal meanings. Let my process of determining my own internal meaning simply proceed to its own limit, and then I shall face Being. I shall not only imitate my object as another, and correspond to it from without: I shall become one with it, and so internally possess it. This is a very technical statement of our present thesis, and of our form of Idealism,—a statement which only our later study can justify. But in making that statement here, I merely call attention to the fact that the process of defining limits is one which mathematical science has not only developed, but in large measure, at the present time, prepared for philosophical adaptation, so that to view the concept of Being in this light is to approach it with an interest for which recent research has decidedly smoothed the way. We shall meet both with false ways of defining the limit, and with true ways.

My second remark is closely related to the first, but is somewhat less technical, and involves a return to the practical aspects of our intended theory. I have just said that the development of the conception of an idea whose internal meaning is fully completed, and whose relation to Being is even thereby defined, will involve a discussion of the way in which our internal, our fragmentary finite meanings, as they appear in our flying moments, are to attain a determined character or are to become, as Hegel would say, *bestimmt,* so as to pass from vagueness to precision. Our theory, as you already see, will identify finite ignorance of Reality with finite vagueness of meaning, will assert that the very Absolute, in all its fulness of life, is even now the object that you really mean by your fragmentary passing ideas, and that the defect of your present human form of momentary consciousness lies in the fact that you just now do not know precisely what you mean. Increase of knowledge, therefore, would really involve increase of determination in your present meaning. The universe you have always with you, as your true internal meaning. Only this, your meaning, you now, in view of the defect of your momentary form of consciousness, realize vaguely, abstractly, without determination. And, as we have further asserted, this indetermination of your ideas also involves a hesitant indeterminateness of your momentary will, a vagueness of conscious ideal as well as of idea, a failure not only to possess, but wholly to know what you want. To pass to your real and completed meaning, to the meaning implied in this very moment's vagueness, would be a passage to absolute determinateness. So to pass would therefore be to know with full determination truths of an often desired type, truths such as: What you yourself are; and, who you are, as this individual; what this individual physical fact now before you is. Yes, it would be to know what the whole individual Being called the World is; and who the Individual of Individuals, namely the Absolute, or God himself, is. Just such final determinateness, just such precision, definiteness, finality of meaning, constitutes that limit of your own internal meaning which our theory will hereafter seek to characterize. And so my present remark hereupon is that, in following our enterprise of defining Being, we shall not be looking for mere abstract principles, but we shall be seeking for the most concrete objects in the world, namely for Individual Beings, and for the system that links them in one Individual Whole,— for Individuals viewed as the limits towards which all ideas of universal meanings tend, and for the Absolute as himself simply the highest fulfilment of the very category of Individuality, the Individual of Individuals.

Will, meaning, individuality, these will prove to be the constant accompaniments and the outcome of our whole theory of ideas, of thought, and of being. And in the light of these remarks we may now be able to anticipate more precisely the form of doctrine to which these lectures are to be devoted.

Idealism in some sense is indeed familiar in modern doctrine. And familiar also to readers of idealistic literature is some such assertion, as that the whole of Reality is the expression of a single system of thought, the fulfilment of a single conscious Purpose, or the realm of one internally harmonized Experience. But what the interested learners ask of idealistic teachers to-day is, as you are all aware, a more explicit statement as to just how Thought and Purpose, Idea and Will, and above all finite thought and will, and absolute thought and will, are, by any idealist, to be conceived as related to each other. My definitions in the foregoing have been deliberately intended to prepare the way for our later direct dealing with just these issues. An idea, in the present discussion, is first of all to be defined in terms of the internal purpose, or, if you choose, in terms of the Will, that it expresses consciously, if imperfectly, at the instant when it comes to mind. Its external meaning, its externally cognitive function as a knower of outer Reality, is thus in these lectures to be treated as explicitly secondary to this its internal value, this its character as meaning the conscious fulfilment of an end, the conscious expression of an interest, of a desire, of a volition. To be sure, thus to define, as we shall see, is not to separate knowing from willing, but it is rather to lay stress, from the outset, upon the unity of knowledge and will, first in our finite consciousness, and later, as we shall see, in the Absolute. Our present statement of our doctrine is therefore not to be accused, at any point, of neglecting the aspect of value, the teleological, the volitional aspect, which consciousness everywhere possesses. We shall reach indeed in the end the conception of an Absolute Thought, but this conception will be in explicit unity with the conception of an Absolute Purpose. Furthermore, as we have just asserted, we shall find that the defect of our momentary internal purposes, as they come to our passing consciousness, is that they imply an individuality, both in ourselves and in our facts of experience, which we do not wholly get presented to ourselves at any one instant. Or in other words, we finite beings live in the search of individuality, of life, of will, of experience, in brief, of meaning. The whole meaning, which is the world, the Reality, will prove to be, for this very reason, not a barren Absolute, which devours individuals, not a wilderness such as Meister Eckhart found in God, a *Stille Wüste, da Nieman heime ist,* a place where there is no definite life, nor yet a whole that absorbs definition, but a whole that is just to the finite aspect of every flying moment, and of every transient or permanent form of finite selfhood,—a whole that is an individual system of rationally linked and determinate, but for that very reason not externally determined, ethically free individuals, who are nevertheless One in God. It is just because all meanings, in the end, will prove to be internal meanings, that this which the internal meaning most loves, namely the presence of concrete fulfilment, of life, of pulsating and originative will, of freedom, and of individuality, will prove, for our view, to be of the very essence of the Absolute Meaning of the world. This, I say, will prove to be the sense of our central thesis; and here will be a contrast between our form of Idealism and some other forms.

And thus, in this wholly preliminary statement, I have outlined our task, have indicated its relation to the problems of religion, have suggested its historical affiliations, and have, in a measure, predicted its course. I have defined in general the problem of the relation of the World as Idea to the World as Fact, and have stated our issue as precisely this relation between Ideas and Reality. In order to assist in clarifying our undertaking, I have also given a general definition of what an idea is, and have stated the logical contrast between the consciously internal and the apparently external meaning of any finite idea. And finally I have asserted that, in dealing with the problem as to how internal and external meaning can be reduced to a consistent whole, we shall be especially guided to fruitful reflection upon the final relation of the World and the Individual. This, then, is our programme. The rest must be the actual task.

I am not unaware how valueless, in philosophy, are mere promises. All, in this field, must turn upon the method of work. The question of philosophy is not about the interest or the hopefulness of your creed, but about your rational grounds for holding your convictions. I accept the decidedly strict limitations imposed by this consideration, and shall try, when we come to the heart of our critical and constructive task, to be as explicit as the allotted time permits, both in expounding the precise sense of the doctrine now loosely and dogmatically sketched in the foregoing statement, and in explaining the grounds that lead me to prefer it, as a solution both of logical and of empirical problems, to its rivals. But the way of detailed argument is long, and the outlook of the whole enterprise may often seem, as we proceed with our difficulties, dark and perplexing. Introductions also have their rights; and I have meant in these opening words merely to recount the dream of which what follows must furnish both the interpretation and, in a measure, the justification.

6 ❧ INDIVIDUALITY AND FREEDOM [1]

I

. . . No accusation is more frequent than an Idealism which has once learned to view the world as a rational whole, present in its actuality to the unity of a single consciousness, has then no room either for finite individuality, or for freedom of ethical action. It was for the sake of preparing the way for a fair treatment of this very problem that we from the beginning defined the nature of ideas in terms at once of experience and of will. As we later passed to the assertion of the unity of the world from the final point of view, we have never lost sight of the fact that this is the unity of a divine Will, or, if you please, of a divine Act, at the same time as it is the unity of the divine Insight. The word "Meaning" has for us, from the outset, itself possessed a twofold implication,—not because we preferred ambiguity, but because, once for all, the facts of consciousness warrant, and in fact demand, this twofold interpretation. Whoever is possessed of any meaning, whoever faces truth, whoever rationally knows, has before his consciousness at once, that which *possesses the unity of a knowing process,* and that which *fulfils a purpose,* or in other words, that which constitutes what we have from the outset called an act of will as well as an act of knowledge. It is essential to our entire understanding of our Fourth Conception of Being, that we should remember the truth in both of these aspects, not dividing the aspects themselves, nor confounding their significance.

A few words of purely psychological analysis may then be, at this point, useful, to clarify the precise relations between intellectual and voluntary processes in our ordinary consciousness.

Popular psychology long since far too sharply sundered the Intellect and the Will in the empirical processes of the finite

[1] Josiah Royce, *The World and the Individual* (New York: The Macmillan Company, 1899, 1901), Vol. I, Lecture X, pp. 433–470.—Editor's note.

136

human mind. Viewing the intellect as a passive reception of the truth, defining the will as the power to alter facts, the popular psychology was forced, almost from the outset, to make an effort to reunite the powers that it had thus falsely separated. For a very little consideration shows not only that we can will to know, but also that we are in general guided, in our intellectual processes, by the very interests which popular pyschology refers to the will. On the other hand, our voluntary processes, if they are conscious, are themselves matters of knowledge. For our conscious volition implies that we know what we will. In consequence of these obvious considerations, a more modern psychology has been led to its well-known doctrine that all such psychological divisions are rather distinctions between different aspects of the same process, than means for telling us of naturally sundered or even of separable processes. If we regard the human subject, in the ordinary psychological way, as a being whose conscious life runs parallel with the highest physical processes of his organism, we get a view of the relation between the intellect and the will which is far more just, at once to the natural history of the mind, and to the deeper meaning of the inner life of our consciousness. View man as a natural being, and you find him adjusting himself to his environment, acting, as they say, in response to stimuli. The world influences his senses, only to awaken him to such functions as express his interest in this world. Now the whole life of the organism is precisely the life of adjustment. The physical activities accompanying consciousness so take place that the organism preserves itself, and expresses its natural bearing towards its world. And the whole life of consciousness, accompanying these adjustments, constitutes a more or less accurate knowledge of what the adjustments are. The life of our consciousness is therefore a life of watching our deeds, of estimating our deeds, of predicting our deeds, and of interpreting our whole world in terms of deeds. We observe no outer facts without at the same time more or less clearly observing our attitude towards those facts, our estimate of their value, our response to their presence, our intentions with respect to our future relations with these facts.

But, within the circle of this general unity of our consciousness, various distinctions indeed arise. Sometimes the outer fact, viewed more or less in abstraction from its value to ourselves, more completely fills the field of our consciousness, and then we are likely to talk of a state of relatively pure Knowledge. If our state is one in which an idea explicitly appears as attempting to correspond to the presupposed object of its own External Meaning, or to its own Other, we call the process one of Thought about External Reality. Sometimes, however, our acts themselves, viewed as efforts to alter the outside facts, come more clearly before us either for deliberate estimate, or for impulsive decision; and in such cases we find the narrow field of our consciousness more clearly taken up by what we call Will. But facts are never known except with reference to some value that they possess for our present or intended activities. And on the other hand, our voluntary activities are never known to us except as referring to facts to which we attribute in one way or another an intellectually significant Being,—a reality other than what is present to us at the moment.

It follows that when, for general purposes, we study, not the psychology, but, as at present, the total significance of our conscious life, we are much less interested in the separation between knowledge and will than in that unity which psychology already recognizes, and which philosophy finds of still more organic importance. Consequently, when, at the outset of these discussions, we pointed out the element of will in the constitution of ideas, we were dwelling upon precisely what for the psychologist appears as the intimate connection between the knowing process of the mind and the motor responses of the organism to its environment. When we know, we have in the first place present to our minds certain contents, certain data, certain facts, it may be of the outer senses, it may be of the memory and the imagination. But if rational knowledge takes place, these data are not merely present, but they also take on forms; they constitute ideal structures; they fulfil our own purposes. These purposes consciously correspond either to what an ordinary observer would call our visible responses to our environment, or to what a psychologist, who looks closer than an ordinary observer, would find also to involve memories, or hints, or fragments, of former adjustments. The result is, so far, that, when we know, the facts both of sense and of imagination unite in our minds, into the expression of a Plan of Action. And thus the knowing process is a process partially embodying our own will. Upon such an analysis of the nature of ideas all the foregoing discussion has been founded; and now we deliberately repeat and emphasize this interpretation in order to make way for a final statement of the place of the will in our doctrine of being.

From this point of view, then, the contrast between knowledge and will, *within* our own conscious field, is so far this; viz., that we speak of our conscious process as a Knowing, in so far as all the data are woven into one unity of consciousness; while we speak of this same process as Will, in so far as this unity of consciousness involves a fulfilment or embodiment of a purpose. The word "Meaning" very properly lays stress upon both of these aspects at once. For what we call a Meaning is at once something observed with clearness as an unity of many facts, and something also intended as the result which fulfils a purpose. But when we take account of *External* Meanings, we speak of Thought in so far as we seek correspondence to our presupposed Other, and of Will in so far as we seek to produce the Other that shall correspond to the Internal Meaning. Yet here the distinction, as we have already seen, is wholly relative to the point of view.

But now it next becomes us to take special note of this latter aspect of the will,—an aspect upon which the popular consciousness lays great stress. For the will is usually regarded as primarily the Cause of something which but for the will would not come into existence. We have already spoken of *acts* of will; and the popular view declares that we are conscious of an activity which *causes states of consciousness to exist within ourselves, and acts to come into existence outside of ourselves,* and which is therefore responsible for the actual production of new Being in the universe. But if, with reference to the scientific value of this popular view, we turn to psychology for advice, we find at the present time, in that science, decidedly opposed interpretations of the sense in which the human will can be regarded as a cause. According to one of these interpretations the word "act" is properly to be applied merely to the physical process by which our organism gets adjusted to its environment. The causes of precisely such physical acts are, from this psychological point of view, themselves physical causes. Our consciousness, according to this same view, is not itself a cause, either of the physical act whereby we express our will, or of the states of mind themselves which constitute our inner intent. Our will merely accompanies our adjustment to the environment, and constitutes our own consciousness of the meaning of a certain portion of this adjustment. Our will is not itself one of the forces or powers of nature.

On the other hand, a traditional doctrine, which has won for itself no small hearing in psychology, regards the volitional, or active, side of our consciousness, not merely as a fact in itself, but as a cause of other facts, both physical and mental. From this point of view, the distinction between intellect and will acquires a fresh importance, and declines to be reduced to that mere distinction of aspects which we have emphasized in the foregoing account. For, as is often said, man, in so far as he is a mere knower, accomplishes nothing; he merely observes. But as doer, as voluntary agent, he is the source of new being; he is an originator. Will, for this view, is nothing if not efficacious. A process that merely accompanies and reflects, without affecting, the adjustments of my organism to its environment, would be no true will. A sort of consciousness which merely observes that from moment to moment my inner life, for me, seems to have meaning, would, as this view asserts, in the end deprive my life of its most important meaning. For above all, as they say, what I mean to be is an originator of facts, and of facts that but for me would not exist. The true problem regarding the place of the will in the universe arises, according to this view, precisely at the point where one asks, Is the will the cause of any existence other than itself?

The two views about the will as cause thus brought into opposition have justly played a great part, both in the psychological and the metaphysical controversies of all periods, ever since the meaning of life began seriously to be considered. And the relation of this whole controversy to the deepest interest of metaphysics is as unquestionable as it is easy to misinterpret. For the word "cause" is a term of very various meaning. So ambiguous and obscure, in fact, is the idea of cause as customarily used, that I have deliberately preferred to avoid even defining the issue about the causality of the will until our concept of Being had first assumed in general a definite form. Moreover, even at the present stage of our inquiry, although we must indeed deal with one aspect of the issue upon its own substantial merits, we shall do best to avoid, on the present occasion, any thorough-going discussion of the varieties of meaning of the word "cause." We shall do best merely to state the sense in which we ourselves regard the Being of facts as *due to the will*, be that will human or divine. We shall then postpone, until our second course of lectures, a more precise distinction of the various forms of causation, which we shall learn to recognize as present in nature and in mind. For the concept of cause, properly regarded, is rather a cosmological than a fundamentally metaphysical conception.

To metaphysics in general belongs, above all, the question that we have been considering,—the question what it is to be. To metaphysics also belongs the problem, What fundamentally different kinds of Being are there? And in this connection the relation between God and the individual is indeed of essential importance. From the metaphysician you may also expect the answer to the question, To what principles is the actual constitution of the world of conscious volition, and of ethically significant life, due? But it is within the realm of what we call Nature,—namely, within the realm of finite experience, with its various phenomenal distinctions of organic and inorganic, of apparently living and apparently lifeless beings,—it is, I say, in case of Nature, that the diversified processes, present to our ordinary experience, arouse questions as to the special kinds of causal linkage that, in any particular case, bind one fact to another. It is in this world,— the phenomenal or natural, the essentially fragmentary world, the realm which cannot contain its whole truth within itself,— it is in this realm, I say, that the special problems concerning physical and mental causation, concerning active and inactive beings, concerning the relation of physical organism and mental phenomena, most properly arise. And we shall do well to keep separate the study of the whole constitution of the universe (conceived in accordance with the general principles of our theory of Being), from a study of the special problems of the phenomenal world. It is not my present purpose, then, to exhaust the theory of the sense in which will is, and is not, an active cause in the natural world. What can at present be asked from us is a general statement of the sense in which what exists expresses, on the one hand, the will of God; and, on the other hand, that individual will which you find at any moment present in a fragmentary way in your own finite consciousness. I shall maintain that both God's will and our own finite will get consciously expressed in the world, and that no contradiction results from this statement.

II

At any moment your ideas, in so far as they are rational, embody a purpose. That we have asserted from the outset. Our

original example, that of the melody sung, for the sake of the
mere delight in singing, remains for us typical of the entire life
of what one may call consciously free and internally unrestricted
finite ideas. Now what we in the first place have asserted in regard to such ideas, is that, precisely in so far as they are whole
ideas, they stand before our consciousness as present fulfilments
of purpose.

Any mere purpose, so far as it is still relatively fragmentary, or
is, so to speak, disembodied, or is a mere striving, begins, in
any such empirical case, the little drama that is acted within the
momentary limits of a finite consciousness. In saying that this,
at first disembodied purpose, becomes expressed, whenever any
consciousness of such an act passes from its earlier to its later
temporal stages,—I merely report what happens. I make as yet
simply no assertion with regard to any psychological or physical
causation. I assert as yet, in such a case, no effective force. I mention nothing of the nature of a physical or psychical tendency
such that, by the mere necessity of its nature, it must work itself
out. What my consciousness finds when I sing or speak is that a
certain meaning actually gets expressed. My act of singing takes
place. At once, then, there are data present, there are facts of
consciousness, and there is this significance which these facts embody. Whether the facts could have come into existence in this
way unless a given nervous organism or a given psychical
entity, endowed with specific powers, subject to general laws,
were already in existence, of all that my finite consciousness in
the present moment tells me nothing. To assert any such thing is
so far to assert a mere psychological or cosmological theory. The
basis of such an assertion, if it has any basis, must be sought
outside of any one moment's experience. On the other hand, in
vain would any psychologist, in vain would any realistic metaphysician, attempt to rob my finite consciousness of the significance which this my own moment of singing or speaking has, for
me, embodied. This significance is a matter of my experience.
Whatever your system of metaphysics, the singer can say: Here
at least the world has meaning, for lo! *I sing.*

Now, as a metaphysical theory, our idealistic doctrine with regard to Being in its wholeness has simply maintained that, without any regard to a doctrine of causation, without regard in the
least to any specific view as to the psychology of mental process,
*the whole universe, precisely in so far as it is, is the expression
of a meaning, is the conscious fulfilment of significance in life,*

precisely as the melody present at a given moment to the singer is for his consciousness the momentary expression of a meaning. And so our theory of Being is not founded upon any prior doctrine of causation. Cause and effect, laws mechanical or laws psychological, fate or freedom, in so far as any of these have Being, are from our point of view subject to the prior conditions of the very concept of Being itself. If nothing can be *except* what embodies a meaning, we are not first required to explain how anything whatever comes into Being, or how anything whatever is caused. For the cause of Being would itself have Being, and could itself exist, if our analysis is correct, only as the actual expression of a meaning.

The unhappy slavery of the metaphysics of the past to the conception of causation has been responsible for some of the most fatal of the misfortunes of religion and of humanity. That the existence of God was to be proved only by the means of the concept of causation, was one of the most characteristic of the presuppositions of an earlier theology, and was often supposed to be maintained on the basis of the authority of Aristotle. As a fact, this method of dealing with the theory of Being was false to the deepest spirit of Aristotle himself. For Aristotle's God is primarily the All-perfect Being, and is only secondarily the subject of which causation could be predicated in any form whatever. But however that may be, the theology which conceives the relation between God and the world, and between the world and the individual, as primarily a causal relation, subordinates the universal to the particular in theory, and the significant to the relatively insignificant in practical doctrine. The inevitable results of any such inversion of the rational order is a world where either fate reigns, or absolute mysteries are the final facts; or where both these unhappy results are combined. That just because the universe is through and through transparently significant, it may later prove to be worth while to regard my will as in this or that respect a cause of certain special results, is intelligible enough. But the genuine significance of my voluntary process is always an affair of my own consciousness regarding the present meaning of my life. You will in vain endeavor to deduce that meaning from the distinctly lower category of causal efficacy. That lower category of causation always implies a comment which somebody else, viewing my act in a relatively external way, may pass upon me from without.

It is indeed metaphysically just to assert that in certain aspects of my life I must needs be regarded as a cause, because I am already known to possess conscious significance, and because some aspects of this significance turn out to be causal. But you can never, on the other hand, discover wherein consists my significance by merely asserting that I am somehow or other a powerful cause. And precisely so it is in the case of God. You can indeed say that this or that fact in the world must be viewed as a result of laws whose source lies in the divine nature. But in asserting this you merely lay stress upon a result of that conscious significance which first of all attaches to the Being of all things, and to the life of God in its wholeness.

I cannot, then, too strenuously insist upon the thought that our own theory of Being places the very significance, both of the whole world and of the individual life, in the actual conscious fulfilment of meaning. Such fulfilment, from our own point of view, is the only reality. We therefore do not explain the existence of meaning in the world by looking, in the end, beyond any meaning for the cause which has brought the significant world to pass. To view the matter in that way would be of the very essence of Realism, and would involve all the contradictions which have already led us to reject the realistic interpretation of Being. Causation will find its place in our world, but as a mere result,—a partial aspect,—a mere item of the very significance of that world itself. For causal connections have a place only as expressing their own aspect of the meaning of things. On the other hand, the mere part, causation, will never appear in our account as the source of the whole; nor will this causation, which is but a very special form of Being, or a name for various special forms of Being, ever appear as that to which either the Being, or the wholeness of the meaning of the world, is due. And so much, then, for the mere causal efficacy, either of God or of man.

In consequence of these considerations, our primary question in regard to the finite human individual, in his relation to the divine life, is merely the question, In what sense does the finite Being retain, despite the unity of the whole divine life, any individual significance of his own, and what is the relation of this finite significance to the meaning and plan of the whole? But for the answer to this, our really important question, we may now be prepared, if we next lay new stress upon certain aspects of the Fourth Conception of Being, to which we have made repeated reference.

III

We have said that a meaning gets wholeness and individuality of expression precisely in so far as it gets, at the same time, conscious determination. An imperfect idea is vague. It is general. But it is so, in our own finite consciousness, in *two* senses. (1) Any finite idea, as we have seen, sends us to some other experience to furnish us yet further instances that are needed for its whole expression. This reference to another for the remainder of itself is characteristic of even the clearest and most precise of our finite ideas, just in so far as they are general. Thus, in counting, the single numbers refer us, further on in the number-series, for the rest of what the counting process implies. If one merely counts the first ten numbers, there are still other numbers to count. A complete consciousness of the whole meaning of the number-series would complete this process of seeking Another by presenting the whole individual meaning of the number concept in a finished form. We have, so far, altogether postponed the discussion of those difficulties about the quantitative Infinite which the conception of a completed knowledge of numbers seems to involve.[2] We have asserted only that the arithmetical or mathematical Being of the number-series cannot be consistently expressed, either in realistic form or in the form of mere valid possibilities of experience. We have consequently asserted that even the realm of mathematical Being involves facts which only our Fourth Conception can adequately express. In what way the whole experience in question gets realized, we have pointed out only in the general fashion indicated in the foregoing lecture. The whole Being in question, as we have said, must be present to the final consciousness in its complete form, or in such wise that no other, beyond, remains to be sought. So much, then, for the first inadequacy of our finite general ideas.

(2) But our finite passing consciousness is incomplete or inadequate to its own purposes not merely by lack of contents adequate to express its wholeness, but by reason of vagueness with regard to its own momentarily conscious purposes. The principal source of actual error, in finite consciousness, we have al-

[2] See the Supplementary Essay to the present volume. [Royce's note.—Ed.]

ready found to be the indetermination of our purposes at any stage in their realization. Now the presupposition of our whole view is that the final expression of purpose is not merely complete as to its contents, *but absolutely determinate as to what meaning these contents fulfil.* Now the finite process, whereby our own consciousness passes from an indeterminate to a relatively determinate state of purpose, of intention, of seeking for contents, is known to us in its psychological manifestations as a process of Selective Attention, growing more and more definite as it proceeds. Precisely in so far as we are conscious of a definite meaning at any instant, we are conscious of contents selected, as it were, from the background of our own finite consciousness, selected as the contents which are such that no other contents would definitely tend to express our will. Now it is the law of conscious growth in ourselves, that greater determination of purpose, and greater wealth of presented contents, are the correlative aspects of any gradual fulfilment of meaning. The more we know and the more richly we find our will fulfilled, the more exclusive and determinate becomes our purpose. The vague purpose is so far not at the instant clear as to whether *this or that* would better fulfil its meaning. The precise purpose selects this *instead* of that. Precise decision is exclusive as well as inclusive. And when I speak of this fact, I refer once more directly to our consciousness as my warrant. I presuppose nothing as to the causal basis, or as to the psychological or physical origin, of attention. I say that one who rationally finds a meaning fulfilled, discovers at once a wealth of contents, and a very sharply specific exclusiveness of interest fulfilled by these contents.

A satisfied will, a fully expressed meaning, would involve, then, the twofold consciousness that we may express by the two phrases, (1) I have all that I seek, and need no other; (2) I need precisely these contents, and so select them as to permit no other to take here and for this purpose their place. As a matter of fact, then, a will satisfied, a precisely determinate meaning expressed in facts, is as selective and exclusive on the one hand, as, on the other hand, it is possessed of an exhaustive wealth of contents which meet its selection.

Now it is this selective character of every rational conscious process, a character as manifest to consciousness as it is ultimately significant for the constitution of all Being,—it is this character, I say, which to my mind is responsible above all for the Individuality which we have already characterized as belonging to the whole of Being, and which we shall now find as equally characteristic of every region of finite Being. Strange as it may at first seem, a closer examination of the nature of truth makes easily manifest that what is, quite apart from any causal theory, must be viewed by the consciousness that faces Being as a selection from abstractly possible contents. The nature of these contents in general is recognized, and is so far present, at the very moment when the realization of this nature in the single shape selected from amongst all possible shapes is, at the same time, experienced.

This general view, that what is, is a selection from possibilities, is in another form as characteristic of Realism, and even in a sense of Mysticism, as it is of our own view of Being.

The discovery that the affirmation of reality is logically based upon the exclusion of the barely possible, is constantly made by common sense, is constantly illustrated by daily experience, and is popularly exemplified by that well-known destruction of possibilities which characterizes the passing of youth, the course of history, the reproduction of every species through relatively chance union of the members of that species, and by countless other instances. The Darwinian theory of the genesis of species by natural selection, is only a single instance of the application of this general concept that the real is a selection from amongst possibilities.

In elementary logic, as we earlier showed, it becomes manifest that all universal judgments are at once, as they say, negatively existential, and involve a destruction of logically possible classes of objects. Thus, let there be what the logicians call an Universe of Discourse, that is, a world of possible beings of which you are discoursing. Into that world let two classes of objects, A and B, be introduced. Then in your universe of discourse it becomes logically possible that there should be four sub-classes of beings, namely, the things which are both A and B, the things which are A but not B, the things which are not A but which are B, and finally the things which are neither A nor B. Thus, for example, if your universe of discourse is to contain righteous men and happy men, there are four sub-classes of men who are righteous and happy, who are righteous and unhappy, who are unrighteous but happy, and who are neither righteous nor happy. Now begin to make universal assertions about the relations amongst these classes. Assert that all the righteous are happy. At once, as we saw in our seventh lecture, this assertion appears as a negative existential assertion, and as the destruction of a possibility. For you can express it by saying that in your universe the sub-class, otherwise possible, of righteous men who are unhappy, has vanished from existence. Your universe has now reduced its realized possibilities to the existence of three sub-classes. The example is trivial. It is but one of a countless number. To know facts is to destroy mere possibilities. To know that there is even a single righteous man in your universe of discourse, is to destroy so far the abstractly possible alternative that that individual man is unrighteous. This result so far holds with absolute generality, and without regard to your special definition of the concept of Being. Accordingly every realist regards the real as the selection from the possible. And in this we too agree with him.

Spinoza, in his curious compromise between realistic and mystical motives, undertook indeed to deny this selective function of reality; and asserted that from the divine point of view all that is possible is real. In vain, however, would one attempt to carry out this doctrine, except by expressly substituting for all other conceptions of being the Third Conception, viz., that of the real as the valid. But even this conception itself is obliged to distinguish between the relatively determinate genuine possibilities of experience, and the absolutely unrestricted products of any passing fancy. For one who develops even his most general ideas so that they have any relative wholeness of meaning, some possibilities seem to be at once excluded. Thus we already saw that in the mathematician's realm numerous abstract possibilities are excluded whenever a specific theorem is demonstrated. Our rejection, however, of the Third Conception of Being as inadequate was due in the end to a recognition of the fact that, so long as you define mere universals, mere general natures of things, you define neither the Being of objects nor the truth of ideas.

But now, as a fact, our whole experience with the concept of Being has shown us that this exclusion of bare or abstract possibilities by the presence of determinate facts does *not* tend to impoverish, but rather to enrich, our consciousness of what is real; for it is by exclusion of vain possibilities that we become able at once to define a conscious purpose and to get it fulfilled in a precise way. The life in which anything whatever can consistently happen, and in which any purpose can be fulfilled in

any way, has in so far no character as a life. So far the experience
of such a life is the experience of nothing in particular,—of no
meaning. It is indeed true that an object which we regard as possible in the sense that it is still lacking, but is needed for a
specific purpose, is precisely the object which our finite experience seeks, longs to possess, regards as beyond itself, calls therefore the desired Other. The absence of such an object is indeed
a lack, a relative defeat of the finite purpose. And from our own
point of view, the Fourth Conception of Being does indeed involve the thesis that there are no valid possibilities which are to
remain in the end, and for God, merely possible and unfulfilled
in *this* sense, namely in the sense that while they are needed for
a specific purpose, they are still regarded as absent or as non-
existent. But, on the other hand, we have also found that what a
given finite purpose desires includes its own specific definition,
as this one purpose rather than another, as this specific way of
selecting facts. Now the more determinate the consciousness of
such a purpose becomes, the more does such consciousness involve a selection of some facts rather than others, or an exclusion
from Being of what is now regarded as merely and vainly or
abstractly possible.

If you ask what manner of partial Being, from the point of
view of our Fourth Conception, such abstractly conceived but
concretely excluded facts possess, I answer, precisely the fragmentary sort of Being which the consciousness of a specific purpose, that is the consciousness of a particular attentive selection,
consciously assigns to them. They are known *as* the excluded
facts. They are defined by consciousness only in relatively general terms. As mere kinds of experience, the facts which attention
thus excludes are themselves part of the very consciousness which
forbids them to have any richer and more concrete Being than
this character of remaining mere aspects of the whole. In this
sense, but in this only, are they facts whose nature is experienced. And once more, in saying this, I refer to consciousness
and to nothing else as my warrant for the meaning that I intend
to convey. When one attends, when one chooses, when one finds
a meaning at once specific and fulfilled, one actually observes, as
an aspect of one's experience, that which one defines as the exclusion of a generally conceived possibility. One's experience of
the general nature of this possibility is itself a part of the contents of one's whole present consciousness. The realization of the

whole present meaning is known by virtue of this very consciousness that one is excluding from complete expression facts whose general nature one still experiences.

Now what I assert is that our Fourth Conception of Being, in conceiving the real as the present fulfilment of meaning, experienced as such fulfilment from the absolute point of view, still expressly recognizes that every such fulfilment involves conscious selection and exclusion. The facts which fulfil the meaning are at once such that no other beyond is still needed to supply a lack, while, on the other hand, no other facts could take their place without precisely a failure to fulfil the purpose. And in this twofold sense is the world of the fulfilled meaning an individual world, a world whose place no other could take. A consciousness which faced a collection of mere possibilities, without selection, would face neither wholeness nor determination of life. The very perfection of experience involves then, as an element, the exclusion of another, whose general nature is indeed a part of the very experience in question. Just as formal logic and traditional Realism have already recognized that to be real involves the exclusion of bare possibilities, so our own conception also expressly recognizes that the life which is, in its wholeness, is exclusive as well as inclusive; and that in this sense, once more, the realm of Being has the character of the complete, but for this very reason of the determinate, Individual. So much then for Exclusion and Selection as aspects of will both in God and in man. We next pass on toward more special comparisons between Absolute and Finite Individuality. For Individuality, as we now begin to see, is, in one aspect, the expression of Selective Interest. Yet for a moment we must still treat of Individuality in general.

IV

The concept of the logical Individual, viewed apart from the question as to the distinctions of the various grades of individuality, finite or infinite, is a problem that frequently has received far too indefinite a treatment in logical discussions. What shall the word "individual" in general mean? As we have often already indicated, the technical answer to this question runs: By an individual being, whatever one's metaphysical doctrine, one means an unique being, that is, a being which is alone of its own type, or is such that no other of its class exists. Now, as we saw in an earlier lecture, our human knowledge begins with immediate data, and with vague ideas. But mere colors and sounds, as such, may indeed indicate individual beings; but they are not yet known as individuals; while our early ideas, in their twofold vagueness, both as ideas needing further determination in order to define their purpose, and as ideas needing further embodiment to complete their expression, are far from being consciously adequate ideas of individual entities. A very little examination of our popular conceptions shows how very general all such conceptions are. A very little study of concrete science reveals how hard it is for any man to get a clear idea of what his science regards as the constitution of any of its individual objects. It is far easier to know something about the circulation of the blood, than to have any adequate knowledge of the medical aspects of the case of an individual man whose circulation is in any way deranged by disease. It is precisely the individual case that constitutes the goal of the physician's knowledge. In general a real knowledge of individual facts is the ideal aim of science, rather than the beginning of any form of human insight; and this one can observe to be true, quite apart from any metaphysical conception of what constitutes individuality.

Yet it is indeed perfectly true that, long before we have any scientific approach to a knowledge of the individual facts of the natural world, we all of us somehow believe that the world contains individual beings. And the historical prominence of the thesis that whatever is, is individual, the prominence, I say, of this thesis in the metaphysics of all ages, is due to deep reasons which seldom come to the clear consciousness of those who are accustomed to talk glibly about individuality. Only our Fourth Conception of Being is able to make the conception at once rational and explicit. It is, so we have asserted, precisely as the final and satisfactory expression of the whole will of an idea that any object can be regarded as unique. But what makes the presupposition that objects are individual precisely in so far as they are real appear so early in human thought, and exercise such a controlling influence over the development of science, is precisely that demand of the finite idea for wholeness of expression, which we have just analyzed in both of its contrasted aspects. Long before we can ever say, with even a shadow of plausibility, that we ourselves have known and experienced the unique presence of any single fact, as such, our restless finite will itself has demanded that the real world wherein our will seeks, and logically speaking, ultimately finds, its fulfilment, shall be altogether determinate, both in so far as nothing further is needed to complete it, and in so far as nothing else would meet the needs which constitute finite ideas.

But owing to our finitude, will, in our own case, far anticipates its own fulfilment. The individual, therefore, as a conceived object of inquiry, of desire, and of knowledge, appears in our finite human thought as something that we early define much more in terms of selective exclusion than of empirically observed completeness. We presuppose the individual in both the foregoing senses; viz., as selected and as complete. But, if you look closely at that region of our consciousness where first we come nearest to facing what we take to be an experience of individuality, you find, I think, that it is our selective attention, especially as embodied in what one may call our exclusive affections, which first brings home to us what we mortals require an individual being to be. How in fact should a finite being, whose experience constantly passes from one partial fulfilment to another, from one vague general idea to another instance of the same generality,—how should such a being, I say, come to be so sure as most of us are that he has actually stood in the presence of individuals, and has faced beings that are unique? Yet every man supposes, to take perfectly ordinary instances, that his own father and mother are real individuals, and that other men, too, even where their individuality has been far less closely scrutinized, are still in themselves somehow individuals. Every man also early believes that the world as a whole, whether he regards it as one or as many, is at all events an individual collection of individuals. Yet to make this assertion is in any case far to transcend any man's actual experience, regarded merely as that experience comes to us. For what we find in our finite wanderings are always cases of types, instances of imperfectly fulfilled meanings. In observing my father, what I each time experience must necessarily be merely the presence to my mind of a certain kind of experience. That the object of this experience is unique, that in all the universe there is no other like it, how should I myself ever experience this fact? That this theorem about individuality is itself true, is precisely what our Fourth Conception of Being has now asserted. For whatever the relation between the finite idea and the whole world may be, this we already know from our Fourth Conception, namely that the world in its unity is an individual whole, such that no other could take its place as an expression of this one purpose.

Our idea of individuality comes to our finite consciousness, therefore, rather on the selective side of this consciousness than upon the side of its present fulfilment. It is not so much what I already know about an individual as what my affections determine to regard as unique in the value of my object, that first brings home to me, in the case of my father or my mother or my home or my personal possessions, or my own life, and later only in the case of indifferent beings, the uniqueness of the object in question. Affection first says in presence of an object, imperfectly presented in experience, not only that there shall be further experience completing and fulfilling this meaning, but also that there shall be in this further experience such unity as constitutes an unique object. Affection first declares that there shall be no other object capable of fulfilling this meaning, beyond the single object whose Being I now presuppose. It is thus, for instance, that the lover says, There shall be none like my beloved. It is thus, too, that the mother says, There shall be no child like my child. It is thus that the loyal friend says, There shall be no friend like my friend. It is thus that the finite Self says, No life shall have precisely the meaning that my life has. It is thus also that the ethical consciousness says, My duty shall be that which nobody but myself can conceivably do. In brief, in our finite life, the sense of the determinate selection of the single object that we shall regard as the fulfilment of our meaning, comes earlier to our consciousness than any specific hope that, in our finite capacity, we shall ever live to see this specific meaning wholly fulfilled.

Now this disposition of our finite will, this tendency to a selection of our objects as unique, is precisely the character which our Fourth Conception regards as also belonging to that Absolute Will which faces the final meaning and fulfilment of the world. For the world as a whole is, from our point of view, an individual fact, not merely by virtue of the completeness of the contents of the Absolute Experience, but by reason of the definiteness of the selection of that object which shall be permitted to fulfil the final meaning. No significant purpose, no element of meaning that finite ideas demand as necessary for their own fulfilment, could indeed be, according to our thesis, wholly ignored from the absolute point of view. But, on the other hand, the very perfection of the fulfilment would logically require of the divine will the sort of determination of purpose of which we too are conscious when we deal with the objects of the exclusive affection. It is will, then, in God and in man, that logically determines the consciousness of individuality. The individual is, primarily, the object and expression of an exclusive interest, of a determinate selection.

From this point of view, the world in its wholeness might indeed be regarded as, so to speak, an only begotten son of the central purpose,—an unique expression,—unique not merely by reason of its wealth, but of its exclusiveness. And thus the category of individuality would be fulfilled in the whole precisely in the sense in which our finite affection presupposes its fulfilment in individual cases.

V

We have thus gradually prepared ourselves to define the relation between the Finite and the Absolute Will. We have studied as aspects of will, both selective attention and the nature of individuality. We have indicated, too, the sense in which, for our Fourth Conception, the world is the fulfilment of purpose. And now, to sum up so far, we do not say that any purpose, divine or human, first existing as a merely separate power, thereupon *causes* its own fulfilment. On the contrary, we say as to God, that from the absolute point of view, the genuine knowledge of the absolute purpose, as an empirical fact, is its own fulfilment. For, according to our central thesis, except as consciously fulfilling a purpose, nothing can, logically speaking, exist at all. In the second place we have also maintained that the fulfilment of the divine purpose is twofold, involving at once wealth of experience conforming to the one meaning, and selection both of the facts which express the meaning, and of the precise and individual determination of the meaning itself. The world that thus expresses meaning appears, from the absolute point of view, as an unique whole, but as also an unique selected whole, such that neither for the whole nor for any of the parts could any other fact be substituted, without failure in the realization of precisely this totality of determinate meaning. And consequently, quite apart from any causal theory, that selective aspect which common sense already regards as essential to the will does indeed appear in our account as a real and logically required character of the divine or absolute will. In the third place, however, we find a similarly selective character belonging to our own will, and an experience of such selection we find in that sort of exclusive interest whereby, even in advance of knowledge, we undertake to define the individuality which we presuppose in all the objects of our more exclusive affection.

If you ask, from this point of view, in what sense the world is to be called rather the expression of the Divine Will, and in what sense it is rather the expression of the Divine Knowledge, I reply that while we have by no means separated these two aspects of the universe, we can now easily see the convenience from many points of view of distinguishing them. The Divine or Absolute Knowledge this world expresses, by virtue of the unity of consciousness in which all its facts are linked, and by virtue too of that universality of meaning which joins all various ideas, in such wise that every finite idea, in so far as it merely refers to another, or has external reference, is general, while the whole expression of these ideas is unique and individual. In this same sense we can also speak of the world, quite accurately, as the expression, or embodiment, or fulfilment, of the Divine Thought. Will, on the other hand, this world expresses, not as if the Divine Will were an external power causing the world, but in so far as the unity of the whole is teleological, is such as ideas intend; or again, in so far as the world attains wholeness, and needs no fact beyond it for its completion; and finally, in so far as this wholeness and uniqueness of the world is the expression of an ideal selection, whose nature is well exemplified by our own exclusive interests, and whose type of fulfilment we all observe whenever we win a rational ideal goal.

Now all these considerations might seem once more to deprive any finite portion, or aspect, of this conscious universe, of any distinguishable private significance. On the contrary, however, precisely the opposite is the true result. For consider. If the whole world is at once the complete expression of a plan, and also the unique expression of such plan, then every fact in it, precisely in so far as we *distinguish* that fact from other facts, and consider its internal meaning, is also inevitably unique, sharing in so far the uniqueness of the whole. For, to illustrate, if in the ordinary empirical world of space, this room is unique, so that by hypothesis there shall be no other room like it in the world, then any definable part of the unique room, by virtue of the very fact that it is different from all the other parts of this same room, has its own unique individuality as opposed to any other fact in the universe.

Or again, let A be any fact. First suppose A to be merely an abstract universal, a general type. Then suppose A to be an individual. If A is as a whole merely a case of a type, so that there are other cases like it, then any part of A is in so far also only a case of a type, and is not unique. But if A is an individual, unique and elsewhere unexampled, then every fragment of A has its part in the individuality of the whole, just as a play of Shakespeare, as this particular expression of the individuality of the poet, has its own uniqueness by sharing in his.

Now, by hypothesis, the world exists only as *such* an expression of the meaning of the divine system of ideas, that no other life than this of the present world could express precisely this system. But suppose that you lay stress upon the facts of any finite life. You have a right to do so, for these facts exist for the Absolute precisely as much as for you. Then you have, in the first place, facts that exist only as an expression of a meaning. If you ask of what meaning they are the expression, the answer is, of the meaning of the very ideas and of the very will, that, in the finite consciousness, accompany these very facts.

Take, for instance, one of your own acts. In part, it expresses one of your own purposes. Now our theory does indeed unite both your act and the idea that your act expresses, along with all other acts and ideas, in the single unity of the absolute consciousness. But this single unity of the absolute consciousness, as we already saw at the last time, is nothing that merely absorbs your individuality, in such wise that you vanish from amongst the facts of the world. You remain from the absolute point of view precisely what you now know yourself to be, namely, the possessor of just this ideal purpose, whose internal meaning is embodied in just so much of conscious life as is yours. Our very theory insists that your internal meanings, your ideas viewed as internally significant, your selections and expressions, are typical instances of facts, and of precisely the facts of whose unity the world consists. Now if the whole world is, as whole, the unique expression of the divine purpose, it follows that every finite purpose, precisely in so far as it is, is a partial expression and attainment of the divine will; and also that every finite fulfilment of purpose, precisely as we finite beings find it, is a partial fulfilment of the divine meaning. For from our point of view, while all finite ideas, in so far as concerns their external meaning, are indeed general, still no fact exists *merely* as a case of a type, or merely as an instance of an universal. The very simplest view of any finite fact already makes it a positive part of the unique divine experience, and therefore, as this part, itself unique. A still deeper view recognizes any finite will, say your own present will, as a stage or case of the expression of the divine purpose at a given point of time; but this expression, too, is once more unique. And this expression is also in one aspect no other than what you find it to be, to wit, your own conscious will and meaning.

Thus the individuality of the whole in such wise dwells in the parts, the individuality of the unique divine purpose is in such wise present in each finite purpose, that no finite purpose, viewed merely as an internal meaning, could have its place taken by another without a genuine alteration of the whole; while, on the other hand, it is equally true that the whole would not be what it is were not precisely this finite purpose left in its own uniqueness to speak precisely its own word—a word which no other purpose can speak in the language of the divine will. In brief, then, our view leaves all the unique meaning of your finite individual life just as rich as you find it to be. You are in God; but you are not lost in God. If every finite pulsation of life, despite its aspect of mere generality, its external meaning, has something unique about it, and if this unique aspect of the finite life expresses an internal meaning, then the meaning of every such fact itself is unique. Or to apply the matter once more to yourself: if every instance of your life expresses a will that is to be found expressed in precisely this way nowhere else in all the world, and if this will is the will of which you are now conscious, then we can say that the verdict of your own consciousness when it regards your life as the expression of your individual will is in no wise refuted, but is only confirmed by our Fourth Conception of Being.

Thus it is then that we deal, in case of the finite will and the divine will, with the problem of the One and the Many. A realistic union of the many different beings in one being we long since found to be impossible. For our present point of view, however, the realistic difficulty of the Many and the One has been wholly set aside. It is not indeed for us a question of how the many *things* could become one *thing*. For us the unity of the world is the unity of consciousness. The variety of the world is the internal, but none the less wealthy and genuine, variety of the purposes and embodiments of purpose present within this unity of the one divine consciousness. Now with regard to the ultimate unity and consequent harmony of all this variety, our Fourth Conception has given us indeed a general formula. The Many must, despite their variety, win harmony and perfection by their coöperation. But this principle, so far, gives us no limit either to the empirical variety of will, or of interest and of experience in the absolute, nor any limit to the relative independence which the uniqueness of the individual elements makes possible. What we see, however, is that every distinguishable portion of the divine life, in addition to all the universal ties which link it to the whole, expresses its own meaning. We see, too, that this meaning is unique, and that this meaning is precisely identical with what each one of us means by his own individual will, so far as that will is at any time determinate, uniquely selected, and empirically expressed. So much then for the general relations of Absolute and of Finite will.

VI

Two expressions, familiar to common sense in speaking of finite will, receive herewith their sufficient and, I believe, their only possible justification. Common sense first asserts that, when my will gets expressed, I individually am *active*. Common sense also, in the second place, asserts that when my will gets inwardly expressed in my choice, I individually am *free*. Now into the endless discussions as to the causal relations of this or that aspect of the human will we have declined in this discussion to go. We have declined, because we have said that all causation, whatever it is, is but a special instance of Being, and never can explain any of the ultimate problems about Being. But when we have asserted, as we have now done, that every moment of every finite consciousness has some unique character, and when we have asserted, as we have also done, that in our rational life our momentary will and its finite expression belong to this very unique aspect of our finite life, we have indeed found, in our finite will, an aspect which *no* causation could ever by any possibility explain. For whatever else causation may be, it implies the explanation of facts by their general character, and by their connections with other facts. Whatever is unique, is as such not causally explicable. The individual as such is never the mere result of law. In consequence, the causal explanation of an object never defines its individual and unique characters as such, but always its general characters. Consequently, *if* the will and the expression of that will in any moment of our finite life possess characters, namely, precisely these individual and uniquely significant characters which no causal explanation can predetermine, then such acts of will, as significant expressions of purpose in our life, constitute precisely what ethical common sense has always meant by free acts. If your finite purpose is now different from that of any other finite being, and if your finite purpose now in any sense uniquely expresses, however inadequately, its own determinate meaning, in its own way, then, you can indeed assert: I alone, amongst all the different beings of the universe, will this act. That it is true that God here also wills in me, is indeed the unquestionable result of the unity of the divine consciousness. But it is equally true that this divine unity is here and now realized by me, and by me only, through my unique act. My act, too, is a part of the divine life that, however fragmentary, is not elsewhere repeated in the divine consciousness. When I thus consciously and uniquely will, it is I then who just here *am* God's will, or who just here consciously act for the whole. I then am so far free.

The other popular conception, in addition to the conception of freedom, which belongs in this connection, is that very conception of Activity which I have just employed. By the term "activity" I regard our ethical common sense as meaning precisely the very fact that our present will, as the will of an individual, is unique. By our activity, then, I mean just the unique significance of the present expression of our will. If a general law,—a merely universal type,—if our characters or temperaments, or some other such universal nature of things, are expressed in our present experience, then, in so far, we are indeed mere cases of types. In so far we do not act. But if this my present expression of my meaning is in such wise unique that, but for this meaning, this expression would have no place in the whole realm of Being, then indeed I may call my present expression of meaning my act. As my act this my present will is as unique as is the whole divine life, as free as is the whole meaning of which the whole world is an expression. *Not* by virtue then of any supposed causal efficacy is the divine will as a power the producer of the world. And just so, not by virtue of its potency as a physical agent is our human action a free cause.

To our later series of lectures must be altogether left the discussion of any sort of causation in its real, but in its extremely subordinate, place in the constitution of reality. But what we at present say to the finite being is: You are at once an expression of the divine will, and by virtue of that very fact the expression here and now, in your life, of your *own* will, precisely in so far as you find yourself acting with a definite intent, and gaining through your act a definite empirical expression. We do not say, Your individuality causes your act. We do not say, Your free will creates your life. For Being is everywhere deeper than causation. What you are is deeper than your mere power as a physical agent. Nothing whatever besides yourself determines either causally or otherwise just what constitutes your individuality, for you are just this unique and elsewhere unexampled expression of the divine meaning. And here and now your individuality in your act *is* your freedom. This your freedom is your unique possession. Nowhere else in the universe is there what here expresses itself in your conscious being. And this is true of you, not in spite of the unity of the divine consciousness, but just because of the very uniqueness of the whole divine life. For all is divine, all expresses meaning. All meaning is uniquely expressed. Nothing is vainly repeated; you too, then, as individual are unique. And (here is the central fact) just in so far as you consciously will and choose, you then and there in so far know what this unique meaning of yours is. Therefore are you in action Free and Individual, just because the unity of the divine life, when taken together with the uniqueness of this life, implies in every finite being just such essential originality of meaning as that of which you are conscious. Arise then, freeman, stand forth in thy world. It is God's world. It is also thine.

7 ❧ THE TEMPORAL AND THE ETERNAL[1]

... There is an ancient distinction of the philosophers between the Temporal and the Eternal. It must be plain at this point, that we ascribe to the true world a certain eternal type of Being. Yet how shall we reconcile this with our equally obvious treatment of the world as existing in time? Plainly we have here a question that is of great importance for any understanding of the categories of experience. It belongs, then, in the context of these earlier discussions of our present series of lectures. Moreover, it is one that will constantly meet us later. The relation of Time to Nature will be of central concern to us. When we come to deal with the individual Self, we shall again have to face the question: In what sense has the Self of the individual a purely Temporal, and in what sense an Eternal type of reality? And before we can answer this question we must be more precise than we have yet been in defining the terms Time and Eternity. The issue here involved has a significance not only theoretical, but also intensely practical. It will need therefore a close and deliberate scrutiny. Time, as we shall soon see, is a concept of fundamentally practical meaning. The definition of the Eternal, on the other hand, has very close relations to the question as to the ultimate significance of all that is practical. Any rational decision as between a pessimistic and an optimistic view of the world, any account of the relations between God and Man, any view of the sense in which the evils and imperfections of the Universe can be comprehended or justified, any account of our ethical consciousness in terms reconcilable with our Idealism,—in brief, any philosophical reconciliation with religion and life, must turn in part upon a distinction between the Temporal and the Eternal, and upon an insight into their unity in the midst of their contrast. The problem at issue is one of the most delicate and, at the same time, one of the simplest of the great issues of phi-

[1] Josiah Royce, *The World and the Individual* (New York: The Macmillan Company, 1899, 1901), Vol. II, Lecture III, pp. 111-151.—Editor's note.

losophy. I shall here have to deal with it at first in a purely theoretical fashion, and shall then proceed to its practical applications. For both aspects of the question we are now fully prepared.

I

Time is known to us, both perceptually, as the psychologists would say, and conceptually. That is, we have a relatively direct experience of time at any moment, and we acknowledge the truth of a relatively indirect conception that we possess of the temporal order of the world. But our conception of time far outstrips in its development and in its organization anything that we are able directly to find in the time that is known to our perceptions. Much of the difficulty that appears in our metaphysical views about time is, however, due to lack of naïveté and directness in viewing the temporal aspects of reality. We first emphasize highly artificial aspects of our conception of time. Then we wonder how these various aspects can be brought into relation with the rest of the real world. Our efforts to solve our problem lead very easily to contradictions. We fail to observe how, in case of our more direct experience of time and of its meaning, various elements are woven into a certain wholeness,— the very elements which, when our artificial conception of time has sundered them, we are prone to view as irreconcilable with one another and with reality.

Our more direct perceptions of time form a complex sort of consciousness, wherein it is not difficult to distinguish several aspects. For the first, some Change is always occurring in our experience. This change may belong to the facts of any sense, or to our emotions, or to our ideas; but for us to be conscious is to be aware of change. Now this changing character of our experience is never the whole story of any of our clearer and more definite kinds of consciousness. The next aspect of the matter lies in the fact that our consciousness of change, wherever it is definite and wherever it accompanies definite successive acts of attention, goes along with the consciousness that for us something comes first, and something next, or that there is what we call a Succession of events. Of such successions, melodies, rhythms, and series of words or of other simple acts form familiar and typical examples. An elementary consciousness of change without such definite successions we can indeed have; but where we observe clearly what a particular change is, it is a change wherein one fact succeeds another.

A succession, as thus more directly experienced by us, involves a certain well-known relation amongst the events that make up the succession. Together these events form a temporal sequence or order. Each one of them is over and past when the next one comes. And this order of the experienced time-series has a determinate direction. The succession passes *from* each event *to* its successor, and not in the reverse direction; so that herein the observed time relations notoriously differ from what we view as space relations. For if in space *b* is next to *a*, we can read the relation equally well as a coexistence of *a* with *b*, and as a coexistence of *b* with *a*. But in case *b* succeeds *a*, as one word succeeds another in a spoken sentence, then the relation is experienced as a passing from *a* to *b*, or as a passing over of *a* into *b*, in such wise that *a* is past,. as an event, before *b* comes. This direction of the stream of time forms one of its most notable empirical characters. It is obviously related to that direction of the acts of the will whose logical aspect interested us in connection with the consideration of our discriminating consciousness.

But side by side with this aspect of the temporal order, as we experience this order, stands still another aspect, whose relation to the former has been persistently pointed out by many psychological writers, and as persistently ignored by many of the metaphysical interpreters of the temporal aspect of the universe. When we more directly experience succession,—as, for instance, when we listen to a musical phrase or to a rhythmic series of drum-beats,—we not only observe that any antecedent member of the series is over and past before the next number comes, but also, and without the least contradiction between these two aspects of our total experience, we observe that this whole succession, with both its former and later members, so far as with relative directness we apprehend the series of drum-beats or of other simple events, is present *at once* to our consciousness, in precisely the sense in which the unity of our knowing mental life always finds present at once many facts. It is, as I must insist, true that for my consciousness *b* is experienced as following *a*, and also that both *a* and *b* are *together* experienced as in this relation of sequence. To say this is no more contradictory than to say that while I experience two parts of a surface as, by virtue of their spatial position, mutually exclusive each of the other, I also may experience the fact that both these mutually exclusive parts go together to form one whole surface. The sense in which they form one surface is, of course, not the sense in which, as parts, they exclude each other, and form different surfaces. Well, just so, the sense in which *b*, as successor of *a*, is such, in the series of events in question, that *a* is over and gone when *b* comes, is not the sense in which *a* and *b* are together elements in the whole experienced succession. But that, in *both* of these senses, the relation of *b* to its predecessor *a* is an experienced fact, is a truth that any one can observe for himself.

If I utter a line of verse, such as

The curfew tolls the knell of parting day,

the sound of the word *day* succeeds the sound of the word *parting*, and I unquestionably experience the fact that, for me, every earlier word of the line is over and past before the succeeding word or the last word, *day*, comes to be uttered or to be heard. Yet this is unquestionably not my whole consciousness about the succession. For I am certainly *also* aware that the *whole* line of poetry, as a succession of uttered sounds (or, at all events, a considerable portion of the line), is present to me at once, and as this one succession, when I speak the line. For only by virtue of experiencing this wholeness do I observe the rhythm, the music, and the meaning of the line. The sense in which the word *parting* is over before the word *day* comes, is like the sense in which one object in space is *where* any other object is *not*, so that the spatial *presence* of one object excludes the presence of another at the same part of space. Precisely so the presence of the word *day* excludes the presence of the word *parting* from its own place in the temporal succession. And, in our experience of succession, each element is *present* in a particular point of the series, in so far as, with reference to that point, other events of the series are either *past*, that is, over and done with, or are *future*, that is, are later in the series, or are *not yet when* this one point of the series is in *this* sense present. Every word of the uttered line of poetry, viewed in its reference to the other words, or to previous and later experiences, is *present* in its own place in the series, is *over and done with* before later events can come, or when they are present, and is *not yet* when the former events of the succession are present. And that all this is true, certainly is a matter of our experience of succession.

But the sense in which, nevertheless, the whole series of the uttered words of the line, or of some considerable portion of the line, is presented to our consciousness *at once,* is precisely the sense in which we apprehend this line as one line, and this succession as one succession. The whole series of words has for us its rhythmic unity, and forms an instance of conscious experience, whose unity we overlook at one glance. And unless we could thus overlook a succession and view at once its serially related and mutually exclusive events, we should never know anything whatever about the existence of succession, and should have no problem about time upon our hands.

This extremely simple and familiar character of our consciousness of succession,—this essentially double aspect of every experience of a present series of events,—this inevitably twofold sense in which the term *present* can be used in regard to our perception of temporal happenings,—this is a matter of the most fundamental importance for our whole conception of Time, and, as I may at once add, for our conception of Eternity. Yet this is also a matter very frequently obscured, in discussion, by various devices often used to express the nature of the facts here in question. Sometimes, for the sake of a laudable attempt to define the term *present* in a wholly unambiguous way, those who are giving an account of our experience of time are led to assert that, since every part or element of any series of temporal events can be *present* only when all the other elements of the series are temporally non-existent, *i.e.* are either past or future, it must therefore be quite impossible for us to be conscious, *at once,* of a present succession involving a series of such elements. For how, they say, can I be conscious of the presense of all the successive words of the verse of poetry, when only one word is actually and temporally present at any one time? To comprehend how I can become in any sense aware of the series of successive words that constitutes the line of verse, such students of our problem are accustomed to say that when any one word as *passing,* or *day,* is present to my mind, the other words, even of the same line, can be present to consciousness *only* as coexistent memories or images of the former words, or as images of the expected coming words. From this point of view, I never really observe any sequence of conscious events as a sequence at all. I merely apprehend each element by itself; and I directly conclude from the images which in my experience are coexistent with this element, that there have been antecedent, and will be subsequent events in the series.

This interpretation of our consciousness of time is, however, directly counter to our time-experience, as any one may observe it for himself. For we do experience succession, and *at once* we do take note of facts that are in different times. For, I ask you, What word of mine is it that, as this single present word, you just *now* hear me speaking? If I pause a little, you perhaps dwell upon the last word that I utter before pausing, and call that the one present word. Otherwise, however, as I speak to you, you are conscious of series of successive words, of whole phrases, of word groups, of clauses. Within each one of these groups of words, you are indeed more or less clearly aware that every element has its own temporal place; and that, *in so far as* each element is taken by itself as present, the other elements either precede or succeed it, and in *this* sense are not in one time with it. But this very fact itself you know merely in so far as you actually experience series, each of which contains several successive words. These series come to you not merely by virtue of remembered facts, but also as experienced facts.

And in truth, were this not so, you could indeed have no experience of succession at all. You would then experience, at any one moment, merely the single word, or something less than any single word, together with the supposed coexistent and contemporaneous images of actually past or of coming words. But how, in that case, would your experience of time-sequences come to seem to you different from any experience whatever of coexistence? Nor is even this the only difficulty about the doctrine which supposes you to be unable to view a series of successive events as all at once presented to your consciousness. A still deeper difficulty results from such an effort to evade the double sense in which the facts of succession are known in your experience. If you can have present to you only *one* event at a time in a series of successive events, how long, or rather how short, must an event be to contain within itself no succession at all, or no difference between former and latter contents? In vain do you suppose that, at any time, you have directly present to your consciousness only one of the successive words that you hear me speak. Not thus do you escape our difficulty. For a spoken word is itself a series of temporally successive sounds. Can you hear at once the whole spoken word, or can you grasp at once this whole series? If so, my own foregoing account is in principle admitted. For then, in this presence of the facts of succession to your consciousness, there are our two former aspects, both of them, involved. *Each* element of the succession (namely, in this case, the elementary sounds that to your consciousness make up the word) is temporally present just when it occurs, but *not* before or afterwards, in so far as it follows previous elements and succeeds later elements; and also *all* the elements are, in the other sense of the term, *present at once* to consciousness, as constituting this whole succession which you call the word. If, however, you deny that you actually hear, apart from memory or from imagery, any single whole word at once, I shall only the more continue to ask you, What is the least or the simplest element of succession that is such as to constitute a merely present experience, with *no* former or latter contents within it? What apart from any memory or any imagery, and wholly apart from ideas of the past or the future of your experience, is present to you, in an indivisible time instant, just *Now?* The question is obviously unanswerable, just because an absolutely indivisible instant of mathematical time, with no former and latter contained within it, neither constitutes nor contains any temporal event, nor presents to you any fact of temporal experience whatever, just as an indivisible point in space could contain no matter, nor itself ever become, in isolation, an object of spatial experience. On the other hand, an event such that in it you were unable to perceive any succession, would help you in no whit to get the idea of time until you experienced it along with other events. What is now before you is a succession, within which are parts; and of these parts each, when and in so far as once your attention fixes it, and takes it in its time relations, is found as a present that in time both precedes and succeeds other facts, while these other facts are also just as truly before you as the observed element called the temporally present one is itself before you. And thus you cannot escape from our twofold interpretation of the experience of temporal succession. You are conscious of a series of successive states presented to you as a whole. You are also aware that each element of the succession excludes the others from its own place in time.

There is, to be sure, another frequent way of describing our consciousness of succession,—and a way that on the whole I find unsatisfactory. According to this view, events come to us in succession in our experience,—let us say the words of a spoken verse,—and *then* something often called the synthetic activity of the mind supervenes, and later binds together into unity, these successive facts, so that when this binding has taken place we *then* recognize the whole fagot of experience as a single succession. This account of the temporal facts, in terms of an activity called a synthesis, helps me, as I must confess, no whit. What I find in consciousness is that a succession, such as a rhythm of drum-beats, a musical phrase, a verse of poetry, comes to me as one present whole, present in the sense that I know it all at once. And I also find that this succession is such that it has *within* it a temporal distinction, or order, of earlier and later elements. While these elements are at once known, they are *also* known as such that at the briefer instant *within* the succession when any one of them is to be temporally viewed as a present fact, none of the others are contemporaneous with that fact, but all are either *no longer* or *not yet* when, and in so far as, that element is taken as the present one. And I cannot make this datum of experience any more definite by calling it a synthesis, or the mere result of a synthesis.

I have now characterized the more directly given features in our consciousness of succession. You see, as a result, that we men experience what Professor James, and others, have called our "specious present," as a serial whole, *within* which there are observed temporal differences of former and latter. And this our "specious present" has, when measured by a reference to time-keepers, a length which varies with circumstances, but which appears to be never any very small fraction of a second, and never more than very few seconds in length. I have earlier referred to this length of our present moments as our characteristic "time-span" of consciousness, and have pointed out how arbitrary a feature and limitation of our consciousness it is. We shall return soon to the question regarding the possible metaphysical significance of this time-span of our own special kind of consciousness.

But it remains here to call closer attention to certain other equally important features of our more direct experience of time-succession. So far, we have spoken, in the main, as if succession were to us a mere matter of given facts, as colors and sounds are given. But all our experience also has relation to the interests whose play and whose success or defeat constitute the life of our will. Every serial succession of which we are conscious therefore has for us some sort of meaning. In it we find our success or our failure. In it our internal meanings are expressed, or hindered, thwarted or furthered. We are interested in life, even if it be, in idle moments, only the dreary interest of won-

dering what will happen next, or, in distressed moments, the
interest in flying from our present fortune, or, in despairing
moments, of wishing for the end; still more then if, in strenuous moments, our interest is in pursuing our ideal. And our
interest in life means our conscious concern in passing on from
any temporal present towards its richer fulfilment, or away
from its relative insignificance. Now that Direction of temporal
succession of which I before made mention, has the most intimate
relations to this our interest in our experience. What is earlier in
a given succession is related to what is later as being that *from*
which we pass *towards* a desired fulfilment, or in search of a
more complete expression of our purpose. We are never content
in the temporal present in so far as we view it as temporal,
that is, as an event in a series. For such a present has its meaning as a transition from its predecessors towards its successors.

Our temporal form of experience is thus peculiarly the form
of the Will as such. Space often seems to spread out before us
what we take to be the mere contents of our world; but time
gives the form for the expression of all our meanings. Facts, in
so far as, with an abstractly false Realism, we sunder them
from their meanings, therefore tend to be viewed, as merely in
relations of coexistence; and the space-world is the favorite region of Realism. But ideas, when conscious, assume the consciously temporal form of inner existence, and appear to us as
constructive processes. The visible world, when viewed as at
rest, therefore interests us little in comparison with the same
world when we take note of its movements, changes, successions.
As the kitten ignores the dead leaves until the wind stirs them,
but then chases them—so facts in general tend to appear to
us all dead and indifferent when we disregard their processes.
But in the movements of things lies for us, just as truly as in
her small way for the kitten, all the glory and the tragedy, all
the life and the meaning of our observed universe. This concern, this interest in the changing, binds us then to the lower
animals, as it doubtless also binds us to beings of far higher
than human grade. We watch the moving and tend to neglect
the apparently changeless objects about us. And that is why
narrative is so much more easily effective than description in
the poetic arts; and why, if you want to win the attention of
the child or the general public, you must tell the story rather
than portray coexistent truths, and must fill time with series of
events, rather than merely crowd the space of experience or of

imagination with manifold but undramatic details. For space furnishes indeed the stage and the scenery of the universe, but the world's play occurs in time.

Now all these familiar considerations remind us of certain of the most essential characters of our experience of time. Time, whatever else it is, is given to us as that within whose successions, in so far as for us they have a direct interest and meaning, every event, springing from, yet forsaking, its predecessors, aims on, towards its own fulfilment and extinction in the coming of its successors. Our experience of time is thus for us essentially an experience of longing, of pursuit, of restlessness. And this is the aspect which Schopenhauer and the Buddhists have found so intolerable about the very nature of our finite experience. Upon this dissatisfied aspect of finite consciousness we ourselves dwelt when, in the former series of lectures, we were first learning to view the world, for the moment, from the mystic's point of view. As for the higher justification of this aspect of our experience, that indeed belongs elsewhere. But as to the facts, every part of a succession is present in so far as when it is, that which is *no longer* and that which is *not yet* both of them stand in essentially significant, or, if you will, in essentially practical relations to this present. It is true, of course, that when we view relatively indifferent time-series, such as the ticking of a watch or the dropping of rain upon the roof, we can disregard this more significant aspect of succession; and speak of the endless flight of time as an incomprehensible brute fact of experience, and as in so far seemingly meaningless. But no series of experiences upon which attention is fixed is wholly indifferent to us; and the temporal aspect of such series always involves some element of expectancy and some sense of something that no longer is; and both these conscious attitudes color our interest in the presented succession, and give the whole the meaning of life. Time is thus indeed the form of practical activity; and its whole character, and especially that direction of its succession of which we have spoken, are determined accordingly.

I I

I have dwelt long upon the time consciousness of our relatively direct experience, because here lies the basis for every deeper comprehension of the metaphysics both of time and of eternity. Our ordinary conception of time as an universal form of existence in the external world, is altogether founded upon a generalization, whose origin is in us men largely and obviously social, but whose materials are derived from our inner experience of the succession of significant events. The conceived relations of Past, Present, and Future in the real world of common-sense metaphysics, appear indeed, at first sight, vastly to transcend anything that we ourselves have ever observed in our inner experience. The infinite and irrevocable past that no longer is, the expected infinite future that has as yet no existence, how remote these ideal constructions, supposed to be valid for all gods and men and things, seem at first sight from the brief and significant series of successive events that occur within the brief span of our actual human consciousness. Yet, as we saw in the ninth lecture of our former Series, common sense, as soon as questioned about special cases, actually conceives the Being of both the past and the future as so intimately related to the Being of the present that every definite conception of the real processes of the world, whether these processes are viewed as physical or as historical or explicitly as ethical, depends upon taking the past, the present, and the future as constituting a single whole, whose parts have no true Being except in their linkage. As a fact, moreover, the term *present,* when applied to characterize a moment or an event in the time-stream of the real world, never means, in any significant application, the indivisible present of an ideal mathematical time. The present time, in case of the world at large, has an unity altogether similar to that of the present moment of our inner consciousness. We may speak of the present minute, hour, day, year, century. If we use the term *present* regarding any one of these divisions of time, but regard this time not as the experienced form of the inner succession of our own mental events, but as the time of the real world in which we ourselves form a part, then we indeed conceive that this present is world-embracing, and that suns move, light radiates between stars, the deeds of all men occur, and the minds of all men are conscious, in this same present time of which we thus make mention. Moreover, we usually view the world-time in question in terms of the conceptions of the World of Description, and so we conceive it as infinitely divisible, as measurable by various mathematical and physical devices, and as a continuous stream of occurrence. Yet in whatever sense we speak of the real present time of the world, this present, whether it is the present second, or the present century, or the present geological period, it is, for our conception, as truly a divisible and connected whole region of time, within which a succession of events take place, as it is a world-embracing and connected time, within whose span the whole universe of present events is comprised. A mathematically indivisible present time, possessing no length, is simply no time at all. Whoever says, "In the universe at large only the present state of things is real, only the present movement of the stars, the present streamings of radiant light, the present deeds and thoughts of men are real; the whole past is dead; the whole future is not yet,"—any such reporter of the temporal existence of the universe may be invited to state how long his real present of the time-world is. If he replies, "The present moment is the absolutely indivisible and ideal boundary between present and future,"—then one may rejoin at once that in a mathematically indivisible instant, having no length, no event happens, nothing endures, no thought or deed takes place,—in brief, nothing whatever temporally exists,—and that, too, whatever conception you may have of Being. But if the real present is a divisible portion of time, then it contains within itself succession, precisely as the "specious present" of psychological time contains such internal succession. But in that case, within the real present of the time-world, there are already contained the distinctions that, in case of the time of experience, we have heretofore observed. If, in what you choose to call the present moment of the world's history, deeds are accomplished, suns actually move from place to place, light waves traverse the ether, and men's lives pass from stage to stage, then *within* what you thus call the present there are distinguishable and more elementary events, arranged in series, such that when any conceived element, or mere elementary portion of any series is taken in relation to its predecessors and successors, it is *not yet* when its antecedents are taken as temporally present, and is *past and gone* when its successors are viewed as present. The world's time is thus in all respects a generalized and extended image and correspondent of the observed time of our inner experience. In the time of our more direct experience, we find a twofold way in which we can significantly call a portion of time a present moment. The present, in our inner experience, means a whole series of events grasped by somebody as having some unity for his consciousness, and as having its own single internal meaning. This was what we meant by the present experience of this musical phrase, this spoken line of verse, this series of rhythmic beats. But, in the other sense of the word, an element within any such whole is present in so far as this element has antecedents and successors, so that they are *no longer* or *not yet* when it is temporally viewed as present, while in turn, in so far as any one of them is viewed as the present element, this element itself is either *not yet* or *no longer*. But precisely so, in the conceptual time of our real world, the Present means any section of the time-stream in so far as, with reference to anybody's consciousness, it is viewed as having relation to this unity of consciousness, and as in a single whole of meaning with this unity. Usually by "our time," or "the real time in which we now live," we mean no very long period of the conceived time-stream of the real world. But we never mean the indivisible *now* of an ideal mathematical time, because, in such an indivisible time-instant, nothing could happen, or endure, or genuinely exist. But within the present, if conceived as a section of the time-stream, there are internal differences of present, past, and future.

For, in a similar fashion, as the actual or supposed length of the "specious present" of our perceptual time is something arbitrary, determined by our peculiar human type of consciousness, so the length of the portion of conceptual time which we call the *present*, in the first sense of that term, namely, in the sense in which we speak of the "present age," is an arbitrary length, determined in this case, however, by our more freely chosen interest in some unity which gives relative wholeness and meaning to this present. If usually the "present age" is no very long time, still, at our pleasure, or in the service of some such unity of meaning as the history of civilization, or the study of geology, may suggest, we may conceive the present as extending over many centuries, or over a hundred thousand years. On the other hand, within the unity of this first present, any distinguishable event or element of an event is *present*, in the second, and more strictly temporal sense in so far as it has predecessors and successors, whereof the first are *no longer*, and the latter *not yet*, when this more elementary event is viewed as happening.

Nor does the parallelism between the perceptual and the conceptual time cease here. The perceptual time was the form in which meaning, and the practically significant aspects of consciousness, get their expression. The same is true of the conceptual time, when viewed in its relations to the real world. Not only is the time of human history, or of any explicitly teleological series of events, obviously the form in which the facts win their particular type of conceived meaning; but even the time of physical science gets its essential characters, as a conception, through considerations that can only be interpreted in terms of the Will, or of our interest in the meaning of the world's happenings.

For the conceived time-series, even when viewed in relation to the World of Description, still differs in constitution from the constitution of a line in space, or from the characters belonging to a mathematically describable physical movement of a body, in ways which can only be expressed in terms of significance. Notoriously, conceptual time has often been described as correspondent in structure to the structure of a line, or as correspondent again, in character, to the character of an uniformly flowing stream, or of some other uniform movement. But a line can be traversed in either direction, while conceptual time is supposed to permit but one way of passing from one instant to another in its course. An uniform flow, or other motion, has, like time, a fixed direction, but might be conceived as returning into itself without detriment to its uniformity. Thus an ideally regular watch "keeps time," as we say, by virtue of the uniformity of its motion; but its hands return ever again to the same places on the face; while the years of conceptual time return not again. And finally, if one supposed an ideally uniform physical flow or streaming in one rectilinear direction only, and in an infinite Euclidean space, the character of this movement might so far be supposed to correspond to that of an ideally conceived mathematical time; except for one thing. The uniformity and unchangeableness of the conceived physical flow would be a merely given character, dependent, perhaps, upon the fact that the physical movement in question was conceived as meeting with no obstacle or external hindrance; but the direction of the flow of time is a character essential to the very conception of time. And this direction of the flow of time can only be expressed in its true necessity by saying that in case of the world's time, as in the case of the time of our inner experience, we conceive the past as leading towards, as aiming in the direction of the future, in such wise that the future depends for its meaning upon the past, and the past in its turn has its meaning as a process expectant of the future. In brief, only in terms of Will, and only by virtue of the significant relations of the stages of a teleological process, has time, whether in our inner experience, or in the conceived world order as a whole, any meaning. Time is the form of the Will; and the real world is a temporal world in so far as, in various regions of that world, seeking differs from attainment, pursuit is external to its own goal, the imperfect tends towards its own perfection, or in brief, the internal meanings of finite life gradually win, in successive stages, their union with their own External Meaning. The general justification for this whole view of the time of the real world is furnished by our idealistic interpretation of Being. The special grounds for regarding the particular Being of time itself as in this special way teleological, are furnished by the foregoing analysis of our own experience of time, and by the fact that the conceptual time in terms of which we interpret the order of the world at large, is fashioned, so to speak, after the model of the time of our own experience.

III

Having thus defined the way in which the conceptual time of the real world of common sense corresponds in its structure to the structure of the time known to our inner perception, we are prepared to sketch our theory both of the sense in which the world of our idealistic doctrine appears to be capable of interpretation as a Temporal order, and of the sense in which, for this same theory, this world is to be viewed as an Eternal order. For, as a fact, in defining time we have already, and inevitably, defined eternity; and a temporal world must needs be, when viewed in its wholeness, an eternal world. We have only to review the structure of Reality in the light of the foregoing analysis in order to bring to our consciousness this result.

And so, first, the real world of our Idealism has to be viewed by us men as a temporal order. For it is a world where purposes are fulfilled, or where finite internal meanings reach their final expression, and attain unity with external meanings. Now in so far as any idea, as a finite Internal Meaning, still seeks its own Other, and consciously pursues that Other, in the way in which, as we have all along seen, every finite idea does pursue its Other, this Other is in part viewed as something beyond, *towards* which the striving is directed. But our human experience of temporal succession is, as we have seen, just such an experience of a pursuit directed towards a goal. And such pursuit demands, as an essential part or aspect of the striving in question, a consciousness that agrees in its most essential respect with our own experience of time. Hence, our only way of expressing the general structure of our idealistic realm of Being is to say that wherever an idea exists as a finite idea, still in pursuit of its goal, there appears to be some essentially temporal aspect belonging to the consciousness in question. To my mind, therefore, time, as the form of the will, is (in so far as we can undertake to define at all the detailed structure of finite reality) to be viewed as the most pervasive form of all finite experience, whether human or extra-human. In pursuing its goals, the Self lives in time. And, to our view, every real being in the universe, in so far as it has not won union with the ideal, is pursuing that ideal; and, accordingly, so far as we can see, is living in time. Whoever, then, is finite, says, "not yet," and in part seeks his Other as involving what, to the seeker, is still future. For the finite world in general, then, as for us human beings, the distinction of past and future appears to be coextensive with life and meaning.

I have advisedly used, however, the phrase that the time-consciousness is a "part" or "aspect" of the striving. For from our point of view, the Other, the completion that our finite being seeks, is not *merely* something beyond the present, and is not merely a future experience, but is also inclusive of the very process of the striving itself. For the goal of every finite life is simply the totality whereof this life, in its finitude, is a fragment. When I seek my own goal, I am looking for the whole of myself. In so far as my aim is the absolute completion of my Selfhood, my goal is identical with the whole life of God. But, in so far as, by my whole individual Self, I mean my whole Self in contrast with the Selves of my fellows,—then the completion of my individual expression, in so far as I am this individual and no other,—*i.e.* my goal, as this Self, is still not any one point or experience in my life, nor any one stage of my life, but the totality of my individual life viewed as in contrast with the lives of other individuals. Consequently, while it is quite true that every incomplete being, every finite striving, regards itself as aiming towards a future, because its own goal is not yet attained; we have, nevertheless, to remember that the attainment of the goal involves more than any future moment, taken by itself, could ever furnish. For the Self in its entirety is the whole of a self-representative or recurrent process, and not the mere last moment or stage of that process. As we shall see, there is in fact no last moment. A life seeking its goal is, therefore, indeed, essentially temporal,—but is so just as music is temporal,—except indeed that music is not only temporal, but temporally finite. For every work of musical art involves significant temporal series, wherein there is progression, and passage from chord to chord, from phrase to phrase, and from movement to movement. But just as any one musical composition has its value not only by virtue of its attainment of its final chord, but also at every stage of the process that leads towards this conclusion; and just as the whole musical composition is, as a whole, an end in itself; so every finite Internal Meaning wins final expression, not merely through the last stage of its life (if it has a last stage), but through its whole embodiment. And, nevertheless, as the music attains wholeness only through succession; so every idea that is to win its complete expression, does so through temporal sequences.

Since, at all events, no other than such a temporal expression of meaning in life is in any wise definable for our consciousness, our Idealism can only express its view of the relation of finite and absolute life by viewing the whole world, and in particular the whole existence of any individual Self, as such a temporal process, wherein there is expressed, by means of a Well-Ordered Series of stages, a meaning that finally belongs to the whole life, but that at every temporal stage of the process in question appears to involve, in part, a beyond,—a something not yet won,—and so a distinction both of the past and the future of this Self from the content of any one stage of the process when that stage is viewed as the present one.

In this sense, therefore, our doctrine is obliged to conceive the entire world-life as including a temporal series of events. When considered with reference to any one of these events, the rest of the events that belong to the series of which any one finite Self takes account, are past and future, that is, they are *no longer* and *not yet;* just as, when viewed with reference to any one chord or phrase in the musical composition, all the other successive elements of the composition are either past or future.

The infinite divisibility of the time of our ordinary scientific conceptions is indeed due to that tendency of our own discriminating attention to an endless interpolation of intermediary stages,—a tendency which we studied in connection with our general account of the World of Description. We have, however, seen reasons, which, applied to time, would lead us to declare that an absolute insight would view the temporal order as a discrete series of facts ordered as any succession of facts expressing one purpose would be ordered, viz. like the whole numbers. On the other hand, we have no reason to suppose that our human consciousness distinctly observes intervals of time that in brevity anywhere nearly approach to the final truth about the temporal order. Within what is for us the least observable happening, a larger insight may indeed discriminate multitudes of events. In dealing with the concept of Nature, we shall see what significant use may be made of the hypothesis that there exists or may exist, finite consciousness for which the series of events that we regard as no longer distinguishable from merely elementary and indivisible happenings, are distinguished so minutely as to furnish content as rich as those which, from our point of view, occupy æons of the world's history. Our right to such hypotheses is incontestable, provided only that they help us to conceive the true unity of experience. Nevertheless, in the last analysis, the Absolute Will must be viewed as expressed in a well-ordered and discrete series of facts, which from our point of view may indeed appear, as we shall still further see, capable of discrimination *ad infinitum*.

But now secondly, and without the least conflict with the foregoing theses, I declare that this same temporal world is, when regarded in its wholeness, an Eternal order. And I mean by this assertion nothing whatever but that the whole real content of this temporal order, whether it is viewed from any one temporal instant as past or as present or as future, is *at once* known, *i.e.* is consciously experienced as a whole, by the Absolute. And I use this expression *at once* in the very sense in which we before used it when we pointed out that to your own consciousness, the whole musical phrase may be and often is known *at once, despite* the fact that each element of the musical succession, when taken as the temporally present one, excludes from its own temporal instant the other members of the sequence, so that they are either *no longer* or *not yet*, at the instant *when* this element is temporally the present one. As we saw before, it is true that, in one sense, each one of the elements or partial events of a sequence excludes the former and the latter elements from being at the time *when* this particular element exists. But that, in another and equally obvious and empirical sense, *all* the members of an actually experienced succession are *at once* to any consciousness which observes the whole succession as a whole, is equally true. The term *present,* as we saw, is naturally used both to name the temporally present when it is opposed to whatever precedes or succeeds this present, and also to name the observed facts of a succession in so far as they are experienced as constituting one whole succession. In so far the term is indeed ambiguous. But even this ambiguity itself is due to the before-mentioned fact that, if you try to find an absolutely simple present temporal fact of consciousness, and still to view it as an event in time, you are still always led, in the World of Description, to observe or to conceive that this temporal fact is a complex event, having a true succession *within* itself. So that the *now* of temporal expression is never a *mere* now, unless indeed it be viewed either as the ideal mathematical instant within which *nothing* takes place, or else as one of the finally simple stages of the discrete series of facts which the absolute insight views as the expression of its Will.

As to the one hypothesis, an absolute instant in the mathematical sense is like a point, an ideal limit, and never appears as any isolated fact of temporal experience. Every *now* within which something happens is therefore *also* a succession; so that every temporal fact, every event, so far as we men can observe it, has to be viewed as present to experience in *both* the senses of the term present; since this fact *when* present may be contrasted with predecessors that are *no longer* and with successors that are *not yet,* while this same fact, when taken as an event occupying time, is viewed as a presented succession with former and latter members contained within it. As to the other hypothesis, it seems clear that we human beings observe no such ultimate and indivisible facts of experience just because, so far as we observe and discriminate facts, we are more or less under the bondage of the categories of the World of Description.

But, in view of the correspondence between the universal time of the world-order, as we conceive it, and the time of our internal experience, as we observe it, the temporal sequences must be viewed as having in the real world, and for the Absolute, the same twofold character that our temporal experiences have for ourselves. *Present,* in what we may call the inclusive sense of the term, is any portion of real time with all its included events, in so far as there is any reason to view it as a whole, and as known in this wholeness by a single experience. *Present,* in what we may by contrast call the exclusive sense, is any one temporal event, in so far as it is contrasted with antecedent and subsequent events, and in so far as it excludes them from coexistence with itself in the same portion of any succession. These two senses of the term *present* do not contradict each other in case of the world-order any more than they do in case of our own inner experience. Both senses express inevitably distinct and yet inseparable connected aspects of the significant life of the conscious will, whether in us, or in the universe at large. Our view declares that all the life of the world, and therefore all temporal sequences, are present at once to the Absolute. Our view also maintains that, without the least conflict with this sense in which the whole temporal order is known at once to the Absolute, there is another sense in which any portion of the temporal sequence of the world may be taken as present, when viewed with reference to the experience of any finite Self whose present it is, and when contrasted with what for this same point of view is the past and the future of the world. Now the events of the temporal order, when viewed in this latter way, are divided, with reference to the point of view of any finite Self, into what *now* is, and what *no longer* is, and what *is to be,* but is *not yet.* These same events, however, in so far as they are viewed at once by the Absolute, are for such view, all equally present. And this their presence is the presence of all time, as a *totum simul,* to the Absolute. And the presence in this sense, of all time at once to the Absolute, constitutes the Eternal order of the world,—eternal, since it is inclusive of all distinctions of temporal past and temporal future,—eternal, since, for this very reason, the totality of temporal events thus present at once to the Absolute has no events that precede, or that follow it, but contains all sequences within it,—eternal, finally, because this view of the world does not, like our partial glimpses of this or of that relative whole of sequence, pass away and give place to some other view, but includes an observation of every passing away, of every sequence, of every event and of whatever in time succeeds and follows that event, and includes all the views that are taken by the various finite Selves.

In order to conceive what, in general, such an eternal view of the temporal order involves, or to conceive in what sense the temporal order of the real world is also an eternal order, we have, therefore, but to remember the sense in which the melody, or other sequence, is known at once to our own consciousness, despite the fact that its elements when viewed merely in their temporal succession are, in so far, *not* at once. As we saw before, the brief span of our consciousness, the small range of succession, that we can grasp at once, constitutes a perfectly arbitrary limitation of our own special type of consciousness. But in principle a time-sequence, however brief, is already viewed in a way that is not *merely* temporal, when, despite its sequence, it is grasped at once, and is thus grasped not through mere memory, but by virtue of actual experience. A consciousness related to the whole of the world's events, and to the whole of time, precisely as our human consciousness is related to a single melody or rhythm, and to the brief but still extended interval of time which this melody or rhythm occupies, —such a consciousness, I say, is an Eternal Consciousness. In principle we already possess and are acquainted with the nature of such a consciousness, whenever we do experience any succession as one whole. The only thing needed to complete our idea of what an actually eternal consciousness is, is the conceived removal of that arbitrary limitation which permits us men to observe indeed at once a succession, but forbids us to observe a succession at once in case it occupies more than a very few seconds.

IV

This definition of the relations of the Temporal and the Eternal accomplishes all the purposes that are usually in mind when we speak of the divine knowledge as eternal. That eternity is a *totum simul,* the scholastics were well aware; and St. Thomas develops our present concept with a clearness that is only limited by the consequences of his dualistic view of the relation of God and the world. For after he has indeed well defined and beautifully illustrated the inclusive eternity of the divine knowledge, he afterwards conceives the temporal existence of the created world as sundered from the eternal life which belongs to God. And hereby the advantages of an accurate definition of the eternal are sacrificed for the sake of a special dogmatic interest.

Less subtle forms of speculation have led to uses of the word *eternal,* whose meaning is often felt to be far deeper than such usages can render explicit. But as these subtle usages are often stated, they are indeed open to the most obvious objections. An eternal knowledge is often spoken of as if it were one for which there is *no* distinction whatever between past, and present, and future. But such a definition is as absurd as if one should speak of our knowledge of a whole musical phrase or rhythm, when we grasped such a whole at once, as if the *at once* implied that there were for us no temporal distinction between the first and the last beat or note of the succession in question. To observe the succession *at once* is to have present with perfect clearness *all* the time-elements of the rhythm or of the phrase just as they are,—the succession, the tempo, the intervals, the pauses, —and yet, without losing any of their variety, to view them at once as one present musical idea. Now for our theory, that is precisely the way in which the eternal consciousness views the temporal order,—not ignoring one jot or tittle of its sharp distinctions of past or of future, of succession or of duration, —but still viewing the whole time-process as the expression of a single Internal Meaning. What we now call past and future are not merely the *same* for God; and, nevertheless, they are viewed *at once,* precisely as the beginning and the end of the rhythm are not the same for our experience, but are yet at once seen as belonging to one and the same whole succession.

Or again, an eternal knowledge is often supposed to be one that abstracts from time, or that takes no account of time; so that, for an eternal point of view it is as if time were not at all. But to say this is as if one were to speak of observing at once the meaning or character of the whole phrase or rhythm by simply failing to take any note at all of the succession as such. The meaning is the meaning of the succession; and is grasped only by observing this succession as something that involves former and latter elements, while these elements in time exclude one another, and therefore follow, each one *after* its predecessor has temporally ceased, and *before* its successor temporally appears. Just so, we assert that the eternal insight observes the whole of time, and all that happens therein, and is eternal only by virtue of the fact that it does know the whole of time.

Or again, some doctrines often speak of an eternal insight as something wholly and inexplicably *different* from any temporal type of consciousness, so that *how* God views His truth as eternal truth, no man can say. But our theory regards the essential relation of an eternal to a temporal type of consciousness as one of the simplest of the relations that are of primal importance for the definition of the Absolute. Listen to any musical phrase or rhythm, and grasp it as a whole, and you thereupon have present in you the image, so to speak, of the divine knowledge of the temporal order. To view all the course of time just as you then and there view the whole of that sequence,—this is to be possessed of an eternal type of insight.

"But," so many hereupon object,—"it appears impossible to see how this sort of eternal insight is possible, since just now, in time, the infinite past,—including, say, the geological periods and the Persian invasion of Greece, is *no longer,* while the future is *not yet.* How then for God shall this difference of past and future be transcended, and all be seen at once?" I reply, In precisely the same sense all the notes of the melody except this note are not *when* this note sounds, but are either *no longer* or *not yet.* Yet you may know a series of these notes at once. Now precisely so God knows the whole time-sequence of the world at once. The difference is merely one of span. You now exemplify the eternal type of knowledge, even as you listen to any briefest sequence of my words. For you, too, know time even by sharing the image of the Eternal.

Or again, a common wonder appears regarding how the divine knowledge can be in such wise eternal as to suffer no change to occur in it. How God should be unchangeable, yet express His will in a changing world, is an ancient problem. Our doctrine answers the question at a stroke. The knowledge of all change is itself indeed unchangeable, just because any change that occurs or that can occur to any being is already included amongst the objects known to the eternal point of view. The knowledge of this melody as one whole does not itself consist in an adding of other notes to the melody. The knowledge of all sequences does not itself follow as another sequence. Hence it is indeed not subject to the fate of sequence.

And finally, a mystery is very generally made of the fact that since time appears to us as inevitably infinite, and as therefore not, like the melody or the rhythm, capable of completion, an eternal knowledge, if it involves a knowledge of the whole of time, must be something that has to appear to us self-contradictory and impossible. Any complete answer to this objection involves, of course, a theory of the infinite. Such a theory I have set forth in the Supplementary Essay, published with the First Series of these lectures. The issue involved, that of the positive concept of an infinite whole, is indeed no simple one, and is not capable of any brief presentation. I can here only report that the considerations set forth in that Supplementary Essay have led me to the thesis that a Well-Ordered Infinite Series, under the sole condition that it embodies a single plan, may be rightly viewed as forming a totality, and as an individual whole, precisely as a musical theme or a rhythm is viewed by our experience as such a whole. That the universe itself is such an infinite series, I have endeavored, in that paper, to show in great detail. If you view the temporal order of the world as also forming such an endless whole, expressing a single plan and Will (as I think you have a right to do), then the argument of the Supplementary Essay in question will apply to our present problem. The whole of time will contain a single expression of the divine Will, and therefore, despite its endlessness, the time-world will be present as such a single whole to the Absolute whose Will this is, and whose life all this sequence embodies.

V

In order to refer, as I close, to the practical interest which has guided me through all the abstract considerations even of this present lecture, I may be permitted to anticipate some of our later results about the Self, and, for the sake of illustration, to point out that from our point of view, as we shall later explain it more fully, your life, your Self, your will, your individuality, your deeds, can be and are present at once to the eternal insight of God; while, nevertheless, it is equally true that not only for you, but for God, your life is a genuine temporal sequence of deeds and strivings, whereof, when you view this life at the present temporal instant, the past is just now *no longer*, while the future is *not yet*. This twofold view of your nature, as a temporal process and as an eternal system of fact, is precisely as valid and as obvious as the twofold view of the melody or of the rhythm. Your temporal present looks back, as Will, upon your now irrevocable past. That past is irrevocable because it is the basis of your seeking for the future, and is the so far finished expression of your unique individual Will. Your future is the *not yet* temporally expressed region wherein you, as finite being, seek your own further expression. That future is still, in one aspect, as we shall see, causally undetermined, precisely in so far as therein something unique, that is yours and yours only, is to appear in the form of various individually designed expressions of your life-purpose,—various individual deeds. Therefore, as we shall be able to maintain, despite all your unquestionable causal and moral determinations, there will be an aspect of your future life that will be free, and yours, and such as no causation can predetermine, and such as even God possesses only in so far as your unique individuality furnishes it as a fact in His world.

And nevertheless, your future and your past, your aspect of individuality, and of freedom, and the various aspects wherein you are dependent upon the rest of the world, your whole life of deeds, and your attainment of your individual goal through your deeds,—all these manifold facts that are yours and that constitute you, are present at once to the Absolute,—as facts in the world, as temporal contents eternally viewed,—as a process eternally finished,—but eternally finished precisely by virtue of the temporal sequence of your deeds. And when you wonder how these aspects can be at once the aspects of your one life,— remember what is implied in the consciousness *at once* of the melody or the rhythm as a sequence,—and you will be in possession of the essential principle whereby the whole mystery is explained.

It is this view, once grasped in its various aspects, that will enable us to define in what sense man is one with God, and in what sense he is to be viewed as at present out of harmony with his own relation to God, and in that sense alienated from his true place in the eternal world. And so, in discussing this most elementary category, we are preparing the way for a most significant result as to the whole life of any man.

The temporal man, viewed just now in time, appears, at first, to be sundered even from his own past and future, and still more from God. He is a seeker even for to-morrow's bread,— still more for his salvation. He knows not just at this instant even his own individuality; still less should he immediately observe his relation to the Absolute in his present deed and in his fleeting experience. Only when he laboriously reflects upon his inmost meaning, or by faith anticipates the result of such reflection, does he become aware of how intimately his life is bound up with an Absolute life. This our finite isolation, is, however, especially and characteristically a *temporal* isolation. That inattention of which we spoke in the last lecture, is especially an inattention to all but this act, as it now appears to me. I am not one with my own eternal individuality, especially and peculiarly because this passing temporal instant is not the whole of time, and because the rest of time is *no longer* or else *not yet when* this instant passes. Herein lies my peculiarly insurmountable human limitation. This is my present form of consciousness. To be sure, I am not wholly thus bound in the chains of my finitude. Within my present form and span of consciousness there is already exemplified an eternal type of insight, whereby the *totum simul* is in many cases and in brief span won. But beyond this my span of presentation, time escapes me as a past and future that is at once real and still either no longer or else not yet. From the eternal point of view, however, just this my life is *at once* present, in its Individuality and its wholeness. And because of this fact, just in so far as I am the eternal or true Individual, I stand in the presence of God, with all my life open before Him, and its meaning revealed to Him and to me. Yet this my whole meaning, while one with His meaning, remains, in the eternal world, still this unique and individual meaning, which the life of no other individual Self possesses. So that in my eternal expression I lose not my individuality, but rather win my only genuine individual expression, even while I find my oneness with God.

Now, in time, I seek, as if it were far beyond me, that goal of my Selfhood, that complete expression of my will, which in God, and for God, my whole life at once possesses. I seek this goal as a far-off divine event,—as my future fortune and success. I do well to seek. Seek and ye shall find. Yet the finding,—it does not occur merely as an event in time. It occurs as an eternal experience of this my whole striving. Every struggle, every tear, every misery, every failure, and repentance, and every rising again, every strenuous pursuit, every glimpse of God's truth,—all these are not mere incidents of the search for that which is beyond. They are all events in the life; they too are part of the fulfilment. In eternity all this is seen, and hereby,—even in and through these temporal failures, I win, in God's presence and by virtue of His fulfilment, the goal of life, which is the whole of life. What no temporal instant ever brings,—what all temporal efforts fail to win, that my true Self in its eternity, and in its oneness with the divine, possesses.

So much it has seemed that I might here venture to anticipate of later results, in order that the true significance of our elementary categories might be, however imperfectly, defined for us from the outset. For all the questions as to our deeper relations to the universe are bound up with this problem of Time and Eternity.

8 ❧ THE HUMAN SELF [1]

The contrast between Matter and Mind is usually regarded as a serious obstacle in the way of any interpretation of the world of experience in terms of a philosophical Idealism. In the last two lectures we have seen that this contrast is not empirically known to be as absolute as our customary fashions of conception often make it seem. The hypothesis concerning Nature which we suggested was partly intended to illustrate precisely this possibility of reconciling Idealism with the generalizations of our ordinary study of Nature. The hypothesis itself, like any other effort towards a Cosmology, is, in its details, provisional and tentative. Only its general type, as an idealistic hypothesis about Nature, seems to me to be a sure representative of the truth. In its special features it is to be subject to the control of further experience. But it provides in its very terms for such further control. The hypothesis asserts, in fact, that all the theories of the special sciences, together with the general theory of Nature suggested by this very hypothesis itself, must be viewed as incidents in the history of man's effort gradually to comprehend the organization of a realm of Mind, of which man himself is a member. Now every idealist holds that there is no dead matter anywhere in the world, and that all that is is the expression of the Spirit. But in what way this thesis is to be applied to the detailed interpretation of Nature, cannot be decided in advance of a careful scrutiny of the facts. And the special way suggested at the last time is the one which to me personally seems to promise most. I am sure that in its most general outlines, this hypothesis is sound. But all its details are subject to correction.

I

Herewith, however, we are led to the threshold of a new enterprise. We have so far stated a general hypothesis regarding Nature. But in forming this hypothesis, I myself have been

[1] Josiah Royce, *The World and the Individual* (New York: The Macmillan Company, 1899, 1901), Vol. II Lecture VI, pp. 245–247, 256–277. —Editor's note.

especially interested in its bearing upon the conception of the place in Nature that is occupied by Man. Now as we know Man, he first of all appears to us as a being whose inner life is that of an individual Self. The Self of each man apparently has had an origin in time, and a development such as makes it dependent, for its contents and its character, upon natural conditions. In its turn, our self-consciousness, when once it has developed, furnishes to us the sort of insight by means of which we may hope for a comprehension of some of the mysteries of Nature. Any deeper criticism of our hypothesis about Nature must therefore depend upon a more exact account of what we mean by the human Self. We must know how we are able, both to conceive this Self as in any sense the outcome of the processes of Nature, and to apply our view of the Self to an explanation of Nature.

My next task must therefore be to state, in outline, a theory of the human Self.

What a man means by himself is notoriously a question to which common sense gives various and ambiguous answers. That by the Self one means a real being, common sense indeed insists. But the nature of this real being forms the topic of the greatest vacillation in all popular metaphysics. . . .

I I

Such considerations ought once for all to give pause to those who have regarded the problem of the true nature of the Self as a matter of direct inner knowledge, or as something to be settled by an appeal to the plain man. But of course these considerations merely indicate a problem, and are by no means decisive as against any metaphysical view which insists upon a true and deeper unity of Selfhood at the basis of all these variations of the apparent Self. But wherein shall our own metaphysical doctrine seek for guidance in this world of complexities?

I reply, The concept of the human Self, like the concept of Nature, comes to us, first, as an empirical concept, founded upon a certain class of experiences. But like the concept of Nature, the concept of the human Self tends far to outrun any directly observable present facts of human experience, and to assume forms which define the Self as having a nature and destiny which no man directly observes or as yet can himself verify. If we consider first the empirical basis of the conception of the Self, and then the motives which lead us beyond our direct experience in our efforts to interpret the Self, we find, as a result of a general survey, three different kinds of conceptions of what it is that one means or ought to mean by the term Self as applied to the individual man. Each of these sorts of conception of the human Self is once more capable of a wide range of variation. Each can be used as a basis of different and, on occasion, of conflicting notions of what the Self is. But the three have their strong contrasts with one another, and each lays stress upon its own aspect of the facts.

First then, there is the more directly empirical way of conceiving the Self. In this sense, by a man's Self, you mean a certain totality of facts, viewed as more or less immediately given, and as distinguished from the rest of the world of Being. These facts may be predominantly corporeal facts, such as not only the man himself but also his neighbors may observe and comment upon. In this sense my countenance and my physical deeds, my body and my clothing,—all these may be regarded as more or less a part of myself. My neighbor so views them. I may and very generally do so view them myself. If you changed or wholly removed such facts, my view of what I am would unquestionably alter. For to my neighbor as to myself, I am this man with these acts, this body, this presence. I cannot see these facts as my neighbor does, nor can he take my view of them. But we all regard such facts, not only as belonging to the Self, but as constituting, in a measure, what we regard as the Self of the present life. In addition to the external or corporeal Self of the phenomenal world, there is the equally empirical and phenomenal Self of the inner life, the series of states of consciousness, the feelings, thoughts, desires, memories, emotions, moods. These, again, both my neighbor and myself regard as belonging to me, and as going to make up what I am. To be sure, within this inner empirical Self, we all make distinctions, now so freely illustrated, between what does and what does not essentially belong to the Self. When a man tells me a piece of interesting news, or expounds to me his opinions, I naturally regard the ideas which then arise in my mind as his and not as mine. I have to reflect in order to observe the somewhat recondite fact that the ideas which he seems to convey to me are in one sense ideas of my own, aroused in me according to laws of association. On the other hand, when I think alone by myself, the ideas which occur to me seem to be primarily mine. I have to reflect in order to remember how largely they have been derived from books, from nature, or from conversation, and how little I can call originally my own. And everywhere in the inner life, as it flits by, I observe a constantly shifting play of what I distinguish as more truly myself, from what I regard as relatively foreign. This feeling or purpose, this mood or this choice, is my own. That other emotion or idea is alien to me. It belongs to another. I do not recognize it as mine. The distinctions, thus empirically made, have no one rational principle. They are often founded upon the most arbitrary and unstable motives. The vacillation of common sense regarding the Self is endlessly repeated in my own inner life. I am constantly sure that there exists a Self, and that there I am, present to my own consciousness as the one whose experiences all these are, and who set myself over against the foreign non-Ego at every moment. But in distinguishing my empirical non-Ego from the Ego, I follow no stateable rule in my inner life from moment to moment. I even voluntarily play with the distinctions of Self and not-Self,—dramatically address myself as if I were another, criticise and condemn myself, and upon occasion observe myself in a relatively impersonal fashion, as if I were a wholly alien personality. On the other hand, there are countless automatic processes that alter or that diminish the immediately given distinctions between Ego and non-Ego. The lover in Locksley Hall somewhat unobservantly tells us how:—

Love took up the harp of life, and smote on all the chords with
    might;
Smote the chord of Self that trembling, passed in music out of
    sight.

The lover admits that in the state which he thus describes, the Self, if invisible in the inner experience, was still able, most decidedly, to make itself heard. And, as a fact, one may well question whether, in view of what the lover in Locksley Hall tells us, the Self of this lover ever passed beyond his own range of vision at all, or was in the least out of sight. But the happy emotional confusion of self-consciousness here in question is familiar indeed to all who know joyous emotion. And in the sadder emotions one also has endless varieties in the intensity, clearness, and outlines which in our empirical consciousness characterize, from moment to moment, the relations of Self and not-Self.

III

But one may now ask, still dwelling upon the empirical Self, what manner of unity is left, in the midst of all these variations, as the unity that the concept of the Self can still be said to possess in our ordinary experience? And by what marks is the Self to be distinguished from the rest of the world? I reply, by pointing out a fact of central importance for the whole understanding of the empirical Ego. The variations of our experience and of our opinion concerning the empirical Self are countless in number. And no purely rational principle guides us in defining the Self from moment to moment in the world of common sense, or in distinguishing it from the not-Self. But there still does remain *one psychological principle* running through all these countless facts, and explaining, in general, both why they vary, and why yet we always suppose, despite the chaos of experiences, that the Self of our inner and outer life preserves a genuine, although to us hidden unity. This psychological principle is the simple one that, in us men, the distinction between Self and not-Self has a predominantly *Social origin,* and implies a more or less obviously present contrast between what we at any moment view as the life of another person, a fellow-being, or, as you may for short in general call him, an Alter, and the life, which, by contrast with that of the Alter, is just then viewed as the life of the present Ego. To state the case more briefly, I affirm that our empirical self-consciousness, from moment to moment, depends upon a series of contrast-effects, whose psychological origin lies in our literal social life, and whose continuance in our present conscious life, whenever we are alone, is due to habit, to our memory of literal social relations, and to an imaginative idealization of these relations. Herein lies a large part of the explanation of those ambiguities of common sense upon which I have so far insisted.

My proof for this view I cannot here give at length. I have stated the psychological aspects of the whole case pretty extensively elsewhere.[2] My friend, Professor Baldwin of Princeton University, has independently worked out a theory of the psychological origin of Self-Consciousness, and a doctrine about the evolution of the relations of Ego and Alter,—a theory which I am on the whole prepared to accept, and which agrees with the considerations that I myself have been led to develop, and, in the places now referred to, to set forth. Here there is time only for a brief indication of what I mean by this theory of the empirical Ego, of its unity in variety, and of its distinction from the world of the non-Ego.

Nobody amongst us men comes to self-consciousness, so far as I know, except under the persistent influence of his social fellows. A child in the earlier stages of his social development, —say from the end of the first to the beginning of the fifth year of life,—shows you, as you observe him, a process of the development of self-consciousness in which, at every stage, the Self of the child grows and forms itself through Imitation, and through functions that cluster about the Imitation of others, and that are secondary thereto. In consequence, the child is in general conscious of what expresses the life of somebody else, before he is conscious of himself. And his self-consciousness, as it grows, feeds upon social models, so that at every stage of his awakening life his consciousness of the Alter is a step in advance of his consciousness of the Ego. His playmates, his nurse, or mother, or the workmen whose occupations he sees, and whose power fascinates him, appeal to his imitativeness, and set him the copies for his activities. He learns his little arts, and as he does so, he contrasts his own deeds with those of his models, and of other children. Now contrast is, in our conscious life, the mother of clearness. What the child does instinctively, and without comparison with the deeds of others, may never come to his clear consciousness as his own deed at all. What he learns imitatively, and then reproduces, perhaps in joyous obstinacy, as an act that enables him to display himself over against others,—this constitutes the beginning of his self-conscious life. And in general, thenceforth, social situations, social emotions, the process of peering into the contents of

---

[2] See my *Studies of Good and Evil*, especially the essay on the Anomalies of Self-consciousness, *op. cit.*, pp. 169–197. Professor Baldwin's very complete treatment of the topic is to be found in the second volume of his well-known work: *Mental Development in the Child and the Race*, where it dominates the entire discussion.

other minds during the child's questioning period, the conflicts of childish sport, the social devices for winning approval,—in brief, the whole life of social harmony and rivalry,—all these things mean an endless series of contrasts between two sets of contents, which retain, amidst all their varieties, *one* psychologically important character. Upon this character the empirical unity and the general continuity of our adult self-consciousness depend.

In any literal social situation, namely, one is aware of ideas, designs, interests, beliefs, or judgments, whose expression is observed in the form of acts, words, looks, and the like, belonging to the perceived organisms of one's fellow-men. In strong contrast, both in the way in which they appear in the field of our sense-perceptions, and in the current interests and feelings with which they are accompanied and blended, are the acts, words, and other expressions, of our own organism, together with the ideas, designs, and beliefs which accompany these acts. Now these two contrasting masses of mental contents simply constitute the Alter and the Ego, the neighbor and the Self, of any empirical instant of our literal social life together. That these sets of contents stand in strong contrast to each other is, for the first, a mere fact of sense and of feeling. One does not reason about this fact from instant to instant. One finds it so. Nor does one appeal to any intuition of an ultimate or of a spiritual Ego, in order to observe the presented fact that my neighbor's words, as he speaks to me, do not sound or feel as my words do when I speak to him, and that the ideas which my neighbor's words at once bring to my consciousness, stand in a strong and presented contrast to the ideas which receive expression in my words as I reply to him. Alter and Ego, in such cases, are found as facts of our direct observation. Were no difference observed between the contents which constitute the observed presence of my neighbor, and the contents which constitute my own life in the same moment, then my sense of my neighbor's presence, and my idea of myself, would blend in my consciousness, and there would be so far neither Alter nor Ego observed.

Now just such social contrast-effects have been occurring in our experience since childhood. The contrasts in question have always retained a certain general similarity, despite wide and countless differences. Just as all color contrasts are in a measure alike, so too are all social contrasts. Always the contents which constitute the Ego, at the very moment of their contrast with the

remaining contents present during the social contrast-effect, have
been associated with certain relatively warm and enduring organic
sensations, viz. sensations coming from within our own bodies.
Always the contents belonging to our consciousness of our neighbors have been relatively free from these accompaniments, and
have had the characters belonging to external sense-perceptions.
And there are still other empirical similarities present in all social
relations. Hence, despite all other changes, the Ego and the Alter
have tended to keep apart, as facts of our empirical observation,
and each of the two has tended towards its own sort of organization as a mass of observed and remembered empirical facts. The
Alter, viewed as a mass of experienced facts,—the words, looks,
and deeds and ideas of other people,—differentiates and inte-
grates into all that I call my experience of mankind; the Ego,
centred about the relatively constant organic sensations, but receiving its type of unity especially through the social contrast-
effects, stands as that totality of inner and outer experience which
I recognize as my own, just because it sharply differs from my experience of any of the rest of mankind, and stands in a certain
permanent sort of contrast thereto.

In origin, then, the empirical Ego is secondary to our social
experience. In literal social life, the Ego is always known as in
contrast to the Alter. And while the permanent character of our
organic sensations aids us in identifying the empirical Ego,
this character becomes of importance mainly because hereby we
find ourselves always in a certain inwardly observable type of
contrast to the whole of our social world.

Now what literal social life thus trains us to observe, the
inner psychological processes of memory and imagination enable us indefinitely to extend and to diversify. The child soon
carries over his plays into more or less ideal realms, lives in
the company of imaginary persons, and thus, idealizing his
social relations, idealizes also the type of his self-consciousness.
In my inner life, I in the end learn ideally to repeat, to vary,
to reorganize, and to epitomize in countless ways, the situations
which I first learned to observe and estimate in literal social
relations. Hereby the contrast between Ego and Alter, no longer
confined to the relations between my literal neighbor and myself, can be refined into the conscious contrasts between present
and past Self, between my self-critical and my naïve Self, between my higher and lower Self, or between my Conscience and
my impulses. My reflective life, as it empirically occurs in me

from moment to moment, is a sort of abstract and epitome of my whole social life, viewed as to those aspects which I find peculiarly significant. And thus my experience of myself gets a certain provisional unity. But never do I observe my Self as any single and unambiguous fact of consciousness.

I V

The empirical Ego has now been, in outline, characterized. The source of its endless varieties has been sketched. Its unity has been found to be not, in our present form of existence, a fact that gets anywhere fully presented, as a rationally determined whole of life or of meaning. The empirical unity of the Ego depends merely upon a certain continuity of our social and of our inner life of experience and memory. The most stable feature about the empirical Ego, is that *sort of contrast in which it stands to the social world, literal and ideal, in which we live.* But precisely as here upon earth we have no abiding city, just so, in our present human form of consciousness, the Self is never presented except as a more or less imperfectly organized series of experiences, whose contrast with those of all other men fascinates us intensely, but whose final meaning can simply never be expressed in the type of experience which we men now have at our disposal. Were our life not hid in an infinitely richer and more significant life behind the veil, we who have once observed the essential fragmentariness of the empirical Ego would indeed have parted with our hope of a true Selfhood.

But the two other types of conception of the Self remain to be characterized. The one of these types, the second in our list of three, need detain us at this stage but little. The third type we shall at once so sketch as to define the momentous task that lies before us in our later lectures.

The second type of the conceptions of the Ego consists of all those views which regard the Self as in some metaphysical sense a real being, without defining the true Being of this Self in strictly idealistic terms. Such conceptions of the human Self as an entity are numerous in the history of philosophy. Their classification and further characterization will receive attention in the next lecture. For the moment I may exemplify them by mentioning as their most familiar examples, those views which conceive the human Self as, in some realistic sense, a distinct and independent entity. For such views the true Self is often essentially a Substance. Its individuality means that in essence it is separable, not only from the body, but from other souls. It preserves its unity despite the chaos of our experiences, just because in itself, and apart from all experience, it *is* One. It lies at the basis of our psychical life; and it must be sharply distinguished from the series of the states of consciousness, and even from their empirical organization. It is the source of all the order of our mental life; and all our self-consciousness is a more or less imperfect indication of its nature.

Such realistic views are well known to you. And you also know now why, without showing the least disrespect to their historical dignity, I can and must simply decline to follow them into their details in these lectures. They are all founded upon the realistic conception of Being. They must therefore all fall with that conception. Their true spirit indeed is often of far deeper moment than their mere letter. What doctrines of Soul-Substance have often meant to express, namely, a respect for human individuality, and an appreciation of its eternal worth in the life of the Universe, our own theory of the human individual will erelong develop in its own fashion. But taken literally, the doctrine that beneath or behind our conscious life there is a permanent substance, itself never either presented or presentable in consciousness, but real, and real in such wise that its Being is independent of any knowledge that from without refers to it,—this whole doctrine, I say, simply perishes, for the purposes of our argument, together with Realism, and only its revised and purified inner meaning can reappear, in quite another guise, in the world of Idealism. Whatever the Self is, it is not a Thing. It is not, in Aristotle's or in Descartes' sense, a Substance. It is not a realistic entity of any type. Whether we men ever rightly come to know it or not, it exists only as somewhere known, and as a part of the fulfilment of meaning in the divine life. We are spared the trouble of proving this thesis here in detail, simply because our general proof of Idealism has discounted the entire issue. We are not comdemning Realism unheard; but only after the most careful analysis of its claims. But with Realism passes away every view which regards the real Self as anything but what every real fact in the universe is: A Meaning embodied in a conscious life, present as a relative whole within the unity of the Absolute life.

Well, there remains the third type of conception of the Self, namely, the strictly idealistic type. And precisely this type it was that I exemplified before, when I spoke of the way in which the Self has been distinguished, even by common sense, into a higher and a lower, a nobler and a baser Self. As stated in ordinary fashion, such concepts, as we saw, remain crude, and lead to frequent inconsistency. Revised with reference to the demands of our Idealism, the concept of the Self will assume a form which will reduce to unity these apparent inconsistencies of ethical common sense, and will also escape from bondage to those empirical complexities forced upon us by the Ego of the passing moment. We shall then see that the concept of the individual Self is, in its higher forms, in large measure an essentially Ethical Conception. And the third type of conceptions of the Ego consists of definitions which have always laid stress upon just this aspect. From this point of view, the Self is not a Thing, but a Meaning embodied in a conscious life. Its individuality, in case of any human being, implies the essential uniqueness of this life. Its unity, transcending as it does what we ever find presented in our present type of consciousness, implies that the true individual Self of any man gets its final expression in some form of consciousness different from that which we men now possess. The empirical variety, complexity, ambiguity, and inconsistency of our present consciousness of the Self, is to be explained as due to the fact that, in the moral order of the universe, no individual Self is or can be isolated, or in any sense sundered from other Selves, or from the whole realm of the inner life of Nature itself. Consequently, even what is most individual about the Self never appears except in the closest connection with what transcends both the meaning and the life of the finite individual. Now, in our present form of conscious existence, we catch mere glimpses of the true meaning of the individual Self, as this meaning gets expressed in our deeds and in our ideals, and we also obtain equally fragmentary glimpses of the way in which this Self is linked to the lives of its fellows, or is dependent for its expression upon its relations to Nature, or is subject to the general moral order of the universe. These various transient flashes of insight constitute our present type of human experience. And it is their variety, their manifoldness, and their fragmentariness, which together are responsible for all those inconsistencies in our accounts of the Self,—inconsistencies which our present discussion has been illustrating. But if you want to free yourself from hopeless bondage to such inconsistencies, you must look, not to some realistic conception of a Soul-Substance, but to some deeper account of the ethical meaning of our present life than we have yet formulated. And from this point of view we get a notion of Selfhood and of individuality which may be summarized at the present stage much as follows.

Our general idealistic theory asserts that the universe in its wholeness is the expression of a meaning in a life. What this view implies about every fragment and aspect of life that your attention may chance to select, or that your human experience may bring before you as the topic of inquiry, we have in former lectures repeatedly pointed out. Any instant of finite consciousness partially embodies a purpose, and so possesses its own Internal Meaning. Any such instant of finite consciousness also seeks, however, for other expression, for other objects, than are now present to just that instant, and so possesses what we have called its External Meaning. Our Idealism has depended, from the first, upon the thesis that the Internal and the External meaning of any finite process of experience are dependent each upon the other, so that if the whole meaning and intent of any finite instant of life is fully developed, and perfectly embodied, this Whole Meaning of the instant becomes identical with the Universe, with the Absolute, with the life of God. Even now, whatever you are or seek, the implied whole meaning of even your blindest striving is identical with the entire expression of the divine Will. And it is in this aspect of the world that we have found the unity of Being. On the other hand, as we have also seen, this unity of the world-life is no simple unity, such as the mystic sought. It is an infinitely complex unity. And of this complexity, of this wealth of life that the complete expression of even your most transient and finite glimpses of meaning implies,—the foregoing facts about the Self are merely instances. If you are in company with a friend, the whole meaning of your thoughts and of your interests while you speak with him, not only requires for its complete expression his inner life as well as yours, and not only requires the genuine and conscious unity of his life and of yours by virtue of the ties of your friendship; but this same meaning also demands that, despite this unity of your life as friends,— yes, even because of this unity, your friend and yourself shall remain also contrasted lives, whose unity includes and presupposes your variety as these two friends. For a friendship is not a simple unity of conscious life, but the unity of two conscious lives each of which contrasts itself with the other, and feels in the other's relative independence the fulfilment of its own purpose. And just so, when your meaning is not friendly but hostile, and when you stand in presence of your opponent, your rival, your enemy, your finite conscious meaning still implies, even in the midst of all its confused illusions, the demand that the very life of your enemy shall exist as the expression of your hostile intent to hold him as your real enemy, while nevertheless this life of his, other than your present conscious experience, and linked with your experience through the ties of meaning, is contrasted with your own life as the life that yours opposes and in so far seeks either to win over to your purposes, or to annul. Finite love and finite hate, and human experience of life in any form, always imply, therefore, that the will now present, but imperfectly expressed, in this passing instant, is genuinely expressed through other conscious life that, from the Absolute point of view, is at once in conscious unity with this instant's purpose, and also in conscious contrast with this instant's purpose.

Primarily then, the contrast of Self and not-Self comes to us as the contrast between the Internal and the External meaning of this present moment's purpose. In the narrowest sense, the Self is just your own present imperfectly expressed pulsation of meaning and purpose,—this striving, this love, this hate, this hope, this fear, this inquiry, this inner speech of the instant's will, this thought, this deed, this desire,—in brief, this idea taken as an Internal Meaning. In the widest sense, the not-Self is all the rest of the divine whole of conscious life,—the Other, the outer World of expressed meaning taken as in contrast with what, just at this instant of our human form of consciousness, is observed, and, relatively speaking, possessed. Any finite idea is so far a Self; and I can, if you please, contrast my present Self with my past or my future Self, with yesterday's hopes or with to-morrow's deeds, quite as genuinely as with your inner life or with the whole society of which I am a member, or with the whole life of which our experience of Nature is a hint, or, finally, with the life of God in its entirety. In every such case, I take account of a true contrast between Self and not-Self. All such contrasts have a common character, namely, that in them an imperfectly expressed will is set over against its own richer expression, while stress is laid upon the fact,—a perfectly genuine fact of

Being,—the fact that the whole expression always retains, and does not merely absorb or transmute, the very contrast between the finite Self and its desired or presupposed Other,—its world of External Meanings. But if you ask how many such contrasts can be made, I reply, An infinite number. In countless ways can the Self of this instant's glimpse of conscious meaning be set into contrast with the not-Self, whose content may be the life of past and future, of friends and of enemies, of the social order and of Nature, of finite life in general, and of God's life in its wholeness.

But if the contrast of Self and not-Self can thus be defined with an infinite variety of emphasis, the unity of each of the two, Self and not-Self, can be emphasized in an equally infinite number of ways, whose depth and whose extent of meaning will vary with the range of life of which one takes account, and with the sort of contrast between Self and not-Self which one leaves still prominent over against the unity. Thus, in the familiar case of our ordinary social self-consciousness, I first view a certain realm of past and future experience as so bound up with the internal meaning of this instant's conscious experience, that I call this temporal whole of life the life of my own human Self, while I contrast this private existence of mine with that of my friends, my opponents, or of my other fellows, or with that of human society in general. The motives that lead to such an identification of the Self of the instant with a certain portion of that which is the instant's not-Self, namely, with a certain portion of past and future experience, are, as we have seen, extremely various, and in our empirical existence, both fickle and transitory. Whoever believes that he has any one rational principle for his usual identification of his past and future with the Self of this instant, has only to consider the psychological variations of self-consciousness before enumerated to discover his error. What will remain, after such an examination of the Self of common sense, will be the really deep and important persuasion that he *ought to possess* or to create for himself, despite this chaos, some one principle, some finally significant contrast, whereby he should be able, with an united and permanent meaning, to identify that portion of the world's life which is to be, in the larger sense, his own, and whereby he should become able to contrast with this, his larger Self, all the rest of the world of life.

And now this very consideration, this fact that one *ought to be able* to select from all the universe a certain portion of re-

membered and expected, of conceived and of intended life as
that of his own true and individual Self, and that one ought
to contrast with this whole of life, with this one's larger or truer
individuality, the life of all other individual Selves, and the life
of the Absolute in its wholeness,—this consideration, I say,
shows us at once the sense in which the Self is an Ethical Category. At this instant, as I have said, you can indeed identify
the Self, if you please, with just the instant's passing glimpse
of Internal Meaning; and in that case you can call all else the
not-Self. To do this is to leave the Self a mere thrill of transient life,—a fragment whose deeper meaning is wholly external
to itself. But you can, and in general you do, first identify a remembered past, and an intended future, with the Self whose
individuality is just now hinted to you; and this enlarged self
of memory and purpose you then oppose to a not-Self whose content is first the world of your fellow-men, and then the world of
Nature and of the Absolute in its wholeness. Now what justification have you for this view of your larger Self? Apart from
the capricious and shifting views of common sense, you can
have, I reply, but one justification, namely this: You regard this
present moment's life and striving as a glimpse of a certain task
now assigned to you, the task of your life as friend, as worker,
as loyal citizen, or in general as man, *i.e.* as one of God's expressions in human form. You conceive that, however far you might
proceed towards the fulfilment of this task, however rich this
individual life of yours might become, it would always remain,
despite its unity with the world-life, in some true sense contrasted with the lives of your fellows, and with the life of God,
just as now you stand in contrast to both. While your whole
meaning is now, and will always remain one with the entire life
of God, you conceive that this whole meaning expresses itself
in the form of an articulate system of contrasting and coöperating lives, of which one, namely your own individual life, is
more closely linked, in purpose, in task, in meaning, with the
life of this instant, than is the life of any other individual. Or
as you can say: "At this instant I am indeed one with God, in
the sense that in him my own absolute Selfhood is expressed.
But God's will is expressed in a manifold life. And this life is
a system of contrasted lives that are various even by virtue of
their significant union. For true unity of meaning is best manifested in variety, just as the most intimate and wealthy friendship is that of strongly contrasting friends. And in the manifold

lives that the world in its unity embodies, there is one, and only one, whose task is here hinted to me as my task, my life-plan,—an ideal whose expression needs indeed the coöperation of countless other Selves, of a social order, of Nature, and of the whole universe, but whose individual significance remains contrasted with all other individual significance. If this is my task, if this is what my past life has meant, if this is what my future is to fulfil, if it is in this way that I do God's work, if my true relation to the Absolute is only to be won through the realization of this life-plan, and through the accomplishment of this unique task, then indeed I am a Self, and a Self who is nobody else, just precisely in so far as my life has this purpose and no other. *By this meaning of my life-plan, by this possession of an ideal, by this Intent always to remain another than my fellows despite my divinely planned unity with them,—by this, and not by the possession of any Soul-Substance, I am defined and created a Self.*"

Such, I say, will be your confession, if once you come to define the Self in the only genuine terms,—namely, in ethical terms. If once you choose this definition, then the endless empirical varieties of self-consciousness, and the caprices of common sense, will not confuse you. You will know that since now we see through a glass darkly, you cannot expect at present to experience your human selfhood in any one consistent and final expression. But, too, you will know that you are a Self precisely in so far as you intend to accomplish God's will by becoming one; and that you are an individual precisely in so far as you purpose to do your Father's business in unique fashion, so that in this instant shall begin a work that can be finished only in eternity,—a work that, however closely bound up it may be with all the rest of the divine life, still remains in its expression distinguishable from all this other life. You will indeed recognize that at every moment you receive from without, and from other Selves, the very experiences that give your Selfhood a chance to possess its meaning. You will know that of yourself alone you would be nothing. You will also know that as co-worker with your fellows, and as servant of God, you have a destiny of which our present life gives us but the dimmest hint.

This is in outline, the doctrine of the ethical Self, to whose development and defence our later lectures shall be devoted.

9 ❧ THE MORAL ORDER [1]

In dwelling at such length, in the third lecture of the present series, upon the contrast between the Temporal and the Eternal aspects of Reality, I was dealing not merely with one of the most frequently misunderstood issues of philosophy, but with one of the most practical of the concerns of life. For in this contrast, and in the unity which underlies it, is involved the solution of the most perplexing problem with which the ethical consciousness of humanity has to deal. I call this problem the general question concerning the sense in which the world is a Moral Order. Our Idealism has declined to accept the world as a real fact merely given, in advance of an analysis of the sense in which the world is to be real. When we therefore now assert that the real has this or that character, our undertaking depends upon a previous analysis of what it is *to be real*. *To be*, we have said, means *to fulfil a purpose*, in fact, to fulfil in final, individual expression, the *only* purpose, namely, the Absolute purpose. Our closer study has shown us that this Absolute purpose is not only One, but also infinitely complex, so that its unity is the unity of many Wills, each one of which finds its expression in an individual life, while these lives, as the lives of various Selves, have an aspect in which they are free, in so far as each, while in many aspects determined, is still in its own measure a determiner of all the rest. We have also further seen that, in so far as we mortals can undertake at all to conceive the expression of the Absolute Purpose, this expression is in one aspect Temporal, in so far as there is a process which has successive stages, such that some are *no longer*, and others *not yet, when* the present stage of the world-process is. In another aspect, as we have seen, the same world-process is Eternal, in so far as the whole of it is viewed at one glance by the Absolute, precisely as we view the whole of any brief rhythmic succession at a glance whenever we observe such successions. That the world has all these inter-

[1] Josiah Royce, *The World and the Individual* (New York: The Macmillan Company, 1899, 1901), Vol. II, Lecture VIII, pp. 335–375. The lecture is reprinted in its entirety.—Editor's note.

related characters at once, we assert, yet not because we *first* recognize that all these characters are given as mere data in a realistic realm, so that only *then* we proceed to try to unify them after admitting their independent Being. No, we assert these various aspects of the world to be real only in so far as we can see that hereby purpose is fulfilled. Hereby each of these characters is deduced from our general concept of Being, as that concept is illustrated by our experience. *One* is the Absolute, because in *mere* multiplicity there would be no finality of insight. *Many* is the Absolute, because in the interrelationships of contrasted expressions of a single Will lies the only opportunity for the embodiment of wholeness of life, and for the possession of Self-consciousness by the Absolute. For the mystic long ago showed us that simple Oneness meant Nothingness. *Individuals* are all the various expressions of the Absolute, in so far as they are Many; just because, where the One is individual, every aspect and element of its self-expression is unique. *Free*, in its own degree, is every individual will amongst all the wills that the world-life expresses, because every such will, as unique, is in some respect underivable from all the others. *Temporal,* is the world order, because, so far as we can know, time is the universal form of the expression of Will. *Eternal* is this same world order, because past, present, and future time equally belong to the Real, and their Being implies, by definition, that they are present, in their wholeness, to the final insight. And Time, surveyed in its wholeness, is Eternity.

So far, then, we have merely developed our central concept of Being, and have attempted to interpret experience in the light of this concept. But now we assert that this world which we have been characterizing is a Moral Order. In what sense, and for what reason, do we assert this?

I

Despite the general exposition and defence that the ethical aspects of our conception of Being received in the former series of these lectures, and despite the frequent illustration that this same aspect has already received in the present series, it still seems necessary to face, more carefully than heretofore, familiar objections which, as experience shows, are sure to be directed

against such a view as ours, whenever it is considered with reference to the moral consciousness of man. These objections, as
I conceive, are founded upon a failure to grasp our doctrine of
Being in its wholeness. Persistently dwelling, now too exclusively
upon this and now too abstractly upon that aspect of our
theory, and neglecting to regard the meaning of all its aspects
together, an objector finds it easy to say, sometimes that the universe which we depict is not sufficiently fixed and final in its
form of Being to meet the demands of common sense, and sometimes that it is far too fixed and moveless in its type of Being to
leave room for any genuinely moral activity. We have defended
ourselves against Realism. Have we found sufficient room for the
demands of a strictly ethical Idealism? We have maintained the
unity of Nature and of Mind. Have we escaped from the danger of making our moral activities the mere incidental phenomena that help to express our own predetermined individual nature? We have vindicated the uniqueness of every human Self.
But have we given the Self any sufficiently significant moral task
to perform in the universe? We have insisted upon the finality
and perfection of the whole life of the Absolute Self. But have
we succeeded as yet in rescuing the individual Selves from being
mere expressions of a preëstablished harmony? We have assigned
both to rigid and unchangeable natural law and to causal determination, a very subordinate place in the universe. But have we
avoided a result equivalent to a sort of ethical fatalism? I conceive that, even after all that precedes, such objections will not
infrequently be urged by some who may have followed so far
our course. The answer, however, to every such objection lies at
present extremely near. Our fuller statement, regarding the relations of the temporal and the eternal aspects of Being, has only
to be applied to the present issues in order to lead at once to a
recognition of the way in which all these ethical doubts are to
be met.

For the moment, however, I must give the ethical objector the
word. He shall undertake to show what he means by calling the
world a Moral Order. He shall attempt to show that the world
which we have been depicting is not a Moral Order, or is not a
complete and sufficient Moral Order. We shall then see how,
from our point of view, such objections are to be met. And first,
then, what is a Moral Order? And secondly, has our Idealism
place for such a Moral Order?

II

"A Moral Order," our objector may first maintain, "depends upon recognizing not only that Selves exist, but that they so exist that they can do good or evil of their own accord, and by means of their own free will. In a true Moral Order, there is indeed law and control present in the universe; but each Self has its own sphere. And within this sphere the Self is not merely an unique voice in a symphony whose divine perfection is preëstablished, but an agent in a realm where one not only can go right but also can err, and where perfections are attained, if at all, by means of the will of the individual. In a Moral Order there can be true progress. But progress, where it has an ethical meaning, involves the production of what never existed before,—of the novel, and not merely of the absolute, of the finite, and not merely of the divine. Moreover, in a Moral Order, any ethical agent can say, 'It is not yet foreordained what I shall accomplish. I must find that out by my own work.' The ethical agent must also be able to say, 'I am needed. Even God needs my help. Without my doing of the right, something would remain forever undone.' The salvation of the individual moral agent must depend in part upon his own free choice. However the divine will may coöperate in the moral world, it is open to the free agent to choose whom he will serve. Above all it is essential, for every moral view of the universe, to conceive that the world can be made better than it is. There is thus an essential opposition, for the moral, even if not for the metaphysical consciousness, between the predicate *ought to be,* and the predicate *is.* Perfection, in the moral sense, is something still to be sought, it cannot be merely found. *The best world for a moral agent is one that needs him to make it better.* The purely metaphysical consciousness in vain, therefore, says of the good, *It is.* The moral consciousness insists upon setting higher than every such assertion the resolve, *Let it be.*[2] The moral consciousness declines to accept, therefore, any metaphysical finality. It rejects every static world. It is dynamic. Nowhere could it say, 'I have found that what is

2 See Mr. Wm. Salter's *Ethical Religion,* p. 13, for an eloquent expression of this attitude.

is altogether good.' Its watchword is, 'Grow better and make better.'

"But now," the objector may continue, "this your idealistic world lacks these essential characteristics of a true Moral Order. In your world everything, including all of what you call the free acts of the moral agents,—everything is present at one glance to the Absolute. And, for the Absolute, no other world than this one is, or in concrete truth can be. For in this world in its wholeness, the Absolute purpose, by your hypothesis, is embodied. Therefore, the whole, when viewed as a whole, is seen to be static, fixed, changeless. The individual agent knows at any instant, first, that what he really means, even in his blindness, is identical with the Absolute Will. He knows, then, that he can neither produce what ought not to be, nor create by his own deed a needed good that ought to be, and that, without his coöperation, would never come to be. For his deed, as your theory teaches, is never anything but one of the incidents in the process through which the Absolute wins the eternal perfection. The individual agent therefore does not find that the world needs him to make it better, except in the one sense, that, according to you, the world is indeed certain to have one of its own incidental finite perfections embodied in whatever the individual agent does. Your moral agent, so called, is therefore unable to sin, or to go wrong, or to be less, at any temporal moment, than he should be.

"Were he other than he is, then, as you maintain, the whole world would indeed also be other than it is. But, according to you, the world, as known to the Absolute, is known as a world that fulfils the Absolute purpose, and that, in so far, cannot be other than it is. Hence, once more, despite all that you have said about uniqueness and freedom, the individual is certain to be, in his own place, best as he is, whatever he is. And your Idealism is therefore, in its optimism, unable to give any genuine moral meaning to life. For in making *whatever is,* the final fulfilment of purpose, you have wholly lost sight of that contrast between *what is* and what *ought to be,* upon which all the moral consciousness depends. Your unique voices in the divine symphony are no more the voices of moral agents than are the stones in a mosaic. And if you relieve the individual from absolute causal determination, you do not relieve him from a fatalism none the less all embracing. You relieve him from absolute causal determination by saying that the purpose to explain him by taking account of his relationships to other beings, is always a purpose of somebody else, of some finite observer who is external to the being explained; and you say that this external purpose of the causal explainer of any agent's life is limited, as to its success, by the fact that this individual agent himself is unique, and that therefore, in some aspect, he is always incapable of being explained through any knowledge of his heredity, or of his environment, or of anything which is not himself. Now suppose that all this is granted. Still, by your idealistic hypothesis, any individual agent, if not explicable by means of anything external to himself, is still included in a perfect whole in such wise that he constitutes, despite his uniqueness, an organic part of that perfect whole. From this fate, according to you, he cannot escape. You have said, yourself, in a former discussion, in these lectures: 'In vain do we wander in darkness. We are eternally at home in God.' According to you, then, we please God, and are ourselves pleased, in our union with God—and pleased too even with ourselves, whatever we are. And this indeed is our fate. As for foreordination in general,—your doctrine of the temporal and the eternal has still to face the ancient difficulty concerning the reconciliation of the divine foreknowledge, and the free will of man.''

I have allowed the objector, so far, to state his case as well as I am able to indicate, from my own experience of such arguments, what that case is likely to be. I can answer only by pointing out, what, to my mind, are the facts regarding the matter here at issue.

III

And first, whatever our ethical doctrine may be, we shall all agree that the moral *Ought*, in its primary sense, is a category of temporal application. However eternal the moral law may be, in its validity and in its relation to the knowledge of man or of the Absolute, it is a law whose reference is to acts, and to intended consequences of action, in so far as they follow one another in a time-sequence, or may be conceived as in such a sequence. Whoever says, "I ought to do thus or thus," stands in a present moment of time, and looks forward to a future. His present decision is to be followed by a course of action. And in a world where there were no succession, there would be no morality. Consequently, the metaphysic of conduct is subject to the same general conditions as govern the metaphysic of any time-process. But, from our point of view, as we have now seen, time has its perfectly definable place in Being. There is succession. And our view of the Eternal has place for just such real view of succession. When one asserts that the future is *not yet,* our view, equally with the view of common sense, maintains that this assertion has truth. When one also asserts that past and future,—what is *no longer* and what is *not yet,* have their place together in the *totum simul* of the eternal order as the Absolute sees it,—we have already observed how and why there is no conflict whatever between this assertion and the assertion that the past and the future are, temporally speaking, *not* present. Hence our view, in recognizing the true nature of the temporal order, and in showing the relation of this order to the eternal order, has already defined as real the general condition upon which all moral activity depends, and has asserted that this condition, namely, the temporal succession of the world's events, is as real a fact for the Absolute as for us. The difference between the human view and the Absolute's view of the temporal order is simply that, for men, only very brief series of successive events can be viewed *totum simul,* while for the Absolute, *all* events are thus viewed, while all events remain, for such an inclusive view, none the less successive than they are for us.

So far, then, as to the mere temporal form in which alone any moral activity can take place. And now, in the next place, as to the more special conditions of moral activity: Our objector has said that, in a moral world, any moral agent can either do right, or choose the wrong. We accept the statement. Let there be any moral agent, *A*. We agree with our opponent that *A* must perform any one of his moral acts at some temporal moment. The act, in order to be a moral act at all, must, despite all of the aspects in which it may be determined by the heredity, environment, etc., of the agent, still possess an aspect in which it is *not* deducible from any external conditions, but is the agent's own present deed. Moreover, in order to be a moral act, this deed must form part of a succession of intentions, and of deeds, in which the agent's own will is progressively expressed. And this individual will of the agent must be so expressed in the deeds that in some genuine respect it lies with the agent himself to determine what nothing else in the world wholly determines, namely, the right or wrong character of this deed, and its conformity or nonconformity to the standard which constitutes the Ought. All this our opponent asserts. All this, however, we too assert. And we have already in general indicated in former discussions why and how we assert just this to be true. Our present purpose is merely to develop and to apply, more specifically, the former results.

Yet now, when our opponent still insists that we have no right to assert that these characters of freedom and of relative self-determination, and of individual power to do right or wrong, belong to the moral agents of our world, we in reply might stubbornly insist, if we chose, that our opponent himself should explain in what sense he regards the freedom and the individual initiative of moral agents as real facts in his own world. We might ask him, in other words, to make articulate his view of the sense in which his Moral Order has any sort of Being whatever. In our former series of lectures, we exhaustively treated the possible meanings of the ontological predicate. Our opponent, if he is to present a rational view, must do likewise. When he asserts the moral agents to be in any sense free, or to have in any sense their individual power of initiative, he becomes responsible for an ontology. He is a realist, or a mystic, or a critical rationalist, or an idealist in his metaphysic, whatever may be the ethical contents whose Being he asserts. We long since saw, then, why he can be consistent in his ontology only in case he is an idealist. But, unless he can set aside our former argument as to the nature of Being, then, whatever his well-warranted enthusiasm for a Moral Order may be, he can assert the Being of that Moral Order only by declaring that it is real simply because the Absolute knows it to be whatever it is, and because the Absolute Will finds in just this individuality, freedom, and initiative of the moral agents, whose acts occur in time, the fulfilment of the highest purpose. Now this is precisely what we ourselves assert. And we assert it for precisely the reason that leads our opponent to assert it,—namely, because, to our view as to his, a world where the temporal succession of acts, despite all its causal connections and its countless general characters, has room for individuality and for initiative, is precisely the sort of world wherein, and wherein alone, the highest purpose can be fulfilled, and the most perfect life expressed.

Yet we shall indeed turn from this more polemic fashion of challenging our opponent to explain in what sense his Moral Order can express any Being at all; and we shall now explain, more fully, in what sense we declare that the temporal acts of individuals involve the power to go right or to go wrong, and in what sense, according to us, what *ought to be* and what *ought not to be,* can with equal possibility occur at any one temporal instant, despite, or in fact, just *because of* the eternal perfection of the whole. The true distinction, and the true connection, between the temporal and the eternal aspects of Being, furnish, in truth, the basis for a solution of this whole problem.

I V

Let us return to the individual moral agent. By his reality, as an individual being, at any moment of time, we now well know what we mean. We mean that just then there is a finite Internal Meaning, which seeks its own Other, and which, in any degree of blindness or of imperfection of insight that you please, is seeking, as this Other, the Absolute itself. We hold that this finite Internal Meaning is, furthermore, the meaning of a Self, which contrasts itself, more or less sharply, with the whole of the rest of the universe, even in seeking to find in this universe its own will expressed. So far we have, if you please so to call it, the fate of every finite Self. To seek anything but the Absolute itself is, indeed, even for the most perverse Self, simply impossible. All life is looking for God, however base the forms of idolatry beneath which the false love of the world may ignorantly hide its own meaning, at any one temporal instant. And now, however you define your moral philosophy, it is indeed true that by the Ought you mean, at any temporal instant, a rule that, if followed, would guide you so to express, at that instant, your will, that you should be thereby made nearer to union with the divine, nearer to a consciousness of the oneness of your will and the Absolute Will, than you would become if you acted counter to this Ought. Now it is enough for our present purpose that a consciousness of such a rule can arise in any Self, at the moment of a moral act. Hereupon, however, there also arises the familiar situation in which conduct counter to the consciousness of the Ought appears, to the temporal Self, to be possible.

This situation, so far as it here concerns us, in this extremely general sketch of the possibility of a Moral Order, is as follows: The Self, inevitably meaning the Absolute as that Other which it seeks to know as the Real, and inevitably seeking, also, to win union with that Absolute wherein its own final will is expressed, and to know the world as its own, and its own life as in harmony with the world, is still, as this present finite Self, conscious of its *contrast* with that world which it views as beyond its present range of experience, or as beyond the circle wherein its Internal Meaning is now consciously expressed. Common sense expresses this contrast by saying that I have one will; while the world seems to have another will, which may to any extent oppose mine. The Ought, under these conditions, comes to our finite consciousness in the form of some principle which, in general, however we may formulate it, says: "Harmonize thy will with the world's Will. Express thyself through obedience. Win thy victory by accepting thy task. The world is already thy Will absolutely expressed. Learn this truth by conforming thy deed to an absolute law." It is enough for us here that this consciousness of the Ought can and does arise; while the essence of it is that the Self is to accomplish the object of its search through obedience to an order which is not of its own momentary creation.

But, as we have said, the Self is known through a contrast-effect. Its own will, as it now is consciously present, is not yet known as in harmony with the Other wherein it inevitably seeks to find its own expression. It is always abstractly possible, therefore, for the Self to conceive its search for self-expression as simply an undertaking not to obey, but to subdue, to its own present purpose, the world which is beyond. Instead of developing its momentary Internal Meaning into harmony with its own External Meaning, it may, in its narrowness, seek to convert the latter into the former. Instead of assuming the attitude that Tennyson expresses by saying:—

> Our wills are ours to make them thine,

the Self may seek its self-expression explicitly in the form of rebellion. Nor is such a rebellious attitude by any means wholly evil. Conscious choice of a total evil is, indeed, impossible. For the Self, at its worst, seeks finality of self-expression, and seeks this self-expression through a life that is at once Other than its present Internal Meaning, and perfected in its form and content. Yet because the consciousness of the Self depends upon a contrast, the overcoming of the oppositions involved in that contrast, while never conceivable in an utterly evil shape, can be conceived, by the finite Self, as in conflict with what a clearer insight knows to be the Ought, since the consciousness of the Ought demands of the Self an overcoming of the opposition through a rational obedience to the law of the Absolute, while the consciousness opposed to the Ought seeks to master the world in the service of the mere caprice of the Self.

Or, to state the conflict in its simplest terms: I always will to become one with my world, and so, with God. But when I explicitly follow the Ought, I seek to transform myself as I now am into the likeness and the expression of God. And when I oppose what a clearer insight would see to be the Ought, I seek to fashion the truth after the image, and to make God the mere tool of myself as I now am. In both cases it is indeed impossible for me to avoid seeking a good, and expressing a truth as I act. For as a fact, I can only assert my finite Self by actively transforming myself; so that I actually obey, in some measure, even while I rebel. For the finite Self cannot seek its own, without passing over into new life. And there is self-sacrifice involved in even the most stubborn rebellion; and courage and endurance are exercised, unwillingly, even by the most cowardly of pleasure-seekers. The soul of goodness in things evil lies deeper than those admit who see not the tie that binds all Being in one. Even in the depths of hell the lost, if such there were, would still, despite themselves, serve God amidst their darkness. Nor can any being wander so far as to escape not only the presence, but the indwelling, of the Absolute. Moreover, even when the finite Self rebelliously seeks to subdue all Being to its own present conscious caprice, it actually expresses, in its own way, a truth. For there is indeed no life, however slight, which makes no difference to the rest of the world; nor is there any caprice, however perverse, that is not an aspect, however fragmentary, of God's perfect meaning. So that when the Self rebels, it can rebel only because the Spirit dwells in it; and when it would fashion all things to its own will, it utters a truth, viz. the truth that, in its own degree, it is the object and expression of the divine interest. But if the rebellious Self expresses thus unwillingly a truth that is already divine, the obedient Self, willingly seeking, even in what is Other, its own will, and surrendering in order that it may possess, acts willingly in accordance with a truth that is final, and is conscious of its own meaning in a form that is far more significant than the one in which the life of the rebellious Self is embodied.

Now it would belong to a system of ethical doctrine to develop what I thus only hint, namely, the positive content of the moral act, and the deeper nature of the contrast between what ought to be and what ought not to be. Here I am only interested in defining the alternative courses of action that are possible in a finite being sufficiently to show that a moral act, when once its content has been defined, can be conceived as occurring at any temporal instant, and in the life of any finite Self. But having defined the general situation which any moral agent faces, we again ask the question, Can our theory find room, in the temporal world, *for free moral choices that conform or do not conform to the Ought?* In other words, can a finite Self, knowing the Ought, in any sense freely choose to rebel or to obey? And is such free choice to do ill consistent with our theory of the perfection of the whole, and the finality of the eternal order?

V

Our question, as thus formulated, assumes several aspects, each of which must now be considered in its turn. Our own statement, in a former lecture, concerning the individuality and freedom of the finite Self, turned upon saying that in the unique whole of the Absolute life, every finite life, as related to that whole, and as one of the aspects of this whole, must be itself unique. Since this uniqueness of each finite life, in other words of each Self, is itself the embodiment of an aspect of the Absolute Will; this aspect in turn appeared as itself an unique will, not elsewhere precisely duplicated, and so as the individual will of this finite Self. As the unique cannot be wholly defined through its external relations, or deduced from them, or causally explained by means of them, we found each finite Self to be, in some aspect of its nature, free. And viewing the same facts in the light of the distinction between the temporal and the eternal, we now assert that each finite Self, in so far as it is an ethical individual, having a continuity of purpose in its life, expresses itself in a series of deeds, each one of which, as a deed that has an unique place in an unique life, is itself, in some measure and in some aspect, however slight,— free,—so that the individuality of every act sets a limit to the possibility of the causal explanation of this act by an external observer. We have now to see how this former theory of the general nature of finite and temporal freedom applies to the case of the moral act, as that act has here been defined. That every such finite freedom of action is a strictly limited freedom, we clearly see. Our question is whether such freedom is sufficient to give finite acts their needed character as a choice between what ought to be done, and what ought not to be done, by the individual agent at any moment.

Our objector may hereupon say: "What you have called the freedom of the finite Self certainly cannot be *moral* freedom. For, according to you, the Self always wills the same essential aim, namely its final union and harmony with its Other, or, in other words, its fulfilment through its oneness with the Absolute. As for the conflict between the Ought, on the one hand, and the rebellious attitude of the finite Self on the other hand,—a conflict whose decision, as you assert, constitutes the content of the moral act,—*such a conflict can depend solely upon ignorance*. The Self seeks its own realization. It *can* seek nothing else. This realization means oneness with God. No other aim is possible. But ignorance of how to reach the goal is possible in a finite being. And, according to you, the rebellious Self is thus ignorant of its own true good, and states its fragment of truth in a false form. The Self that follows what a higher insight sees to be the Ought, on the other hand, merely knows the truth, and knowing follows. Your so-called moral acts are thus *mere expressions of knowledge or of ignorance,—not of freedom.*"

To this objection I reply that, by our hypothesis, whenever an individual acts, his deed is at once, and inseparably, an act of knowledge and an expression of purpose,—an insight and a choice. And the sense in which it is both knowledge and will at once is just here best indicated by remembering the sense in which every act of will, and every process of knowledge, involves what the psychologist calls Attention. To attend, is to be at once guided in your momentary deed by what you know, and determined in your knowledge by what you do. And, as Professor James has so successfully pointed out, and as we ourselves have maintained from the outset of the present series, the central feature of every voluntary deed, the constitutive principle of every finite life, is a process of Attention. An idea arises in your mind. The idea already involves a nascent deed. Attend to that idea rather than to any other, and at once the idea, filling the whole circle of your consciousness, turns into its appropriate completed deed. In a moment of temptation, the man who has his opportunity to embezzle, begins to think of how he could misappropriate the funds intrusted to him. The idea, already possessed of its ominous Internal Meaning, comes to consciousness as already the nascent deed of a Self rebellious against what is, for a higher insight, the Ought,— against the law of honor that here binds the Self to the truth, and to the Absolute. Does the conceived deed win possession of the whole field of consciousness? Then, indeed, by what thenceforth appears to the externally observant psychologist as an altogether automatic process, the deed is carried out in the man's conduct. In other words, if the man thinks of nothing so much as of his opportunity to embezzle, then, if the opportunity also persists, and the physical power to accomplish the deed remains, he inevitably embezzles. On the other hand, if he thinks rather of the law of the obedient Self, of his honor, and of the tie that, when fully comprehended, is seen to be a tie that binds him to God, the deed remains undone, and the nascent evil Self is suppressed by the wiser Self. The only field of choice, in such a case, is therefore *the field of attention.*

But an act of attention, I repeat, is at once an act by which we come to know a truth, and an act by which we are led to an outward deed. Such outward deed may be (as in the case earlier dwelt upon in our discussion of the World of Description), a deed whereby we come to seem, to an external observer, inactive, and merely observant of our world. But such inactivity, if it be deliberately chosen, is itself a sort of activity. As a man attends, so is he, so he knows, and so too, he acts, or voluntarily refrains from action. Therefore it is vain, in case of any true choice, to separate, at just that instant, the knowledge which guides and the voluntary activity which then and there expresses this knowledge. What I potentially know, can indeed be, for any one abstract purpose, pretty sharply sundered from what I am able to do. Thus my memory has stores of possible knowledge that I do not now recall. And on the other hand, my acts could create outer objects that I have never yet made. And when one thus views the realm of what I can know, as for instance my storehouse of memories; and the realm of what I can do, namely, the possible new objects that my will could produce, knowledge and will seem far apart. But, in our present consciousness, knowledge and will are, as we long ago saw, merely two aspects of the present unity of conscious life. What we now know means whatever is at present a discriminated fact in the unity of consciousness. What we now do means whatever we win through the present expression of our purposes in knowing. But the process whereby our present knowledge alters to meet our purposes, and is known as thus altering, is the process of attention. This process involves, then, an alteration of present knowledge to suit our purpose. It also, and inevitably, involves an acting according to our present knowledge.

In the second lecture of the present series, we considered our discriminating attention in its theoretical aspect, as something relatively opposed to definite action. But this opposition, as we saw, comes to light in cases where we so far lack the knowledge that is sufficient to guide us in a definite course of action. Here, however, we have to consider attention in so far as it means *a deliberate and free dwelling upon, or ignoring of, plans of action which we are supposed already to possess.* In this case, our attention appears not in its theoretical, but in its practical aspect. This attention is our choice to narrow the field of our own consciousness in a particular way at a particular moment.

It is indeed true that, according as a man now views the relation of the Self to the world, so, just now, he acts. It is equally true that, since every conscious act is a present act of attention, which is directed to some aspect of the relation between the Self and the world, therefore, according as a man now consciously acts, so, at this instant, he comes to view this very relation between the world and his individual Self. A morally ignorant man, who has never learned the law, or conceived in some particular sense of his own higher good, we acquit of moral defect, just in so far as he acts in this so far invincible ignorance. He must first get knowledge, as we say, before he can choose the right course of acting. It does not, however, follow that his knowledge of the good, when it comes, will deprive his good deeds of their free character. For in performing any one good deed, if he acts voluntarily, he will act by virtue of his own conscious attention to the good. So long as he clearly thinks of nothing so much as of his already known relation to the world and to God, he will indeed inevitably act accordingly, and be not the rebellious, but the obedient Self; precisely as while the tempted man thinks of nothing so much as of his temptation to embezzle, he will inevitably steal whenever the opportunity offers. But, in both cases, knowledge will determine outer deed, precisely in so far as the inner deed of attention gets its purpose expressed in a particular kind of present knowledge.

To our objector we consequently here reply: According to our view, all beings, everywhere, serve the Absolute purpose precisely in so far as then and there they know that purpose. Nor can any, even the worst beings, act without in some measure relating their momentary deed to what, however blindly, they then and there know of that purpose. But, on the other hand, *all conscious beings, at any instant, know what they are conscious of, precisely in so far as they attend to an ideal.* But the act of attention of just this instant, taken together with the resulting knowledge, is peculiarly apt to be the expression of just this instant's unique, and accordingly free, will. In one aspect, as we saw before (in our second lecture), our consciousness at this instant is made narrow, our attention is centred upon just *these* facts, by virtue of conditions which we *cannot* now control. But in another aspect, our voluntary narrowing of the field of our attention, at this instant, *does* alter the range of what we now know. Now it is in *this* aspect that our attention, and so our will, can be, at any one instant, morally free. Hence when a being, by virtue of his training, and of the present grade of his consciousness, has at any instant present to him some form of the conflict between the Ought and the rebellious Self, *what he then does turns upon, and is the expression of, the way in which he then and there attends to one or to the other of the warring interests.* If he chooses to think of nothing so much as that it is just the private Self, as it now is, whose fulfilment, at any cost, he seeks, he comes to lack, in so far, the moralizing knowledge. His caprice, for himself, becomes then the only hint of the divine that tends to remain in sight. In so far as this tendency excludes everything else from sight, he forgets God as God, forgets the Ought as the Ought, and acts with a *viciously acquired naïveté.* Such a deed can never be wholly bad, simply because nothing absolutely evil exists, and because, as we metaphorically said, even in the depths of hell they still unwillingly serve God. But if, on the other hand, the attention *fixes* nothing so much as the truer relation of the present temporal Self to the Other, upon whose definition the Ought depends, then just such attention wins its expression in the obedient and self-surrendering deed. *What is in any such case done is, therefore, indeed the expression of present knowledge. But in this case the present state of knowledge is the expression of the present attention. And the attention is the will of the instant.* Our theory is, that, despite all the causal de-

pendence of the Self upon its own past, and upon all its social
and natural conditions, just this act of attention, at this temporal instant, never occurred before, and will never occur again,
and is, in so far, unique, individual, incapable of any complete
causal explanation, and is, in consequence, the free act of this
self. And thus, despite all the objections, we vindicate for our
theory the power to deduce the possibility of temporal acts that
possess a true moral significance.

The sole possible free moral action is then a freedom that relates to the present fixing of attention upon the ideas of the Ought
which are already present. To sin is *consciously to choose to
forget,* through a narrowing of the field of attention, an Ought
that one already recognizes. For while I cannot avoid acting
in accordance with the Ought so long as I clearly know it, I
can, through voluntary *inattention,* freely choose to forget it.
And while, again, the truth as far as I know it compels my
deed, I do the good freely in so far as I freely choose to *continue* my already existent attention to the already recognized
truth concerning the good. All sin, then, is sin against the light
by a free choice to be inattentive to the light already seen. Or
again, all sin is a free choosing of the *sort* of narrowness which,
in our second lecture, we found to be, in one aspect, the
natural fate of the human being. That is, sin depends upon a
narrowing of consciousness, so that a present ignorance of what
one *ought to know* occurs. Now a certain narrowness of consciousness we before found to be our fate. But *freely chosen*
and vicious narrowness,—a deliberate forgetting of what one
already knows of God and the truth, this is of the very essence
of sin. All free choice of the good, on the other hand, is
voluntary persistence in attending to the good already known.
Moral freedom is simply this freedom to hold by attention, or
to forget by inattention, an Ought already present to one's finite
consciousness. But such freedom is, upon our view, possible and
actual.

V I

Yet the objector's strongest argument remains still insufficiently emphasized. "Not thus," he may say, "do you escape
from the moral fatalism which was urged against you at the
outset. What you have so far made out, if your argument be

altogether granted, is, that, at any one point of time, a given
moral agent, *A,* may freely so act, through his attentive process,
as to emphasize either a false, or else a true view, of his relations to the Other that he seeks, namely, to the final expression
of his whole will in the eternal order. The consequence may
be a deed that a moralist will call an evil act or a good one,
according as the agent decides by his choice in attending or not
attending to the Ought as he knows it. But you have done
well to admit that according to your metaphor, even in hell
they unwillingly serve God. Those who make the hellish choice
serve God ignorantly. But then, according to you, *God knows
that they do so.* And in him even their own whole intent, together with the more conscious and obedient intent of those
whom the moralist calls the good, is completely brought to
light, and is eternally fulfilled, in an unique whole which, as
you have repeatedly insisted, is such that no other fulfils or,
speaking in terms of the concrete will, can fulfil, the one absolute purpose. In this unique whole, as you have also pointed
out, every finite life and intent has its own individual place, a
place that no other could take. And this place is, by hypothesis,
a place in an absolutely perfect whole. The sinners, then, even
by all their worst efforts to forget the good, cannot accomplish
anything that makes the world less than perfect. Nor can the
good do anything but express by their persistent attention their
own consciousness that the whole is perfect. They cannot make
the world better. Now where the world is such that the eternal
perfection is predetermined, whatever the moral agent does, the
situation is one of a moral fatalism."

I reply that here at last we reach the point where the distinction of the temporal and the eternal order becomes of most
critical importance. Moral acts, as I have pointed out, occur in
time. It is with reference to time, and in particular, to the
time which any moral agent views as his future, that the agent
himself, or any one who judges him, estimates any act as good
or as ill. The free agent, whose temporal act (as an attentive
choice between a persistence in knowing the Ought, and a free
forgetting of Ought in favor of the evil), we have already characterized, is told by the moralist, that by his deed he can make
his world better, or worse. The emphasis here is laid, and
rightly laid, upon *his* world, upon the world *as he can view it
in relation to his deed,*—upon an aspect of Reality as such, and
not upon the eternal whole of Reality taken as a whole. The

moral agent is explicitly this Self as contrasted with other Selves. He is this individual among other individuals. You cannot indeed separate him from other individuals; but you recognize him as this individual by contrasting what he intends and effects, with what other individuals intend and effect.

Now once considering the individual as acting in time, what you have a right to say to him is, that, if he intends evil results, —let us say, repeating our former example,—if he intends embezzlement, in a region of the temporal world where embezzlement is possible, and is accordingly an evil,—then, just in so far as he succeeds in carrying out his end, he produces what, at just that point of time, is indeed an actual evil. Now, in one of the lectures of our former Series, in speaking of death and similar evils, we already briefly considered how our Idealism has to view the general nature and the possibility of actual finite ills. Our examples of such ills were chosen, at that stage, not from the region of human conduct, but from our experiences of what seem to be natural ills,—ills whose source and true meaning are in large part unknown to us. Of such natural ills, death is a classic instance, and we used it, in the discussion to which I here refer, as our principal instance. Let us recall the main features of our view as there stated, reminding ourselves, for the moment, not so much of the sense in which moral ills or sins are possible, but rather of the general sense in which any evil can be said to have a place in Being.

A finite ill is a fact of experience whose fragmentariness makes our universal search for the Other, for what lies beyond, for the context, explanation, justification, and supplement of this fact, peculiarly pathetic and eager. In the most general sense of the word evil, *all* finite facts, viewed as such, are indeed evil, precisely in so far as, when taken in themselves, they have no complete meaning, and leave us in disquietude, searching still for the Other, *i.e.,* for true Being in its wholeness. To this aspect of finite life we long since called attention. It is not satisfactory to be finite. On the other hand, for our view, no finite fact is a total evil, for taken in its eternal context, as aspect of the whole, it ultimately implies, demands, or, if you please, *means* all other finite facts, and forms together with them, the total life in which the Absolute Will is fulfilled. In the more special sense of the word, however, we apply the term *evil* to facts which are *so* disquieting that they especially emphasize, as it were, their own finitude and ours, in so far as our experience is confined to them. When we face such facts anywhere in the temporal order, and are conscious of them as evils, we very especially desire to change our own experience of them. This we desire, just because these facts send us so imperatively to some Other, wherein we hope to find the features by virtue of which the positive value of the world shall become plain to us. In the presence of such ills, as for instance, pain and death, we inevitably say, "If this were all, then indeed better no world at all than this one." And thus, in so far, an evil is a fact that very loudly proclaims, as it were, to our consciousness. "In me, Being in its wholeness and finality is not to be found. Elsewhere, elsewhere, lies the experience of the final truth."

Now how such ills can have any place in Being, we in a measure have seen from the very moment when, in refuting the abstractions of pure Mysticism, we first observed that unless the finite is real, the Absolute itself has no Reality. If Being is a final whole of experience, there must be that experience of which it is the whole, that striving of which it is the finality, that imperfection of which it is the completion. Or, to state the matter in less technical terms, unless the Absolute knows what we know when we endure and wait, when we love and struggle, when we long and suffer, the Absolute in so far is less and not more than we are. For all these states of ours mean something. The meaning of the world is the meaning of life, not of the lifeless; and attainment is not won except as the attainment of the goal of painful endeavors. And the more significant the endeavors, the deeper the experience of finitude, and so of evil, that they include. But nothing that is known to the finite is lost to the Absolute; and finitude is a condition for the attainment of perfection, in precisely the sense in which the temporal is a condition for the consciousnes of the eternal, or, to use our former simile, precisely as the successive chords of the music are a condition of the beauty of the whole succession when it is viewed *as* a whole. What ills find their place in finite Being, and what place any particular evil finds,—these are topics for special consideration. But of ill in general, this is the idealistic theory.

But from such an indication as to the nature of ill in general, we return to the special case of moral evil. If evil in general can exist, in any finite and temporal region of our idealistic world, then evil can be the work of some finite moral agent.

And this is as true for us as for our opponents. For when we call the evil the work of any agent, we mean that it expresses that agent's will, as he embodied his will at some temporal moment of his life. Now for us it is as true, as for our opponents, that the will of a finite being can win an actual temporal expression. And in consequence of what we have already said concerning the uniqueness and the individuality of the free agent's temporal act, it is quite as possible for us as it is for our opponents to conceive that a just observer, aware of the facts, could say to a given finite agent, regarding a particular ill: "This is what you have done. And but for you, and for you only, amongst all those who act in the world, this ill,—just this temporal fact that dissatisfies, never would have been."

"But," says our opponent, "according to you, the nature of Being, viewed in its wholeness, is fatally so constituted that this ill, which a given finite agent does, is so supplemented, so overcome, so included in a richer life, so taken up into the Other which this ill, even as it is, already means and implies, —that the whole is perfect despite the ill." Yes, I reply, but *how* is this ill included and reconciled within the perfect whole? Not, according to our hypothesis, by virtue of the fact that the evil deed expresses the finite agent's evil will, but *because his will is supplemented, is overcome, is thwarted, is overruled*, by what expresses some other will than his finite will was, in so far as he himself, at the moment of acting, consciously defined that will. For the supposition is that what he intended, just in so far as he opposed what he then viewed as his own interest to the world's interest, and just in so far as this deed expressed his will, was the ill, and not the Absolute life; the finite rebellion, and not the final harmony,—the embezzlement, for instance, and not the Ought. If *per impossibile* he had won might over Being, as he did win in his own measure and time, a momentary self-expression, the whole universe would have been an ill, and in fact, since nothing finally ill can exist as a whole at all, the universe would have been destroyed. For, by the very nature of Being and of evil, every sin, in its intention is, in essence, world-destroying. For in conscious intent, as an act of choosing to narrow attention so as to ignore what ought to be known and then to act in accordance with this vicious ignorance, it is inconsistent with the very conditions which make Being as a whole possible. What the ill-doer accomplished, then, was an actual ill, and an ill that would not have been, and that need not have been, but for his individual choice in narrowing his attention as he did. And in so far as his will was effective, there was that in the universe that had to be atoned for, and thwarted. Only through the conquest over this evil-doer and his deed, is the final perfection won. His deed is related to the goodness of the whole, much as the dread that in itself is cowardly, and is destructive of courage, is related to the courage that consists in enduring and in overcoming this dread, and that in so far depends, for its very perfection, upon that dread.

In the temporal world, then, the evil-doer's will is, according to our hypothesis, possessed of a measure, both of individuality and of freedom. It is in its own time and degree morally effective. What it produces is, in its temporal reality as this act or series of finite acts, an evil. This evil is due to the evil-doer, and without his choice it need not have occurred at all. Therefore, any free moral agent, in so far as he is free, may either choose or avoid evil deeds by choosing to attend to the good that he now knows, or to narrow his attention and ignore this good. Consequently, such an agent's own world, that is, the world of the facts which express his finite will, precisely in so far as he himself distinguishes himself from all the rest of the Absolute life,—*his* world, I say, is, for our doctrine, as for our opponent's doctrine, a world which this finite agent can make worse or better if he chooses, and, within his own range of efficacy, *as* he chooses. The *means* by which he can freely do this we have seen, viz. his free attention or inattention to the good. As for the consequences of this free choice of his, they may, in a closely linked world, prove to be as grave, extended, and as lasting as temporal conditions may determine.

So much then for the possibility of free and significant moral choices of good and of ill. Consequently, as to the charge that our view is a moral fatalism, what *we* say to the moral agent is this: You act as you will, just in so far as you are free. And you are free in the before-defined sense. That is, you are free to attend or not attend to the Ought as you already, at any moment, have come to know it. If you do ill, the world-order will, indeed, in the end make good the ill you have done, and in *that* sense will make naught of your deed,—yet not because you are unable to do any ill at all, but because elsewhere, in the temporal order, other agents, seeking to overcome the disquieting ill which your will has chosen as its expression, will somewhere and somehow succeed. You yourself may,—yes, doubt-less will, in the end, come to join in this self-conquering task. The moral order of your idealistic world means, then, not that no moral ill can be done, but that, in the temporal order, *every evil deed must somewhere and at some time be atoned for, by some other than the agent, if not by the agent himself,* and that this atonement, this overcoming of the evil deed, will in the end make possible that which in the eternal order is directly manifest, namely, the perfection of the whole.

Now it is decidedly the condition of a moral order that evil should be, in the end, overruled for good. And precisely this is the result that our own theory defines and necessitates. When we then say that, in the eternal order, the whole is good, we do not say that this evil-doer is wholly good, or that his deed has no ill effects, or that any fate predetermines how he shall take his place in the good order. We assert that he becomes a part of the perfect whole in so far as his evil deed is over-ruled for good, either by another, or later, by his individual Self.

VII

We have herewith in substance dealt with our opponent's case. We may return, however, in conclusion, to his original statements in their order as we stated them. "For the Absolute," our objector (referring to our own view of the Absolute) said, "no other world than this one is, or in concrete truth can be." Hence, as our opponent insisted, the whole, when viewed as a whole, is "static, fixed, changeless." And therefore the deed of any moral agent is powerless to change this perfect world for good or for ill. Our reply here runs that the world, seen from the eternal point of view, is indeed not *further* subject to change. Yet this is only because the eternal point of view includes in its single glance the whole of time, and therefore includes a knowledge and estimate of all the changes that finite agents, acting in time, really work in *their own world,* namely, in the temporal world that is future to their own deeds, and subject to their own will. The totality of temporal changes, forms in-deed, in one sense, a static whole, namely, in so far as no *further* series of events succeeds the whole of the temporal order of succession. But in another sense our world is as full of morally significant novelties as the nature of any world in any wise permits. For at every instant of time, according to our hypothesis, something novel, significant, individual, and in its own measure free, occurs, and leads to new results for which the choices of finite moral agents are responsible.

Our objector further insisted that, for our view, "The individual knows at any instant that what he really means, even in his blindness, is identical with the Absolute Will." Our reply is that here all turns upon the sense in which the word *identical* is used. The identity of the finite and the Absolute meaning is, for us, no mere identity without difference. I now know that, however blindly I strive, I suffer, or sin, my meaning, when fully interpreted in the light of all other life, of all the events that I now ignore, of all the future through which I and my fellows are yet to pass, of all the atoning deeds that shall yet reconcile my stubborn will to God's will, and of all the acts that shall overrule for good my worst intent,—that my meaning, I say, when included in one whole with all these endless differences, is identical with God's will. But taken by myself, as now I am, I am, indeed, remote enough, in my passing consciousness, both from my own self-expression, and from my final conscious union with my Other, namely with the Absolute.

"But," said the objector, "the agent's deed, as your theory teaches, is never anything but one of the incidents in the process through which the Absolute wins the eternal perfection. Therefore your agent is unable to sin, or to go wrong, or to be less, at any temporal moment, than he should be." I respond, The conclusion does not follow. Whatever I do, in my finitude, at this point of time, is, indeed, an incident in a process. The moral question is, *What sort of incident?* Viewed in itself the incident may be an evil deed. In that case, by the very definition of evil, and because the process, in its eternal completion, is good, the incident will be one that is turned to the good only by a further temporal process of overcoming the consequences of this deed, and of atoning therefor. The agent, then, according to us, is able to go wrong and to sin. If he sins, the eternal perfection includes his condemnation and the overcoming of his evil will, just as the hero condemns and overcomes his own dread, and thereby attains the perfection of courage.

"Were the agent other than he is," urges the objector, "the whole world would, indeed, be other than it is. But according to you, the world as known to the Absolute, is known as a world that fulfils the Absolute purpose, and that in so far *cannot* be other than it is." Hence the individual, as our objector also urged, cannot, without a failure of the Absolute purpose, be other than he is, and "is certain to be, in his own place, best as he is, whatever he is."

Our answer here insists simply upon a closer examination of the situation before us. There is an agent, *A,* whose will is, in some aspect, determined by nothing external to or other than himself, as he, at some moment of time, consciously is and acts. Were he other than he is, all the rest of the universe would in some sense be altered. Now he is an element in a perfect whole. But he is so merely because, in so far as evil appears in any region of that whole, this evil, by its very nature, demands, and finds, some Other, which so supplements it that it is overruled for good. As an evil, it cannot exist in isolation. Its supplement appears in the form of deeds of atonement, reparation, control, condemnation, and in the end, fulfilment. Such deeds in general are made necessary, by the evil deed, although their actual accomplishment will involve, by our hypothesis, the expression of individuality that is in some sense or aspect other than the individuality that accomplishes the evil deed. These amending deeds will themselves, therefore, possess, in some measure, the character of free will acts. They will occur, in the temporal order, subsequently to the evil deed. They will, as common sense would word the situation, "make good" the evil done. Only by virtue of these deeds, and because in the end they not merely offer external palliations to the ill done, but so include and control the will of the evil-doer himself that he comes to be related to the whole much as the dread of the hero is to the hero's courage,—only *thus* does the evil-doer enter into and become one with the perfect whole. In himself considered, however, the evil-doer, as evil-doer, is not, for our view, "best as he is." And if he had done otherwise, just these amending, atoning, reconciling, and perfecting deeds need never have occurred. If the evil-doer replies, "Yes, but the Absolute Will wrought even in and through me when I did ill," we reply, The Absolute Will wrought in you, as Absolute Will, *in so far as it was indeed well that you, as temporal individual actor, should just then be, in your own measure, free* and individual. For freedom and individuality are aspects of every element in a perfect whole. But the Absolute Will, as

such, was just what, in the evil deed, in so far as it was your
free deed, you *denied* at the moment of your act; for, declining
to attend to it, you made as if it were not. The amending and
atoning deeds are not yours, in so far as you temporally chose
the ill, but are acts either of your own Self at a later time, or
of the other Selves. In brief, the Absolute Will wins through
your condemnation and overcoming of your ill, and not through
your coöperation, so long as, and whenever, your temporal
act is not one of coöperation.

"But you lose sight," continues the objector, "of that contrast between what is and what ought to be, upon which all
the moral consciousness depends." My reply here is that what
ought to be and what is, can and do indeed fall asunder *at any
one instant of the temporal order.* For that is the very nature
of time, viz. that what is just now, at this instant of time, is
not yet what ought to be, but needs Another to supplement it.
Therefore is time the very form of the restless, finite Will. But
what ought to be at any or at every point of the temporal order, is real in the eternal order in its wholeness. The world is
not *now* good, nor is Being at this instant a temporally present
whole, nor does either God or man at this instant of time see
what *now* is as a fulfilment, or as right. Hence the future is
needed to supplement the present. Hence it is that hope springs
eternal in every finite instant. Hence it also is that, as the pes-
simists so mournfully observe, every hope for temporal good
brings always its measure of disappointment. Nowhere in time
is the good finally found. It is found, as the final good, only
in the eternal order.

"According to you," the objector had still insisted, "we please
God, and are ourselves pleased, in our union with God,—
and pleased too with ourselves, whatever we are." I respond,
God is pleased, if so you wish to express the fact, and we
too, in our union with God, are pleased, *with the eternal triumph of the good over the evil.* But this final satisfaction presupposes and includes just that dissatisfaction with evil, which
requires that every temporal evil deed shall meet its true adjustment to the good order through the deeds of atoning efficacy,
or, in general terms, through the presence of that Other which
every evil deed, when once seen as evil, demands. We are indeed pleased, in our union with God, in the eternal order, to
see that our own evil deeds have been overruled for good. But

just herein lies the essence of the moral order of the universe, viz. in that we, too, however we wander, come in eternity freely to our home.

"Yet your doctrine," the objector finally urged, "has still to face the ancient difficulty concerning the reconciliation of the divine foreknowledge and the free will of man." My response to this last objection is that, for our Idealism this ancient difficulty simply does not exist. We do not conceive that God, first preëxisting and foreknowing, then in time creates a world that is real beyond himself, and that, in time, is subsequent in its events to his preëxistent foreknowledge. For us, *God does not temporally foreknow anything, excepting in so far as he is expressed in us finite beings.* The knowledge that exists in time is the knowledge that finite Selves possess, in so far as they are finite. And no such foreknowledge can predict the special features of individual deeds precisely in so far as they are unique. Foreknowledge in time is possible only of the general, and of the causally predetermined, and not of the unique and the free. Hence neither God nor man can perfectly foreknow, at any temporal moment, what a free-will agent is yet to do. On the other hand, the Absolute *possesses a perfect knowledge at one glance of the whole of the temporal order, present, past, and future.* This knowledge is ill-called foreknowledge. It is eternal knowledge. And as there is an eternal knowledge of all individuality, and of all freedom, free acts are known as occurring like the chords in the musical succession, precisely when and how they actually occur.

So much then for the detail of our objector's arguments, so far as we here need recall them. His general principles have before been duly met. We conclude then, that our idealistic realm is a moral order, wherein any moral agent has his place, his task, his effectiveness, his freedom, and his individual worth, and has all these just by virtue of his unity with all Being, and with God. His acts are his own, even because God's Will is in him as the very heart of his freedom. And his deeds· are not indifferent to the whole universe, which wins through his free aid when he coöperates, and through the overruling of his caprice when he withstands. Yet it wins by regarding and including his freedom.

10 ⚘ THE STRUGGLE
WITH EVIL [1]

All finite life is a struggle with evil. Yet from the final point of view the Whole is good. The Temporal Order contains at no one moment anything that can satisfy. Yet the Eternal Order is perfect. We have all sinned, and come short of the glory of God. Yet in just our life, viewed in its entirety, the glory of God is completely manifest. These hard sayings are the deepest expressions of the essence of true religion. They are also the most inevitable outcome of philosophy. We have by this time laid the foundation for an understanding of the sense in which all these propositions are true. In doing so we have offered our principal contribution to the interests of Natural Religion. In the bare assertion of just these truths, that appear to our ordinary consciousness a stumbling-block and foolishness, the wisest of humanity, in India, in Greece, and in the history of Christian thought, are agreed. But the philosophical problem has always been to reconcile these doctrines with reason. An idealistic philosophy, when once understood, gives to all of them its own peculiar interpretation, but then makes them seem almost commonplaces.

Yet we have still further to develop and to illustrate, in the final stage of our argument, the precise way in which these central truths are to be held and applied. Nothing in philosophy appears more discouraging than any serious theoretical misstatement of the problem of evil. Yet nothing is more opposed to the interests of the awakened soul than to refuse every attempt to understand that problem in philosophical terms. In its purely ethical aspects this problem concerned us at the last time. In its more general relations we shall now finally consider its meaning and its bearing upon the great virtues of courage, endurance, resignation, and hope. Hereby we shall be led to the

[1] Josiah Royce, *The World and the Individual* (New York: The Macmillan Company 1899, 1901), Vol. II, Lecture IX, pp. 379–394, 405–411. —Editor's note.

view of the Union of God and Man which shall form the topic
of our concluding lecture.

I

In speaking of moral evil, at the last time, we assumed,
without special analysis, and as a result of ethical doctrine, the
meaning of the Ought, and the sense in which the conduct of a
moral agent is to be judged as good or as evil according as it
does or does not conform to the standard of the Ought. Upon
the present occasion, where I shall have to deal with the general problem of evil, we shall less depend upon the special doctrines of Ethics. We shall use a more general and simpler definition of evil, in terms of our Theory of Being,—a definition
which has repeatedly come to our notice. An evil is, in general,
a fact that sends us to some Other for its own justification, and
for the satisfaction of our will. This account of what it is to be
an evil, we have now repeatedly illustrated. The account, when
taken strictly, obviously applies, without exception, to every
finite fact, *quâ* finite, and especially to every fact in the temporal
order, when that fact is viewed in relation to its own future.
Any temporal fact, as such, is essentially more or less dissatisfy-
ing, and so evil. The only question, in this regard, about any
temporal event, is how great an evil it makes manifest to our
experience. But that in Time there is, for the will, no conscious
satisfaction, is a thesis that, according to our view, is the necessary correlative of the thesis that Time is the form of the will.
The future of our experience is that region to which, in our
finite dissatisfaction, we proceed, seeking therein our fuller expression. To say this is simply to affirm that Time possesses
the idealistic type of Being, and no other type. If one rejects,
as we do, any realistic account of Time, as of every other aspect of Being, one finds no other way than this to view the nature
of Time, or to define the relations of the present to the future.
For future time exists for me, in my finite capacity, either as
that to which I have a conscious relation, or as that to which
I have relations whereof I am just now unconscious. In the
latter sense, the future time when, for instance, I shall be
sleeping, or shall be dead, appears to me indeed at this moment, as a time whose order is to go on without any reference
to my will; and in so far, the law that every present has its

future, and that to every instant another succeeds, seems to be capable of a purely realistic interpretation. Time, when so viewed, is regarded as the fate of the world,—as the devourer, the destroyer, of whatever now is. But the reasons that led us to abandon Realism have long since led us to declare that our conscious and not our merely fatal relations to Time, are the ones that give us our only genuine glimpses of the true nature of the temporal order. And, thus interpreted, future time is that realm of Being in which my will is yet to be expressed, or in which the other finite wills that I view, through the social contrast, or through my knowledge of Nature, as contemporaneous with mine, are also yet to be expressed. But if our will is yet to be expressed, then it certainly is not yet fully expressed in our experience. And this means that our finite will is now dissatisfied. Our original idealistic formula here recurs. Were the will satisfied with its present expression in experience, the whole of Being would now be present. No Other would be or be conceived. There would be no future; for future time would have neither meaning nor place in Being. As it is, a brief abstract and epitome of every finite conscious life in the temporal world might be given in the words, "Dissatisfied with what now is, I press on towards what is yet to come."

It follows that dissatisfaction is the universal experience of every temporal being. How this dissatisfaction empirically appears, under what form, with what intensity,—this is a matter that the more concrete experience of life, taken in all its various aspects, has to decide. Vast ranges of finite ill, namely, those that are filled with physical suffering, have characters which we men are of course unable, at present, to explain in detail by any such abstract formula as the foregoing. Yet in those cases where our life is already largely under voluntary control, and where we are therefore more conscious of what life's meaning is, we are able ourselves more directly to observe that the conscious ills, which, in such cases, still beset our fortune, are in a large measure due to the very magnitude and ideality of our undertakings themselves, to the very loftiness of our purposes, and even to the very presence of our active control over our deeds. For all these more ideal aspects of our consciousness mean that we set our standard high, and strive beyond the present more ardently. And in such cases our ideals actually imply our present dissatisfaction, and so contribute to our consciousness of temporal ill. In such instances, too, we see that the principal defect

of these higher regions of our life is a defect of the very form
of our present consciousness, and of any consciousness which is
limited to some temporal present. For the type of consciousness
that we now possess, and any type of temporally limited consciousness, is too narrow for our higher purposes. It never can
contain what shall adequately and finally express our present
ideas. Hence the larger our ideals, the more we understand *why*
it is that nothing temporal can satisfy us.

On the other hand, it is indeed true that the abstract formula
just stated does not enable us to comprehend why, quite apart
from our consciousness of our ideals, sometimes pain over-
whelms, or sorrow besets, or fortune bears down heavily upon
us, while at other times the conscious course of the time-stream
appears relatively smooth, and we are even disposed, at some de-
luded moments, to say, with Othello, "My soul has found her
rest so absolute." I have no intention of using our merely general formula about temporal evil as a means for predicting or
for explaining in detail our special human experience of ill.
I admit at once that man's Selfhood is bound by the most manifold ties to the life of universal Nature. In consequence, man
constantly has fortunes that have no definite relations to his own
conscious ideals. Man echoes, in his passing experiences of good
and of ill, the fortunes, the interests, and the ideals of vast
realms of other conscious and finite life, whose dissatisfactions become, as it were, *per accidens,* part of each individual
man's life, even when the man concerned cannot himself, at
present, see how or why his own ideals, or what he takes to be
his own concerns, are directly such as to make these dissatisfactions his fate. And this is true, first, in so far as man,
the social being, echoes the joys and sorrows of his fellow-
men, without regard to whether he consciously knows how
these joys and sorrows stand related to his own ideal interests.
But this echoing of other finite life than ours extends, secondly,
as my hypothesis about Nature supposes, to all those relations
with the life of Nature upon which I earlier dwelt, when we
were stating our cosmological theory. Thus, for instance, our
organic pains, and our more instinctive emotions, have a depth
and a manifoldness that I should hypothetically explain, in
accordance with the theory of Nature earlier expounded, as
due to the fact that vast strivings,—expressing the Will of the
race rather than of the individual, and of Nature-Life in its
wholeness rather than of the life of any one man,—strivings,

that in themselves are conscious and ideal, are at any moment, in our narrow present consciousness, merely echoed and hinted, by many of our profounder, but less rational joys and sorrows, repugnances and attractions. According as these vaster interests that pervade the processes of Nature, and that constitute the various meanings of its temporal occurrences, become more or less indirectly represented in our conscious life, we have experiences of such joys, and of such griefs, of such successes and of such failures, as we ourselves cannot directly explain in ideal or conscious terms. In so far, our dissatisfactions are indeed not recognized by ourselves as due to the temporal non-fulfilment of our own plans; and, therefore, in precisely these cases, our fortunes seem unearned. And so, owing to the vast extent and to the complexity of these our relatively opaque relations to Nature, no one formula for the fortunes of life can possibly prove adequate to explain to ourselves, in our present form of consciousness, the wealth of our experiences of evil and of good, and the detail of these experiences.

And yet, apart from these endless complications, the abstract formula does hold good that all finite and temporal processes of will must inevitably involve dissatisfaction. And the truth is also verifiable that, in so far as we can consciously grasp the meaning of our own lives, we know why they not only are, but, in the temporal order, must be, and, I may add, *ought to be* unsatisfactory, just because our ideals are so much vaster than our present form of experience, with its brief present instants, can ever adequately express, and just because the realm of finite life to which we belong is full of ideal strivings, so that the whole creation, seeking its own fulfilment, groaneth and travaileth together in pain until now.

On the other hand, for our idealistic Theory of Being, this very presence of ill in the temporal order is the condition of the perfection of the eternal order. The most general reason why this is true we have now repeatedly stated. Simple Oneness is nothingness. Simple finality, apart from the process towards finality, is equally unintelligible. Attainment of a goal means a consciousness that a certain process wins its own completion. But this process is essentially a struggle towards the goal. Where there is the aim, there is also a consciousness that includes incompleteness, and that contrasts this with the completion of the very process which itself embodies the various stages of the aim. The only way to give our view of Being rationality is to see that we long for the Absolute only in so far as in us the Absolute also longs, and seeks, through our very temporal striving, the peace that is nowhere in Time, but only, and yet absolutely, in Eternity. Were there then no longing in Time, there would be no peace in Eternity. When the prayer is uttered that God's will may be done on earth as it is in heaven, we do well to remember that the meaning, which here appears in the form of a petition, is identical with what philosophy must report as a simple fact, directly implied by our Theory of Being. Were not God's Will in its totality, triumphant in the struggle that goes on upon the earth, it would never be done in heaven at all. For heaven, if taken as the name for a realm where the Absolute Will is directly expressed, means simply the Eternal Order in its wholeness. While earth, taken as a region where the same Will at each instant appears as yet struggling with evil, is nothing whatever but a portion or aspect of the Temporal Order. But, as we have seen, these two orders are not divided in their Being. Realism would have sundered them. We simply cannot. The Temporal Order, taken in its wholeness, is for us identical with the Eternal Order. There are, then, not two regions sundered in their Being, in one of which the divine Will reigns supreme, while in the other the success of the divine plan is essentially doubtful. These two realms of Being are merely the same realm, viewed in one aspect as a temporal succession, wherein the particular present Being of each passing instant is contrasted with the *no longer* and *not yet* of past and future, so that fulfilment never at one present instant is to be found; while, in the other aspect, this same realm is to be viewed, in its entirety, as one life-process completely present to the Absolute consciousness, precisely as the musical succession is present at a glance to whoever appreciates a phrase of the music.

II

Thus, in its most abstract aspect, we have before us our idealistic method of viewing the ills of fortune, just as, at the last time, in speaking of the Moral Order, we endeavored to set before ourselves the idealistic way of viewing the nature and place of moral ills. But herewith we are indeed led to dwell upon yet another aspect of the problem of evil. The two undertakings just mentioned are not to be sundered. Our former study here again concerns us. Every ill of human fortune, since for our view it must be regarded as the expression, in the temporal order, of some finite will, is not explicable merely in abstract terms as due to the general nature of temporal Being. For it is also, presumably, either directly due to the magnitude and ideality of our finite plans, or else is more or less directly the expression of the morally defective intent of some human or extra-human moral agent, or of the inadequacy of such an agent to his own ideals.

In regard to the question: Whence and by whose deed or defect came just this ill-fortune?—we have indeed seldom any right to venture upon any detailed speculations. For since the Internal Meaning of the processes of Nature is, in general, hidden from man, we do well, in considering our natural misfortunes, rather to observe how best to adjust our skill to the actual ways of Nature, than to waste our time in a practically vain blaming of unknown hostile agencies for their blind or intentional interference with the life of man. Man's practical business is with the direction of his own will to the service of God. And he does this most wholesomely when he least concerns himself with the misdeeds, if such there be, of extra-human finite agents. Not even in case of the consequences of human conduct is it wholesome to judge our fellows, except within the narrow range where the facts are inevitably known to us, or where our judgment can lead to the improvement of the conduct of our fellows. Still less is the search for the origin, and for the specific nature of what one might call, in traditional speech, the diabolical elements in the finite world at large, any profitable search for us mortals. The wise man contents himself, as far as possible, with the knowing, in general, that there is an indefinitely vast range of voluntary finite evil-doing which, in the temporal order, has to be endured, and for which atonement must be temporally rendered, in order that the divine will may be eternally accomplished.

On the other hand, it is indeed plain that the moral ill of any agent, when once it has to be recognized as such, is thereby seen at once to become the source of ill fortune to other finite moral agents. For just because this world is a moral order, we suffer together. Nor can it be wholly indifferent to any righteous man that his neighbor sins. In a sense the sin of every evil-doer amongst us taints all of us. For if I am a man, and if nothing human is alien to me, then, however much my individual free will may be set against any direct consent to the evil-doer's particular purpose, this my free will, by virtue of our very definition of individuality, is in no sense absolutely independent of the common human nature that I share with the sinner. All human sin is therefore indeed in some sense my own. It is at least my ill fortune, even where it is not at all my own individual choice. And in this sense every wise man, in contemplating sin and its consequences, in all cases where he must needs know of them, hears the echo of the word, *That art thou,* sounding in his own heart in a tone which is as tragic, as the assertion itself is here one-sided, but in its own partial measure, true, even for the saintliest of men. No man amongst us is wholly free from the consequences, or from the degradation, involved in the crimes of his less enlightened or less devoted neighbors; and the solidarity of mankind links the crimes of each to the sorrows of all.

Morally evil deeds, and the ill fortune of mankind, are thus inseparably linked aspects of the temporal order. To know this in the right sense is not to be predisposed to a hasty moral judgment of our fellows, nor to the wanton imputation of blame to agencies either human or extra-human; but it is rather to learn to judge our own life-task more seriously. Let an ill fortune come, in such wise that I myself can impute to my own free will no conscious share in provoking this ill fortune. In general, I shall then be entering upon a vain search, if I try, in my finitude, to discover whose guilt or whose defect it is, whereof I now suffer the consequences. Yet since the whole temporal order is the expression of will, and since even the processes of external Nature, for our own view, embody the intent of finite agents, whose life is linked to ours by ties to us at present mysterious, I can indeed say, in general, that all ill fortune results from the defects, or at least from the defective expression, of some finite will. This finite will is in general unknown to me. I do well not to trouble myself to impute blame. Yet presumably every such defect of finite will has, like our own defects, a genuinely moral significance. I am therefore right in holding that, when I suffer an ill fortune due to external natural agencies (however meaningless that ill fortune may appear to me), I am enduring a part of the burden of the world's struggle with temporal finitude, or with sin and with its consequences. Hence my endurance becomes, to my wiser view, no merely self-centred Stoicism, intended only to show my own powers, but a willingness to coöperate, whenever I can, in the divine task of giving meaning even to the seeming chaos of our present temporal experience. My willingness to bear hardness, as a good soldier, when I possess such willingness, is therefore never content to be merely passive, or to remain a mere matter of personal pride. I shall undertake to atone for the ill that the unknown agent has done, and so to show how even the seemingly accidental natural ill can be made an element in a life of significant devotion and of positive meaning. The soul of goodness in things evil I shall not merely assume, but shall try actively to find out, through my very effort either to coöperate in removing this natural ill, or so to face it, that I shall come to work all the more serviceably and loyally because of its very presence in my life.

On the other hand, when I inevitably am obliged to know *whose* sin it is whereof I endure the consequences when I suffer, I shall then remember, once for all, that all men are brothers, and that no man's fault can really be wholly indifferent to my Being; and I shall even rejoice, when I have the strength, that to me the opportunity is here given to join consciously in the common task of atoning for this sin.

Were I at this point a realist, I might no doubt rebel to find that my essentially independent moral entity had been, by ill fortune, somehow yoked by external and by arbitrary ties to my fellow's evil deeds, so that I seemed to myself to be dragging about with me the corpse of another man's crimes even while my deserts were wholly sundered from his. But I am no realist. I know that I have no Being whatever which can be sundered from the Being of my fellow-man. I know that I have moral individuality only in so far as I have my unique share in the identically common ideal task of endurance, and of seeking for the expression of the Eternal Will. My individuality is therefore parted by no chasm from my fellow's life. My responsibility, while not that of my fellow, is in no sense any absolutely independent fact in the universe, but is most intimately linked with my fellow's deeds and fortunes. I shall therefore indeed rejoice when, quite apart from any idle desire to impute blame, I become conscious of this, as of all other truth. And I do become conscious thereof whenever I am forced to observe that my sufferings are due to my fellow's misdeeds. I do not indeed rejoice that he did these evil deeds. But that wherein I rejoice is to have thus indicated to me the common human task of undertaking, in company with my fellows, to make good just this evil. I do not go out of my way to learn even this sort of truth. For it is, I repeat, not my human business to seek to impute blame, but to serve God however and whenever I can; and search for the source of an evil deed is in general an idle task, in a world where fortune constantly teaches me quite as much about such matters as I just now need to know. Yet to pry into the guilt of my neighbor is one matter; to rejoice that I have found a human office is quite another. And when the knowledge of my neighbor's fault is forced upon me through my own resulting misfortune, I rejoice, if I am wise, to discover at least one case where my share in the atoning work of our common humanity is clearly laid out before me.

But further, this knowledge of the intimate, although often to us so mysterious, relation of ill fortune and sin, renders especially serious my view of my own moral task. No sin of mine is wholly indifferent to my fellows. All future life is in some wise other because of my misdeeds, whether finite beings observe the fact or not. This our whole definition of Being necessarily implies. I constantly carry about with me a genuine, if in one sense strictly limited, responsibility for the whole world's fortunes; for what is deed to me is in some sense fortune for all other Selves. My visible sphere of action cannot then be so narrow that I am wholly without influence upon the whole realm of Being, and upon every region thereof. And thus the significance of my moral existence, however petty my apparent range of influence, and however limited in one sense my powers may be, extends, in another sense, without limit, through the whole range of the future temporal order. In brief, it is with your moral efficacy as with your physical efficacy when viewed in accordance with the ideal theory of gravitation. According to that theory, when you move, you move, however little, the whole earth and the sun and the stars.

And thus we have sketched, in general terms, our idealistic view of the solidarity of the moral order, and of the interrelation between evil doing and ill fortune. All that we have herewith asserted is in strict accord with the definite, but also limited, range that our foregoing lecture gave to the moral freedom of the Individual. Our doctrine of individuality demands that every Self shall be in some respect free. Our doctrine of the unity of Being implies that all Selves are known, without any true separation, in the organism of a single world life. And so far from there being any opposition between these two aspects of our idealistic realm, they are strictly reciprocal aspects. The one World and the free Individual imply each the other. For the proof and the significance of individuality are to be found, not in any independence and separateness of soul, but in the very fact that since the Absolute life is One, every region of this life has unique relations to the whole, while uniqueness of will and meaning imply everywhere a measure of finite freedom. On the other hand, the proof of the Absolute unity is statable only in terms of the principle that whatever is, is the final expression of the fully developed internal meaning of any finite idea; so that the Absolute is needed in order to give meaning to any Self, and no Self can be wholly independent of any other.

. . . . .

V

I return afresh to our own idealistic view. I state again its theses and their consequences,—but this time in a directly practical form.

I suffer. Why? In general because I am an agent whose will is not now completely expressed in a present conscious life. I seek in the Beyond my fulfilment. The higher my ideals, the more far-reaching my plans, the more I am full of the longing for perfection, the more there is in me of one kind of sorrow,—namely, of sorrow that my present temporal life is not yet what I mean it to be. Moreover, the narrowness of my present form of consciousness not only limits my ideal search for the fulfilment that I conceive in the future. It also sets bounds to my conscious retention of my former attainments. What I have won, I too often forget and forsake. My past is no longer mine, just because my consciousness is of such narrow span. I lose my own past, just as I struggle in vain to win what is still my future. Thus I am beset with temporal ill behind and before. The *no longer* and the *not yet* equally baffle me.

Now is there any good in all this essential, and, nevertheless, ideally colored, misfortune that besets the best deeds and meanings of my present form of consciousness? Yes. There is, indeed, one very great good. For in respect of this better aspect of my life, I suffer because of the very magnitude and the depth of my meanings. I am in ideal larger than my human experience permits me, in present fact, to become. My evil is the result of this my highest present good. Can I improve this my state of temporal ill? Yes, by every serious effort to live in better accord with my ideal. To be sure, there is no infallible rule for winning temporal good fortune; for my fortunes, and my actual power to attain my temporal goals, depend upon my infinitely complex natural relations with other life. No act of my finite individuality has created, or can transform, my temperament, my heredity, my environment, or can free me from the burden that I must cheerfully accept,—the burden of being this man, weighted with the presence of this organism, this inheritance of human sorrow and sin, this task in a world of cares. But one thing lies in my power. And that is, to be devoted to my life's task, namely, to the Eternal. For me the readiness is all. But I can be ready, ready to accept the dear sorrow of possessing ideals, and of taking my share of the divine task.

But in all this my own struggle with evil, wherein lies my comfort? I answer—my true comfort can never lie in my temporal attainment of my goal. For it is my first business, as a moral agent, and as a servant of God, to set before myself a goal that, in time, simply cannot be attained. Woe unto them that are at ease in Zion. Yes, woe unto them, for they are essentially self-contradictory in the blindness of their self-assertion. They assert that they win peace in their temporal doings; but temporal peace is a contradiction in terms. We approach such peace nearest of all when we have least of ideal significance in our consciousness. We attain it only in deep sleep, while the restlessly beating heart suggests that nature is even then dissatisfied with and in every present state of what men call our organism; but while we, as mere finite human individuals, will nothing, think nothing, and for just that time are nothing. Whoever is awake, is content with the present precisely in so far as the world means little to him. The more the world means, at any moment, to our consciousness, the more we go onward towards some goal. The more then are we discontent with the instant.

Our comfort cannot, therefore, be at once significant, and yet a matter of purely temporal experience. Wherein, then, can comfort truly be found? I reply, In the consciousness, first, that the ideal sorrows of our finitude are identically God's own sorrows, and have their purpose and meaning in the divine life as such significant sorrows; and in the assurance, secondly, that God's fulfilment in the eternal order—a fulfilment in which we too, as finally and eternally fulfilled individuals, share,— is to be won, not as the mystic supposed, without finitude and sorrow, but through the very bitterness of tribulation, and through overcoming the world. In being faithful to our task we, too, are temporally expressing the triumph whereby God overcomes in eternity the temporal world and its tribulations.

I say, our sorrows are identically God's own sorrows. This consequence flows directly from our Idealism. And we accept this consequence heartily. It contains the only ground for a genuine Theodicy. The Absolute knows all that we know, and knows it just as we know it. For not one instant can we suppose our finite experience first "absorbed" or "transmuted" and then reduced, in an ineffable fashion, to its unity in the divine life. The eternal fulfilment is not won by ignoring what we find present to ourselves when we sorrow, but by including this our experience of sorrow in a richer life. And, on the other hand, nothing in our life is external to the divine life. As the Absolute is identically our whole Will expressed, our experience brought to finality, our life individuated, so, on the other hand, we are the divine as it expresses itself here and now; and no item of what we are is other than an occurrence within the whole of the divine existence. In our more ideal sorrows we may become more clearly aware *how* our intention, our plan, our meaning, is one with the divine intent, and *how* our experience is a part of the life through which God wins in eternity his own. And the comfort of this clearer insight lies precisely here:—I sorrow. But the sorrow is not only mine. This same sorrow, just as it is for me, is God's sorrow. And yet, since my will is here also, and consciously, one with the divine Will, God who here, in me, aims at what I now temporally miss, not only possesses, in the eternal world, the goal after which I strive, but comes to possess it even through and because of my sorrow. Through this my tribulation the Absolute triumph, then, is won. Moreover, this triumph is also eternally mine. In the Absolute I am fulfilled. Yet my very fulfilment, and God's, implies, includes, demands, and therefore can transcend, this very sorrow.

For now, secondly, I assert, even in all this, that the divine fulfilment in eternity can be won only through the sorrows of time. For, as a fact, we ourselves, even in our finitude, know that the most significant perfections include, as a part of themselves, struggle, whereby opposing elements, set by this very struggle into contrast with one another, become clearly conscious. Such perfections also include suffering, because in the conquest over suffering all the nobler gifts of the Spirit, all the richer experiences of life, consist. As there is no courage without a dread included and transcended, so in the life of endurance there is no conscious heroism without the present tribulations in whose overcoming heroism consists. There is no consciousness of strength without the presence of that resistance which strength alone can master. Even love shows its glory as love only by its conquest over the doubts and estrangements, the absences and the misunderstandings, the griefs and the loneliness, that love glorifies with its light amidst all their tragedy. In a world where there was no such consciousness as death suggests to us mortals, love would never consciously know the wealth and the faithfulness of its own deathless meaning. Whoever has not at some time profoundly despaired, knows not the blessed agony of rising from despair and of being more than the demonic powers that are wrecking his life. Art, which in its own way often gives us our brief glimpses of the eternal order, delights to display to us all this dignity of sorrow. The experience of life, amidst all the chaos of our present form of consciousness, brings home to us this great truth that the perfection of the Spirit is a perfection through the including and transcending of sorrow,—and brings it home in a form that leaves us no doubt that unless God knows sorrow, he knows not the highest good, which consists in the overcoming of sorrow.

So much then for our sorrows, so far as they have to us, as we are, a consciously ideal meaning. But, you may say, much of sorrow, such as mere physical pain, and such as our more degrading ill fortune, has not this quality. To us as we are such sorrow seems in no wise ennobling. What comfort have we for ills that seem not to have, for our present consciousness, any ideal meaning? Do they link us with the divine? Do they help us onwards in the task of life? Do they not rather tend to drive us to forget our goals, and to lose sight of life's meaning? Can such sorrows thus be justified?

I have already, in substance, replied to this objection. Man, as he is, lives not only his more consciously ideal human life. Linked as he is to countless processes of nature, and of his fellows, he echoes, in his passing experiences, the sorrows of the world. He cannot now know the ideal meaning of the vast realms of finite life in whose fortunes he is at present mysteriously doomed to share. His comfort here lies in knowing that in all this life ideals are sought, and meanings temporally expressed,—with incompleteness at every instant, with the sorrow of finitude in every movement of the natural world, but with the assurance of the divine triumph in Eternity lighting up the whole.

In brief, then, nowhere in Time is perfection to be found. Our comfort lies in the knowledge of the Eternal. Strengthened by that knowledge, we can win the most enduring of temporal joys, the consciousness that makes us delight to share the world's grave glories and to take part in its divine sorrows,—sure that these sorrows are the means of the eternal triumph, and that these glories are the treasures of the house of God. When once this comfort comes home to us, we can run and not be weary, and walk and not faint. For our temporal life is the very expression of the eternal triumph.

11 ☼ THE UNION OF GOD AND MAN [1]

For better or for worse, the investigation to which our two series of lectures have been devoted now draws to its close. Our case has been presented. A theory of Being, itself founded upon an interpretation of human experience, has been applied to special problems, such as human life constantly offers to our notice. The result has been an outline of the basis of a Philosophy of Religion. We began our first series of lectures by stating our general problem as that of the World and the Individual,—of their nature and their relations. As we close, we are chiefly interested in that aspect of this problem which now, in view of the immediately preceding lectures, lies nearest to us; viz., the question as to the relations between God and Man.

I

Our account of the human Self has endeavored to be as just as our space permitted to the complexity, the temporal instability, and the natural dependence, of Man the finite being, when he is viewed in the context of the physical world. There is a sense in which man is a product of Nature, and in which his life is but one incident in a vast process of Evolution,—a process whose inner meaning in great part at present escapes us. We have tried to see the extent to which just this is true. There is also a sense in which man's life as a Self appears to be a mere series of relatively accidental experiences, and of shifting social contrast-effects. We have attempted to show how far this also is the case. There is a philosophical truth in saying, as tradition and common sense long ago said, that man is a prey of fortune,—that his life is a shadow, that all his essence seems insubstantial,

[1] Josiah Royce, *The World and the Individual* (New York: The Macmillan Company, 1899, 1901), Vol. II, Lecture X, pp. 415–452. The lecture is reprinted in its entirety.—Editor's note.

transient, and uncertain, and that, so far as you find law govern-
ing his life, it appears to the external observer to be a merely natural law, indifferent to the meanings and ideals that man himself most prizes. And to such truth also we have endeavored to
be just. But when we were led to emphasize all these limitations
of human nature, our interpretation of them was from the outset determined by the inevitable consequences of our general
theory of Being. None of these aspects of man's existence could
appear to us startling or strange, or even disappointing, because
we had long since learned in what sense, and in what sense only,
these very facts could possess any Being whatever. For in thinking of this world, where his natural place in the temporal order
is so insignificant, man finds that the very link which binds the
whole universe to this instant's knowledge is a link that predetermines what meaning the whole must itself possess, and consequently what meaning man's life, despite its apparent pettiness,
must illustrate.

To the individual man we have accordingly said: Conceive
yourself, in the light of your science, as this seeming plaything
of natural destiny. Know your frame. Remember not only that
you are dust, in the ancient sense of that word, but also that you
are in your inner life, in the way that psychological analysis has
now rendered familiar,—an insubstantial series of psychical conditions, physically and socially determined, precisely in so far
as such determination is possible,—a being whose nature has
only such permanence as may prove to be involved in the permanent meaning of those fleeting conditions themselves, in case
they indeed may possess any such meaning. View yourself as
an incident, or at best an episode, in the world-embracing process
of evolution. And then, when you have done all this, ask afresh
this one question: How can I know all these things? And how
can all these facts themselves possess any Being? You will find
that the only possible answer to your questions will take the
form of asserting, in the end, that you can know all this, and
that all this can be real, only by reason of an ontological relation
that, when rightly viewed, is seen to link yourself, even in all
your weakness, to the very life of God, and the whole universe
to the meaning of every Individual. In God you possess your individuality. Your very dependence is the condition of your freedom, and of your unique significance. The one lesson of our entire course has thus been the lesson of the unity of finite and of
infinite, of temporal dependence, and of eternal significance, of

the World and all its Individuals, of the One and the Many, of God and Man. Not only in spite, then, of our finite bondage, but because of what it means and implies, we are full of the presence and the freedom of God.

But now, emphasizing the especially human aspect of our ontology, and the especially ethical significance of our theoretical results, we must expound a little more fully some of these our characteristic theses. And the particular further task of this closing lecture must be to bring together the various threads of our argument, in so far as they bear upon the doctrine of the individual Self, and of the more practical aspects of this its union with God. We have laid our basis. Let us indicate some of the consequences of our theory.

II

And next, as to our whole definition of the nature of the Divine Life. If our foregoing argument has been sound, our Idealism especially undertakes to give a theory of the general place and of the significance of Personality in the Universe. Personality, to our view, is an essentially ethical category. A Person is a conscious being, whose life, temporally viewed, seeks its completion through deeds, while this same life, eternally viewed, consciously attains its perfection by means of the present knowledge of the whole of its temporal strivings. Now from our point of view, God is a Person. Temporally viewed, his life is that of the entire realm of consciousness in so far as, in its temporal efforts towards perfection, this consciousness of the universe passes from instant to instant of the temporal order, from act to act, from experience to experience, from stage to stage. Eternally viewed, however, God's life is the infinite whole that includes this endless temporal process, and that consciously surveys it as one life, God's own life. God is thus a Person, because, for our view, he is self-conscious, and because the Self of which he is conscious is a Self whose eternal perfection is attained through the totality of these ethically significant temporal strivings, these processes of evolution, these linked activities of finite Selves. We have long since ceased, indeed, to suppose that this theory means to view God's perfection, or his self-consciousness, as the temporal result of any process of evolution, or as an event occurring at the end of time, or at the end of any one process, however extended, that occurs in time. The melody does not come into existence contemporaneously with its own last note. Nor does the symphony come into full existence only when its last chord sounds. On the contrary, the melody is the whole, whereof the notes are but abstracted fragments; the symphony is the totality, to which the last chord contributes no more than does the first bar. And precisely so it is, as we have seen, with the relation between the temporal and the eternal order. God in his totality as the Absolute Being is conscious, not *in* time, but *of* time, and of all that infinite time contains. In time there follow, in their sequence, the chords of his endless symphony. For him is this whole symphony of life at once. Moreover there is indeed, for our doctrine, no temporal conclusion of the world's successive processes,—no one temporal goal of evolution,—no single temporal event to which the whole creation moves. For as, even in the finite symphony, every chord restlessly strives after a musical perfection that in itself it only hints, and that it does not yet finally contain, but as nevertheless this very perfection is in the whole symphony itself, viewed as a whole,—so, in the universe, every temporal instant contains a seeking after God's perfection. Yet never, at any instant of time, is this perfection attained. It is present only to the consciousness that views the infinite totality of this very process of seeking.

Such has been our doctrine concerning the divine life, when taken in its character as the life of the Absolute. That a conception of an endless temporal process which nevertheless constitutes one whole, present to one consciousness, is a possible conception, and that this conception is free from the self-contradictions which have usually been ascribed to the idea of the Infinite,—all this I have endeavored to show at length. But in consequence of this endlessness which I ascribe to the temporal order, and in consequence of the fact that no last event, no final occurrence in the sequence of the world's life, is to my mind possible, and in consequence of the wholeness of meaning which I nevertheless attribute to the divine consciousness itself, I am led to add here a word as to the general significance of historical progress, and of the evolutionary processes of the universe,—a word that will prove necessary for the purposes of this our concluding lecture.

At every instant, in the temporal order, God's will is in process of expressing itself. Now since this is true of every instant of time, it follows that every stage of the world-process, viewed as God views it, stands in an immediate relation to God's whole purpose. Hence there is, indeed, always progress in the universe in so far as at any instant some specific finite end is nearing or is winning its temporal attainment. Yet those are wrong who lay such stress upon the conception of progress as to assert that, in order for the world to attain a divine meaning at all, it is necessary to suppose whatever comes later in time to be in all respects better, or to be in every way nearer to God's perfection, than is what comes earlier in time. To make this assertion is to declare that in the divine order of the universe there is a Law of Universal Progress in time, so that all temporal things grow, by God's will, in all respects better as the world goes on. But our view does not make this assertion. Unquestionably, in the temporal order, if this is indeed, as we have asserted, a Moral Order, there is always in some respects Progress, because there is always a seeking of some new form and partial expression of Being, and a passing on towards such new forms and expressions. Moreover, as we have seen, there are new Ethical Individuals originating in time, and thenceforth adding their significance to the world's process. But if the temporal world thus always contains progress, it none the less obviously always involves, for any temporally limited conscious view, decay. Temporal progress, then, is only one aspect of the temporal order. For, as we pass on into our own future, we lose closer conscious touch with our own past. The growth of the man involves the death of his own childhood, with its special suggestions of divine beauty. The maturity of age means the loss of youth. For us mortals, every new temporal possession includes the irrevocable loss of former conscious possessions. Now this same tendency, as we have earlier seen, seems to hold true of all the irreversible process of universal Nature. For in Nature, too, nothing recurs. The broken china will not mend. The withered flowers bloom no more. The sun parts forever with its heat. Tidal friction irrevocably retards the revolution of the earth. And all these things, while they include the very conditions of progress, also involve decay.

In brief, it is, with the occurrences of the successive movements of time, or with the stages of life, precisely as it is with whatever else in the universe you learn to conceive as an individual fact. One finite individual, taken as such, never possesses the precise and unique perfections of its fellow, *i.e.*, of any other individual. Hence whenever you have to pass, in your finite experience, from a partial view of one individual fact to a similar view of another individual fact, you lose something as well as gain something; and of this truth you become more clearly aware the nearer you come to an insight into the true natures of the objects concerned. Nothing can really be spared from the whole, *i.e.,* from the universe. Hence every transition, such as we make in our finite experience, is a loss as well as a gain. No progress therefore is mere progress. Every growth is also a decay. Every attainment of temporal good is also the suffering of a temporal ill. And just that is what every mother observes when she learns to mourn because her children win the very maturity that she has all the while longed and striven to help them win. Just such is our experience too when we listen to music. In hearing the Heroic Symphony of Beethoven, how easily, during the Funeral March,—yes, even during the triumphant glories of the closing movement,—how easily, I say, may not the hearer wish himself back again in the midst of the striving life that the opening theme of the first movement introduces. Finite gain is also finite loss. This is the axiom of the temporal world, in so far as you view its events under the conditions of any finite span of conscious survey. Hence mere Progress,—Progress without any admixture of temporal decay and loss,—is not the law of the sequent events of the world.

On the other hand, in so far as any finite consciousness seeks, in its own future, a temporal goal that it has not yet won, and then approaches that goal,—for just this consciousness, in view of just this goal, there is indeed Progress. Now from our point of view, the general rationality of the world's temporal processes assures us that at all times there is, on the whole, and despite countless hindrances and evils, precisely this sort of attainment of significant goals occurring in the world. Hence Progress is, in one sense, but by no means in every sense, a fact always present in time. It is always present in the sense that at every moment of time some new and significant goal, that never before was attained, is approached by the finite agents whose will is just now in question. They seek new good, and, despite all evil, they always tend to win good, and always have some measure of success in striving intelligently for such good. On the other hand, Progress is not universal, if by universal Progress you mean a condition in which the temporal world should be in all essential respects better at any one moment than it ever was before. On the contrary, you can always say that in *some* respects the finite universe of any one temporal instant is worse than it ever was before, since it has irrevocably lost all those perfections that the past contained, and that now are sought for in vain, while with every new temporal instant of the world more and still more of such perfections become lost beyond recall in the past. For instance, Progress for mankind here on earth is not universal; for, remember, we have lost, beyond earthly human recall, the Greeks, and the constructive genius of a Shakespeare or of a Goethe; and these are, indeed, for us mortals, simply irreparable losses. Yet, on the other hand, Progress in a sense is universal for mankind; for daily civilization, retaining some of its ancient treasures, adds new ones; and, aiming at goods never yet won, attains them.

The one most essentially progressive aspect of the temporal order is that which is due to the appearance of new Ethical Individuals. For their perfections are additions to the world's stock of ideal goods; and they, as we shall see, do not pass away. Yet it has to be remembered that a new Ethical Individual, considered in any one temporal stage of his life, is not *merely* an added perfection, that the world never possessed before. He is *also* an added problem,—a new source of conflict and of often painful endeavor. Only from the eternal point of view is he finally viewed as a perfection. In time he may appear, for a long while, as a new evil.

Now, it is worth while to recall such considerations, simple as they are, whenever we are concerned to conceive the relation of Progress, or of that still more generally conceived realm of processes called Evolution, to the divine life. As a fact, all ages are present at once as elements in an infinite significant process to the divine insight. Every age therefore has, as the historian Ranke once said of the ages of human history, its "unmittelbare Beziehung auf die Gottheit." All things always work together for good from the divine point of view; and whoever can make this divine point of view in any sense his own, just in so far sees that they do so, despite the inevitable losses and sorrows of the temporal order.

I I I

So much, then, for some results of our general view of the divine Personality, and of the relation between the temporal and eternal aspects of its life. And now, in the next place, for our view of the human Person. Man, too, in our view, is a Person. He is not, indeed, an Absolute Person; for he needs his conscious contrast with his fellows, and with the whole of the rest of the universe, to constitute him what he is. He is, however, a conscious being, whose life, temporally viewed, seeks its completion through deeds. That from the eternal point of view this same life of the individual man, viewed as intentionally contrasted with the life of all the rest of the world, consciously attains its perfection by means of the knowledge of the whole of its temporal strivings,—this is, indeed, a corollary of our foregoing doctrine, a corollary which we have yet more precisely to develop. It is just this corollary which constitutes the basis of the philosophical theory of Immortality,—a theory which we have here briefly to characterize and to explain.

The human Self, as we earlier saw, is not a Thing, nor yet a Substance, but a Life with a Meaning. I, the individual, am what I am by virtue of the fact that my intention, my meaning, my task, my desire, my hope, my life, stand in contrast to those of any other individual. If I am any Reality whatever, then I am doing something that nobody else can do, and meaning something that nobody else can mean; and I have my relatively free will that nobody else can possess. The uniqueness of my meaning is the one essential fact about me.

But when with this consideration in mind we turn to ask about the relation of the human Self to Time, our first impression is that our doctrine gives no positive decision as to how long a temporal process is needed for the complete expression of the whole life and the entire meaning of any one human Self. And as a fact, if we take the term "Self" with reference to those varieties of meaning that before engaged our attention when we discussed the empirical Ego, we see at once that there is a sense in which what can be called a particular finite Ego gets its temporal expression, so far as you view that expression apart from the rest of the universe, only within some very limited portion of time. The Self, as we said, can be arbitrarily limited, if you will, to this instant's passing selfhood, taken as in contrast to all the rest of the universe of Being. The Self of this finite idea, of this passing thrill of Internal Meaning, is, indeed, if you choose so to regard it, something that, from God's point of view, and in its relation to God, is seen as a genuine Self,—an Individual. For, as we have from the outset observed, the Self of this instant's longing has its true and conscious relations to all the rest of the infinite realm of Being. We men are, indeed, just now not wholly conscious of the true individual meaning of even this passing moment. But in God this meaning becomes conscious.

For this instant has its twofold aspect, the temporal and the eternal. Viewed temporally, it is just something that now occurs, and that, seen as God sees it, has its own unique contrast with every other event in the universe, and that also is in so far no other event, and no other Self. Nowhere else in time will its precise contents recur. Viewed eternally, it finds the complete and individual expression of its whole meaning in God's entire life. In so far as it is conscious of its true relations to the divine, it is this unique prayer for the coming of the kingdom of heaven. And in the eternal wholeness of the divine life, this prayer is answered. Browning's wonderful little poem, *The Boy and the Angel,* well expresses this aspect of the twofold meaning of every instant of finite individuality. Here and now, and not merely elsewhere and in the far-off future, this instant's song of praise, this moment's search after God, is the temporal expression of a value that is unique, and that would be missed as a lost perfection of the eternal world if it were not known to God as just this finite striving. The temporal brevity of the instant is here no barrier to its eternal significance. And in so far, the lesson of our whole theory is that, when you are viewed as just this momentary Self, working here in the darkness of your finitude upon the task of your earthly life, you have not to endure temporally, for a long time, in order to be linked to God. In him you are even now at home. For you here mean, by every least act of service, infinitely more than you find presented to your human form of consciousness; and in God this meaning of yours, just as the true meaning of this temporal instant's deed, wins its eternal and self-conscious expression.

But now, of course, as we have long since seen, the Self of the single temporal instant is far from being the whole human Self as we rightly come to contrast that Self of the Individual with all the rest of the world. The whole human Self, as we have seen, is the Self of the unique life-plan. And this Self needs a temporally extended expression, which no single instant of our human experience contains. The Self thus viewed has a meaning that seeks unity with God only through the temporal attainment of goals in a series of successive deeds. And of course the Self, taken in this sense, is a far truer expression of what we mean by our individuality than is the Self of any one temporal instant. Yet here again the length of temporal expression that is required for the embodiment of any one type of finite individuality varies with the temporal significance of the ideal that may be in ques-

tion in defining the Self. A life-plan, in so far as it is conscious
only of brief temporal purposes, needs only a brief life to accomplish its little task. The Self that merely reads this lecture to
you, on the present occasion, is indeed, from the eternal point
of view, an individual. But it is so far an individual of limited
finite duration. The Self of the mere reader of this lecture has
no endurance beyond to-day. It is defined by a contrast with
the rest of the universe that is especially determined by the conditions of just this temporal academic appointment. Its particular
social contrast is with your present Selfhood as hearers. Its work
is done when the hour closes. Nowhere else, in time, has just
that individuality its task, its duty, its deed, or its expression. On
the other hand, the ethical continuity of just this selfhood with
the selfhood of other tasks, of former lectures, of the writing of
these lectures, and of my personal obligations to you and to the
University, is so essential a fact in my life, as I *ought* to view my
life, that here the sundering of one fragment of temporal processes from other processes seems especially arbitrary and useless. Yet, whenever we undertake any task, however transient its
temporal expression, that view of the union of God and Man,
of the Eternal and the Temporal, upon which our whole teaching here depends, requires us steadfastly to bear in mind that
every fragment of life, however arbitrarily it may be selected, has
indeed its twofold aspect. It is what it temporally is, in so far as
it is this linked series of events, present in experience, and somehow contrasted with all other events in the universe. It is what
it eternally is, by virtue of those relations which appear not
now, in our human form of consciousness, but which do appear,
from the divine point of view, as precisely the means of giving
their whole meaning to these transient deeds of ours. To view
even the selfhood that passes away, even the deeds of the hour,
as a service of God, and to regard the life of our most fragmentary selfhood as the divine life taking on human form,—this is
of the deepest essence of religion. From this point of view it is
indeed true that now, even through these passing deeds, we are
expressing what has at once its eternal and its uniquely individual Being. Here God's will shall be done as elsewhere in the temporal universe it can never again be done, and has never yet been
done:—so to resolve is to view our daily duty as our duty, and
this passing selfhood, even in its transiency, as possessing eternal meaning.

Yet not thus do we discover the adequate view of the relation of the Human Self to time. For the Ethical Self, as we have already seen, has its meaning defined in terms of an activity to which no temporal limits can be set without a confession of failure. When I aim to do my duty I aim to accomplish, not merely the unique, but such a service that I could never say, at any one temporal instant: "There is no more for me to accomplish; my work is done. I may rest forever." For that is of the very essence of Ethical Selfhood, namely, to press on to new tasks, to demand new opportunity for service, and to accept a new responsibility with every instant. It follows that the same considerations which imply the intimate union of every temporal instant's passing striving with the whole life of God, equally imply that an individual task which is ideal, which is unique, and which means the service of God in a series of deeds such as can never end without an essential failure of the task, can only be linked with God's life, and can only find its completion in this union with God, in an individual life which is the life of a conscious Self, and which is a deathless life. And thus at length we are led to the first formulation of our conception of human Immortality.

IV

As a fact, the sense in which the human Individual, taken in his wholeness, as one ethical Person amongst other Persons, is to be viewed as Immortal, may be more precisely defined, at the present stage of our inquiry, by means of three distinct yet closely linked considerations.

The first is a consideration founded upon our whole theory of the nature of Individuality, as we set forth that theory in defining the doctrine of Being.

We know Being from three sides. Whatever is, is something that in one aspect forms a content of experience. Nothing has a place in the realm of Reality which is not, in one aspect, something presented, found, verified, as a fact known to God, and given as a datum of the Absolute Experience. This is the first aspect of Reality. But secondly, nothing is real which is not also, in another aspect, an object conforming to a type,—an object possessing definable general characters, and embodying Thought,— an object expressive of the ideas that the Divine Wisdom contemplates. These two aspects of Being we studied at length in our foregoing series of lectures. But we found that these two aspects of Being are not the only ones. A third is not less essential, and is in fact the most significant of the three. What is real is not only a content of experience, and not only the embodiment of a type, but it is an individual content of experience, and the unique embodiment of a type. And we found, as the most essential result of our whole analysis of Being, that neither in terms of mere experience, which contains only contents immediately given, nor yet in terms of mere abstract thinking, which defines only general types, can the true nature of this third aspect of Being, viz. of the individuality of any given fact, be expressed or discovered. Individuality is a category of the satisfied Will. *This fact* is an individual fact only in so far as *no other* fact than this could meet the purpose that the world as a whole, and consequently every fact in the world, expresses. I can then never merely experience that *this fact* is unique, or that this individual is unique. Nor can I ever merely, by abstract thinking, define what there is about the type of *this fact* which demands that it should be unique, or should be an individual at all. In so far then as I merely feel the presence of contents of experience, I can postulate that they stand for or hint the existence of individuals. But as mere observer I never empirically find that this is so. In so far as, once having thus felt the presence of facts of experience, I proceed, as for instance in my study of science, to describe the types and the laws of these contents of my experience, I can once more postulate that I am indeed thinking about realities which, in themselves, are individual. But I can never discover, by my thinking process taken as such, what constitutes their individuality. When I become aware of the presence of one of my fellow-beings, I never either feel or abstractly conceive why this being is such that no other can take his place in Being. For if I observe how he looks and acts, I so far do not observe in him any reason why another might not look and act precisely as he does. And if I proceed abstractly to conceive the fashions and laws of his behavior, I expressly define only general types. It is precisely the *no other* character, the uniqueness, of this individual, the character whereby he is this man and nobody else, which neither my observation nor my description of my fellow can compass.

Hence, as we long since saw, for us, creatures of fragmentary consciousness, and of dissatisfied will, as we here in the temporal order are, the individuality of all things remains a postulate, constitutes for us the central mystery of Being, and is rather the object that our exclusive affections seek, that our ethical con-

sciousness demands, that love presupposes, than any object which
we in our finitude ever attain. Now this, our relation to the true
individuality of the beings of our whole world, holds as well in
case of the Self of each one of us, as of the remotest star or of
God himself. The individual is real; but under our finite conditions of dissatisfied longing, the individual is never found.

Just here, however, lies the first of the three considerations
whereby our general theory of Being has a bearing upon the
doctrine of Immortality. The Self, however you take it,—
whether as the Self of this instant's longing, or the Self of any
temporal series of deeds and of experiences, is in itself real. It
possesses individuality. And it possesses this individuality, as
we have seen, in God and for God. In its relation, namely,
to the whole universe of experiences and of deeds, this Self
occupies its real and unique place as such that no other can take
that place, or can accomplish that task, or can fulfil that aim.
Now the consciousness which faces the true individuality of
this Self is, by our whole hypothesis, continuous with, and
directly one with, the finite and fragmentary consciousness that
the Self possesses of its own present life. The Self can say: "As
human Self, here and now in time, I know not consciously
what my own individuality is, or what I really am. But God
knows. And now God knows this not in so far as he is another
than myself, *i.e.*, another individual than the Self that I am.
He knows me in so far as, in the eternal world, in my final
union with him, I know myself as real. In him, namely, and as
sharing in his perfect Will, my will comes consciously to find
wherein lies precisely what satisfies my will, and so makes my
life, this unique life, distinct from all other lives. Here, now,
in the human form, my life so imperfectly expresses for my
present consciousness, my will, that I indeed intend to stand in
contrast to all other individuals, and to be unique; but still find,
in my finite dissatisfaction, that I am not here aware *how* my
will wins its unique expression. But in God's Will, and as
united to him, my will does win this unique expression. What
is, however, in the idealistic world, is somewhere known. The
knowing, however, that my will wins unique expression in my
life, and in my life as distinct from all other individual lives,
is, *ipso facto*, my individual and conscious knowing. Hence in
God, in the eternal world, and in unity, yet in contrast with all
other individual lives, my own Self, whose consciousness is
here so flickering, attains an insight into my own reality and
uniqueness."

The inevitable consequence is that every Self, in the eternal world, wins a consciousness of its own individual meaning, by virtue of the very fact that it sees itself as this unique individual, at one with God's whole life, and fulfilling his Will through its own unique share in that Will. However mysterious our individuality is here, in our temporally present consciousness, we, in the eternal world, are aware of what our individuality is. We ourselves, and not merely other individuals, become, in God, conscious of what we are, because, in God, we become aware of how our wills are fulfilled through our union with him, and of how his Will wins its satisfaction only by virtue of our unique share in the whole. "I shall be satisfied," the finite and dissatisfied will may indeed say, "when I awake in thy likeness." And in our union with God, we are, in the eternal world, awake. [2]

So far, however, we make a statement of the conscious aspect of our union with God,—a statement that, in its reference to the temporal endurance of the Self, appears still ambiguous. What we so far assert is that, in God, every individual Self, however insignificant its temporal endurance may seem, eternally possesses a form of consciousness that is wholly other than this our present flickering form of mortal consciousness. And now, precisely such an assertion is indeed the beginning of a philosophical conception of Immortality. In brief, so far, we assert that individuality is real, and belongs to all our life, but that individuality does not appear to us as real individuality in our present human form of consciousness. We accordingly assert that our life, as hid from us now, in the life of God, has another form of consciousness than the one which we now possess; so that while now we see through a glass darkly, in God we know even as we are known. This doctrine, as we shall soon find, implies far more regarding the temporal endurance of the Self than we have yet made wholly manifest.

V

But now this first consideration may be supplemented by a second. By the arbitrary selection, and isolation, of any one finite

---

[2] To the development of the aspect of the problem of Immortality that has here been summarized I have devoted my Ingersoll Lecture on the *Conception of Immortality*, published in 1900.

Internal Meaning, you can, as we have said, regard any temporally brief series of conscious finite ideas as a Self. And so regarded, this arbitrarily selected Self appears as implying, so far, no long continuance. It dies with its own moment, or hour, or year, or age, of the world's history. We have indeed just seen that in order to be at all, however transiently, such a Self has to be an individual fact in the realm of Being, and that, as an individual, it is inevitably linked in God with a form of self-consciousness in which its own life and meaning and place in the universe become manifest to it as its own. Even such a Self, then, possesses, in the eternal world, a form of consciousness far transcending that of our present human type of momentary insight. In your eternal union with God you see what even your present life and purposes mean; and they mean, even as they are, infinitely more than your human type of consciousness makes manifest to yourself. But there is, indeed, another aspect of even your most transient life as a changing and apparently passing Self. And this aspect comes to light when you ask in what way, and in what sense, any finite Self can come to a temporal end, can die, can cease to be. A very neglected problem of applied metaphysics here awaits our treatment. In our seventh lecture of the present series we touched upon it briefly in speaking of the selective process in nature and in conscious life. It recurs here in another form.

This problem is the one of the very Possibility of Death. The statement of the problem in these terms may surprise. Yet what is our whole metaphysical inquiry but a seeking to comprehend the possibility of even the most commonplace facts? That death occurs, we know. What death is, common sense cannot tell us. I propose to take up the question here in its most general form, and as a question of metaphysics. The physical death of a man is but a special case of the law of the universal transiency of all temporal facts. We have studied that law, in former lectures, in several aspects. The most universal law of Nature we found to be that of the constant occurrence of events that, once past, are irrevocable. We found that the most general reason for this irrevocableness of every temporal event is simply the individual character of that event as a real fact. What once has occurred can never occur again, simply because whatever is real is individual, is unique, and therefore, in its individuality, is incapable of repetition elsewhere in the world than precisely where it occurs. The very reason that makes us often regard the past as dead beyond recall is then the fact, presupposed, but never experienced by us in our finite capacity, namely, the fact that the past is a realm where unique and individual occurrences have found their place. Because all temporal happenings, or real events, are incapable of being twice present in the world, therefore new times must always bring new happenings; and what has once taken place returns not. In this sense, in the temporal world, individuality and transiency are intimately linked aspects of the universe.

In dealing with the problem of time, we have therefore already dealt, in a sense, with the general problem that underlies this whole question about death. But here we indeed undertake this problem in a more concrete form. In a sense, indeed, the life of every temporal instant dies with that instant, yet what interests us at present is the fact of the temporal termination, not of any and every instant's life, but of certain significant series of life-processes, whose continuance from moment to moment, from year to year, from age to age, we indeed often desire, or regard even as necessary, if our human world is to win for us any adequate meaning, while nevertheless, as a fact, these processes prove to be, from our human point of view, of limited duration. Thus springtime dies, youth passes away, love loses its own; evolution, as we have just seen, goes hand in hand with decay; and above all, the lives of human individuals meet with a termination in physical death,—a termination which is, from our point of view, so meaningless and irrational that it stands as the one classic instance of the might of fate, and of the apparently hopeless bondage of our human form of existence.

And now, taking these concrete instances of death in our temporal world, and viewing them as peculiarly impressive and pathetic examples of temporal transiency, I once more ask, How, from our idealistic point of view, is such death possible at all as a real event? Here is a finite fragment of life,—I care not what it is, so long as it shall possess, for our present human purposes, some deep internal meaning. It may be the life of a mother's love for her infant; it may be the life of two lovers, dreaming of a supernatural happiness; it may be the enthusiasm that inspires a soldier's devotion for his flag, or an artist's longing for his ideal; or finally, it may be the whole personal human life of a hero, of a statesman, or of a saint. Now the law of our human realm of experience is that any such life some day, so far as we can see, comes to an end, and is lost beyond human recall. The mother's love for the present infant becomes a dear memory, while the infant, perhaps, grows into an evil and pain-inspiring maturity. The lovers part, or perhaps forget. Fate of all sorts cuts short, sooner or later, the soldier's, the artist's, the hero's, the saint's activities. Now in all such cases, whether or no what we call physical death intervenes, the same essential problem appears. This is the problem of death in a concrete, but still generalized form. Something with a meaning comes to an end *before* that meaning is worked out to its completion, or is expressed with its intended individual wholeness. The problem presented by such cases is not to be answered by the purely general statement, already made, —the statement that everything temporal is transient, and that only the eternal whole passes not away. That most general statement, by virtue of our theory of the temporal order, does indeed point out that the eternal perfection of the world of the divine Will can only be expressed in a realm of temporal deeds, each one of which, as temporal, is transient, and, as an individual deed, is irrevocable. But what now is our problem is furnished by those series of events in which something individual is attempted, but is, within our ken, never finished at all. We ask about the death which does not apparently result from the mere nature of the time-process, from the mere necessity that every finite and individual event should occupy its one place in the temporal realm. No, the death which here concerns us is the ending that seems to defeat all the higher types of individual striving known to us. And now, we state this problem, as idealists, thus, How can such death as this have any place at all in Being?

Our clew to the answer is, however, furnished to us by our whole Theory of Being. A realist would not venture to raise our question, if once he recognized the fact of death as a real fact at all. For him, death would be an independently real fact; and of no such fact could he consistently ask the reason. A mystic would indeed not leave unanswered our problem. He would reply, "Death is an illusion." But then, for the mystic, *all* is illusion. A critical rationalist would simply say: "It is the valid law of Being. All finite things pass away." But we, as idealists, have another task whenever we attribute Being to any object. For us, to be means to fulfil a purpose. If death is real at all, it is real only in so far as it fulfils a purpose. But now, what purpose can be fulfilled by the ending of a life whose purpose is so far unfulfilled? I answer at once, the purpose that can be fulfilled by the ending of such a life is necessarily a purpose that, in the eternal world, *is consciously known and seen as continuous with, yes, as inclusive of, the very purpose whose fulfilment the temporal death seems to cut short.* This larger purpose may indeed involve, as we have long since seen, the relative inhibition and defeat of the lesser purpose. But in our idealistic world it cannot involve the mere *ignoring* of that lesser purpose. The thwarting of the lesser purpose is always included within the fulfilment of the larger and more integral purpose. The possibility of death depends upon the transcending of death through a life that is richer and more conscious than is the life which death cuts short, and the richer life in question is, in meaning, if not in temporal sequence, continuous with the very life that death interrupts.

Or, to put the case otherwise: A conscious process, with a meaning, but with a meaning still imperfectly expressed, is cut short, and left with its purpose still disembodied. So far we have a fact, namely, the fact of death, but so characterized that its Being is stated in merely negative terms. We, as idealists, ask, What is this death? If real, it is a positive fact; it is not something merely negative. But what positive fact? For us, all facts are known facts, are facts of consciousness and ultimately of the consciousness of the Absolute. The defeated purpose is such only in so far as it is known, and then is known as terminated. But is known, I insist, by whom? In terms of what individual conscious life does even the Absolute know of the finite life that has ended? I answer, the defeated purpose is known by some conscious being who can say: "This was my purpose, but temporally I no longer seek its embodiment. I have abandoned it. It is no longer a purpose of my life." The life that is ended is thus viewed by the Absolute as followed, at some period of time, by another life that in its meaning is continuous with the first. This new life it is which says, "No longer is that terminated purpose pursued by me." But now, in our world, where only the fulfilment of purpose has any Being whatever, the new consciousness, in and for which the old life is terminated, must say, "That ceasing of my former purpose, that ending of my past life, has its meaning; and this meaning is continuous with my own larger meaning. My former Self is dead, only in so far as my new Self sees the meaning of that death." Or in other words, the new Self is really inclusive of and able to transcend the meaning of the old Self; or, in fact, the two Selves really form stages in the development of one Individual. Thus from our point of view, even the selective process which we before studied in Nature is a process involving survival as well as death.

Not otherwise, in our idealistic world, is death possible. I can temporally die; but I myself, as larger individual, in the eternal world, see *why* I die; and thus, in essence, my whole individuality is continuous in true meaning with the individuality that dies. The lovers may part, but in the eternal world, individuality that is temporally sequent to theirs, and continuous in meaning with theirs, is found as consciously knowing why they parted. Was it faithlessness? Then it was sin; and in the eternal world, this larger individuality is found viewing the parting as their fault, for which, as for all sin, atoning deeds are needed. Was it wisdom that they should part? Then, in the eternal world the sorrow of their parting is continuous with a willing bearing of this parting, as one of time's sorrows. It is so with the mother's loss of the infant, or with the hero's or artist's pursuit of his ideal. It is so too with physical death. How, and in what way, the deathless individuality sees itself as including and fulfilling the selfhood whose struggles death terminates, we do not in any detail at present know. That this larger selfhood is in the end in unity with the divine Selfhood we know; but we know too that it is not as something lost in God, that the dead Self of our human life wins its unity with the divine. For our theory implies that when I die, my death is possible as a real fact only in so far as, in the eternal world, at some time after death, an individual lives who consciously says: "It was my life that there temporally terminated unfinished, its meaning not embodied in its experience. But I now, in my higher Self-expression, see why and how this was so; and in God I attain, otherwise, my fulfilment and my peace."

The Possibility of Death, as a metaphysical fact, in a world where all facts are facts of consciousness, and where even the worst sorrows and defeats exist only as partial expressions of a divine meaning, depends, then, upon the deeper fact that whoever dies with his meanings unexpressed, lives, as individual, to see, in the eternal world, just his unique meaning finally expressed, in a life sequent to, although not necessarily temporally continuous with, the life that death terminated. I shall finally die, in time, only when I come to say to myself, "My work is consciously and absolutely accomplished."

V I

But this brings us to our third consideration, which, in fact, has been already expressed in our former words, both in this and in foregoing lectures. An ethical task is essentially one of which I can never say, "My work is finished." Special tasks come to an end. The work of offering my unique service, as this Individual, to God and to my fellows, can never be finished in any time, however great. For always, at any future moment, if I know my union with God, I shall know, whatever my form of consciousness, that there are my fellows beyond me, different from myself, and yet linked by the ties of the divine unity to my life and my destiny. I shall know then that I have not yet accomplished all of the relations to them which my ethical tasks involve. To be an ethical individual is to live a life with one goal, but contrasted with all other lives. Every deed emphasizes the contrast, and so gives opportunity for new deeds. A consciously last moral task is a contradiction in terms. For whenever I act, I create a new situation in the world's life, a situation that never before was, and that never can recur. It is of the essence of the moral law to demand, however, that whenever a new deed of service is possible, I should undertake to do it. But a new deed is possible whenever my world is in a new situation. My moral tasks spring afresh into life whenever I seek to terminate it. To serve God is to create new opportunities for service. My human form of consciousness is indeed doubtless a transient incident of my immortal life. Not thus haltingly, not thus blindly, not thus darkly and ignorantly, shall I always labor. But the service of the eternal is an essentially endless service. There can be no last moral deed.

And thus, in three ways, our union with God implies an immortal and individual life. For first, in God, we are real individuals, and really conscious Selves,—a fact which neither human thought nor human experience, nor yet any aspect of our present form of consciousness, can make present and obvious to our consciousness, as now it is. But since this very fact of our eternal and individual Selfhood is real as a conscious fact, in God, we too, in him, are conscious of our individuality in a form higher than that now accessible to us. And secondly, the death of an individual is a possible fact, in an idealistic world, only in case such death occurs as an incident in the life of a larger individual, whose existence as this Self and no other, in its individual contrast with the rest of the world, is continuous in meaning with the individuality that death cuts short. No Self, then, can end until itself consciously declares, "My work is done, here I cease." But, thirdly, no ethical Self, in its union with God, can ever view its task as accomplished, or its work as done, or its individuality as ceasing to seek, in God, a temporal future. In Eternity all is done, and we too rest from our labors. In Time there is no end to the individual ethical task.

VII

But now these considerations lead us, in our closing words, to dwell briefly upon an aspect of the life of the Ethical Individual which has grown more and more obvious as we have proceeded.

We have often spoken of the Human Individual as a finite being. In the temporal order, he everywhere remains so; for he has a temporal beginning; and at any moment of time he has so far lived but for a finite period, has so far accomplished but a finite task, and seeks, as one whose life is unfinished, his own temporal future, which is not yet. The same can be said of any temporal being, of whatever degree of dignity or of wisdom, whose life is considered from any period of time onwards, and up to any point of time. But now what of the completed Self, of the Ethical Individual, as it comes consciously to distinguish itself from all others, in the eternal world, and as it finds itself fully expressed in its own unique aspect of the life of the Absolute? Is it still to be called a finite Self?

The plain answer of course is that, as the complete expression of a Self-representative System of purpose and fulfilment, it is there, viz. in the eternal world, no longer finite, but infinite. Yet it differs from the Absolute Self in being *partial,* in requiring the other individuals as its own supplement, and in distinguishing itself from them in such wise as to make their purposes not wholly and in every sense its own. It is, as Spinoza would have said of his divine attributes, "infinite in its own kind"; only that, to be sure, its existence is not independent of that of the other Individuals, as the Spinozistic attributes were independent of one another. For it is not related to these other selves *merely* through the common relation to God; on the contrary, it is just as truly related to God *by means of* its relation to them. Its life with them is an eternally fulfilled social life, and the completion of this eternal order also means the self-conscious expression of God, the Individual of Individuals, who dwells in all, as they in him.

There is needed a convenient term for expressing the nature of an individual being which, although "infinite in its own kind" (that is, infinite as a complete expression of its own self-representative purpose), is still essentially but a part of a larger system, involving still other purposes and beings. The word "finite" suggests, indeed, the character of *needing a relatively external Other.* In *this* sense, however, it remains certainly true that the Ethical Individual profoundly needs, in the eternal world, as its Other, without which it can neither be nor be conceived, the universe of the other Ethical Individuals. And it needs them not merely as parts of itself, but as its comrades. If then the term "finite" could be used without ambiguity in this special sense, one could indeed say that in contrast with the Absolute Individual, who is the sole *completely integrated* Self, the single Ethical Individual remains finite, since it is, even in the eternal world, essentially dependent, even for the expression of its own will, upon the other Individuals beyond itself, in contrast with whom it defines itself. But since the word "finite" is, with technical accuracy, used for systems that are *not* self-representative in type, the best way is not to attempt any unauthorized use of the term, but to characterize the eternal ethical Individual as *infinite but partial.* Its fellows, in the self-conscious organism of the Absolute, are, as we have seen, infinite in number, since the Absolute must possess an infinite wealth of self-representation. On the other hand, the various individual Selves may, and in an infinite number of cases *must,* as the various self-expressions of the same system, interpenetrate in the most manifold ways, sharing in countless instances the same immediate contents of experience, even while viewing these contents in different orders, and as the expressions of different, although interrelated, individual life-purposes. The possibility, and in fact the necessity, of some such structure, in the completed self-representative system, we discussed, in a very inadequate fashion, in our Supplementary Essay.[3] Had we time here to illustrate the complications which the recent in-

---

[3] p. 517, *sqq.,* p. 546, of the former series.

vestigations of self-representative systems have shown to be characteristic of their structure, we should see clearly that, although the world of the Absolute Individual is, from our point of view, an individual selection from an infinitely wealthy realm of unrealized possibilities, its internal structure, in order that it should be self-representative at all, must involve the sort of formal complexity here suggested, and must therefore make inevitable that interpenetration of the lives of countless and various Selves which our own theory of the origin and social nature of the ethical Self demands. It is this interpenetration, in various ways and degrees, of the lives of the completed Selves in the eternal world which, according to our hypothesis concerning Nature, would presumably be manifested, in a phenomenal way, in the temporal world, by the processes of intercommunication amongst the various members of any social order, or amongst what to us seem widely sundered regions of Nature. For according to our hypothesis, no actual relations of various minds are merely external and mechanically determined; but all are due to the fact that every Self, representing in its own way the Absolute, represents also other Selves in a way and order that may, in the temporal world, appear to any extent as a process whose individual instances are determined by special physical conditions.

The *infinity* and the accompanying *partial* character of each Ethical Individual suggests, however, still one more consideration that older theological doctrines have very generally failed to recognize as a possibility. Yet the modern theory of Infinite Assemblages makes it almost a commonplace of exact thinking, when once any system has been recognized as infinitely complex in structure, to take note of this consideration in dealing with such a system.

To an infinite collection of objects, as we saw in the Supplementary Essay, *the axiom that the part cannot be equal to the whole does not apply.* There is a perfectly definite sense [4] in which a part of an infinitely complex system can remain, not only a part that excludes from itself *some* portion of the whole, but a part that is only one of an infinite number of mutually

---

[4] See, concerning the mathematical consideration here in question, the recent reports of Schönfliess: "Die Entwickelung der Lehre von den Punktmannigfaltigkeiten," in the *Jahresbericht der deutschen Mathematiker-Vereinigung,* Bd. VIII, Heft II, in particular, p. 4, *sq.,* p. 10, *sqq.,* and p. 18, *sqq.*

exclusive parts of this whole. Thus, to give a purely formal instance of what I here have in mind, let me ask you to consider the whole numbers. Amongst the whole numbers you can select at pleasure a relatively very small sub-class, or *part;* viz., *those whole numbers which are powers of* 2, that is, 2 itself, as the *first* power, the *square* of 2, the *cube* of 2, and so on. You can then select *another* part; viz., *the whole numbers which are powers of* 3; and a third part; viz., *those which are powers of* 5. You can suppose this process of selection carried on so that each one of the demonstrably infinite collection of prime numbers, 2, 3, 5, 7, 11, 13, etc., shall form the basis of a selection of a partial collection of whole numbers, viz. its own powers. Thus the powers of 7, of 11, of 13, and so on, would form a system of collections of whole numbers. Now consider these resulting *partial collections of whole numbers.* Each collection is *precisely as infinite* as the entire series of whole numbers. For 2, or 3, or 5, or whatever other prime number you have taken, has a *first* power, a *second* power, a *third* power, and so on without end. For every whole number defines a new power of the prime numbers in question. Each of the partial collections of whole numbers thus defined has, in consequence, one number to correspond to *every whole number* without exception, namely, its first number, its second, its third, and so on without end. And yet no two of these partial collections contain *any* whole numbers in common; for no power of any prime number is equal to any power of another prime number. All of the partial collections contain nothing, however, *but* whole numbers; and there are an infinity of these infinite partial collections, although each of them is, in its own internal complication, precisely equal to the whole from which they are all alike selected. Nor do even they, if taken together, in the least exhaust the original collection of whole numbers; since there are countless equally infinite collections of whole numbers which are *not* powers of any prime number, but which are products of various powers of prime numbers. And so we can define an infinite system such that it contains an infinity of mutually exclusive parts, while each of these parts is equal to the whole in internal complexity of structure, and in the multitude of its own parts.

This instance, taken by itself, is formal and seemingly trivial. It assumes metaphysical importance, however, as soon as you remember that, from our point of view, the infinity of the real system of the Self, whether in case of the Ethical Individual, or in case of the Absolute, is an actual, and, in the eternal world, a completed infinity. We see then that, from our point of view, the Ethical Individual, however small a part of the infinite System of Individuals he may be, yet may be conceived as strictly equal in infinity of structure and of variety of content to the Absolute, having a series of experiences precisely as rich in its details, a knowledge precisely as multitudinous, a meaning precisely as complex, as the Absolute Self in its wholeness. Yet the Ethical Individual may be none the less *only* a part,—*only* one of an infinite number of equally partial Individuals, whose lives, to be sure, are not in every respect mutually exclusive, but who are not at all confounded either with one another or with the Absolute in its wholeness.

We therefore *need not conceive the eternal Ethical Individual, however partial he may be, as in any sense less in the grade of complication of his activity or in the multitude of his acts of will than is the Absolute.* And thus we see, in a new way, how the individual Self may recognize that in God it finds its own fulfilment, while still it clearly distinguishes other Selves, within the Absolute, as in one sense beyond it. It may be conceived then as a Part equal to the Whole, and finally united, as such equal, to the Whole wherein it dwells.

—But we must turn from the eternal back to our temporal world. The special, the very finite, and imperfect task of these lectures is indeed accomplished. We have dealt with the nature of God, with the origin and meaning of man's life, and with the union of God and Man. Our result is this:—Despite God's absolute unity, we, as individuals, preserve and attain our unique lives and meanings, and are not lost in the very life that sustains us, and that needs us as its own expression. This life is real through us all; and we are real through our union with that life. Close is our touch with the eternal. Boundless is the meaning of our nature. Its mysteries baffle our present science, and escape our present experience; but they need not blind our eyes to the central unity of Being, nor make us feel lost in a realm where all the wanderings of time mean the process whereby is discovered the homeland of Eternity.

PART III

SELECTIONS FROM

The Philosophy
of Loyalty

12 ❧ THE NATURE AND THE NEED OF LOYALTY [1]

One of the most familiar traits of our time is the tendency to revise tradition, to reconsider the foundations of old beliefs, and sometimes mercilessly to destroy what once seemed indispensable. This disposition, as we all know, is especially prominent in the realms of social theory and of religious belief. But even the exact sciences do not escape from the influence of those who are fond of the reëxamination of dogmas. And the modern tendency in question has, of late years, been very notable in the field of Ethics. Conventional morality has been required, in company with religion, and also in company with exact science, to endure the fire of criticism. And although, in all ages, the moral law has indeed been exposed to the assaults of the wayward, the peculiar moral situation of our time is this, that it is no longer either the flippant or the vicious who are the most pronounced or the most dangerous opponents of our moral traditions. Devoted reformers, earnest public servants, ardent prophets of a coming spiritual order,—all these types of lovers of humanity are represented amongst those who to-day demand great and deep changes in the moral standards by which our lives are to be governed. We have become accustomed, during the past few generations,—during the period of Socialism and of Individualism, of Karl Marx, of Henry George, of Ibsen, of Nietzsche, of Tolstoi,—to hear unquestionably sincere lovers of humanity sometimes declaring our traditions regarding the rights of property to be immoral, and sometimes assailing, in the name of virtue, our present family ties as essentially unworthy of the highest ideals. Individualism itself, in many rebellious forms, we often find asserting that it speaks in the name of the true morality of the future. And the movement begun in Germany by Nietzsche—the tendency towards what that philosophical rhapsodist called the "transmutation

1 Josiah Royce, *The Philosophy of Loyalty* (New York: The Macmillan Company, 1908), Lecture I, pp. 3–28, 30–42.—Editor's note.

of all moral values"—has in recent years made popular the
thesis that all the conventional morality of the past, whatever
may have been its inevitableness, or its temporary usefulness,
was in principle false, was a mere transition stage of evolution,
and must be altered to the core. "Time makes ancient good
uncouth": in this well-known word one might sum up the
spirit of this modern revolt against moral traditions.

Now when we review the recent moral controversies that express this sort of questioning, some of us find ourselves especially
troubled and bewildered. We all feel that if the foundations
of the exact sciences are to be criticised by the restless spirit of
our reforming age, the exact sciences are indeed well able to
take care of themselves. And as for religion,—if its fortunes
have indeed, of late, deeply troubled and perplexed many
gentle hearts, still both believers and doubters have now generally come to view with a certain resignation this aspect of
the fate of our time, whether they regard religious doubt as the
result of God's way of dealing with a wayward world, or as a
sign of man's transition to a higher stage of enlightenment.

But restlessness regarding the very foundations of morality
—that seems to many of us especially discouraging. For that
concerns both the seen and the unseen world, both the truths
that justify the toil spent upon exact science, and the hopes for
the love of which the religions of men have seemed dear. For
what is science worth, and what is religion worth, if human
life itself, for whose ennoblement science and religion have
both labored, has no genuine moral standards by which one
may measure its value? If, then, our moral standards themselves
are questioned, the iron of doubt—so some of us feel—seems
to enter our very hearts.

I

In view, then, of the fact that the modern tendency to revise traditions has inevitably extended itself, in new ways, to
the region of morals, I suppose that a study of some of the
foundations of the moral life is a timely undertaking. It is
such an undertaking that I propose as the task of the present
course of lectures. My purpose, in these discussions, is both a
philosophical and a practical purpose. I should indeed be glad,
if there were time, to attempt, in your company, a systematic

review of all the main problems of philosophical ethics. That is, I should like, were that possible, to discuss with you at length the nature, the foundation, and the truth of the moral law, approaching that problem from all those various sides which interest philosophers. And, as a fact, I shall indeed venture to say something, in the course of these lectures, regarding each of these topics. But I well know that there is no space, in eight lectures, for any adequate treatment of that branch of philosophy which is called Ethics. Nor do you come here merely or mainly for the sake of hearing what a student of philosophy chances to think about the problems of his own calling. Accordingly, I shall not try, in this place, to state to you any system of moral philosophy. Rather is it the other aspect of my purpose in appealing to you—the practical aspect, which I must especially try to bear in mind throughout these lectures.

Our age, as I have said, is a good deal perplexed regarding its moral ideals and its standards of duty. It has doubts about what is really the best plan of human life. This perplexity is not wholly due to any peculiar waywardness of our time, or to any general lack of moral seriousness. It is just our moral leaders, our reformers, our prophets, who most perplex us. Whether these revolutionary moral teachers are right or wrong, they beset us, they give us no rest, they call in doubt our moral judgments, they undertake to "transmute values." And the result, for many of us, is a practical result. It tends to deprive us of that confidence which we all need in order to be ready to do good works. It threatens to paralyze the effectiveness of many conscientious people. Hence any effort to reason calmly and constructively about the foundations of the moral life may serve, not merely to clarify our minds, but to give vigor to our deeds. In these lectures, then, I shall ask you to think indeed about moral problems, but to think for the sake of action. I shall try to give you some fragments of a moral philosophy; but I shall try to justify the philosophy through its application to life. I do not much care whether you agree with the letter of any of my philosophical formulas; but I do want to bring to your consciousness, by means of these formulas, a certain spirit in terms of which you may henceforth be helped to interpret the life that we all in common need to live. Meanwhile, I do not want merely to refute those reformers and prophets of whose perplexing assaults upon our moral traditions I have just spoken, nor yet do I want to join myself with them in perplexing you still further.

I want, as far as I can, to indicate some ways whereby we may clarify and simplify our moral situation.

I indeed agree with the view that, in many ways, our traditional moral standards ought to be revised. We need a new heaven and a new earth. We do well to set out to seek for both, however hard or doubtful may be the quest. In so far as our restlessness about moral matters—our unsettlement—implies a sense of this need, it is a good thing. To use a comparison suggested by modern Biblical criticism—our conventional morality is indeed a sort of Pentateuch, made up of many ancient documents. It has often been edited afresh. It needs critical reëxamination. I am a student of philosophy. My principal business has always been criticism. I shall propose nothing in this course which I have not tried to submit to critical standards, and to revise repeatedly.

But, on the other hand, I do not believe that unsettlement is finality. Nor to my mind is the last word of human wisdom this: that the truth is inaccessible. Nor yet is the last word of wisdom this: that the truth is merely fluent and transient. I believe in the eternal. I am in quest of the eternal. As to moral standards, in particular, I do not like that mere homesickness and spiritual estrangement, and that confusion of mind about moral ideals, which is nowadays too common. I want to know the way that leads our human practical life homewards, even if that way prove to be infinitely long. I am discontented with mere discontent. I want, as well as I can, not merely to help you to revise some of your moral standards, but to help you to give to this revision some definitive form and tendency, some image and hint of finality.

Moreover, since moral standards, as Antigone said, are not of to-day or yesterday, I believe that revision does not mean, in this field, a mere break with the past. I myself have spent my life in revising my opinions. And yet, whenever I have most carefully revised my moral standards, I am always able to see, upon reviewing my course of thought, that at best I have been finding out, in some new light, the true meaning that was latent in old traditions. Those traditions were often better in spirit than the fathers knew. We who revise may sometimes be able to see this better meaning that was latent in forms such as are now antiquated, and perhaps, in their old literal interpretation, even mischievous. Revision does not mean mere destruction. We can often say to tradition: That which thou sowest is not quickened except it die. But we can sometimes see in the world of opinion a sort of resurrection of the dead, —a resurrection wherein what was indeed justly sown in dishonor is raised in honor,—glorified,—and perhaps incorruptible. Let us bury the natural body of tradition. What we want is its glorified body and its immortal soul.

II

I have entitled these lectures, "The Philosophy of Loyalty." I may as well confess at once that my title was suggested to me, early last summer, by a book that I read—a recent work by a distinguished ethnologist, Dr. Rudolf Steinmetz of The Hague, entitled "The Philosophy of War." War and loyalty have been, in the past, two very closely associated ideas. It will be part of the task of these lectures to break up, so far as I can, in your own minds, that ancient and disastrous association, and to show how much the true conception of loyalty has been obscured by viewing the warrior as the most typical representative of rational loyalty. Steinmetz, however, accepts, in this respect, the traditional view. According to him, war gives an opportunity for loyal devotion so notable and important that, if war were altogether abolished, one of the greatest goods of civilization would thereby be hopelessly lost. I am keenly conscious of the sharp contrast between Steinmetz's theory of loyalty and my own. I agree with Steinmetz, as you will later see, regarding the significance of loyalty as a central principle of the moral life. I disagree with him very profoundly as to the relation of war both to true loyalty and to civilization in general. The very contrast has suggested to me the adoption of the form of title which Steinmetz has used.

The phrase, "Philosophy of Loyalty," is intended to indicate first, that we are here to consider loyalty as an ethical principle. For philosophy deals with first principles. And secondly, my title means to suggest that we are to view the matter critically and discriminatingly, as well as practically. For philosophy is essentially a criticism of life. Not everything, then, that calls itself loyalty, and not every form of loyalty, shall be put in our discussion on the same level with every other moral quality that uses or that deserves the ancient name in question. Moreover, the term "loyalty" comes to us as a good old popular word, without any exact definition. We are hereafter to define our term as precisely as possible, yet so as to preserve the spirit of the former usage. In estimating the place of loyalty in the moral life, we are, moreover, to follow neither traditional authority nor the voice of private prejudice. We are to use our reason as best we can; for philosophy is an effort to think out the reasons for our opinions. We are not to praise blindly, nor to condemn according to our moods. Where loyalty seems to be a good, we are to see why; when what men call loyalty leads them astray, we are to find wherein the fault lies. Since loyalty is a relative term, and always implies that there is some object, some cause, to which any given loyalty is to be shown, we must consider what are the fitting objects of loyalty. In attempting an answer to these various questions, our philosophy of loyalty must try to delve down to the roots of human conduct, the grounds for our moral standards, as far as our time permits.

But when all these efforts have been made towards a philosophical treatment of our topic, when certain discriminations between true and mistaken loyalty have been defined, when we have insisted upon the fitting objects of loyalty, and have throughout indicated our reasons for our theses, there will then stand out one great practical lesson, which I shall try to illustrate from the start, and to bring to its fruition as our lectures close. And the lesson will be this: *In loyalty, when loyalty is properly defined, is the fulfilment of the whole moral law.* You can truthfully centre your entire moral world about a rational conception of loyalty. Justice, charity, industry, wisdom, spirituality, are all definable in terms of enlightened loyalty. And, as I shall maintain, this very way of viewing the moral world —this deliberate centralization of all the duties and of all the virtues about the one conception of rational loyalty—is of great service as a means of clarifying and simplifying the tangled moral problems of our lives and of our age.

Thus, then, I state the task which our title is intended to set before us. The rest of this opening lecture must be devoted to clearing our way—and to a merely preliminary and tentative view of our topic. I must first attempt a partial and provisional definition of the term "loyalty" as I shall use that term. I wish that I could begin with a final and adequate definition; but I cannot. Why I cannot, you will see in later lectures. At the moment I shall try to direct your minds, as well as I can, merely to some of the features that are essential to my conception of loyalty.

III

Loyalty shall mean, according to this preliminary definition: *The willing and practical and thoroughgoing devotion of a person to a cause.* A man is loyal when, first, he has some *cause* to which he is loyal; when, secondly, he *willingly* and *thoroughly* devotes himself to this cause; and when, thirdly, he expresses his devotion in some *sustained and practical way*, by acting steadily in the service of his cause. Instances of loyalty are: The devotion of a patriot to his country, when this devotion leads him actually to live and perhaps die for his country; the devotion of a martyr to his religion; the devotion of a ship's captain to the requirements of his office when, after a disaster, he works steadily for his ship and for the saving of his ship's company until the last possible service is accomplished, so that he is the last man to leave the ship, and is ready if need be to go down with his ship.

Such cases of loyalty are typical. They involve, I have said, the willingness of the loyal man to do his service. The loyal man's cause is his cause by virtue of the assent over his own will. His devotion is his own. He chooses it, or, at all events, approves it. Moreover, his devotion is a practical one. He does something. This something serves his cause. Loyalty is never mere emotion. Adoration and affection may go with loyalty, but can never alone constitute loyalty. Furthermore, the devotion of the loyal man involves a sort of restraint or submission of his natural desires to his cause. Loyalty without self-control is impossible. The loyal man serves. That is, he does not merely follow his own impulses. He looks to his cause for guidance. This cause tells him what to do, and he does it. His devotion, furthermore, is entire. He is ready to live or to die as the cause directs.

And now for a further word about the hardest part of this preliminary definition of loyalty: A loyal man, I have said, has a cause. I do not yet say that he has a good cause. He might have a bad one. I do not say, as yet, what makes a cause a good one, and worthy of loyalty. All that is to be considered hereafter. But this I now premise: If one is loyal, he has a cause which he indeed personally values. Otherwise, how could he be devoted to it? He therefore takes interest in the cause, loves it, is well pleased with it. On the other hand, loyalty never means the mere emotion of love for your cause, and never means merely following your own pleasure, viewed *as* your private pleasure and interest. For if you are loyal, your cause is viewed by you as something outside of you. Or if, like your country, your cause includes yourself, it is still much larger than your private self. It has its own value, so you as a loyal person believe. This essential value it would keep (so you believe) even if your private interest were left out of account. Your cause you take, then, to be something objective—something that is not your private self. It does not get its value merely from your being pleased with it. You believe, on the contrary, that you love it just because of its own value, which it has by itself, even if you die. That is just why one may be ready to die for his cause. In any case, when the loyal man serves his cause, he is not seeking his own private advantage.

Moreover, the cause to which a loyal man is devoted is never something *wholly* impersonal. It concerns other men. Loyalty is social. If one is a loyal servant of a cause, one has at least possible fellow-servants. On the other hand, since a cause, in general, tends to unite the many fellow-servants in one service, it consequently seems to the loyal man to have a sort of impersonal or superpersonal quality about it. You can love an individual. But you can be loyal only to a tie that binds you and others into some sort of unity, and loyal to individuals only through the tie. The cause to which loyalty devotes itself has always this union of the personal and the seemingly superindividual about it. It binds many individuals into one service. Loyal lovers, for instance, are loyal not merely to one another as separate individuals, but to their love, to their union, which is something more than either of them, or even than both of them viewed as distinct individuals.

So much for a preliminary view of what loyalty is. Our definition is not complete. It raises rather than solves problems about the nature of loyalty. But thus indeed we get a first notion of the general nature of loyalty.

IV

But now for a next step. Many people find that they have a need of loyalty. Loyalty is a good thing for them. If you ask, however, why loyalty may be needed by a given man, the answer may be very complex. A patriot may, in your opinion, need loyalty, first because his country needs his service, and, as you add, he actually owes this service, and so needs to do his duty, viz. to be loyal. This first way of stating a given man's need of a given loyalty, turns upon asserting that a specific cause rightly requires of a certain man a certain service. The cause, as one holds, is good and worthy. This man actually ought to serve just that cause. Hence he stands in need of loyalty, and of just this loyalty.

But in order thus to define this man's need of loyalty, you have to determine what causes are worthy of loyalty, and why this man ought to serve his own cause. To answer such questions would apparently presuppose a whole system of morals,—a system which at this stage of our argument we have not yet in sight.

But there is another,—a simpler, and, at the outset, a lower way of estimating the value of loyalty. One may, for the time, abstract from all questions as to the value of causes. Whether a man is loyal to a good cause or to a bad cause, his own personal attitude, when he is loyal, has a certain general quality. Whoever is loyal, whatever be his cause, is devoted, is active, surrenders his private self-will, controls himself, is in love with his cause, and believes in it. The loyal man is thus in a certain state of mind which has its own value for himself. To live a loyal life, whatever be one's cause, is to live in a way which is certainly free from many well-known sources of inner dissatisfaction. Thus hesitancy is often corrected by loyalty; for the cause plainly tells the loyal man what to do. Loyalty, again, tends to unify life, to give it centre, fixity, stability.

Well, these aspects of loyalty are, so far as they go, good for the loyal man. We may therefore define our need of loyalty in a certain preliminary way. We may take what is indeed a lower view of loyalty, regarding it, for the moment, in deliberate abstraction from the cause to which one is loyal. We may thus regard loyalty, for the moment, just as a personal attitude, which is good for the loyal man himself.

Now this lower view of our need of loyalty is the one to which in the rest of this lecture I want you to attend. All that I now say is preliminary. Results belong later. Let us simply abstract from the question whether a man's cause is objectively worthy of his loyalty or not. Let us ask: What does a man gain by being loyal? Suppose that some cause, outside of and also inclusive of his private self, so appeals to a man that he believes it to be worthy, and becomes heartily loyal to it. What good does he get personally out of his loyalty? In order to answer this question, even in this preliminary way, I must indeed go rather far afield, and define for you, still very tentatively, one of the best-known and hardest of the problems of our personal life.

V

What do we live for? What is our duty? What is the true ideal of life? What is the true difference between right and wrong? What is the true good which we all need? Whoever begins seriously to consider such questions as these soon observes certain great truths about the moral life which he must take into account if his enterprise is to succeed, that is, if he is ever to answer these questions.

The first truth is this: We all of us first learned about what we ought to do, about what our ideal should be, and in general about the moral law, through some authority external to our own wills. Our teachers, our parents, our playmates, society, custom, or perhaps some church,—these taught us about one or another aspect of right and wrong. The moral law came to us from without. It often seemed to us, in so far, something other than our will, something threatening or socially compelling, or externally restraining. In so far as our moral training is still incomplete, the moral law may at any moment have to assume afresh this air of an external authority merely in order to win our due attention. But if we have learned the moral law, or any part of it, and if we do not ask any longer how we first learned, or how we may still have to learn afresh our duty, but if, on the contrary, we rather ask: "What reason can I now give to myself why a given act is truly right? What reason can I give why my duty is my duty?"—then, indeed, we find that no external authority, viewed merely as external, can give one any reason why an act is truly right or wrong. Only a calm and reasonable view of what it is that I myself really will,—only this can decide such a question. My duty is simply my own will brought to my clear self-consciousness. That which I can rightly view as good for me is simply the object of my own deepest desire set plainly before my insight. For your own will and your own desire, once fully brought to self-consciousness, furnish the only valid reason for you to know what is right and good.

This comment which I now make upon the nature of the moral law is familiar to every serious student of ethics. In one form or another this fact, that the ultimate moral authority for each of us is determined by our own rational will, is admitted even by apparently extreme partisans of authority. Socrates long ago announced the principle in question when he taught that no man is willingly base. Plato and Aristotle employed it in developing their ethical doctrines. When St. Augustine, in a familiar passage in his Confessions, regards God's will as that in which, and in which alone, our wills can find rest and peace, he indeed makes God's will the rule of life; but he also shows that the reason why each of us, if enlightened, recognizes the divine will as right, is that, in Augustine's opinion, God has so made us for himself that our own wills are by nature inwardly restless until they rest in harmony with God's will. Our restlessness, then, so long as we are out of this harmony, gives us the reason why we find it right, if we are enlightened, to surrender our self-will.

If you want to find out, then, what is right and what is good for you, bring your own will to self-consciousness. Your duty is what you yourself will to do in so far as you clearly discover who you are, and what your place in the world is. This is, indeed, a first principle of all ethical inquiry. Kant called it the Principle of the Autonomy or self-direction of the rational will of each moral being.

But now there stands beside this first principle a second principle, equally inevitable and equally important. This principle is, that I can never find out what my own will is by merely brooding over my natural desires, or by following my momentary caprices. For by nature I am a sort of meeting place of countless streams of ancestral tendency. From moment to moment, if you consider me apart from my training, I am a collection of impulses. There is no one desire that is always present to me. Left to myself alone, I can never find out what my will is. . . .

VI

So far, then, we have a rather paradoxical situation before us. Yet it is the moral situation of every one of us. If I am to know my duty, I must consult my own reasonable will. I alone can show myself why I view this or this as my duty. But on the other hand, if I merely look within myself to find what it is that I will, my own private individual nature, apart from due training, never gives me any answer to the question: What do I will? By nature I am a victim of my ancestry, a mass of world-old passions and impulses, desiring and suffering in constantly new ways as my circumstances change, and as one or another of my natural impulses comes to the front. By nature, then, apart from a specific training, I have no personal will of my own. One of the principal tasks of my life is to learn to have a will of my own. To learn your own will,—yes, to create your own will, is one of the largest of your human undertakings.

Here, then, is the paradox. I, and only I, whenever I come to my own, can morally justify to myself my own plan of life. No outer authority can ever give me the true reason for my duty. Yet I, left to myself, can never find a plan of life. I have no inborn ideal naturally present within myself. By nature I simply go on crying out in a sort of chaotic self-will, according as the momentary play of desire determines.

Whence, then, can I learn any plan of life? The moral education of any civilized person easily reminds you how this question is, in one respect, very partially, but, so far as ordinary training goes, constantly answered. One gets one's various plans of life suggested through the models that are set before each one of us by his fellows. Plans of life first come to us in connection with our endless imitative activities. These imitative processes begin in our infancy, and run on through our whole life. We learn to play, to speak, to enter into our social realm, to take part in the ways and so in the life of mankind. This imitative social activity is itself due to our instincts as social beings. But in turn the social activities are the ones that first tend to organize all of our instincts, to give unity to our passions and impulses, to transform our natural chaos of desires into some sort of order—usually, indeed, a very imperfect order. It is our social existence, then, as imitative beings,—it is this that suggests to us the sorts of plans of life which we get when we learn a calling, when we find a business in life, when we discover our place in the social world. And so our actual plans of life, namely, our callings, our more or less settled daily activities, come to us from without. We in so far learn what our own will is by first imitating the wills of others.

Yet no,—this, once more, is never the whole truth about our social situation, and is still less the whole truth about our moral situation. By ourselves alone, we have said, we can never discover in our own inner life any one plan of life that expresses our genuine will. So then, we have said, all of our plans get suggested to us by the social order in which we grow up. But on the other hand, our social training gives us a mass of varying plans of life,—plans that are not utterly chaotic, indeed, but imperfectly ordered,—mere routine, not ideal life. Moreover, social training tends not only to teach us the way of other people, but to heighten by contrast our vague natural sense of the importance of having our own way. Social training stimulates the will of the individual self, and also teaches this self customs and devices for self-expression. We never merely imitate. Conformity attracts, but also wearies us. Meanwhile, even by imitation, we often learn how to possess, and then to carry out, our own self-will. For instance, we learn speech first by imitation; but henceforth we love to hear ourselves talk; and our whole plan of life gets affected accordingly. Speech has, indeed, its origin in social conformity. Yet the tongue is an unruly member, and wags rebelliously. Teach men customs, and you equip them with weapons for expressing their own personalities. As you train the social being, you make use of his natural submissiveness. But as a result of your training he forms plans; he interprets these plans with reference to his own personal interests; he becomes aware who he is; and he may end by becoming, if not original, then at least obstreperous. And thus society is constantly engaged in training up children who may, and often do, rebel against their mother. Social conformity gives us social power. Such power brings to us a consciousness of who and what we are. Now, for the first time, we begin to have a real will of our own. And hereupon we may discover this will to be in sharp conflict with the will of society. This is what normally happens to most of us, for a time at least, in youth.

You see, so far, how the whole process upon which man's moral life depends involves this seemingly endless play of inner and outer. How shall my duty be defined? Only by my own will, whenever that will is brought to rational self-consciousness. But what is my will? By nature I know not; for by birth I am a mere eddy in the turbulent stream of inherited human passion. How, then, shall I get a will of my own? Only through social training. That indeed gives me plans, for it teaches me the settled ways of my world. Yet no,—for such training really teaches me rather the arts whereby I may express myself. It makes me clever, ambitious, often rebellious, and in so far it teaches me how to plan opposition to the social order. The circular process thus briefly indicated goes on throughout the lives of many of us. It appears in new forms at various stages of our growth. At any moment we may meet new problems of right and wrong, relating to our plans of life. We hereupon look within, at what we call our own conscience, to find out what our duty is. But, as we do so, we discover, too often, what wayward and blind guides our own hearts so far are. So we look without, in order to understand better the ways of the social world. We cannot see the inner light. Let us try the outer one. These ways of the world appeal to our imitativeness, and so we learn from the other people how we ourselves are in this case to live. Yet no,—this very learning often makes us aware of our personal contrast with other people, and so makes us self-conscious, individualistic, critical, rebellious; and again we are thrown back on ourselves for guidance. Seeing the world's way afresh, I see that it is not my way. I revive. I assert myself. My duty, I say, is my own. And so, perhaps, I go back again to my own wayward heart.

It is this sort of process which goes on, sometimes in a hopelessly circular way, when, in some complicated situation, you are morally perplexed, and after much inner brooding give up deciding by yourself and appeal to friends for advice. The advice at first pleases you, but soon may arouse your self-will more than before. You may become, as a result, more wayward and sometimes more perplexed, the longer you continue this sort of inquiry. We all know what it is to seek advice, just with the result of finding out what it is that we do not want to do.

Neither within nor without, then, do I find what seems to me a settled authority,—a settled and harmonious plan of life, —unless, indeed, one happy sort of union takes place between the inner and the outer, between my social world and myself, between my natural waywardness and the ways of my fellows. This happy union is the one that takes place whenever my mere social conformity, my docility as an imitative creature, turns into exactly that which, in these lectures, I shall call loyalty. Let us consider what happens in such cases.

VII

Suppose a being whose social conformity has been sufficient to enable him to learn many skilful social arts,—arts of speech, of prowess in contest, of influence over other men. Suppose that these arts have at the same time awakened this man's pride, his self-confidence, his disposition to assert himself. Such a man will have in him a good deal of what you can well call social will. He will be no mere anarchist. He will have been trained into much obedience. He will be no natural enemy of society, unless, indeed, fortune has given him extraordinary opportunities to win his way without scruples. On the other hand, this man must acquire a good deal of self-will. He becomes fond of success, of mastery, of his own demands. To be sure, he can find within himself no one naturally sovereign will. He can so far find only a general determination to define some way of his own, and to have his own way. Hence the conflicts of social will and self-will are inevitable, circular, endless, so long as this is the whole story of the man's life. By merely consulting convention, on the one hand, and his disposition to be somebody, on the other hand, this man can never find any one final and consistent plan of life, nor reach any one definition of his duty.

But now suppose that there appears in this man's life some one of the greater social passions, such as patriotism well exemplifies. Let his country be in danger. Let his elemental passion for conflict hereupon fuse with his brotherly love for his own countrymen into that fascinating and blood-thirsty form of humane but furious ecstacy, which is called the war-spirit. The mood in question may or may not be justified by the passing circumstances. For that I now care not. At its best the war-spirit is no very clear or rational state of anybody's mind. But one reason why men may love this spirit is that when it comes, it seems at once to define a plan of life,—a plan which solves the conflicts of self-will and conformity. This plan has two features: (1) it is through and through a social plan, obedient to the general will of one's country, submissive; (2) it is through and through an exaltation of the self, of the inner man, who now feels glorified through his sacrifice, dignified in his self-surrender, glad to be his country's servant and martyr,—yet sure that through this very readiness for self-destruction he wins the rank of hero.

Well, if the man whose case we are supposing gets possessed by some such passion as this, he wins for the moment the consciousness of what I call loyalty. This loyalty no longer knows anything about the old circular conflicts of self-will and of conformity. The self, at such moments, looks indeed *outwards* for its plan of life. "The country needs me," it says. It looks, meanwhile, *inwards* for the inspiring justification of this plan. "Honor, the hero's crown, the soldier's death, the patriot's devotion—these," it says, "are my will. I am not giving up this will of mine. It is my pride, my glory, my self-assertion, to be ready at my country's call." And now there is no conflict of outer and inner.

How wise or how enduring or how practical such a passion may prove, I do not yet consider. What I point out is that this war-spirit, for the time at least, makes self-sacrifice seem to be self-expression, makes obedience to the country's call seem to be the proudest sort of display of one's own powers. Honor now means submission, and to obey means to have one's way. Power and service are at one. Conformity is no longer opposed to having one's own will. One has no will but that of the country.

As a mere fact of human nature, then, there are social passions which actually tend to do at once two things: (1) to intensify our self-consciousness, to make us more than ever determined to express our own will and more than ever sure of our own rights, of our own strength, of our dignity, of our power, of our value; (2) to make obvious to us that this our will has no purpose but to do the will of some fascinating social power. This social power is the cause to which we are loyal.

Loyalty, then, fixes our attention upon some one cause, bids us look without ourselves to see what this unified cause is, shows us thus some one plan of action, and then says to us, "In this cause is your life, your will, your opportunity, your fulfilment."

Thus loyalty, viewed merely as a personal attitude, solves the paradox of our ordinary existence, by showing us outside of ourselves the cause which is to be served, and inside of ourselves the will which delights to do this service, and which is not thwarted but enriched and expressed in such service. . . .

13 ❧ LOYALTY TO LOYALTY [1]

The two foregoing lectures have been devoted to defending the thesis that loyalty is, for the loyal individual himself, a supreme good, whatever be, for the world in general, the worth of his cause. We are next to consider what are the causes which are worthy of loyalty.

I

But before I go on to this new stage of our discussion, I want, by way of summary of all that has preceded, to get before your minds as clear an image as I can of some representative instance of loyalty. The personal dignity and worth of a loyal character can best be appreciated by means of illustrations. And I confess that those illustrations of loyalty which my earlier lectures used must have aroused some associations which I do not want, as I go on to my further argument, to leave too prominent in your minds. I chose those instances because they were familiar. Perhaps they are too familiar. I have mentioned the patriot aflame with the war-spirit, the knight of romance, and the Japanese Samurai. But these examples may have too much emphasized the common but false impression that loyalty necessarily has to do with the martial virtues and with the martial vices. I have also used the instance of the loyal captain standing by his sinking ship. But this case suggests that the loyal have their duties assigned to them by some established and customary routine of the service to which they belong. And that, again, is an association that I do not want you to make too prominent. Loyalty is perfectly consistent with originality. The loyal man may often have to show his loyalty by some act which

[1] Josiah Royce, *The Philosophy of Loyalty* (New York: The Macmillan Company, 1908), Lecture III, pp. 101–107, 116–138.—Editor's note.

no mere routine predetermines. He may have to be as inventive of his duties as he is faithful to them.

Now, I myself have for years used in my own classes, as an illustration of the personal worth and beauty of loyalty, an incident of English history, which has often been cited as a precedent in discussions of the constitutional privileges of the House of Commons, but which, as I think, has not been sufficiently noticed by moralists. Let me set that incident now before your imagination. Thus, I say, do the loyal bear themselves: In January, 1642, just before the outbreak of hostilities between King Charles I and the Commons, the King resolved to arrest certain leaders of the opposition party in Parliament. He accordingly sent his herald to the House to demand the surrender of these members into his custody. The Speaker of the House in reply solemnly appealed to the ancient privileges of the House, which gave to that body jurisdiction over its own members, and which forbade their arrest without its consent. The conflict between the privileges of the House and the royal prerogative was herewith definitely initiated. The King resolved by a show of force to assert at once his authority; and, on the day following that upon which the demand sent through his herald had been refused, he went in person, accompanied by soldiers, to the House. Then, having placed his guards at the doors, he entered, went up to the Speaker, and, naming the members whom he desired to arrest, demanded, "Mr. Speaker, do you espy these persons in the House?"

You will observe that the moment was an unique one in English history. Custom, precedent, convention, obviously were inadequate to define the Speaker's duty in this most critical instance. How, then, could he most admirably express himself? How best preserve his genuine personal dignity? What response would secure to the Speaker his own highest good? Think of the matter merely as one of the Speaker's individual worth and reputation. By what act could he do himself most honor?

In fact, as the well-known report, entered in the Journal of the House, states, the Speaker at once fell on his knee before the King and said: "Your Majesty, I am the Speaker of this House, and, being such, I have neither eyes to see nor tongue to speak save as this House shall command; and I humbly beg your Majesty's pardon if this is the only answer that I can give to your Majesty."

Now, I ask you not, at this point, to consider the Speaker's reply to the King as a deed having historical importance, or in fact as having value for anybody but himself. I want you to view the act merely as an instance of a supremely worthy personal attitude. The beautiful union of formal humility (when the Speaker fell on his knee before the King) with unconquerable self-assertion (when the reply rang with so clear a note of lawful defiance); the willing and complete identification of his whole self with his cause (when the Speaker declared that he had no eye or tongue except as his office gave them to him),—these are characteristics typical of a loyal attitude. The Speaker's words were at once ingenious and obvious. They were in line with the ancient custom of the realm. They were also creative of a new precedent. He had to be inventive to utter them; but once uttered, they seem almost commonplace in their plain truth. The King might be offended at the refusal; but he could not fail to note that, for the moment, he had met with a personal dignity greater than kingship,— the dignity that any loyal man, great or humble, possesses whenever he speaks and acts in the service of his cause.

Well—here is an image of loyalty. Thus, I say, whatever their cause, the loyal express themselves. When any one asks me what the worthiest personal bearing, the most dignified and internally complete expression of an individual is, I can therefore only reply: Such a bearing, such an expression of yourself as the Speaker adopted. Have, then, your cause, chosen by you just as the Speaker had chosen to accept his office from the House. Let this cause so possess you that, even in the most thrilling crisis of your practical service of that cause, you can say with the Speaker: "I am the servant of this cause, its reasonable, its willing, its devoted instrument, and, being such, I have neither eyes to see nor tongue to speak save as this cause shall command." Let this be your bearing, and this your deed. Then, indeed, you know what you live for. And you have won the attitude which constitutes genuine personal dignity. What an individual in his practical bearing can be, you now are. And herein, as I have said, lies for you a supreme personal good.

• • • • •

III

. . . If loyalty is a supreme good, the mutually destructive conflict of loyalties is in general a supreme evil. If loyalty is a good for all sorts and conditions of men, the war of man against man has been especially mischievous, not so much because it has hurt, maimed, impoverished, or slain men, as because it has so often robbed the defeated of their causes, of their opportunities to be loyal, and sometimes of their very spirit of loyalty.

If, then, we look over the field of human life to see where good and evil have most clustered, we see that the best in human life is its loyalty; while the worst is whatever has tended to make loyalty impossible, or to destroy it when present, or to rob it of its own while it still survives. And of all things that thus have warred with loyalty, the bitterest woe of humanity has been that so often it is the loyal themselves who have thus blindly and eagerly gone about to wound and to slay the loyalty of their brethren. The spirit of loyalty has been misused to make men commit sin against this very spirit, holy as it is. For such a sin is precisely what any wanton conflict of loyalties means. Where such a conflict occurs, the best, namely, loyalty, is used as an instrument in order to compass the worst, namely, the destruction of loyalty.

It is true, then, that some causes are good, while some are evil. But the test of good and evil in the causes to which men are loyal is now definable in terms which we can greatly simplify in view of the foregoing considerations.

If, namely, I find a cause, and this cause fascinates me, and I give myself over to its service, I in so far attain what, for me, if my loyalty is complete, is a supreme good. But my cause, by our own definition, is a social cause, which binds many into the unity of one service. My cause, therefore, gives me, of necessity, fellow-servants, who with me share this loyalty, and to whom this loyalty, if complete, is also a supreme good. So far, then, being loyal myself, I not only get but give good; for I help to sustain, in each of my fellow-servants, his own loyalty, and so I help him to secure his own supreme good. In so far, then, my loyalty to my cause is also a loyalty to my fellows' loyalty. But now suppose that my cause, like the family in a feud, or like the pirate ship, or like the aggressively warlike nation, lives by the destruction of the loyalty of other families, or of its own community, or of other communities. Then, indeed, I get a good for myself and for my fellow-servants by our common loyalty; but I war against this very spirit of loyalty as it appears in our opponent's loyalty to his own cause.

And so, a cause is good, not only for me, but for mankind, in so far as it is essentially a *loyalty to loyalty*, that is, is an aid and a furtherance of loyalty in my fellows. It is an evil cause in so far as, despite the loyalty that it arouses in me, it is destructive of loyalty in the world of my fellows. My cause is, indeed, always such as to involve some loyalty to loyalty, because, if I am loyal to any cause at all, I have fellow-servants whose loyalty mine supports. But in so far as my cause is a predatory cause, which lives by overthrowing the loyalties of others, it is an evil cause, because it involves disloyalty to the very cause of loyalty itself.

I V

In view of these considerations, we are now able still further to simplify our problem by laying stress upon one more of those very features which seemed, but a moment since, to complicate the matter so hopelessly. Loyalty, as we have defined it, is the willing devotion of a self to a cause. In answering the ethical individualists, we have insisted that all of the higher types of loyalty involve autonomous choice. The cause that is to appeal to me at all must indeed have some elemental fascination for me. It must stir me, arouse me, please me, and in the end possess me. Moreover, it must, indeed, be set before me by my social order as a possible, a practically significant, a living cause, which binds many selves in the unity of one life. But, nevertheless, if I am really awake to the significance of my own moral choices, I must be in the position of accepting this cause, as the Speaker of the House, in the incident that I have narrated, had freely accepted his Speakership. My cause cannot be merely forced upon me. It is I who make it my own. It is I who willingly say: "I have no eyes to see nor tongue to speak save as this cause shall command." However much the cause may seem to be assigned to me by my social station, I must coöperate in the choice of the cause, before the act of loyalty is complete.

Since this is the case, since my loyalty never is my mere fate, but is always also my choice, I can of course determine my loyalty, at least to some extent, by the consideration of the actual good and ill which my proposed cause does to mankind. And since I now have the main criterion of the good and ill of causes before me, I can define a principle of choice which may so guide me that my loyalty shall become a good, not merely to myself, but to mankind.

This principle is now obvious. I may state it thus: In so far as it lies in your power, so choose your cause and so serve it, that, by reason of your choice and of your service, there shall be more loyalty in the world rather than less. And, in fact, so choose and so serve your individual cause as to secure thereby the greatest possible increase of loyalty amongst men. More briefly: *In choosing and in serving the cause to which you are to be loyal, be, in any case, loyal to loyalty.*

This precept, I say, will express how one should guide his choice of a cause, in so far as he considers not merely his own supreme good, but that of mankind. That such autonomous choice is possible, tends, as we now see, not to complicate, but to simplify our moral situation. For if you regard men's loyalty as their fate, if you think that a man must be loyal simply to the cause which tradition sets before him, without any power to direct his own moral attention, then indeed the conflict of loyalties seems an insoluble problem; so that, if men find themselves loyally involved in feuds, there is no way out. But if, indeed, choice plays a part,—a genuine even if limited part, in directing the individual's choice of the cause to which he is to be loyal, then indeed this choice may be so directed that loyalty to the universal loyalty of all mankind shall be furthered by the actual choices which each enlightened loyal person makes when he selects his cause.

V

At the close of our first discussion we supposed the question to be asked, Where, in all our complex and distracted modern world, in which at present cause wars with cause, shall we find a cause that is certainly worthy of our loyalty? This question, at this very moment, has received in our discussion an answer which you may feel to be so far provisional,—perhaps unpractical,—but which you ought to regard as, at least in principle, somewhat simple and true to human nature. Loyalty is a good, a supreme good. If I myself could but find a worthy cause, and serve it as the Speaker served the House, having neither eyes to see nor tongue to speak save as that cause should command, then my highest human good, in so far as I am indeed an active being, would be mine. But this very good of loyalty is no peculiar privilege of mine; nor is it good only for me. It is an universally human good. For it is simply the finding of a harmony of the self and the world,—such a harmony as alone can content any human being.

In these lectures I do not found my argument upon some remote ideal. I found my case upon taking our poor passionate human nature just as we find it. This "eager anxious being" of ours, as Gray calls it, is a being that we can find only in social ties, and that we, nevertheless, can never fulfil without a vigorous self-assertion. We are by nature proud, untamed, restless, insatiable in our private self-will. We are also imitative, plastic, and in bitter need of ties. We profoundly want both to rule and to be ruled. We must be each of us at the centre of his own active world, and yet each of us longs to be in harmony with the very outermost heavens that encompass, with the lofty orderliness of their movements, all our restless doings. The stars fascinate us, and yet we also want to keep our own feet upon our solid human earth. Our fellows, meanwhile, overwhelm us with the might of their customs, and we in turn are inflamed with the naturally unquenchable longing that they should somehow listen to the cries of our every individual desire.

Now this divided being of ours demands reconciliation with itself; it is one long struggle for unity. Its inner and outer realms are naturally at war. Yet it wills both realms. It wants them to become one. Such unity, however, only loyalty furnishes to us,—loyalty, which finds the inner self intensified and exalted even by the very act of outward looking and of upward looking, of service and obedience,—loyalty, which knows its eyes and its tongue to be never so much and so proudly its own as when it earnestly insists that it can neither see nor speak except as the cause demands,—loyalty, which is most full of life at the instant when it is most ready to become weary, or even to perish in the act of devotion to its own. Such loyalty unites private passion and outward conformity in one life. This is the very essence of loyalty. Now loyalty has these characters in any man who is loyal. Its emotions vary, indeed, endlessly with the temperaments of its adherents; but to them all it brings the active peace of that rest in a painful life,—that rest such as we found the mystic, Meister Eckhart, fully ready to prize.

Loyalty, then, is a good for all men. And it is in any man just as much a true good as my loyalty could be in me. And so, then, if indeed I seek a cause, a worthy cause, what cause could be more worthy than the cause of loyalty to loyalty; that is, the cause of making loyalty prosper amongst men? If I could serve that cause in a sustained and effective life, if some practical work for the furtherance of universal human loyalty could become to me what the House was to the Speaker, then indeed my own life-task would be found; and I could then be assured at every instant of the worth of my cause by virtue of the very good that I personally found in its service.

Here would be for me not only an unity of inner and outer, but an unity with the unity of all human life. What I sought for myself I should then be explicitly seeking for my whole world. All men would be my fellow-servants of my cause. In principle I should be opposed to no man's loyalty. I should be opposed only to men's blindness in their loyalty, I should contend only against that tragic disloyalty to loyalty which the feuds of humanity now exemplify. I should preach to all others, I should strive to practise myself, that active mutual furtherance of universal loyalty which is what humanity obviously most needs, if indeed loyalty, just as the willing devotion of a self to a cause, is a supreme good.

And since all who are human are as capable of loyalty as they are of reason, since the plainest and the humblest can be as true-hearted as the great, I should nowhere miss the human material for my task. I should know, meanwhile, that if indeed loyalty, unlike the "mercy" of Portia's speech, is not always mightiest in the mightiest, it certainly, like mercy, becomes the throned monarch better than his crown. So that I should be sure of this good of loyalty as something worthy to be carried, so far as I could carry it, to everybody, lofty or humble.

Thus surely it would be humane and reasonable for me to define my cause to myself,—if only I could be assured that there is indeed some practical way of making loyalty to loyalty the actual cause of my life. Our question therefore becomes this: Is there a practical way of serving the universal human cause of loyalty to loyalty? And if there is such a way, what is it? Can we see how personally so to act that we bring loyalty on earth to a fuller fruition, to a wider range of efficacy, to a more effective sovereignty over the lives of men? If so, then indeed we can see how to work for the cause of the genuine kingdom of heaven.

VI

Yet I fear that as you have listened to this sketch of a possible and reasonable cause, such as could be a proper object of our loyalty, you will all the while have objected: This may be a definition of a possible cause, but it is an unpractical definition. For what is there that one can do to further the loyalty of mankind in general? Humanitarian efforts are an old story. They constantly are limited in their effectiveness both by the narrowness of our powers, and by the complexity of the human nature which we try to improve. And if any lesson of philanthropy is well known, it is this, that whoever tries simply to help mankind as a whole, loses his labor, so long as he does not first undertake to help those nearest to him. Loyalty to the cause of universal loyalty—how, then, shall it constitute any practical working scheme of life?

I answer at once that the individual man, with his limited powers, can indeed serve the cause of universal loyalty only by limiting his undertakings to some decidedly definite personal range. He must have his own special and personal cause. But this cause of his can indeed be chosen and determined so as to constitute a deliberate effort to further universal loyalty. When I begin to show you how this may be, I shall at once pass from what may have seemed to you a very unpractical scheme of life, to a realm of familiar and commonplace virtuous activities. The only worth of my general scheme will then lie in the fact that, in the light of this scheme, we can, as it were, see the commonplace virtues transfigured and glorified by their relation to the one highest cause of all. My thesis is *that all the commonplace virtues, in so far as they are indeed defensible and effective, are special forms of loyalty to loyalty,* and are to be justified, centralized, inspired, by the one supreme effort to do good, namely, the effort to make loyalty triumphant in the lives of all men.

The first consideration which I shall here insist upon is this: Loyalty, as we have all along seen, depends upon a very characteristic and subtle union of natural interest, and of free choice. Nobody who merely follows his natural impulses as they come is loyal. Yet nobody can be loyal without depending upon and using his natural impulses. If I am to be loyal, my cause must from moment to moment fascinate me, awaken my muscular vigor, stir me with some eagerness for work, even if this be painful work. I cannot be loyal to barren abstractions. I can only be loyal to what my life can interpret in bodily deeds. Loyalty has its elemental appeal to my whole organism. My cause must become one with my human life. Yet all this must occur not without my willing choice. I must control my devotion. It will possess me, but not without my voluntary complicity; for I shall accept

the possession. It is, then, with the cause to which you personally
are loyal, as it was with divine grace in an older theology. The
cause must control you, as divine grace took saving control of
the sinner; but only your own will can accept this control, and
a grace that merely compels can never save.

Now that such an union of choice with natural interest is possible, is a fact of human nature, which every act of your own, in
your daily calling, may be used to exemplify. You cannot do
steady work without natural interest; but whoever is the mere
prey of this passing interest does no steady work. Loyalty is a
perfect synthesis of certain natural desires, of some range of
social conformity, and of your own deliberate choice.

In order to be loyal, then, to loyalty, I must indeed first
choose forms of loyal conduct which appeal to my own nature.
This means that, upon one side of my life, I shall have to
behave much as the most unenlightened of the loyal do. I shall
serve causes such as my natural temperament and my social
opportunities suggest to me. I shall choose friends whom I like.
My family, my community, my country, will be served partly
because I find it interesting to be loyal to them.

Nevertheless, upon another side, all these my more natural
and, so to speak, accidental loyalties, will be controlled and
unified by a deliberate use of the principle that, whatever my
cause, it ought to be such as to further, so far as in me lies, the
cause of universal loyalty. Hence I shall not permit my choice of
my special causes to remain a mere chance. My causes must
form a system. They must constitute in their entirety a single
cause, my life of loyalty. When apparent conflicts arise
amongst the causes in which I am interested, I shall deliberately
undertake, by devices which we shall hereafter study in these
lectures, to reduce the conflict to the greatest possible harmony.
Thus, for instance, I may say, to one of the causes in which I am
naturally bound up:—

> I could not love thee, dear, so much,
> Loved I not honour more.

And in this familiar spirit my loyalty will aim to be, even within
the limits of my own personal life, an united, harmonious devotion, not to various conflicting causes, but to one system of
causes, and so to one cause.

Since this one cause is my choice, the cause of my life, my

social station will indeed suggest it to me. My natural powers and preferences will make it fascinating to me, and yet I will never let mere social routine, or mere social tradition, or mere private caprice, impose it upon me. I will be individualistic in my loyalty, carefully insisting, however, that whatever else I am, I shall be in all my practical activity a loyal individual, and, so far as in me lies, one who chooses his personal causes for the sake of the spread of universal loyalty. Moreover, my loyalty will be a growing loyalty. Without giving up old loyalties I shall annex new ones. There will be evolution in my loyalty.

The choice of my cause will in consequence be such as to avoid unnecessary conflict with the causes of others. So far I shall indeed negatively show loyalty to loyalty. It shall not be my cause to destroy other men's loyalty. Yet since my cause, thus chosen and thus organized, still confines me to my narrow personal range, and since I can do so little directly for mankind, you may still ask whether, by such a control of my natural interests, I am indeed able to do much to serve the cause of universal loyalty.

Well, it is no part of the plan of this discourse to encourage illusions about the range of influence that any one poor mortal can exert. But that by the mere force of my practical and personal loyalty, if I am indeed loyal, I am doing something for the cause of universal loyalty, however narrow my range of deeds, this a very little experience of the lives of other people tends to teach me. For who, after all, most encourages and incites me to loyalty? I answer, any loyal human being, whatever his cause, so long as his cause does not arouse my hatred, and does not directly injure my chance to be loyal. My fellow's special and personal cause need not be directly mine. Indirectly he inspires my by the very contagion of his loyalty. He sets me the example. By his loyalty he shows me the worth of loyalty. Those humble and obscure folk of whom I have before spoken, how precious they are to us all as inspiring examples, because of their loyalty to their own.

From what men, then, have I gained the best aid in discovering how to be myself loyal? From the men whose personal cause is directly and consciously one with my own? That is indeed sometimes the case. But others, whose personal causes were apparently remote in very many ways from mine, have helped me to some of my truest glimpses of loyalty.

For instance: There was a friend of my own youth whom I

have not seen for years, who once faced the choice between a scholarly career that he loved, on the one hand, and a call of honor, upon the other,—who could have lived out that career with worldly success if he had only been willing to conspire with his chief to deceive the public about a matter of fact, but who unhesitatingly was loyal to loyalty, who spoke the truth, who refused to conspire, and who, because his chief was a plausible and powerful man, thus deliberately wrecked his own worldly chances once for all, and retired into a misunderstood obscurity in order that his fellow-men might henceforth be helped to respect the truth better. Now, the worldly career which that friend thus sacrificed for the sake of his loyalty is far from mine; the causes that he has since loyally served have not of late brought him near to me in worldly doings. I am not sure that he should ever have kept our interests in close touch with one another even if we had lived side by side. For he was and is a highly specialized type of man, austere, and a little disposed, like many scholars, to a life apart. For the rest, I have never myself been put in such a place as his was when he chose to make his sacrifice, and have never had his great choice set before me. Nor has the world rewarded him at all fairly for his fidelity. He is, then, as this world goes, not now near to me and not a widely influential man. Yet I owe him a great debt. He showed me, by the example of his free sacrifice, a good in loyalty which I might otherwise have been too blind to see. He is a man who does not love flattery. It would be useless for me now to offer to him either words of praise or words of comfort. He made his choice with a single heart and a clear head, and he has always declined to be praised. But it will take a long time, in some other world, should I meet him in such a realm, to tell him how much I owe to his example, how much he inspired me, or how many of his fellows he had indirectly helped to their own loyalty. For I believe that a good many others besides myself indirectly owe far more to him than he knows, or than they know. I believe that certain standards of loyalty and of scientific truthfulness in this country are to-day higher than they were because of the self-surrendering act of that one devoted scholar.

Loyalty, then, is contagious. It infects not only the fellow-servant of your own special cause, but also all who know of this act. Loyalty is a good that spreads. Live it and you thereby cultivate it in other men. Be faithful, then, so one may say, to the loyal man; be faithful over your few things, for the spirit of loyalty, secretly passing from you to many to whom you are a stranger, may even thereby make you unconsciously ruler over many things. Loyalty to loyalty is then no unpractical cause. And you serve it not by becoming a mere citizen of the world, but by serving your own personal cause. We set before you, then, no unpractical rule when we repeat our moral formula in this form: Find your own cause, your interesting, fascinating, personally engrossing cause; serve it with all your might and soul and strength; but so choose your cause, and so serve it, that thereby you show forth your loyalty to loyalty, so that because of your choice and service of your cause, there is a maximum of increase of loyalty amongst your fellow-men. . . .

14 ❧ CONSCIENCE [1]

... The reproach that moral philosophers have fine-sounding principles to report, but can never tell us how these principles practically apply, except when the cases are such as common sense has already decided,—this is an old objection to philosophical ethics. I want to show you how I myself meet that objection, and in what way, and to what extent, as I think, the principle of loyalty to loyalty does express the true dictates of conscience, and does tell us what to do in doubtful cases.

What is conscience? You will all agree that the word names a mental possession of ours which enables us to pass some sort of judgment, correct or mistaken, upon moral questions as they arise. My conscience, then, belongs to my mental equipment, and tells me about right and wrong conduct. Moreover, my conscience approves or disapproves my conduct, excuses me or accuses me. About the general nature and office of the conscience we all of us, as I suppose, so far agree. Our differences regarding our conscience begin when questions arise of the following sort: Is our conscience inborn? Is it acquired by training? Are its dictates the same in all men? Is it God-given? Is it infallible? Is it a separate power of the mind? Or is it simply a name for a collection of habits of moral judgment which we have acquired through social training, through reasoning, and through personal experience of the consequences of conduct?

IV

In trying to meet these questions so far as they here concern us, it is important next to note a few fundamental features which characterize the personal life of all of us. The first of these features appears if one, instead of stopping with the question, "What is my conscience?" goes deeper still and asks the question, "Who and what am I?" This latter question also has indeed

1 Josiah Royce, *The Philosophy of Loyalty* (New York: The Macmillan Company, 1908), Lecture IV, pp. 165–196.—Editor's note.

countless aspects, and a complete answer to it would constitute an entire system of metaphysics. But for our present purpose it is enough to note that I cannot answer the question, "Who am I?" except in terms of some sort of statement of the plans and purposes of my life. In responding to the question, "Who are you?" a man may first mention his name. But his name is a mere tag. He then often goes on to tell where he lives, and where he comes from. His home and his birthplace, however, are already what one may call purposeful aspects of his personality. For dwelling-place, country, birthplace, and similar incidental facts about a man tend to throw light upon his personality mainly because they are of importance for a further knowledge of his social relations, and so of his social uses and activities.

But the answer to the question, "Who are you?" really begins in earnest when a man mentions his calling, and so actually sets out upon the definition of his purposes and of the way in which these purposes get expressed in his life. And when a man goes on to say, "I am the doer of these and these deeds, the friend of these friends, the enemy of these opposing purposes, the member of this family, the one whose ideals are such and such, and are so and so expressed in my life," the man expresses to you at length whatever is most expressible and worth knowing in answer to the question, "Who are you?"

To sum up, then, I should say that a person, an individual self, may be defined as a human life lived according to a plan. If a man could live with no plan at all, purposelessly and quite passively, he would in so far be an organism, and also, if you choose, he would be a psychological specimen, but he would be no personality. Wherever there is personality, there are purposes worked out in life. If, as often happens, there are many purposes connected with the life of this human creature, many plans in this life, but no discoverable unity and coherence of these plans, then in so far there are many glimpses of selfhood, many fragmentary selves present in connection with the life of some human organism. But there is so far no one self, no one person discoverable. You are one self just in so far as the life that goes on in connection with your organism has some one purpose running through it. By the terms "this person" and "this self," then, we mean this human life in so far as it expresses some one purpose. Yet, of course, this one purpose which is expressed in the life of a single self need not be one which is defined by this self in abstract terms. On the contrary, most of us are aware that our lives are unified, after a fashion, by the very effort that we more or less vaguely make to assert ourselves somehow as individuals in our world. Many of us have not yet found out how it would be best to assert ourselves. But we are trying to find out. This very effort to find out gives already a certain unity of purpose to our lives.

But in so far as we have indeed found out some cause, far larger than our individual selves, to which we are fully ready to be loyal, this very cause serves to give the required unity to our lives, and so to determine what manner of self each of us is, even though we chance to be unable to define in abstract terms what is the precise nature of this very cause. Loyalty may be sometimes almost dumb; it is so in many of those obscure and humble models of loyalty of whom I have already spoken. They express their loyalty clearly enough in deeds. They often could not very well formulate it in words. They could not give an abstract account of their business. Yet their loyalty gives them a business. It unifies their activities. It makes of each of these loyal beings an individual self,—a life unified by a purpose. This purpose may in such cases come to consciousness merely as a willing hunger to serve the cause, a proud obedience to the ideal call. But in any case, wherever loyalty is, there is selfhood, personality, individual purpose embodied in a life.

And now, further, if the argument of our first and second lectures is right, wherever a human selfhood gets practically and consciously unified, there is some form of loyalty. For, except in terms of some sort of loyal purpose, as we saw, this mass of instincts, of passions, of social interests, and of private rebelliousness, whereof the nature of any one of us is originally compounded, can never get any effective unity whatever.

To sum up so far,—a self is a life in so far as it is unified by a single purpose. Our loyalties furnish such purposes, and hence make of us conscious and unified moral persons. Where loyalty has not yet come to any sort of definiteness, there is so far present only a kind of inarticulate striving to be an individual self. This very search for one's true self is already a sort of life-purpose, which, as far as it goes, individuates the life of the person in question, and gives him a task. But loyalty brings the individual to full moral self-consciousness. It is devoting the self to a cause that, after all, first makes it a rational and unified self, instead of what the life of too many a man remains,—namely, a cauldron of seething and bubbling efforts to be somebody, a cauldron which boils dry when life ends.

V

But what, you may now ask, has all this view of the self to do with conscience? I answer that the nature of conscience can be understood solely in terms of such a theory of the self as the one just sketched.

Suppose that I am, in the foregoing sense, a more or less completely unified and loyal self. Then there are two aspects of this selfhood which is mine. I live a life; and I have, as a loyal being, an ideal. The life itself is not the ideal. They are and always remain in some sense distinct. For no one act of my life, and no limited set of acts of mine, can ever completely embody my ideal. My ideal comes to me from my cause, as the ideal of the Speaker of the House of Commons, in the story that we have already used to illustrate loyalty, came to him from the House. My cause, however, is greater than my individual life. Hence it always sets before me an ideal which demands more of me than I have yet done,—more, too, than I can ever at any one instant accomplish. Even because of this vastness of my ideal, even because that to which I am loyal is so much greater than I ever become, even because of all this can my ideal unify my life, and make a rational self of me.

Hence, if I am indeed one self, my one ideal is always something that stands over against my actual life; and each act of this life has to be judged, estimated, determined, as to its moral value, in terms of the ideal. My cause, therefore, as it expresses itself to my own consciousness through my personal ideal,—my cause and my ideal taken together, and viewed as one, perform the precise function which tradition has attributed to conscience. My cause, then, for our philosophy of loyalty, *is* my conscience,— my cause as interpreted through my ideal of my personal life. When I look to my cause, it furnishes me with a conscience; for it sets before me a plan or ideal of life, and then constantly bids me contrast this plan, this ideal, with my transient and momentary impulses.

To illustrate: Were I a loyal judge on the bench, whose cause was my official function, then my judicial conscience would be

simply my whole ideal as a judge, when this ideal was contrasted with any of my present and narrower views of the situation directly before me. If, at a given moment, I tended to lay
unfair stress upon one side of a controversy that had been brought
into my court, my ideal would say: But a judge is impartial. If I
were disposed to decide with inadvised haste, the ideal would
say: But a judge takes account of the whole law bearing on the
case. If I were offered bribes, my judicial conscience would reject them as being once for all ideally intolerable. In order to
have such a judicial conscience, I should, of course, have to be
able to view my profession as the carrying out of some one purpose, and so as one cause. This purpose I should have learned, of
course, from the traditions of the office. But I should have had
willingly to adopt these traditions as my own, and to conceive
my own life in terms of them, in order to have a judicial conscience of my own. Analogous comments could be made upon
the conscience of an artist, of a statesman, of a friend, or of a
devoted member of a family, of any one who has a conscience.
To have a conscience, then, is to have a cause, to unify your life by
means of an ideal determined by this cause, and to compare the
ideal and the life.

If this analysis is right, your conscience is simply that ideal of
life which constitutes your moral personality. In having your conscience you become aware of your plan of being yourself and
nobody else. Your conscience presents to you this plan, however,
in so far as the plan or ideal in question is distinct from the
life in which you are trying to embody your plan. Your life as it
is lived, your experiences, feelings, deeds,—these are the embodiment of your ideal plan, in so far as your ideal plan for
your own individual life as this self gets embodied at all.

But no one act of yours ever expresses your plan of life perfectly. Since you thus always have your cause beyond you, there is
always more to do. So the plan or ideal of life comes to stand over
against your actual life as a general authority by which each
deed is to be tested, just as the judicial conscience of the judge
on the bench tests each of his official acts by comparing it with
his personal ideal of what a judge should be. My conscience,
therefore, is the very ideal that makes me this rational self, the
very cause that inspires and that unifies me. Viewed as something within myself, my conscience is the spirit of the self, first
moving on the face of the waters of natural desire, and then
gradually creating the heavens and the earth of this life of the

individual man. This spirit informs all of my true self, yet is nowhere fully expressed in any deed. So that, in so far as we contrast the ideal with the single deed, we judge ourselves, condemn ourselves, or approve ourselves.

Our philosophy of loyalty thus furnishes us with a theory of a certain kind of consciousness which, in any case, precisely fulfils the functions of the traditional conscience. I need hardly say that the conscience which I have now described is not in its entirety at all innate. On the contrary, it is the flower rather than the root of the moral life. But unquestionably we should never get it unless we possessed an innate power to become reasonable, unless we were socially disposed beings, unless we were able so to develop our reason and our social powers as to see that the good of mankind is indeed also our own good, and, in brief, unless we inherited a genuine moral nature.

With this view of the nature of conscience, what can we say as to the infallability of such a conscience? I answer: My conscience is precisely as fallible or as infallible as my choice of a cause is subject to error, or is of such nature as to lead me aright. Since loyalty, in so far as it is loyalty, is always a good, the conscience of any loyal self is never wholly a false guide. Since loyalty may be in many respects blind, one's conscience also may be in many respects misleading. On the other hand, your conscience, at any stage of its development, is unquestionably the best moral guide that you then have, simply because, so far as it is viewed as an authority outside of you, it is your ideal, your cause, set before you; while, in so far as it is within you, it is the spirit of your own self, the very ideal that makes you any rational moral person whatever. Apart from it you are a mere pretence of moral personality, a manifold fermentation of desires. And as you have only your own life to live, your conscience alone can teach you how to live that life. But your conscience will doubtless grow with you, just as your loyalty and your cause will grow. The best way to make both of them grow is to render up your life to their service and to their expression.

Conscience, as thus defined, is for each of us a personal affair. In so far as many of us are fellow-servants of the same cause, and, above all, in so far as all of us, if we are enlightened, are fellow-servants of the one cause of universal loyalty, we do indeed share in the same conscience. But in so far as no two of us can live the same life, or be the same individual human self, it follows that no two of us can possess identical consciences, and that no two of us should wish to do so. Your conscience is not mine; yet I share with you the same infinite realm of moral truth, and we are subject to the same requirement of loyalty to loyalty. This requirement must interpret itself to us all in endlessly varied ways. The loyal are not all monotonously doing the same thing. Yet they individually partake of the one endlessly varied and manifold spirit of loyalty.

As to whether conscience is in any sense divine, we shall learn something in our closing lecture upon the relations of Loyalty and Religion.

VI

So far as is needful for our present practical purpose, the theory of the conscience which our philosophy of loyalty requires is now before you. We needed this theory in order to prepare the way for answering the question: In how far does the law, *Be loyal to loyalty,* enable us to decide cases of moral doubt? In how far does this principle furnish a means of discovering these special precepts about single cases which common sense calls the "dictates of conscience"?

How do moral doubts arise in the mind of a loyal person? I answer: Moral doubts arise in the loyal mind when there is an apparent conflict between loyalties. As a fact, that cause, which in any sense unifies a life as complex as my human life is, must of course be no perfectly simple cause. By virtue of my nature and of my social training, I belong to a family, to a community, to a calling, to a state, to humanity. In order to be loyal to loyalty, and in order to be a person at all, I must indeed unify my loyalty. In the meantime, however, I must also choose special causes to serve; and if these causes are to interest me, if they are to engross and to possess me, they must be such as together appeal to many diverse sides of my nature; they must involve me in numerous and often conflicting social tasks; they can form one cause only in so far as they constitute an entire system of causes. My loyalty will be subject, therefore, to the ancient difficulty regarding the one and the many. Unless it is one in its ultimate aim, it will be no loyalty to universal loyalty; unless it is just to the varied instincts and to the manifold social interests of a being such as I am, it cannot engross me.

Despite this great difficulty, however, the loyal all about us show us that this union of one and many in life is, at least in great portions of long human careers, a possible thing. We never completely win the union; we never realize to the full the one loyal life; but in so far as we are loyal, we win enough of this unity of life to be able to understand the ideal, and to make it our own guide. Our question still remains, however, this: Since the only loyal life that we can undertake to live is so complex, since the one cause of universal loyalty can only be served, by each of us, in a personal life wherein we have to try to unify various special loyalties, and since, in many cases, these special loyalties seem to us to conflict with one another,—how shall we decide, as between two apparently conflicting loyalties, which one to follow? Does our principle tell us what to do when loyalties thus seem to us to be in conflict with one another?

It is, of course, not sufficient to answer here that loyalty to loyalty requires us to do whatever can be done to harmonize apparently conflicting loyalties, and to remove the conflict of loyalties from the world, and to utilize even conflict, where it is inevitable, so as to further general loyalty. That answer we have already considered in an earlier passage of this discussion. It is a sound answer; but it does not meet those cases where conflict is forced upon us, and where we ourselves must take sides, and must annul or destroy one or two conflicting loyalties. One or two illustrations of such a type will serve to show what sorts of moral doubts our own philosophy of loyalty has especially to consider.

At the outset of our Civil War, many men of the border states, and many who had already been in the service of the Union, but who were conscious of special personal duties to single states of the Union, found themselves in presence of a well-known conflict of loyalties. Consider the personal problem that the future General Lee had to solve. Could the precept, *Be loyal to loyalty, and to that end, choose your own personal cause and be loyal thereto,*—could this principle, you may say, have been of any service in deciding for Lee his personal problem at the critical moment?

Or again, to take a problem such as some of my own students have more than once urged, in various instances, as a test case for my theory of loyalty to decide: A young woman, after a thorough modern professional training, begins a career which promises not only worldly success, but general good to the community in which she works. She is heartily loyal to her profession. It is a beneficent profession. She will probably make her mark in that field if she chooses to go on. Meanwhile she is loyal to her own family. And into the home, which she has left for her work, disease, perhaps death, enters. Her younger brothers and sisters are now unexpectedly in need of such care as hers; or the young family of her elder brother or sister, through the death of their father or mother, has come to be without due parental care. As elder sister or as maiden aunt this young woman could henceforth devote herself to family tasks that would mean very much for the little ones in question. But this devotion would also mean years of complete absorption in these family tasks, and would also mean an entire abandonment of the profession so hopefully begun, and of all the good that she can now be fairly sure of doing if she continues in that field.

What are the dictates of conscience? How shall this young woman solve her problem? How shall she decide between these conflicting loyalties? To be loyal to the family, to the needs of brothers, sisters, nephews, nieces,—surely this is indeed devotion of a self to a cause. But to be loyal to her chosen profession, which, in this case, is no mere hope, but which is already an actual and successful task,—is not that also loyalty to a cause? And does the principle, *Be loyal to loyalty,* decide which of these two causes is the one for this young woman to serve?

These two cases of conscience may serve as examples of the vast range of instances of a conflict of loyalties. And now you may ask: What will our principle do to decide such cases?

VII

I reply at once by emphasizing the fact that the precept, *Be loyal to loyalty,* implies two characteristics of loyal conduct which are, to my mind, inseparable. The first characteristic is Decisiveness on the part of the loyal moral agent. The second characteristic is Fidelity to loyal decisions once made, in so far as later insight does not clearly forbid the continuance of such fidelity. Let me indicate what I mean by these two characteristics.

Loyalty to loyalty is never a merely pious wish. It is personal devotion. This devotion shows itself by action, not by mere sentiments. Loyalty to loyalty hence requires the choice of some definite mode of action. And this mode of action involves, in

critical cases, some new choice of a personal cause, through which
the loyal agent undertakes to serve henceforth, as best he can,
the general cause of the loyalty of mankind. Now, my special
choice of my personal cause is always fallible. For I can never
know with certainty but that, if I were wiser, I should better
see my way to serving universal loyalty than I now see it. Thus, if
I choose to be loyal to loyalty by becoming a loyal clerk or a
watchman or a lighthouse keeper, I can never know but that, in
some other calling, I might have done better. Now, it is no part
of the precept, *Be loyal to loyalty*, to tell me, or to pretend to tell
me, what my most effective vocation is. Doubts about that topic
are in so far not moral doubts. They are mere expressions of my
general ignorance of the world and of my own powers. If I
indeed happen to know that I have no power to make a good
clerk or a good watchman, the precept about loyalty then tells
me that it would be disloyal to waste my powers in an undertaking
for which I am so unfit. If, of various possible ways of undertaking to be loyal to loyalty, my present insight already tells me
that one will, in my case, certainly succeed best of all, then,
indeed, the general principle of loyalty requires me to have
neither eyes to see nor tongue to speak save as this best mode
of service commands. But if, at the critical moment, I cannot
predict which of two modes of serving the cause of loyalty to
loyalty will lead to the more complete success in such service, the
general principle certainly cannot tell me which of these two
modes of service to choose.

And, nevertheless, the principle does not desert me, even at
the moment of my greatest ignorance. It is still my guide. For it
now becomes the principle, *Have a cause; choose your cause; be
decisive.* In this form the principle is just as practical as it would
be if my knowledge of the world and of my own powers were
infallible. For it forbids cowardice; it forbids hesitancy beyond
the point where further consideration can be reasonably expected, for the present, to throw new light on the situation. It
forbids me to play Hamlet's part. It requires me, in a loyal spirit
and in the light of all that I now know, to choose and to proceed
to action, not as one who believes himself omniscient, but as one
who knows that the only way to be loyal is to act loyally,
however ignorantly one has to act.

Otherwise stated, the case is this. I hesitate at the critical moment between conflicting causes. For the sake of loyalty to
loyalty, which one of two conflicting special causes shall I hence-

forth undertake to serve? This is my question. If I knew what is
to be the outcome, I could at once easily choose. I am ignorant of
the outcome. In so far I indeed cannot tell which to choose. But
in one respect I am, nevertheless, already committed. I have
already undertaken to be loyal to loyalty. In so far, then, I
already have my cause. If so, however, I have neither eyes to see
nor tongue to speak save as this my highest cause commands.
Now, what does this my highest cause, loyalty to loyalty, command? It commands simply but imperatively that, since I must
serve, and since, at this critical moment, my only service must take
the form of a choice between loyalties, I shall choose, even in
my ignorance, what form my service is henceforth to take. The
point where I am to make this choice is determined by the obvious fact that, after a certain waiting to find out whatever I can
find out, I always reach the moment when further indecision
would of itself constitute a sort of decision,—a decision,
namely, to do nothing, and so not to serve at all. Such a decision
to do nothing, my loyalty to loyalty forbids; and therefore my
principle clearly says to me after a fair consideration of the case:
*Decide, knowingly if you can, ignorantly if you must, but in any
case decide, and have no fear.*

The duty of decisiveness as to one's loyalty is thus founded
upon considerations analogous to those which Professor James
has emphasized, in speaking of certain problems about belief in
his justly famous essay on the Will to Believe. *As soon as further
indecision would itself practically amount to a decision to do
nothing,*—and so would mean a failure to be loyal to loyalty,—
then at once decide. This is the only right act. If you cannot decide knowingly, put your own personal will into the matter, and
thereupon decide ignorantly. For ignorant service, which still
knows itself as a willing attempt to serve the cause of universal
loyalty, is better than a knowing refusal to undertake any service whatever. The duty to decide is, in such cases, just that upon
which our principle insists.

Decision, however, is meaningless unless it is to be followed
up by persistently active loyalty. Having surrendered the self to
the chosen special cause, loyalty, precisely as loyalty to loyalty,
forbids you to destroy the unity of your own purposes, and to set
the model of disloyalty before your fellows, by turning back from
the cause once chosen, unless indeed later growth in knowledge
makes manifest that further service of that special cause would
henceforth involve unquestionable disloyalty to universal loy-

alty. Fidelity to the cause once chosen is as obvious an aspect of a thorough devotion of the self to the cause of universal loyalty, as is decisiveness.

Only a growth in knowledge which makes it evident that the special cause once chosen is an unworthy cause, disloyal to universal loyalty,—only such a growth in knowledge can absolve from fidelity to the cause once chosen. In brief, the choice of a special personal cause is a sort of ethical marriage to this cause, with the exception that the duty to choose some personal cause is a duty for everybody, while marriage is not everybody's duty. The marriage to your cause is not to be dissolved unless it becomes unquestionably evident that the continuance of this marriage involves positive unfaithfulness to the cause of universal loyalty. But like any other marriage, the marriage of each self to its chosen personal cause is made in ignorance of the consequences. Decide, then, in the critical case, and, "forsaking all others, cleave to your own cause." Thus only can you be loyal to loyalty.

If you once view the matter in this way, you will not suppose that our principle would leave either the future General Lee or our supposed young professional woman without guidance. It would say: Look first at the whole situation. Consider it carefully. See, if possible, whether you can predict the consequences to the general loyalty which your act will involve. If, after such consideration, you still remain ignorant of decisive facts, then look to your highest loyalty; look steadfastly at the cause of universal loyalty itself. Remember how the loyal have always borne themselves. Then, with your eyes and your voice put as completely as may be at the service of that cause, arouse all the loyal interests of your own self, just as they now are, to their fullest vigor; and hereupon firmly and freely decide. Henceforth, with all your mind and soul and strength belong, fearlessly and faithfully, to the chosen personal cause until the issue is decided, or until you positively know that this cause can no longer be served without disloyalty. So act, and you are morally right.

Now, that is how Lee acted. And that, too, is how all the loyal of our own Northern armies acted. And to-day we know how there was indeed loyalty to loyalty upon both sides, and how all those loyal actually served the one cause of the now united nation. They loyally shed their blood, North and South, that we might be free from their burden of hatred and of horror. Precisely so should the young woman of our ideal instance choose.

It is utterly vain for another to tell her which she ought to choose, —her profession or her family. But it would be equally vain, and an insult to loyalty, lightly to say to her: Do as you please. One can say to her: Either of these lives,—the life of the successful servant of a profession, or the life of the devoted sister or aunt,—either, if loyally lived, is indeed a whole life. Nobody ought to ask for a more blessed lot than is either of these lives,— however obscure the household drudgery of the one may be, however hard beset by cares the worldly success of the other may prove, or however toilsome either of them in prospect is, so long as either is faithfully lived out in full devotion. For nobody has anything better than loyalty, or can get anything better. But one of them alone can you live. No mortal knows which is the better for your world. With all your heart, in the name of universal loyalty, choose. And then be faithful to the choice. So shall it be morally well with you.

Now, if this view of the application of our precept is right, you see how our principle is just to that mysterious and personal aspect of conscience upon which common sense insists. Such a loyal choice as I have described demands, of course, one's will,— one's conscious decisiveness. It also calls out all of one's personal and more or less unconsciously present instincts, interests, affections, one's socially formed habits, and whatever else is woven into the unity of each individual self. Loyalty, as we have all along seen, is a willing devotion. Since it is willing, it involves conscious choice. Since it is devotion, it involves all the mystery of finding out that some cause awakens us, fascinates us, reverberates through our whole being, possesses us. It is a fact that critical decisions as to the direction of our loyalty can be determined by our own choice. It is also a fact that loyalty involves more than mere conscious choice. It involves that response of our entire nature, conscious and unconscious, which makes loyalty so precious. Now, this response of the whole nature of the self, when the result is a moral decision, is what common sense has in mind when it views our moral decisions as due to our conscience, but our conscience as a mysterious higher or deeper self.

As a fact, the conscience is the ideal of the self, coming to consciousness as a present command. It says, *Be loyal.* If one asks, *Loyal to what?* the conscience, awakened by our whole personal response to the need of mankind replies, *Be loyal to loyalty.* If, hereupon, various loyalties seem to conflict, the conscience says:

Decide. If one asks, *How decide?* conscience further urges, *Decide as I, your conscience, the ideal expression of your whole personal nature, conscious and unconscious, find best.* If one persists, *But you and I may be wrong,* the last word of conscience is, *We are fallible, but we can be decisive and faithful; and this is loyalty.*

15 ❧ TRAINING FOR LOYALTY [1]

IV

The true sphere of a complete loyalty is mature life. We constantly need, all of us, individual training in the art of loyalty. How is this work accomplished in the social order? In answering this question, let history and our daily social experience be our guides. The main lessons that these guides teach us, as I think, are three: First, our loyalty is trained and kept alive by the influence of personal leaders. Secondly, the higher forms of training for loyalty involve a momentous process which I shall call the Idealizing of the Cause. Thirdly, loyalty is especially perfected through great strains, labors, and sacrifices in the service of the cause.

Of the three factors here mentioned, the first and second are inseparable and universal. If we are to be made loyal, we want personal leaders, and highly idealized causes. In exceptional cases a man may seem to be his own sole leader in loyalty. But this is rare. Always, to be sure, a loyal man uses his own leadership, since, as we saw in our fourth lecture, his conscience is his leader. But usually he needs the aid of other personal leaders besides himself. . . .

VI

. . . And how shall we be surest of finding such personal leaders? Shall we look exclusively to those who are fellow-servants of our own chosen special causes? We all do this. Yet this is often not enough. Familiarity and personal misunderstandings often interfere with the guidance that our fellow-

[1] Josiah Royce, *The Philosophy of Loyalty* (New York: The Macmillan Company, 1908), Lecture VI, pp. 268–269, 286–288, 288–298.—Editor's note.

servants give us. We need the wider outlook. Close friendships
are amongst the most powerful supports of loyalty. Yet when
people confine themselves to regarding their close friends as
their leaders in loyalty, they often become narrow and forget
the cause of universal loyalty. Much of the art of loyalty, consequently, depends upon training yourself to observe the loyal
who are all about you, however remote their cause is from yours,
however humble their lives. It is well also, whenever you have to
fight, to learn the art of honoring your opponent's loyalty, even
if you learn of it mainly through feeling the weight and the
sharpness of his sword. "It is a deep cut; but a loyal enemy was
he who could give it to me"—to think in such terms is to lighten
the gloom of conflict with what may sometimes be more precious
than a transient victory; for at such moments of honoring the
loyally dangerous enemy, we begin to learn that all the loyal are
in spirit serving, however unwittingly, the same universal cause.
To be sure, when men have once sufficiently learned that lesson,
they cease to fight. But while fighting lasts, if you cannot love
your enemy, it is a beautiful thing to be able to enjoy the sight of
his loyalty.

But men have not to fight one another in order to display loyalty. Open your eyes, then, to observe better the loyalty of the
peaceful, as well as of the warriors. Consider especially the loyalty of the obscure, of the humble, of your near neighbors, of the
strangers who by chance come under your notice. For such ex-
emplars of loyalty you always have. Make them your leaders.
Regard every loyal man as your leader in the service of the cause
of universal loyalty.

VII

. . . We need not only leaders. We need to idealize our causes;
that is, to see in them whatever most serves to link them to the
cause of universal loyalty. And the procedure whereby our causes
are to be idealized is one involving a range of possible experiences and activities far too vast to be adequately surveyed in our
present discussion. Here belong all those practically valuable
relations between loyalty and art, and between loyalty and religion, which the history of mankind illustrates and which we can
use in our own training for loyalty. Art supports loyalty whenever it associates our cause with beautiful objects, whenever it

sets before us the symbols of our cause in any worthy expression, and whenever, again, by showing us any form of the beautiful, it portrays to us that very sort of learning and unity that loyalty ceaselessly endeavors to bring into human life. Thus viewed, art may be a teacher of loyalty. To say this is in no wise to prejudge the famous question regarding the main purpose of art, and the relation of this purpose of art to the moral life. I am attempting here no theory of art. But it belongs to our present province merely to insist that part of our education in loyalty is to be won through whatever love of beauty and whatever knowledge of the beautiful we possess. The monuments of any cause that possesses monuments should associate our love of this cause with our love for beauty. Our personal causes, if they are worthy at all, need beautiful symbols to express to us their preciousness. Whatever is beautiful appears to us to embody harmonious relations. And the practical search for harmony of life constitutes loyalty. And thus training for loyalty includes the knowledge of the beautiful.

Still more universal in its efficacy as an idealizer of private and personal causes is religion. In how far a genuinely religious experience results from loyalty, and in how far loyalty bears witness to any religiously significant truth, we have hereafter to see. Our closing lectures will deal with the bearing of loyalty upon religion. But we have here to mention, in passing, the converse relation; namely, the influence of religion upon loyalty. We have to point out how large a part of the function of religion in human affairs consists in the idealizing of our loyalties, by linking our causes, whatever they are, to a world which seems to us to be superhuman.

VIII

Art and religion, however, are not our only means for teaching ourselves to view our personal causes as linked with universal human interests, and with an unseen superhuman world. Sorrow, defeat, disappointment, failure, whenever these result from our efforts to serve a cause, may all be used to teach us the same lesson. How such lessons have been taught to humanity at large, the history of those lost causes which have been, even because of the loss, transformed into causes of permanent and world-wide importance, has now shown us. This lesson of the history of the lost causes is, however, one that has deep importance for our individual training. We do not always read this lesson aright. To keep our loyalty steadfast through defeat is something that we often view as a sort of extra strain upon loyalty,—the overcoming of a painful hindrance to loyalty. We ought not so to view the matter. Defeat and sorrow, when they are incurred in the service of a cause, ought rather to be a positive aid to loyalty. If we rightly view them, they will prove to be such an aid. For they enable us to see whether we have really given ourselves to the cause, or whether what we took for loyalty was a mere flare of sanguine emotion. When sorrow over a defeat in the service of our cause reverberates all through us, it can be made to reveal whatever loyalty we have. Let us turn our attention to this revelation, even while we suffer. We shall then know for what we have been living. And whoever, once deliberately dwelling upon his cause at a moment of defeat, does not find the cause dearer to him because of his grief, has indeed yet to learn what loyalty is. The cause, furthermore, when viewed in the light of our sorrow over our loss of its present fortunes, at once tends to become idealized,—as the lost throne of David was idealized by Israel, and as the departed Master's cause was idealized by the early church.

The disciples, in the well-known story, say concerning their lost Master to the stranger whom they meet on the lonely road to Emmaus: "We had trusted that it was he who should have redeemed Israel." But soon after "their eyes were opened, and they knew him, and he vanished out of their sight." Amongst all the legends of the risen Lord, this one most completely expresses the spirit of that loyalty which, triumphing even through defeat, winning the spirit even through the loss of a visible presence, was thereafter to conquer its world.

Now, the lesson of such experiences, as history records them, relates not merely to great movements and to mankind at large. It is a personal lesson. It concerns each one of us. I repeat: View your sorrow by itself, and it is a blind and hopeless fact; view your cause in the light of your sorrow, and the cause becomes transfigured. For you learn hereby that it was not this or that fortune, nor even this or that human life which constituted your cause. There was from the beginning, about your cause, something that to human vision seems superpersonal, unearthly as well as earthly. Now the memory of whatever is lost about your cause is peculiarly adapted to bring to your consciousness what this superpersonal element has been. I have already mentioned the merely psychological aspects of the process that, in such cases, goes on. The glamour which memory throws about the past, the awakening of the imagination when some visible presence is removed, the stimulating reaction from the first stroke of sorrow whenever we are able once more to think of our cause itself, the transformation of our own ideas about the cause, by virtue of the very fact that, since our loss has so changed life, the cause can no longer be served in the old way, and must be the object of new efforts, and so of some new form of devotion,—all these are the idealizing motives which are present when defeat comes. I insist,—human loyalty can never be perfected without such sorrow. Regard defeat and bereavement, therefore, as loyalty's opportunity. Use them deliberately as means for idealizing the cause, and so far bringing your personal cause into closer touch with the cause of universal loyalty.

The most familiar of all those blows of fortune which seem to us, for the moment, to make our personal cause a lost cause, is death, when it comes to those with whom our personal cause has so far been bound up. And yet what motive in human life has done more to idealize the causes of individuals than death has done? Death, viewed as a mere fact of human experience, and as a merely psychological influence, has been one of the greatest idealizers of human life. The memory of the dead idealizes whatever interest the living have in former days shared with the departed. Reverence for the dead dignifies the effort to carry on the work that they began, or that, if they died in childhood, our fond desire would have had them live to do. From the beginning a great portion of the religious imagination of mankind has centered about the fact of death. And the same motive works to-day in the minds of all the loyal, whatever their faith.

Idealize your cause. This has been our maxim for the present aspect of our personal training in loyalty. I have offered merely some hints as to how this maxim may be carried into effect. How science can join with art and with religion, how joyous friendly intercourse can in its own place coöperate with our experiences of sorrow to teach us the lessons of idealizing our common causes, —all this I can only indicate.

And thus we have before us two of the methods whereby individual loyalty is trained. The deliberate fixing of our attention upon the doings of loyal people, the deliberate use of those methods of human nature which tend to idealize our cause,—these are means for training in loyalty.

Yet one method remains,—it is the most commonplace, yet often the hardest of all. Loyalty means giving the Self to the Cause. And the art of giving is learned by giving. Strain, endurance, sacrifice, toil,—the dear pangs of labor at the moments when perhaps defeat and grief most seem ready to crush our powers, and when only the very vehemence of labor itself saves us from utter despair,—these are the things that most teach us what loyalty really is. I need not enlarge here upon an ancient and constantly repeated lesson of life,—a lesson which is known to all of you. The partisans of war often glorify war as a moralizer of humanity, because, as they say, only the greatest strains and dangers can teach men true loyalty. I do not think that war is needed for such lessons. The loyalty of the most peaceful enables us all to experience, sooner or later, what it means to give, whatever it was in our power to give, for the cause, and then to see our cause take its place, to human vision, amongst the lost causes. When such experiences come, let us face them without hesitation. For all these things together,—our personal friends who inspire us to the service of our own causes, the hosts of the loyal whom we know so little, but who constitute the invisible church of those who live in the spirit, the griefs that teach us the glory of what our human vision has lost from its field, the imagination that throws over all the range of human life its idealizing light, the labors that leave us breathless, the crushing defeats that test our devotion,—well, these, these are all only the means and the ministers whereby we are taught to enter the realm of spiritual truth.

16 ✿ LOYALTY, TRUTH, AND REALITY [1]

In closing my last lecture I said that whatever trains us in the arts of loyalty enables us to enter into a world of spiritual truth. These words were intended to indicate that the loyal life has another aspect than the one hitherto most emphasized in these lectures. Our foregoing account has been deliberately one-sided. We have been discussing the moral life as if one could define a plan of conduct without implying more about man's place in the real universe than we have yet made explicit in these lectures. Hence our discussion, so far, is open to obvious objections.

For, in talking about the good of loyalty, we have indeed appealed to human experience to show us wherein that good consists. But our very appeal also showed us that loyalty is good for a man precisely because he believes that his cause itself, even apart from his service, is good, and that both his cause and its goodness are realities, founded in facts which far transcend his individual life and his personal experience. Now, one may well doubt whether this belief of a loyal man is, in any individual case, a well-founded belief. And if it is not well founded, one may well question whether the loyal man's good is not, after all, an illusory good, which will vanish from his experience as soon as he becomes enlightened. Since any instance of loyalty is subject to this sceptical inquiry, one may doubt whether even what we have called the supreme cause, that of loyalty to loyalty, is a good cause. For any or all loyalties may be founded in illusion, and then it would be an illusion that the fostering of loyalty amongst men is a finally worthy undertaking.

I

. . . To sum up: So far we have defined the moral life as loyalty, and have shown why the moral life is for us men the best life. But now we want to know what truth is behind and

[1] Josiah Royce, *The Philosophy of Loyalty* (New York: The Macmillan Company, 1908), Lecture VII, pp. 301–302, 306–313, 340–346.—Editor's note.

beneath the moral life. . . . We want to see the relation of
loyalty to the real universe.

II

What must be true about the universe if even loyalty itself is
a genuine good, and not a merely inevitable human illusion?

Well, loyalty is a service of causes. A cause, if it really is
what our definition requires, links various human lives into the
unity of one life. Therefore, if loyalty has any basis in truth, human lives can be linked in some genuine spiritual unity. Is such
unity a fact, or is our belief in our causes a mere point of view, a
pathetic fallacy? Surely, if any man, however loyal, discovers that
his cause is a dream, and that men remain as a fact sundered
beings, not really linked by genuine spiritual ties, how can
that man remain loyal? Perhaps his supreme good indeed lies
in believing that such unities are real. But if this belief turns out
to be an illusion, and if a man detects the illusion, can he any
longer get the good out of loyalty?

And as for even this personal good that is to be got out of
loyalty, we have all along seen that such good comes to a loyal
man's mind in a very paradoxical way. A loyal man gets good,
but since he gets it by believing that his cause has a real existence outside of his private self, and is of itself a good thing, he
gets the fascination of loyalty not as a private delight of his own,
but as a fulfilment of himself through self-surrender to an externally existing good,—through a willing abandonment of the
seeking of his own delight. And so the loyal man's good is
essentially an anticipation of a good that he regards as not his
own, but as existent in the cause. The cause, however, is itself
no one fellow-man, and no mere collection of fellow-men. It is a
family, a country, a church, or is such a rational union of many
human minds and wills as we have in mind when we speak of a
science or an art. Now, can such causes contain any good which
is not simply a collection of separate human experiences of pleasure or of satisfaction? Thus, then, both the reality and the good
of a loyal man's cause must be objects of the loyal man's belief
in order that he should be able to get the experience of loyalty.
And if his loyalty is indeed well founded, there must be unities
of spiritual life in the universe such that no one man ever, by
himself, experiences these unities as facts of his own consciousness. And these higher unities of life must possess a degree and
a type of goodness,—a genuine value, such that no one man, and

no mere collection of men, can ever exhaustively experience this goodness, or become personally possessed of this value.

How paradoxical a world, then, must the real world be, if the faith of the loyal is indeed well founded! A spiritual unity of life, which transcends the individual experience of any man, must be real. For loyalty, as we have seen, is a service of causes that, from the human point of view, appear superpersonal. Loyalty holds these unities to be good. If loyalty is right, the real goodness of these causes is never completely manifested to any one man, or to any mere collection of men. Such goodness, then, if completely experienced at all, must be experienced upon some higher level of consciousness than any one human being ever reaches. If loyalty is right, social causes, social organizations, friendships, families, countries, yes, humanity, as you see, must have the sort of unity of consciousness which individual human persons fragmentarily get, but must have this unity upon a higher level than that of our ordinary human individuality.

Some such view, I say, must be held if we are to regard loyalty as in the end anything more than a convenient illusion. Loyalty has its metaphysical aspect. It is an effort to conceive human life in an essentially superhuman way, to view our social organizations as actual personal unities of consciousness, unities wherein there exists an actual experience of that good which, in our loyalty, we only partially apprehend. If the loyalty of the lovers is indeed well founded in fact, then they, as separate individuals, do not constitute the whole truth. Their spiritual union also has a personal, a conscious existence, upon a higher than human level. An analogous unity of consciousness, an unity superhuman in grade, but intimately bound up with, and inclusive of, our apparently separate personalities, must exist, if loyalty is well founded, wherever a real cause wins the true devotion of ourselves. Grant such an hypothesis, and then loyalty becomes no pathetic serving of a myth. The good which our causes possess, then, also becomes a concrete fact for an experience of a higher than human level. That union of self-sacrifice with self-assertion which loyalty expresses becomes a consciousness of our genuine relations to a higher social unity of consciousness in which we all have our being. For from this point of view we are, and we have our worth, by virtue of our relation to a consciousness of a type superior to the human type. And meanwhile the good of our loyalty is itself a perfectly concrete good, a good which is present to that higher experience, wherein our cause is viewed in its truth, as a genuine unity of life. And because of this fact we can straightforwardly say: We are loyal not for the sake of the good that we privately get out of loyalty, but for the sake of the good that the cause—this higher unity of experience—gets out of this loyalty. Yet our loyalty gives us what is, after all, our supreme good, for it defines our true position in the world of that social will wherein we live and move and have our being.

I doubt not that such a view of human life,—such an assertion that the social will is a concrete entity, just as real as we are, and of still a higher grade of reality than ourselves,—will seem to many of you mythical enough. Yet thus to view the unity of human life is, after all, a common tendency of the loyal. That fact I have illustrated in every lecture of this course. That such a view need not be mythical, that truth and reality can be conceived only in such terms as these, that our philosophy of loyalty is a rational part of a philosophy which must view the whole world as one unity of consciousness, wherein countless lesser unities are synthesized,—this is a general philosophical thesis which I must next briefly expound to you.

. . . . .

VI

. . . In seeking truth we do not seek the mere crumbling successes of the passing instants of human life. We seek a city out of sight. What we get of success within our passing experience is rationally as precious to us as it is, just because we believe that attainment to be a fragment of an essentially superhuman success, which is won in the form of a higher experience than ours, —a conspectus wherein our human experiences are unified. But what warrant have we for this belief?

I will tell you how I view the case. We need unity of life. In recognizing that need my own pragmatism   ᴊists. Now, we never find unity present to our human experience in more than a fragmentary shape. We get hints of higher unity. But only the fragmentary unity is won at any moment of our lives. We therefore form ideas—very fallible ideas—of some unity of experience, an unity such as our idea of any science or any art or any united people or of any community or of any other cause, any other union of many human experiences in one, defines. Now, if our ideas are in any case indeed true, then such an unity is as a fact successfully experienced upon some higher level than ours and is experienced in some conspectus of life which wins what we need, which approves our loyalty, which fulfils our rational will, and which has in its wholeness what we seek. And then we ourselves with all our ideas and strivings are in and of this higher unity of life. Our loyalty to truth is a hint of this unity. Our transient successes are fragments of the true success. But suppose our ideas about the structure of this higher unity to be false in any of their details. Suppose, namely, any of our causes to be wrongly viewed by us. Then there is still real that state of facts, whatever it is, which, if just now known to us, would show us this falsity of our various special ideas. Now, only an experience, a consciousness of some system of contents, could show the falsity of any idea. Hence this real state of facts, this constitution of the genuine universe, whatever it is, must again be a reality precisely in so far as it is also a conspectus of facts of experience.

We therefore already possess at least one true idea, precisely in so far as we say: "The facts of the world are what they are; the real universe exposes our errors and makes them errors." And when we say this, we once more appeal to a conspectus of experience in which ours is included. For I am in error only in case my present ideas about the true facts of the whole world of experience are out of concord with the very meaning that I myself actively try to assign to these ideas. My ideas are in any detail false, only if the very experience to which I mean to appeal, contains in its conspectus contents which I just now imperfectly conceive. In any case, then, the truth is possessed by precisely that whole of experience which I never get, but to which my colleague [2] also inevitably appeals when he talks of the "long run," or of the experiences of humanity in general.

Whatever the truth, then, or the falsity of any of my special convictions about this or that fact may be, the real world, which refutes my false present ideas in so far as they clash with its wholeness, and which confirms them just in so far as they succeed in having significant relations to its unity,—this real world, I say, is a conspectus of the whole of experience. And this whole of experience is in the closest real relation to my practical life, precisely in so far as, for me, the purpose of my life is to get into unity with the whole universe, and precisely in so far as the universe itself is just that conspectus of experience that we all mean to define and to serve whatever we do, or whatever we say.

[2] Royce is referring to William James.—Editor's note.

But the real whole conspectus of experience, the real view of the totality of life, the real expression of that will to live in and for the whole, which every assertion of truth and every loyal deed expresses—well, it must be a conspectus that includes whatever facts are indeed facts, be they past, present, or future. I call this whole of experience an eternal truth. I do not thereby mean, as my colleague seems to imagine, that the eternal first exists, and that then our life in time comes and copies that eternal order. I mean simply that the whole of experience includes all temporal happenings, contains within itself all changes, and, since it is the one whole that we all want and need, succeeds in so far as it supplements all failures, accepts all, even the blindest of services, and wins what we seek. Thus winning it is practically good and worthy.

But if one insists, How do you know all this? I reply: I know simply that to try to deny the reality of this whole of truth is simply to reaffirm it. Any special idea of mine may be wrong, even as any loyal deed may fail, or as any cause may become, to human vision, a lost cause. But to deny that there is truth, or that there is a real world, is simply to say that the whole truth is that there is no whole truth, and that the real fact is that there is no fact real at all. Such assertions are plain self-contradictions. And on the other hand, by the term "real world," defined as it is for us by our ideal needs, we mean simply that whole of experience in which we live, and in unity with which we alone succeed.

Loyalty, then, has its own metaphysic. This metaphysic is expressed in a view of things which conceives our experience as bound up in a real unity with all experience,—an unity which is essentially good, and in which all our ideas possess their real fulfilment and success. Such a view is true, simply because if you deny its truth you reaffirm that very truth under a new form.

Truth, meanwhile, means, as pragmatism asserts, the fulfilment of a need. But we all need the superhuman, the city out of sight, the union with all life,—the essentially eternal. This need is no invention of the philosophers. It is the need which all the loyal feel, whether they know it or not, and whether they call themselves pragmatists or not. To define this need as pragmatism in its recent forms has done, to reduce truth to expediency, is to go about crying *cash, cash,* in a realm where there is no cash of the sort that loyalty demands, that every scientific inquiry presupposes, and that only the unity of the experiences of many in one furnishes. . . .

17 ❧ LOYALTY AND RELIGION [1]

I

. . . In the last lecture we undertook to consider this larger realm of spiritual unities which must be real in case our loyalty is not based upon illusion. And we attempted to sketch a general theory of truth which might show us that such spiritual unities are indeed realities, and are presupposed by our every effort to define truth. Thus our ethical theory has transformed itself into a general philosophical doctrine; and loyalty now appears to us not only as a guide of life but as a revelation of our relation to a realm which we have been obliged to define as one of an eternal and all-embracing unity of spiritual life.

We have called this realm of true life, and of genuine and united experience,—this realm which, if our argument at the last time was sound, includes our lives in that very whole which constitutes the real universe,—we have called this realm, I say, an eternal world,—eternal, simply because, according to our theory, it includes all temporal happenings and strivings in the conspectus of a single consciousness, and fulfils all our rational purposes together, and is all that we seek to be. For, as we argued, this realm of reality is conscious, is united, is self-possessed, and is perfected through the very wealth of the ideal sacrifices and of the loyal devotion which are united so as to constitute its fulness of being. In view of the philosophy that was thus sketched, I now propose a new definition of loyalty; and I say that this definition results from all of our previous study: *Loyalty is the will to manifest, so far as is possible, the Eternal, that is, the conscious and superhuman unity of life, in the form of the acts of an individual Self.* Or, if you prefer to take the point of view of an individual human self, if you persist in looking at the world just

[1] Josiah Royce, *The Philosophy of Loyalty* (New York: The Macmillan Company, 1908), Lecture VIII,, pp. 355–358, 360–372, 373–398.—Editor's note.

as we find it in our ordinary experience, and if you regard the
metaphysical doctrine just sketched merely as an ideal theory of
life, and *not* as a demonstrable philosophy, I can still hold to my
definition of loyalty by borrowing a famous phrase from the dear
friend and colleague some of whose views I at the last time
opposed. I can, then, simply state my new definition of loyalty
in plainer and more directly obvious terms thus: *Loyalty is the
Will to Believe in something eternal, and to express that belief in
the practical life of a human being.*

This, I say, is my new definition of loyalty, and in its
metaphysical form, it is my final definition. Let me expound it
further, and let me show a little more in detail how it results
from the whole course of our inquiry.

I I

. . . We all of us have to admit, I think, that our daily life depends upon believing in realities which are, in any case, just as truly
beyond the scope of our ordinary individual experience as any
spiritual realm could possibly be. We live by believing in one
another's minds as realities. We give credit to countless reports,
documents, and other evidences of present and past facts; and
we do all this, knowing that such credit cannot be adequately
verified by any experience such as an individual man can obtain.
Now, the usual traditional account of all these beliefs of ours is
that they are forced upon us, by some reality which is, as people
say, wholly independent of our knowledge, which exists by itself
apart from our experience, and which may be, therefore, entirely
alien in its nature to any of our human interests and ideals.

But modern philosophy,—a philosophy in whose historical
course of development our recent pragmatism is only a passing
incident,—that philosophy which turns upon analyzing the bases
of our knowledge, and upon reflectively considering what our
human beliefs and ideas are intended to mean and to accomplish,
has taught us to see that we can never deal with any wholly
independent reality. The recent pragmatists, as I understand
them, are here in full and conscious agreement with my own
opinion. We can deal with no world which is out of relation to
our experience. On the contrary, the real world is known to us in
terms of *our* experience, is defined for us by *our* ideas, and is the
object of *our* practical endeavors. Meanwhile, to declare anything

real is to assert that it has its place in some realm of experience, be this experience human or superhuman. To declare that anything whatever is a fact, is simply to assert that some proposition, which you or I or some other thinking being can express in the form of intelligible ideas, is a true proposition. And the truth of propositions itself is nothing dead, is nothing independent of ideas and of experience, but is simply the successful fulfilment of some demand,—a demand which you can express in the form of an assertion, and which is fulfilled in so far, and only in so far, as some region of live experience contains what meets that demand. Meanwhile, every proposition, every assertion that anybody can make, is a deed; and every rational deed involves, in effect, an assertion of a fact. If the prodigal son says, "I will arise and go to my father," he even thereby asserts something to be true about himself, his father, and his father's house. If an astronomer or a chemist or a statistician or a man of business reports "this or this is a fact," he even thereby performs a deed,—an act having an ideal meaning, and embodying a live purpose; and he further declares that the constitution of experience is such as to make this deed essentially reasonable, successful, and worthy to be accepted by every man.

The real world is therefore *not* something independent of us. It is a world whose stuff, so to speak,—whose content,—is of the nature of experience, whose structure meets, validates, and gives warrant to our active deeds, and whose whole nature is such that it can be interpreted in terms of ideas, propositions, and conscious meanings, while in turn it gives to our fragmentary ideas and to our conscious life whatever connected meaning they possess. Whenever I have purposes and fail, so far, to carry them out, that is because I have not yet found the true way of expressing my own relation to reality. On the other hand, precisely in so far as I have understood some whole of reality, I have carried out successfully some purpose of mine.

There is, then, no merely theoretical truth, and there is no reality foreign, in its nature, to experience. Whoever actually lives the whole conscious life such as *can* be lived out with a definitely reasonable meaning,—such a being, obviously superhuman in his grade of consciousness, not only knows the real world, but *is* the real world. Whoever is conscious of the whole content of experience possesses all reality. And our search for reality is simply an effort to discover what the whole fabric of experience is into which our human experience is woven, what the system of truth is in which our partial truths have their place, what the ideally significant life is for the sake of which every deed of ours is undertaken. When we try to find out what the real world is, we are simply trying to discover the sense of our own individual lives. And we can define that sense of our lives only in terms of a conscious life in which ours is included, in which our ideas get their full meaning expressed, and in which what we fail to carry out to the full is carried out to the full.

III

Otherwise stated, when I think of the whole world of facts,— the "real world,"—I inevitably think of something that is *my own* world, precisely in so far as that world is any object of any reasonable idea of mine. It is true, of course, that, in forming an idea of my world of facts, I do not thereby give myself, at this instant, the least right to spin out of my inner consciousness any adequate present ideas of the detail of the contents of my real world. In thinking of the real world, I am indeed thinking of the whole of that very system of experience in which my experience is bound up, and in which I, as an individual, have my very limited and narrow place. But just now I am not in possession of that whole. I have to work for it and wait for it, and faithfully to be true to it. As a creature living along, from moment to moment, in time, I therefore indeed have to wait ignorantly enough for coming experience. I have to use as I can my fallible memory in trying to find out about my own past experience. I have no way of verifying what your experience is, except by using tests— and again the extremely fallible tests—which we all employ in our social life. I need the methods of the sciences of experience to guide me in the study of whatever facts fall within their scope. I use those practical and momentary successes upon which recent pragmatism insists, whenever I try to get a concrete verification of my opinions. And so far I stand, and must rightly stand, exactly where any man of common sense, any student of a science, any plain man, or any learned man stands. I am a fallible mortal, simply trying to find my way as I can in the thickets of experience.

And yet all this my daily life, my poor efforts to remember and to predict, my fragmentary inquiries into this or that matter of science or of business, my practical acknowledgment of your presence as real facts in the real world of experience, my personal

definition of the causes to which I devote myself,—these are all
undertakings that are overruled, and that are rendered significant,
simply in so far as they are reasonable parts of one all-embracing
enterprise. This enterprise is my active attempt to find out my
true place in the real world. But now I can only define my real
world by conceiving it in terms of experience. I can find my place
in the world only by discovering where I stand in the whole
system of experience. For what I mean by a fact is something that
somebody finds. Even a merely possible fact is something only in
so far as somebody actually *could* find it. And the sense in which
it *is* an actual fact that somebody *could* find in his experience a
determinate fact, is a sense which again can only be defined in
terms of concrete, living, and not merely possible experience, and
in terms of some will or purpose expressed in a conscious life.
Even possible facts, then, are *really* possible only in so far as
something is actually experienced, or is found by somebody.
Whatever is real, then, be it distant or near, past or future, present
to your mind or to mine, a physical fact or a moral fact, a fact of
our possible human experience, or a fact of a superhuman type
of experience, a purpose, a desire, a natural object or an ideal
object, a mechanical system or a value,—whatever, I say, is real,
is real as a content present to some conscious being. Therefore,
when I inquire about the real world, I am simply asking what
contents of experience, human or superhuman, are actually and
consciously found by somebody. My inquiries regarding facts,
of whatever grade the facts may be, are therefore inevitably an
effort to find out *what the world's experience is.* In all my common sense, then, in all my science, in all my social life, I am
trying to discover what the universal conscious life which constitutes the world contains as its contents, and views as its own.

But even this is not the entire story of my place in the real
world. For I cannot inquire about facts without forming my own
ideas of these facts. In so far as my ideas are true, my own personal ideas are therefore active processes that go on within the
conscious life of the world. If my ideas are true, they succeed in
agreeing with the very world consciousness that they define. But
this agreement, this success, if itself it is a fact at all, is once
more a fact of experience,—yet not merely of my private experience, since I myself never personally find, within the limits
of my own individual experience, the success that every act of
truth seeking demands. If I get the truth, then, at any point of
my life, my success is real only in so far as some conscious life,

which includes my ideas and my efforts, and which also includes the very facts of the world whereof I am thinking, actually observes my success, in the form of a conspectus of the world's facts, and of my own efforts to find and to define them.

In so far, then, as I get the truth about the world, I myself am a fragmentary conscious life that is included within the conscious conspectus of the world's experience, and that is in one self-conscious unity with that world consciousness. And it is in this unity with the world consciousness that I get my success, and am in concord with the truth.

But of course any particular idea of mine, regarding the world, or regarding any fact in the world, may be false. However, this possibility of my error is itself a real situation of mine, and involves essentially the same relation between the world and myself which obtains in case I have true ideas. For I can be in error about an object only in case I really mean to agree with that object, and to agree with it in a way which only my own purposes, in seeking this agreement, can possibly define. It is only by virtue of my own undertakings that I can fail in my undertakings. It is only because, after all, I am loyal to the world's whole truth that I can so express myself in fallible ideas, and in fragmentary opinions that, as a fact, I may, at any moment, undertake too much for my own momentary success to be assured, so that I can indeed in any one of my assertions fail justly to accord with that world consciousness which I am all the while trying to interpret in my own transient way. But when I thus fail, I momentarily fail *to interpret my place in the very world consciousness whose life I am trying to define.* But my failure, when and in so far as it occurs, is once more a fact,—and therefore a fact for the world's consciousness. If I blunder, but am sincere, if I think myself right, but am not right, then my error is a fact for a consciousness which includes my fallible attempts to be loyal to the truth, but which sees how they just now lose present touch with their true cause. Seeing this my momentary defeat, the world consciousness sees, however, my loyalty, and in its conspectus assigns, even to my fragmentary attempts at truth, their genuine place in the single unity of the world's consciousness. My very failure, then, like every loyal failure, is still a sort of success. It is an effort to define my place in the unity of the world's conspectus of all conscious life. I cannot fall out of that unity. I cannot flee from its presence. And I err only as the loyal may give up their life for their cause. Whether I get truth, then, or whether I err in detail, *my loyal search for truth insures the fact that I am in a significant unity with the world's conscious life.*

The thesis that the world is one whole and a significant whole of conscious life is, for these reasons, a thesis which can only be viewed as an error, by reinstating this very assertion under a new form. For any error of mine concerning the world is possible only in so far as I really mean to assert the truth about the world; and this real meaning of mine can exist only as a fact within the conspectus of consciousness for which the real whole world exists, and within which I myself live.

This, then, in brief, is my own theory of truth. This is why I hold this theory to be no fantastic guess about what may be true, but a logically inevitable conclusion about how every one of us, wise or ignorant, is actually defining his own relation to truth, whether he knows the fact or not. . . .

IV

We first came in sight of this theory of truth, in these discussions, for a purely practical reason. Abstract and coldly intellectual as the doctrine, when stated as I have just stated it, may appear, we had our need to ask what truth is, because we wanted to know whether the loyal are right in supposing, as they inevitably do suppose, that their personal causes, and that their cause of causes, namely, universal loyalty, that any such causes, I say, possess genuine foundation in truth. Loyalty, as we found, is a practical service of superhuman objects. For our causes transcend expression in terms of our single lives. If the cause lives, then all conscious moral life—even our poor human life—is in unity with a superhuman conscious life, in which we ourselves dwell; and in this unity we win, in so far as we are loyal servants of our cause, a success which no transient human experience of ours, no joyous thrill of the flying moment, no bitterness of private defeat and loss, can do more or less than to illustrate, to illumine, or to idealize.

We asked: Is this faith of the loyal in their causes a pathetic fallacy? Our theory of truth has given us a general answer to this intensely practical question. The loyal try to live in the spirit. But, if thereupon they merely open their eyes to the nature of the reasonable truth, they see that it is in the spirit only that they do or can live. They would be living in this truth, as mere passing fragments of conscious life, as mere blind series of mental processes, even if they were not loyal. For all life, however dark and fragmentary, is either a blind striving for conscious unity with the universal life of which it is a fragment, or else, like the life of the loyal, is a deliberate effort to express such a striving in the form of a service of a superhuman cause. *And all lesser loyalties, and all serving of imperfect or of evil causes, are but fragmentary forms of the service of the cause of universal loyalty.* To serve universal loyalty is, however, to view the interests of all conscious life as one; and to do this is to regard all conscious life as constituting just such an unity as our theory of truth requires. Meanwhile, since truth seeking is indeed itself a practical activity, what we have stated in our theory of truth is itself but an aspect of the very life that the loyal are leading. Whoever seeks any truth is loyal, for he is determining his life by reference to a life which transcends his own. And he is loyal to loyalty; for whatever truth you try to discover is, if true, valid for everybody, and is therefore worthy of everybody's loyal recognition. The loyal, then, are truth seekers; and the truth seekers are loyal. And all of them live for the sake of the unity of all life. And this unity includes us all, but is superhuman.

Our view of truth, therefore, meets at once an ethical and a logical need. The real world is precisely that world in which the loyal are at home. Their loyalty is no pathetic fallacy. Their causes are real facts in the universe. The universe as a whole possesses that unity which loyalty to loyalty seeks to express in its service of the whole of life.

Herewith, however, it occurs to us to ask one final question. Is not this real world, whose true unity the loyal acknowledge by their every deed, and whose conscious unity every process of truth seeking presupposes,—is not this also the world which religion recognizes? If so, what is the relation of loyalty to religion?

The materials for answering this question are now in our hands. We have been so deliberate in preparing them for our present purpose, just for the sake of making our answer the simpler when it comes.

V

We have now defined loyalty as the will to manifest the eternal in and through the deeds of individual selves. As for religion,—

in its highest historical forms (which here alone concern us),—
religion, as I think, may be defined as follows. Religion (in these
its highest forms) *is the interpretation both of the eternal and of
the spirit of loyalty through emotion, and through a fitting activity
of the imagination.*

Religion, in any form, has always been an effort to interpret
and to make use of some superhuman world. The history, the
genesis, the earlier and simpler forms of religion, the relations
of religion and morality in the primitive life of mankind, do not
here concern us. It is enough to say that, in history, there has
often been a serious tension between the interests of religion and
those of morality. For the higher powers have very generally
seemed to man to be either nonmoral or immoral. This very
tension, only too frequently, still exists for many people to-day.
One of the greatest and hardest discoveries of the human mind
has been the discovery of how to reconcile, not religion and
science, but religion and morality. Whoever knows even a small
portion of the history of the cults of mankind is aware of the
difficulties to which I refer. The superhuman has been conceived
by men in terms that were often far enough from those which
loyalty requires. Whoever will read over the recorded words of a
writer nowadays too much neglected, the rugged and magnifi-
cently loyal Old Testament prophet Amos, can see for himself
how bravely the difficulty of conceiving the superhuman as the
righteous, was faced by one of the first who ever viewed the
relation of religion and morality as our best teachers have
since taught us to view them. And yet such a reader can also see
how hard this very task of the prophet was. When we remember
also that so great a mind as that of the originator of Buddhism,
after all the long previous toil of Hindoo thought upon this
great problem, could see no way to reconcile religion and morality, except by bringing them both to the shores of the mysterious
and soundless ocean of Nirvana, and sinking them together in
it depths (an undertaking which Buddha regarded as the salvation of the world), we get a further view of the nature of the
problem. When we remember that St. Paul, after many years of
lonely spiritual struggle, attempted in his teaching to reconcile
morality and religion by an interpretation of Christianity
which has ever since kept the Christian world in a most inspiring
ferment of theological controversy and of practical conflict, we
are again instructed as to the seriousness of the issue. But as a fact,
the experience of the civilized man has gradually led him to see

how to reconcile the moral life and the religious spirit. Since this reconciliation is one which our theory of truth, and of the constitution of the real world, substantially justifies, we are now ready for a brief review of the entire situation.

People often say that mere morality is something very remote from true religion. Sometimes people say this in the interests of religion, meaning to point out that mere morality can at best make you only a more or less tolerable citizen, while only religion can reconcile you, as such people say, to that superhuman world whose existence and whose support alone make human life worth living. But sometimes almost the same assertion is made in the interest of pure morality, viewed as something independent of religion. Some people tell you, namely, that since, as they say, religion is a collection of doubtful beliefs, of superstitions, and of more or less exalted emotions, morality is all the better for keeping aloof from religion. Suffering man needs your help; your friends need as much happiness as you can give them; conventional morality is, on the whole, a good thing. Learn righteousness, therefore, say they, and leave religion to the fantastic-minded who love to believe. The human is what we need. Let the superhuman alone.

Now, our philosophy of loyalty, aiming at something much larger and richer than the mere sum of human happiness in individual men, has taught us that there is no such sharp dividing line between the human and the superhuman as these attempts to sunder the provinces of religion and morality would imply. The loyal serve something more than individual lives. Even Nietzsche, individualist and ethical naturalist though he was, illustrates our present thesis. He began the later period of his teaching by asserting that "God is dead"; and (lest one might regard this as a mere attack upon monotheism, and might suppose Nietzsche to be an old-fashioned heathen polytheist) he added the famous remark that, in case any gods whatever existed, he could not possibly endure being himself no god. *"Therefore,"* so he reasoned, *"there are no gods."* All this seems to leave man very much to his own devices. Yet Nietzsche at once set up the cult of the ideal future being called the *Uebermensch* or Superman. And the *Uebermensch* is just as much of a god as anybody who ever throned upon Olympus or dwelt in the sky. And if the doctrine of the "Eternal Recurrence," as Nietzsche defined it, is true, the *Uebermensch* belongs not only to the ideal future, but has existed an endless number of times already.

If our philosophy of loyalty is right, Nietzsche was not wrong in this appeal to the superhuman. The superhuman we indeed have always with us. Life has no sense without it. But the superhuman need not be the magical. It need not be the object of superstition. And if we are desirous of unifying the interests of morality and religion, it is well indeed to begin, as rugged old Amos began, by first appreciating what righteousness is, and then by interpreting righteousness, in a perfectly reasonable and non-superstitious way, in superhuman terms. Then we shall be ready to appreciate what religion, whose roots are indeed by no means wholly in our moral nature, nevertheless has to offer us as a supplement to our morality.

VI

Loyalty is a service of causes. But, as we saw, we do not, we cannot, wait until somebody clearly shows us how good the causes are in themselves, before we set about serving them. We first practically learn of the goodness of our causes through the very act of serving them. Loyalty begins, then, in all of us, in elemental forms. A cause fascinates us—we at first know not clearly why. We give ourselves willingly to that cause. Herewith our true life begins. The cause may indeed be a bad one. But at worst it is our way of interpreting the true cause. If we let our loyalty develop, it tends to turn into the service of the universal cause. Hence I deliberately declined, in this discussion, to *base* my theory of loyalty upon that metaphysical doctrine which I postponed to my latest lectures. It is a very imperfect view of the real world which most youth get before them before they begin to be loyal. Hosts of the loyal actually manifest the eternal in their deeds, and know not that they do so. They only know that they are given over to their cause. The first good of loyalty lies, then, in the fact which we emphasized in our earlier lectures. Reverberating all through you, stirring you to your depths, loyalty first unifies your plan of life, and thereby gives you what nothing else can give,—your self as a life lived in accordance with a plan, your conscience as your plan interpreted for you through your ideal, your cause expressed as your personal purpose in living.

In so far, then, one can indeed be loyal without being consciously and explicitly religious. One's cause, in its first intention, appears to him human, concrete, practical. It is *also* an ideal. It is *also* a superhuman entity. It also really *means* the service of the eternal. But this fact may be, to the hard-working, and especially to the unimaginative, and, in a worldly sense, fairly successful man, a latent fact. He then, to be sure, gradually idealizes his cause as he goes; but this idealizing in so far becomes no very explicitly emphasized process in his life, although, as we have seen, some tendency to deify the cause is inevitable.

Meanwhile, such an imperfectly developed but loyal man may also accept, upon traditional grounds, a religion. This religion will then tell him about a superhuman world. But in so far the religion need not be, to his mind, an essential factor in his practical loyalty. He may be superstitious; or he may be a religious formalist; or he may accept his creed and his church simply because of their social respectability and usefulness; or, finally, he may even have a rich and genuine religious experience, which still may remain rather a mysticism than a morality, or an æsthetic comfort rather than a love of his cause.

In such cases, loyalty and religion may long keep apart. But the fact remains that loyalty, if sincere, involves at least a latent belief in the superhuman reality of the cause, and means at least an unconscious devotion to the one and eternal cause. But such a belief is also a latent union of morality and religion. Such a service is an unconscious piety. The time may come, then, when the morality will consciously need this union with the religious creed of the individual whose growth we are portraying.

This union must begin to become an explicit union whenever that process which, in our sixth lecture, we called the idealizing of the cause, reaches its higher levels. We saw that those higher levels are reached in the presence of what seems to be, to human vision, a lost cause. If we believe in the lost cause, we become directly aware that we are indeed seeking a city out of sight. If such a cause is real, it belongs to a superhuman world. Now, every cause worthy, as we said, of lifelong service, and capable of unifying our life plans, shows sooner or later that it is a cause *which we cannot successfully express in any set of human experiences of transient joys and of crumbling successes.* Human life taken merely as it flows, viewed merely as it passes by in time and is gone, is indeed a lost river of experience that plunges down the mountains of youth and sinks in the deserts of age. Its significance comes solely through its relations to the air and the ocean and the great deeps of universal experience. For by such

poor figures I may, in passing, symbolize that really rational relation of our personal experience to universal conscious experience,
—that relation to which I have devoted these last two lectures.

Everybody ought to serve the universal cause in his own individual way. For this, as we have seen, is what loyalty, when it
comes to know its own mind, really means. But whoever thus
serves inevitably *loses* his cause in our poor world of human
sense-experience, because his cause is too good for this present
temporal world to express it. And that is, after all, what the old
theology meant when it called you and me, as we now naturally
are, lost beings. Our deepest loyalty lies in devoting ourselves to
causes that are just now lost to our poor human nature. One can
express this, of course, by saying that the true cause is indeed real
enough, in the higher world, while it is our poor human nature
which is lost. Both ways of viewing the case have their truth.
Loyalty means a transformation of our nature.

Lost causes, then, we must serve. But as we have seen, in our
sixth lecture, loyalty to a lost cause has two companions, grief and
imagination. Now, these two are the parents of all the higher
forms of genuinely ethical religion. If you doubt the fact, read
the scriptures of any of the great ethical faiths. Consult the
psalter, the hymns, the devotional books, or the prayers of
the church. Such religion interprets the superhuman in forms
that our longing, our grief, and our imagination invent, but also
in terms that are intended to meet the demands of our highest
loyalty. For we are loyal to that unity of life which, as our truer
moral consciousness learns to believe, owns the whole real world,
and constitutes the cause of causes. In being loyal to universal
loyalty, we are serving the unity of life.

This true unity of the world-life, however, is at once very near
to us and very far from us. Very near it is; for we have our being
in it, and depend upon it for whatever worth we have. Apart
from it we are but the gurgling stream soon to be lost in the
desert. In union with it we have individual significance in and
for the whole. But we are very far from it also, because our human
experience throws such fragmentary light upon the details of our
relation to its activities. Hence in order to feel our relations to it
as vital relations, we have to bring it near to our feelings and to
our imaginations. And we long and suffer the loneliness of this
life as we do so. But because we know of the details of the
world only through our empirical sciences, while these give us
rather materials for a rational life than a view of the unity of life,

we are indeed left to our imagination to assuage grief and to help in the training of loyalty. For here, that is, precisely as to the *details* of the system of facts whereby our life is linked to the eternal, our science forsakes us. We can know *that* we are thus linked. *How* we are linked, our sciences do not make manifest to us.

Hence the actual content of the higher ethical religions is endlessly rich in legend and in other symbolic portrayal. This portrayal is rich in emotional meaning and in vivid detail. What this portrayal attempts to characterize is, in its general outline, an absolute truth. This truth consists in the following facts: *First, the rational unity and goodness of the world-life; next, its true but invisible nearness to us, despite our ignorance; further, its fulness of meaning despite our barrenness of present experience; and yet more, its interest in our personal destiny as moral beings; and finally, the certainty that, through our actual human loyalty, we come, like Moses, face to face with the true will of the world, as a man speaks to his friend.* In recognizing these facts, we have before us what may be called the creed of the Absolute Religion.

You may well ask, of course, whether our theory of truth, as heretofore expounded, gives any warrant to such religious convictions. I hold that it does give warrant to them. The symbols in which these truths are expressed by one or another religion are indeed due to all sorts of historical accidents, and to the most varied play of the imaginations both of the peoples and of the religious geniuses of our race. But that our relations to the world-life are relations wherein we are consciously met, from the other side, by a superhuman and yet strictly personal conscious life, in which our own personalities are themselves bound up, but which also is not only richer but is more concrete and definitely conscious and real than we are,—this seems to me to be an inevitable corollary of my theory of truth.

VII

And now, finally, to sum up our whole doctrine of loyalty and religion. Two things belonging to the world-life we know— two at least, if my theory is true: *it is defined in terms of our own needs; and it includes and completes our experience.* Hence, in any case, it is precisely as live and elemental and concrete as we are; and there is not a need of ours which is not its own. If you

ask why I call it good—well, the very arguments which recent
pragmatism has used are, as you remember, here my warrant. A
truth cannot be a merely theoretical truth. True is that which successfully fulfils an idea. Whoever, again, is not succeeding, or is
facing an evil, or is dissatisfied, is inevitably demanding and defining facts that are far beyond him, and that are not yet consciously his own. A knower of the totality of truth is therefore, of
necessity, in possession of the fulfilment of all rational purposes.
If, however, you ask why this world-life permits any evil whatever, or any finitude, or any imperfections, I must indeed reply
that here is no place for a general discussion of the whole problem of evil, which I have repeatedly and wearisomely considered
in other discussions of mine. But this observation does belong
here. Our theory of evil is indeed no "shallow optimism," but is
founded upon the deepest, the bitterest, and the dearest moral
experience of the human race. The *loyal,* and they alone, know the
one great good of suffering, of ignorance, of finitude, of loss, of
defeat—*and that is just the good of loyalty,* so long as the cause
itself can only be viewed as indeed a living whole. Spiritual
peace is surely no easy thing. We win that peace only through
stress and suffering and loss and labor. But when we find the
preciousness of the idealized cause emphasized through grief,
we see that, whatever evil is, it at least *may* have its place in an
ideal order. What would be the universe without loyalty; and
what would loyalty be without trial? And when we remember that,
from this point of view, our own griefs are the griefs of the very
world consciousness itself, in so far as this world-life is expressed
in our lives, it may well occur to us that the life of loyalty with
all its griefs and burdens and cares may be the very foundation of
the attainment of that spiritual triumph which we must conceive
as realized by the world spirit.

Perhaps, however, one weakly says: "If the world will attains
in its wholeness what we seek, why need we seek that good at
all?" I answer at once that our whole philosophy of loyalty in-
stantly shows the vanity of such speech. Of course, the world-life
does *not* obtain the individual good that is involved in my willing loyalty unless indeed *I am loyal.* The cause may in some way
triumph without me, but not as *my* cause. We have never defined
our theory as meaning that the world-life is *first* eternally complete, but *then* asks us, in an indifferent way, to copy its perfections. Our view is that each of us who is loyal is doing his unique
deed in that whole of life which we have called the eternal simply

because it is the conspectus of the totality of life, past, present, and future. If my deed were not done, the world-life would miss my deed. Each of us can say that. The very basis of our theory of truth, which we found upon the deeds, the ideas, the practical needs, of each of us, gives every individual his unique place in the world order—his deed that nobody else can do, his will which is his own. "Our wills are ours to make them thine." The unity of the world is *not* an ocean in which we are lost, but a life which is and which needs all our lives in one. Our loyalty defines that unity for us as a living, active unity. We have come to the unity through the understanding of our loyalty. It is an eternal unity only in so far as it includes all time and change and life and deeds. And therefore, when we reach this view, since the view simply fulfils what loyalty demands, our loyalty remains as precious to us, and as practical, and as genuinely a service of a cause, as it was before. It is no sort of "moral holiday" that this whole world-life suggests to us. It is precisely as a whole life of ideal strivings in which we have our places as individual selves and are such selves only in so far as we strive to do our part in the whole,—it is thus, and thus only, that our philosophy of loyalty regards the universe.

Religion, therefore, precisely in so far as it attempts to conceive the universe as a conscious and personal life of superhuman meaning, and as a life that is in close touch with our own meaning, is eternally true. But now it is just this *general* view of the universe as a rational order that is indeed open to our rational knowledge. No part of such a doctrine gives us, however, the present right as human beings to determine with any certainty the details of the world-life, except in so far as they come within the scope of our scientific and of our social inquiries. Hence, when religion, in the service of loyalty, interprets the world-life to us with symbolic detail, it gives us indeed merely symbols of the eternal truth. That this truth is indeed eternal, that our loyalty brings us into personal relations with a personal world-life, which values our every loyal deed, and needs that deed, all this is true and rational. And just this is what religion rightly illustrates. But the parables, the symbols, the historical incidents that the religious imagination uses in its portrayals,—these are the more or less sacred and transient *accidents* in which the "real presence" of the divine at once shows itself to us, and hides the detail of its inner life from us. These accidents of the religious imagination endure through many ages; but they also vary from place to place and from one nation or race of men to another, and they ought to do so. Whoever sees the living truth of the personal and conscious and ethical unity of the world *through* these symbols is possessed of the absolute religion, whatever be his nominal creed or church. Whoever overemphasizes the empirical details of these symbols, and then asks us to accept these details as literally true, commits an error which seems to me simply to invert that error whereof, at the last time, I ventured to accuse my pragmatist friends. Such a literalist, who reads his symbols as revelations of the detailed structure of the divine life, seems to me, namely, to look for the eternal *within* the realm of the mere data of human sense and imagination. To do this, I think, is indeed to seek the risen Lord in the open sepulchre.

Concerning the living truth of the whole conscious universe, one can well say, as one observes the special facts of human sense and imagination: "He is not here; he is arisen." Yet equally from the whole circle of the heaven of that entire self-conscious life which *is* the truth, there comes always, and to all the loyal, the word: "Lo, I am with you always, even unto the end of the world."

PART IV

SELECTIONS FROM

The Problem of Christianity

AND

The Hope of the Great Community

18 ❦ PREFACE [1]

The present book is the result of studies whose first outcome appeared, in 1908, in my "Philosophy of Loyalty." Since then, two volumes of my collected philosophical essays have dealt, in part, with the same problems as those which "The Philosophy of Loyalty" discussed. Of these two latter volumes, one is entitled "William James and other Essays on the Philosophy of Life"; and contains, amongst other theses, the assertion that the "spirit of loyalty" is able to supply us not only with a "philosophy of life," but with a religion which is "free from superstition" and which is in harmony with a genuinely rational view of the world. In 1912 were published, by the Scribners in New York, the "Bross Lectures," which I had delivered, in the autumn of 1911, at Lake Forest University, Illinois, on "The Sources of Religious Insight." One of these "Bross Lectures" was entitled "The Religion of Loyalty"; and the volume in question contained the promise that, in a future discussion, I would, if possible, attempt to "apply the principles" there laid down to the special case of Christianity. The present work redeems that promise according to the best of my ability.

I

The task of these two volumes is defined in the opening lecture of the first volume. The main results are carefully summed up in Lectures XV and XVI, at the close of the second volume. This book can be understood without any previous reading of my "Philosophy of Loyalty," and without any acquaintance with my "Bross Lectures." Yet in case my reader finds himself totally at variance with the interpretation of Christianity here expounded, he should not finally condemn my book without taking the trouble to compare its principal theses with those which my various preliminary studies of "loyalty," and of the religion of loyalty, contain.

[1] Josiah Royce, *The Problem of Christianity* (New York: The Macmillan Company, 1913), Vol. I, Preface, pp. vii–xxii.—Editor's note.

In brief, since 1908, my "philosophy of loyalty" has been growing. Its successive expressions, as I believe, form a consistent body of ethical as well as of religious opinion and teaching, verifiable, in its main outlines, in terms of human experience, and capable of furnishing a foundation for a defensible form of metaphysical idealism. But the depth and vitality of the ideal of loyalty have become better known to me as I have gone on with my work. Each of my efforts to express what I have found in the course of my study of what loyalty means has contained, as I believe, some new results. My efforts to grasp and to expound the "religion of loyalty" have at length led me, in this book, to views concerning the essence of Christianity such that, if they have any truth, they need to be carefully considered. For they are, in certain essential respects, novel views; and they concern the central life-problems of all of us.

II

What these relatively novel opinions are, the reader may, if he chooses, discover for himself. If he is minded to undertake the task, he will be aided by beginning with the "Introduction," which immediately follows the "Table of Contents" in the first volume of this book. This introduction contains an outline of the lectures,—an outline which was used, by my audience, when the text of this discussion was read at Manchester College, Oxford, between January 13 and March 6, 1913.

But a further brief and preliminary indication is here in order to prepare the reader a little better for what is to follow.

This book is not the work of an historian, nor yet of a technical theologian. It is the outcome of my own philosophical study of certain problems belonging to ethics, to religious experience, and to general philosophy. In spirit I believe my present book to be in essential harmony with the bases of the philosophical idealism set forth in various earlier volumes of my own, and especially in the work entitled "The World and the Individual" (published in 1899–1901). On the other hand, the present work contains no mere repetition of my former expressions of opinion. There is much in it which I did not expect to say when I began the task here accomplished. As to certain metaphysical opinions which are stated, in outline, in the second volume of this book, I now owe much more to our great and unduly neglected American logician, Mr. Charles Peirce, than I do to the common tradition of recent idealism, and certainly very much more than I ever have owed, at any point of my own philosophical development, to the doctrines which, with technical accuracy, can be justly attributed to Hegel. It is time, I think, that the long customary, but unjust and loose usage of the adjective "Hegelian" should be dropped. The genuinely Hegelian views were the ones stated by Hegel himself, and by his early followers. My own interpretation of Christianity, in these volumes, despite certain agreements with the classical Hegelian theses, differs from that of Hegel, and of the classical Hegelian school, in important ways which I can, with a clear conscience, all the more vigorously emphasize, just because I have, all my life, endeavored to treat Hegel both with careful historical justice and with genuine appreciation. In fact the present is a distinctly new interpretation of the "Problem of Christianity."

One of the most thoughtful and one of the fairest of the reviewers of my "Spirit of Modern Philosophy" said of my former position, as stated, in 1892, in the book thus named, that I then came nearer to being a follower of Schopenhauer than a disciple of Hegel. As far as it went this statement gave a just impression of how I then stood. I have never, since then, been more of an Hegelian than at that time I was. I am now less so than ever before.

III

One favorite and facile way of disposing of a student of idealistic philosophy who writes about religion is to say that he has first formed a system of "abstract conceptions," whose interest, if they have any interest, is purely technical, and whose relation to the concrete religious concerns of mankind is wholly external and formal; and that he has then tried to steal popular favor by misusing traditional religious phraseology, and by identifying his "sterile intellectualism," and these his barren technicalities, with the religious beliefs and experiences of mankind, through taking a vicious advantage of ambiguous words.

I can only ask any one who approaches this book to read Volume I before he undertakes to judge the metaphysical discussions which form the bulk of Volume II; and also to weigh the relations between my metaphysical and my religious phraseology in the light of the summary contained in Lectures XV and XVI of the second volume.

If after such a reading of my actual opinions, as set down in this book, he still insists that I have endeavored artificially to force a set of foreign and preconceived metaphysical "abstractions" upon the genuine religious life of my brethren, I cannot supply him with fairness of estimate, but ought to remain indifferent to his manner of speech.

As a fact, this book is the outcome of experience, and, in its somewhat extended practical sections, it is written (if I may borrow a phrase from the Polish master of romance, Sienkiewicz), "for the strengthening of hearts." That some portions of the discussion are technically metaphysical is a result of the deliberate plan of the whole work; and technical assertions demand, as a matter of course, technical criticisms. The novelty of some of my metaphysical theses in my second volume, and the lack of space for their adequate statement in this book, have made their exposition, as I here have time to give it, both incomplete, and justly subject to many objections, some of which I have anticipated in my text. But, in any case, I have not been merely telling anybody's old story over again.

Since I have been writing from the life, I of course owe a great deal to the inspiration that I long ago obtained from William James's "Varieties of Religious Experience." I even venture to hope that (while I have of course laid stress upon no interests which I could recognize as due to merely private concerns of my own) I might still be addressing at least some few readers who are able to understand, and perhaps sometimes to echo, a cry of genuine feeling when they hear it. For, after all, it is more important that we should together recognize in religion our own common personal needs and life-interests than that we should agree about our formulas. So I have indeed tried, in this book, to speak as one wanderer speaks to another who is his friend, when the way is long and obscure.

Yet in one very important respect the religious experience upon which, in this book, I most depend, differs very profoundly from that whose "varieties" James described. He deliberately confined himself to the religious experience of individuals. My main topic is a form of social religious experience, namely, that form which, in ideal, the Apostle Paul viewed as the experience of the Church. This social form of experience is that upon which loyalty depends. James supposed that the religious experience of a church must needs be "conventional," and consequently must be lacking in depth and in sincerity.

This, to my mind, was a profound and a momentous error in the whole religious philosophy of our greatest American master in the study of the psychology of religious experience. All experience must be *at least* individual experience; but unless it is *also* social experience, and unless the whole religious community which is in question unites to share it, this experience is but as sounding brass, and as a tinkling cymbal. This truth is what Paul saw. This is the rock upon which the true and ideal church is built. This is the essence of Christianity.

If indeed I myself must cry "out of the depths" before the light can come to me, it must be my Community that, in the end, saves me. To assert this and to live this doctrine constitute the very core of Christian experience, and of the "Religion of Loyalty." In discussing "the varieties of religious experience," which here concern us, I have everywhere kept this thesis in mind.

IV

The assertion just made summarizes the single thought to whose discussion, illustration, defence, and philosophy this book is devoted. This assertion is the one which, in my "Philosophy of Loyalty," I was trying, so far as I then could, to expound and to apply. We are saved, if at all, by devotion to the Community, in the sense of that term which these two volumes attempt to explain and to defend. This is what I mean by loyalty. Because the word "loyalty" ends in *ty,* and because what a "Community" is, is at present so ill understood by most philosophers, my former discussions of this topic have been accused of basing all the duties of life upon an artificial abstraction. When I now say that by loyalty I mean the *practically devoted love of an individual for a community,* I shall still leave unenlightened those who stop short at the purely verbal fact that the word "community" also ends in *ty.* But let such readers wait until they have at least read Lectures I, III, and VII of my first volume. Then they may know what is at issue.

This book, if it is nothing else, is at least one more effort to tell what loyalty is. I also want to put loyalty—this love of the individual for the community—where it actually belongs, not only at the heart of the virtues, not only at the summit of the mountains which the human spirit must climb if man is really to be saved, but also (where it equally belongs) at the turning-point of human history,—at the point when the Christian ideal was first defined,—and when the Church Universal,—that still invisible Community of all the faithful, that homeland of the human spirit, "which eager hearts expect," was first introduced as a vision, as a hope, as a conscious longing to mankind. I want to show what loyalty is, and that all this is true of the loyal spirit.

Some of my main theses, in this book, are the following: First, Christianity is, in its essence, the most typical, and, so far in human history, the most highly developed religion of loyalty. Secondly, loyalty itself is a perfectly concrete form and interest of the spiritual life of mankind. Thirdly, this very fact about the meaning and the value of universal loyalty is one which the Apostle Paul learned in and from the social and religious life of the early Christian communities, and then enriched and transformed through his own work as missionary and teacher. Still another of my theses is this: Whatever may hereafter be the fortunes of Christian institutions, or of Christian traditions, the religion of loyalty, the doctrine of the salvation of the otherwise hopelessly lost individual through devotion to the life of the genuinely real and Universal Community, must survive, and must direct the future both of religion and of mankind, if man is to be saved at all. As to what the word "salvation" means, and as to why I use it, the reader can discover, if he chooses, from the text of these lectures.

V

The doctrines of the Community, of Loyalty, of the "lost state of the natural individual," and of Atonement as the function in which the life of the community culminates, appear, in the volumes of this book, in two forms, whose clear distinction and close connection ought next to be emphasized in this preface. First, these doctrines, and the ideas in terms of which they are expressed, are verifiable results of the higher social religious experience of mankind. Were there no Christianity, were there no Christians in the world, all these ideas would be needed to express the meaning of true loyalty, the saving value of the right relation of any human individual to the community of which he is a member, and the true sense of life. These doctrines, then, need no dogmas of any historical church to define them, and no theology, and no technical metaphysical theory, to furnish a foundation for them. In the second place, however, these Christian ideas are based upon deep metaphysical truths whose significance is more than human.

Historically speaking, the Christian church first discovered the Christian ideas. The founder of Christianity, so far as we know what his teachings were, seems not to have defined them adequately. They first came to a relatively full statement through the religious life of the Pauline Churches; and the Pauline epistles contain their first, although still not quite complete, formulation. Paul himself was certainly not the founder of Christianity. But the Pauline communities first were conscious of the essence of Christianity.

Consequently those are right who have held, what the "modernists" of the Roman Church were for a time asserting,— before officialism turned its back, in characteristic fashion, upon the really new and deeply valuable light which these modernists were, for the time, bringing to their own communion. Those, I say, are right who have held that the Church, rather than the person of the founder, ought to be viewed as the central idea of Christianity.

On the other hand, neither the "modernists" of recent controversy, nor any other of the apologists for the traditions of the historical Christian church, have yet seen the meaning of the "religion of loyalty" as the Apostle Paul, in certain of his greatest moments and words, saw and expressed that meaning. The apostle's language, regarding this matter, is as imperishable as it is well warranted by human experience, and as it is also separable from the accidents of later dogmatic formulation, and inexhaustible in the metaphysical problems which it brings to our attention.

Hence the most significant task for a modern revision of our estimate of what is vital in Christianity depends upon the recognition of certain aspects of Christian social experience and of human destiny, aspects to whose exposition and defence, first in empirical terms, and then in the light of a reëxamination of certain fundamental metaphysical ideas, these two volumes are devoted. . . .

19 ❧ THE COMMUNITY
AND THE
TIME-PROCESS [1]

The present situation of the Philosophy of Religion is dominated by motives and tendencies which are at once inspiring and confusing. It is the task of a student of this branch of philosophy to do whatever he can towards clarifying our outlook. Some of our recent leaders of opinion have turned our attention to new aspects of human experience, and have enriched philosophy with a wealth of fascinating intuitions. These contributions to the philosophy of our time have obvious bearings upon the interests of religion. If religion depended solely upon intuition and upon novelty, our age would already have proved its right to be regarded as a period of great advances in religious insight.

In fact, however, religion is concerned, not merely with our experience, but also with our will. The true lover of religion needs a conscience, as well as a joy in living—a coherent plan of action as well as a vital impulse. Now, in the present phase of the philosophy of religion, the religious aspect of the conscience is, as I believe, too seldom made a central object of inquiry. The interests of a coherent plan of life are too much neglected. I believe that both our ethical and our distinctly religious concerns tend to suffer in consequence of these tendencies of recent thought to which I thus allude. I believe that much can be done to profit by the novelties and by the intuitions of our day, without losing ourselves in the wilderness of caprices into which recent discussion has invited us to make the future home of our philosophy.

I

Because I view the problems of the philosophy of religion in this general way, I have undertaken, in the foregoing lectures, a

[1] Josiah Royce, *The Problem of Christianity* (New York: The Macmillan Company, 1913), Vol. II, Lecture IX, pp. 3–18, 35–53.—Editor's note.

study of the problem of Christianity which has been intended to accomplish three distinct, but closely connected tasks:—

First, in a fashion that has shown, as I hope, some genuine sympathy with the tendencies now prevalent, both in the whole field of philosophy, and, in particular, in the study of religion, I have tried to interpret some of the more obviously human and practical aspects of the religious beliefs of our fathers. In other words, I have approached the problem of Christianity from the side, not of metaphysics and of traditional dogmas, but of religious life and of human experience.

Secondly, even in using this mode of approach, I have laid stress upon the fact that Christianity—viewed as a doctrine of life —is not merely a religion of experience and of sentiment, but also a religion whose main stress is laid upon the unity and the coherence of the common experience of the faithful, and upon the judgment which a calm and farseeing conscience passes upon the values of life. The freedom of spirit to which Christianity, in the course of its centuries of teaching, has trained the civilizations which it has influenced, has been the freedom which loves both a wide outlook and a well-knit plan of action. In brief, I have insisted that Christianity, whatever its metaphysical basis may be, and however rich may be the wealth of intuitions which it has opened to its followers, has all the seriousness of purpose, and all the strenuousness of will, which make it indeed a religion of loyalty.

Thirdly, I have, from the outset, said that our view of the mission and the truth of the Christian doctrine of life would not be complete without a study of the metaphysical basis of the Christian ideas.

In the last two lectures we have considered how the modern mind stands related to the human interests which the Christian doctrine of life expresses. Our fathers, however, held Christianity to be, not merely a plan for the salvation of man, but a revelation concerning the origin and fate of the whole cosmos. From this point onwards, in our study, we must face anew the problem which the old faith regarded as solved. We, too, must take account of the universe. We must consider what is the consistent position for the modern mind to accept when the inquiry arises: Has the Christian doctrine of life a more than human meaning and foundation? Does this doctrine express a truth, not only about man, but about the whole world, and about God?

II

The modern man has long since learned not to confine himself to a geocentric view of the universe, nor to an anthropocentric view of the affairs of this planet of ours. For minds trained as ours now are, it has become inevitable to imagine how human concerns would seem to us if we heard of them from afar, as dwellers in other solar or stellar systems might be supposed to hear of them. We have been taught to remember that at some time,—a time not nearly so distant from us in the future as the Miocene division of the Tertiary period is now distant from us in the past, man will probably be as extinct as is now the sabre-toothed tiger. But such considerations as these arouse further queries about Christian doctrine—queries which no modern mind can wholly ignore. Let all be admitted which we urged at the last time regarding the close relation of the Christian doctrine of life to the deepest needs of humanity. Then this will indeed show that Christianity, viewed simply *as* such a doctrine of life, need not fear social changes, so long as civilized man endures; and will remain as a spiritual guide of future generations, however vast the revolutions to which they may be subject, so long as the future generations view life largely and seriously.

But such considerations will not meet all the legitimate questions of a philosophy of religion. For religion, although it need not depend for its appeal to the human heart upon solving the problems of the cosmos, inevitably leads to a constantly renewed interest in those problems. Let it be granted that the salvation of mankind indeed requires some form of religion whose essential ideas are in harmony with the Christian ideas which we have examined; still, that fact will not quite supply an answer to our natural inquiries, if indeed mankind is destined simply to fail,—as the sabre-toothed tiger failed. And if mankind, in the vast cosmos, is as much alone amongst the beings that people the universe as the earth seems to be alone amongst the countless worlds,—what shall it profit us if we seem to be saving our own souls for a time, but actually remain, after all, what we were before,—utterly insignificant incidents in a world-process that neither needs men nor heeds them?

Traditional theology could long ignore such considerations, because it could centre all the universe about the earth and man. But the modern man must think of his kind as thus really related to an immeasurably vast cosmic process, at whose centre our planet does not stand, and in whose ages our brief human lives play a part as transient, relatively speaking, as is, for our own eyes, the flickering of the northern lights.

The task to which we must now devote ourselves is thus determined, for our age, and for the modern man, by the enlarged perspective in which we have to view human history. Our doctrine of life is not so readily to be connected with our picture of the universe as would be the case if we still lived under the heavenly spheres of an ancient cosmology. Yet we shall find that the difference which is here in question will not prove to be so great in its meaning as the quantitative differences between the ancient and modern world seem, at first, to imply. Our fathers also faced the problem of the infinity of the universe, much as they often tried to ignore or to minimize that problem. And, in the spiritual world, mere quantity, however vast, is not the hardest of obstacles to overcome.

III

In any case, however, the part of our undertaking upon which we thus enter, corresponds to those chapters of traditional theology which dealt with the existence and nature of God, and with God's relation to the world, and with the origin and destiny of the human individual. Our own attempt to study these well-worn problems begins with one, and perhaps with only one, advantage over the best-known traditional modes of expounding a philosophical theology. We, namely, set out under the guidance of our foregoing study of the Christian ideas. Central among these ideas is that of the Universal Community. For us, then, theology, if we are to define any theology at all, must depend upon the metaphysical interpretation and foundation of the community. If that ideal of one beloved and united community of all mankind whose religious value we have defended, has a basis, not merely in the transient interests of us mortals, but also in whatever is largest and most lasting in the universe, then indeed the doctrine of the community will prove to be a doctrine about the being and nature and manifestation of God; and our estimate of the relation of the modern mind to the spirit of a Christian creed will be altered and completed accordingly. This one doctrine will indeed not suffice to make us literal followers of tradition; but it will bring us into a sympathy with some of the most essential features of the Christian view of the divine being.

I V

What interests are at stake when this aspect of the problems of theology is emphasized, I can best remind you by recalling the fact which we mentioned in comparing Buddhism and Christianity in a former lecture. The most characteristic feature by which the Christian doctrine of life stands contrasted with its greatest religious rival, we found to be the one summarized in the words of the creed: "I believe in the Holy Ghost, the Holy Catholic Church, the communion of saints." In our former lecture, when we commented upon these words, we laid no stress upon the special traditions of the historical Church. We considered only the universally human significance of the ideal which has always constituted the vital principle of the historical Church,—far away as the adequate embodiment of that ideal in any visible human institution still seems to be. At the present stage of our inquiry,—since we are, of necessity, entering for the time the world of metaphysical abstractions, we have also to abstract from still another aspect of the meaning which the words of the creed intend to convey. For neither the historical Church, nor the distinctively human ideal which it expresses, shall be, in these metaphysical lectures, at the centre of our attention. We are here to ask: For what truth, if any, regarding the whole nature of things, does that article of the creed stand? Our answer must be found, if at all, in some metaphysical theory of the community and of its relation, if such relation it possesses, to the divine being. In other words, the central problem in our present attempt at a theology must be that problem which traditional Christian theology has so strangely neglected,—the problem of what the religious consciousness has called the Holy Spirit.

V

The philosophy of religion, in dealing with the problem of Christianity, has often elaborately expounded and criticised the arguments for the existence of God. Such philosophical arguments have in general to do with the concept of the Deity viewed quite apart from the Christian doctrine of the Trinity. In other cases, and for obvious historical reasons, the philosophy of religion has had much to say about the doctrine of the Logos. This doctrine, when treated as a part of Christian theology, is usually taken to be the theory of the second person of the Trinity. But the traditional doctrine of the Holy Spirit, neglected by the early theologians of the Church, even when the creeds were still in the formative period of their existence, has remained until this day in the background of inquiry, both for the theologians and for the philosophers. A favorite target for hostile, although often inarticulate, criticism on the part of the opponents of tradition, and a frequent object of reverential, but confessedly problematic and often very vague, exposition on the part of the defenders of the faith,—the article of the creed regarding the Holy Spirit is, I believe, the one matter about which most who discuss the problem of Christianity have least to say in the way of definite theory.

Yet, if I am right,—this is, in many respects, the really distinctive and therefore the capital article of the Christian creed, so far as that creed suggests a theory of the divine nature. This article, then, should be understood, if the spirit of Christianity, in its most human and vital of features, is to be understood at all. And this article should be philosophically expounded and defended, if any distinctively Christian article of the creed is to find a foundation in a rationally defensible metaphysical theory of the universe.

Apart from the doctrine of the ideal community, and of the divine Spirit as constituting the unity and the life of this community, Theism can be, as for many centuries it has been, defined and defended. But such theism, which "knows not so much as whether there is any Holy Ghost," is not distinctively Christian in its meaning. And the Logos-doctrine, except when viewed in unity with the doctrine of the Spirit, is indeed what some of its recent hostile critics (such as Harnack) have taken it to be,— a thesis of Greek philosophy, and not a characteristically Christian opinion. The Logos-doctrine of the Fourth Gospel, as we earlier saw, is indeed no mere following of Greek metaphysics; for the Fourth Gospel identifies the Logos with the spirit of the community. Here, then, in this doctrine of the spirit, lies the really central idea of any distinctively Christian metaphysic.

To approach the problems of the philosophy of religion from the side of the metaphysical basis of the idea of the community is therefore, I believe, to undertake a task as momentous as it is neglected.

V I

Moreover, as we shall soon find, this mode of beginning the metaphysical part of our task promises to relieve us, for the time, from the need of using some terms and of repeating some discussions, which recent controversy may well have made wearisome to many of us. The altogether too abstractly stated contrast between Monism and Pluralism—a contrast which fills so large a place in the polemical metaphysical writings of the day, does not force itself to the front, in our minds and in our words, when we set out to inquire into the real basis of the idea of the community. For a community immediately presents itself to our minds both as one and as many; and unless it is both one and many, it is no community at all. This fact does not, by itself, solve the problem of the One and the Many. But it serves to remind us how untrue to life is the way in which that problem is frequently stated.

In fact, as I believe, the idea of the community, suggested to us by the problems of human social life, but easily capable of a generalization which possesses universal importance, gives us one of our very best indications of the way in which the problem of the One and the Many is to be solved, and of the level of mental life upon which the solution is actually accomplished. . . .

I X

We may be aided in making a more decisive advance towards understanding what a community is by emphasizing at this point a motive which we have not before mentioned, and which no doubt plays a great part in the psychology of the social consciousness.

Any notable case wherein we find a social organization which we can call, in the psychological sense, either a highly developed community or the creation or product of such a community, is a case where some process of the nature of a history—that is, of coherent social evolution—has gone on, and has gone on for a long time, and is more or less remembered by the community in question. If, ignoring history, you merely take a cross-section of the social order at any one moment; and if you thus deal with social groups that have little or no history, and confine your attention to social processes which occur during a short period of time,—for example, during an hour, or a day, or a year,—what then is likely to come to your notice takes either the predominantly pluralistic form of the various relatively independent doings of detached individuals, or else the social form of the confused activities of a crowd. A crowd, whether it be a dangerous mob, or an amiably joyous gathering at a picnic, is not a community. It has a mind, but no institutions, no organization, no coherent unity, no history, no traditions. It may be an unit, but is then of the type which suggests James's mere blending of various consciousnesses,—a sort of mystical loss of personality on the part of its members. On the other hand, a group of independent buyers at market, or of the passers-by in a city street, is not a community. And it also does not suggest to the onlooker any blending of many selves in one. Each purchaser seeks his own affairs. There may be gossip, but gossip is not a function which establishes the life of a community. For gossip has a short memory. But a true community is essentially a product of a time-process. A community has a past and will have a future. Its more or less conscious history, real or ideal, is a part of its very essence. A community requires for its existence a history and is greatly aided in its consciousness by a memory.

If you object that a Pauline church, such as I have so often used as an ideal instance of a community, was an institution that had been but very recently founded when the apostle wrote his epistles, then I reply at once that a Pauline church was instructed by the apostle to regard its life as a phase in the historical process of the salvation of mankind. This process, as conceived by Paul and his churches, had gone on from Adam unto Moses, from Moses unto Christ; and the very life of the community was bound up with its philosophy of history. That the memory of this community was in part legendary is beside the point. Its memory was essential to its life, and was busy with the fate of all mankind and with the course of all time.

The psychological unity of many selves in one community is bound up, then, with the consciousness of some lengthy social process which has occurred, or is at least supposed to have occurred. And the wealthier the memory of a community is, and the vaster the historical processes which it regards as belonging to its life, the richer—other things being equal—is its consciousness that it *is* a community, that its members are somehow made one in and through and with its own life.

The Japanese are fond of telling us that their imperial family, and their national life, are coeval with heaven and earth. The boast is cheerfully extravagant; but its relation to a highly developed form of the consciousness of a community is obvious. Here, then, is a consideration belonging to social psychology, but highly important for our understanding of the sense in which a community is or can be possessed of one mental life.

X

If we ask for the reason why such a real or fancied history, possessing in general a considerable length and importance, is psychologically needed in case a group consisting of many individual human beings is to regard itself as an united community, our attention is at once called to a consideration which I regard as indeed decisive for the whole theory of the reality of the community. Obvious as it is, however, this consideration needs to be explicitly mentioned, because the complexity of the facts often makes us neglect them.

The rule that time is needed for the formation of a conscious community is a rule which finds its extremely familiar analogy within the life of every individual human self. Each one of us knows that he just now, at this instant, cannot find more than a mere fragment of himself present. The self comes down to us from its own past. It needs and is a history. Each of us can see that his own idea of himself as this person is inseparably bound up with his view of his own former life, of the plans that he formed, of the fortunes that fashioned him, and of the accomplishments which in turn he has fashioned for himself. A self is, by its very essence, a being with a past. One must look lengthwise backwards in the stream of time in order to see the self, or its shadow, now moving with the stream, now eddying in the currents from bank to bank of its channel, and now strenuously straining onwards in the pursuit of its own chosen good.

At this present moment I am indeed here, as this creature of the moment,—sundered from the other selves. But nevertheless, if considered simply in this passing moment of my life, I am hardly a self at all. I am just a flash of consciousness,—the mere gesticulation of a self,—not a coherent personality. Yet memory links me with my own past,—and not, in the same way, with the past of any one else. This joining of the present to the past reveals a more or less steady tendency,—a sense about the whole process of my remembered life. And this tendency and sense of my individual life agree, on the whole, with the sense and the tendencies that belong to the entire flow of the time-stream, so far as it has sense at all. My individual life, my own more or less well-sundered stream of tendency, not only is shut off at each present moment by various barriers from the lives of other selves,—but also constitutes an intelligible sequence in itself, so that, as I look back, I can say: "What I yesterday intended to pursue, that I am to-day still pursuing." "My present carries farther the plan of my past." Thus, then, I am one more or less coherent plan expressed in a life. "The child is father to the man." My days are "bound each to each by mutual piety."

Since I am this self, not only by reason of what now sunders me from the inner lives of other selves, but by reason of what links me, in significant fashion, to the remembered experiences, deeds, plans, and interests of my former conscious life, I need a somewhat extended and remembered past to furnish the opportunity for my self to find, when it looks back, a long process that possesses sense and coherence. In brief, my idea of myself is an interpretation of my past,—linked also with an interpretation of my hopes and intentions as to my future.

Precisely as I thus define myself with reference to my own past, so my fellows also interpret the sense, the value, the qualifications, and the possessions of my present self by virtue of what are sometimes called my antecedents. In the eyes of his fellow-men, the child is less of a self than is the mature man; and he is so not merely because the child just now possesses a less wealthy and efficient conscious life than a mature man possesses, but because the antecedents of his present self are fewer than are the antecedents of the present self of the mature man. The child has little past. He has accomplished little. The mature man bears the credit and the burden of his long life of deeds. His former works qualify his present deeds. He not only possesses, but in great part is, for his fellow-men, a record.

These facts about our individual self-consciousness are indeed well known. But they remind us that our idea of the individual self is no mere present datum, or collection of data, but is based upon an interpretation of the sense, of the tendency, of the coherence, and of the value of a life to which belongs the memory of its own past. And therefore these same facts will help us to see how the idea of the community is also an idea which is impressed upon us whenever we make a sufficiently successful and fruitful effort to interpret the sense, the coherent interest, and the value of the relations in which a great number of different selves stand to the past.

XI

Can many different selves, all belonging to the present time, possess identically the same past as their own personally interesting past life? This question, if asked about the recent past, cannot be answered in the affirmative, unless one proposes either to ignore or in some way to set aside the motives which, in our present consciousness, emphasize, as we have seen, the pluralism of the social selves. Quite different, however, becomes the possible answer to this question if, without in the least ignoring our present varieties and sunderings, one asks the question concerning some past time that belongs to previous generations of men. For then each of two or more men may regard the same fact of past life as, in the same sense, a part of his own personal life. Two men of the present time may, for instance, have any number of ancestors in common. To say this is not to ignore the pluralistic view of the selves, but only to make mention of familiar facts of descent. But now if these men take great interest in their ancestors, and have a genuine or legendary tradition concerning the ancestors, each of the two men of the present time may regard the lives, the deeds, the glory, and perhaps the spiritual powers or the immortal lives of certain ancestors, now dwelling in the spirit-world, as a part of his own self. Thus, when the individual Maori, in New Zealand, in case he still follows the old ways, speaks of the legendary canoes in which the ancestors of old came over from the home land called Hawaiki to New Zealand, he says, choosing the name of the canoe according to his own tribe and tradition, "*I* came over in the canoe Tai-Nui." Now any two members of a tribe whose legendary ancestors came over in Tai-Nui, possess, from their own point of view, identically the same past, in just this respect. Each of the two men in question has the same reason, good or bad, for extending himself into the past, and for saying, "I came over in that canoe." Now the belief in this identity of the past self of the ancestor of the canoe, belonging to each of the two New

Zealanders, does not in the least depend upon ignoring, or upon minimizing, the present difference between these two selves. The present consciousnesses do not in the least tend to interpenetrate. Neither of the two New Zealanders in question need suppose that there is now any compounding of consciousness. Each may keep aloof from the other. They may be enemies. But each has a reason, and an obvious reason, for extending himself into the ancestral past.

My individual self extends backwards, and is identified with my remembered self of yesterday, or of former years. This is an interpretation of my life which in general turns upon the coherence of deeds, plans, interests, hopes, and spiritual possessions in terms of which I learn to define myself. Now my remembered past is in general easily to be distinguished from the past of any other self. But if I am so interested in the life or in the deeds of former generations that I thus extend, as the Maori extends, my own self into the ancestral past, the self thus extended finds that the same identical canoe or ancestor is part of my own life, and also part of the ideally extended life of some fellow-tribesman who is now so different a being, and so sharply sundered from my present self.

Now, in such a case, how shall I best describe the unity that, according to this interpretation of our common past, links my fellow-tribesmen and myself? A New Zealander says, "We are of the same canoe." And a more general expression of such relations would be to say, in all similar cases, "We are of the same community."

In this case, then, the real or supposed identity of certain interesting features in a past which each one of two or of many men regards as belonging to his own historically extended former self, is a ground for saying that all these many, although now just as various and as sundered as they are, constitute, with reference to this common past, a community. When defined in such terms, the concept of the community loses its mystical seeming. It depends indeed upon an interpretation of the significance of facts, and does not confine itself to mere report of particulars; but it does not ignore the present varieties of experience. It depends also upon an interpretation which does not merely say, "These events happened," but adds, "These events belong to the life of this self or of this other self." Such an interpretation we all daily make in speaking of the past of our own familiar individual selves. The process which I am now using as an illustration,— the process whereby the New Zealander says, "I came over in that canoe,"—extends the quasi-personal memory of each man into an historical past that may be indefinitely long and vast. But such an extension has motives which are not necessarily either mystical or monistic. We all share those motives, and use them, in our own way, and according to our ideals, whenever we consider the history of our country, or of mankind, or of whatever else seems to us to possess a history that is significantly linked with our personal history.

XII

Just as each one of many present selves, despite the psychological or ethical barriers which now keep all of these selves sundered, may accept the same past fact or event as a part of himself, and say, "That belonged to my life," even so, each one of many present selves, despite these same barriers and sunderings, may accept the same future event, which all of them hope or expect, as part of his own personal future. Thus, during a war, all of the patriots of one of the contending nations may regard the termination of the war, and the desired victory of their country, so that each one says: "I shall rejoice in the expected surrender of that stronghold of the enemy. That surrender will be my triumph."

Now when many contemporary and distinct individual selves so interpret, each his own personal life, that each says of an individual past or of a determinate future event or deed: "That belongs to my life;" "That occurred, or will occur, to me," then these many selves may be defined as hereby constituting, in a perfectly definite and objective, but also in a highly significant, sense, a community. They may be said to constitute a community *with reference* to that particular past or future event, or group of events, which each of them accepts or interprets as belonging to his own personal past or to his own individual future. A community constituted by the fact that each of its members accepts as part of his own individual life and self the same *past* events that each of his fellow-members accepts, may be called a *community of memory*. Such is any group of persons who individually either remember or commemorate the same dead,—each one finding, because of personal affection or of reverence for the dead, that those whom he commemorates form for him a part of his own past existence.

A community constituted by the fact that each of its members accepts, as part of his own individual life and self, the same expected *future* events that each of his fellows accepts, may be called a *community of expectation,* or upon occasion, a *community of hope.*

A community, whether of memory or of hope, exists relatively to the past or future facts to which its several members stand in the common relation just defined. The concept of the community depends upon the interpretation which each individual member gives to his own self,—to his own past,—and to his own future. Every one of us does, for various reasons, extend his interpretation of his own individual self so that from his own point of view, his life includes many faraway temporal happenings. The complex motives of such interpretations need not now be further examined. Enough,—these motives may vary from self to self with all the wealth of life. Yet when these interests of each self lead it to accept any part or item of the same past or the same future which another self accepts as its own,—then pluralism of the selves is perfectly consistent with their forming a community, either of memory or of hope. How rich this community is in meaning, in value, in membership, in significant organization, will depend upon the selves that enter into the community, and upon the ideals in terms of which they define themselves, their past, and their future.

With this definition in mind, we see why long histories are needed in order to define the life of great communities. We also see that, if great new undertakings enter into the lives of many men, a new community of hope, unified by the common relations of its individual members to the same future events, may be, upon occasion, very rapidly constituted, even in the midst of great revolutions.

The concept of the community, as thus analyzed, stands in the closest relation to the whole nature of the time-process, and also involves recognizing to the full both the existence and the significance of individual selves. In what sense the individual selves constitute the community we can in general see, while we are prepared to find that, for the individual selves, it may well prove to be the case that a real community of memory or of hope is necessary in order to secure their significance. Our own definition of a community can be illustrated by countless types of political, religious, and other significant communities which you will readily be able to select for yourselves. Without ignoring our ordinary social pluralism, this definition shows how and why many selves may be viewed as actually brought together in an historical community. Without presupposing any one metaphysical interpretation of experience, or of time, our definition shows where, in our experience and in our interpretation of the time-process, we are to look for a solution of the problem of the community. Without going beyond the facts of human life, of human memory, and of human interpretation of the self and of its past, our definition clears the way for a study of the constitution of the real world of the spirit.

20 ❧ THE BODY AND THE MEMBERS [1]

Henceforth, in these lectures, I shall restrict the application of the term "community" to those social groups which conform to the definition stated at the close of our last lecture. Not every social group which behaves so that, to an observer, it seems to be a single unit, meets all the conditions of our definition. Our new use of the term "community" will therefore be more precise and restricted than was our earlier employment of the word. But our definition will clear the way for further generalizations. It will enable us to express our reasons for much that, in our study of the Christian doctrine of life, had to be stated dogmatically, and illustrated rather than intimately examined.

We have repeatedly spoken of two levels of human life, the level of the individual and the level of the community. We have now in our hands the means for giving a more precise sense to this expression, and for furnishing a further verification of what we asserted about these two levels of life. We have also repeatedly emphasized the ethical and religious significance of loyalty; but our definition will help us to throw clearer light upon the sources of this worth. And by thus sharpening the outlines of our picture of what a real community is, we shall be made ready to consider whether the concept of the community possesses a more than human significance. Let us recall our new definition to mind, and then apply it to our main problems.

I

Our definition presupposes that there exist many individual selves. Suppose these selves to vary in their present experiences and purposes as widely as you will. Imagine them to be sundered from one another by such chasms of mutual mystery and inde-

[1] Josiah Royce, *The Problem of Christianity* (New York: The Macmillan Company, 1913), Vol. II, Lecture X, pp. 57–73, 78–105.—Editor's note.

pendence as, in our natural social life, often seem hopelessly to divide and secrete the inner world of each of us from the direct knowledge and estimate of his fellows. But let these selves be able to look beyond their present chaos of fleeting ideas and of warring desires, far away into the past whence they came, and into the future whither their hopes lead them. As they thus look, let each one of them ideally enlarge his own individual life, extending himself into the past and future, so as to say of some far-off event, belonging, perhaps, to other generations of men, "I view that event as a part of my own life." "That former happening or achievement so predetermined the sense and the destiny which are now mine, that I am moved to regard it as belonging to my own past." Or again: "For that coming event I wait and hope as an event of my own future."

And further, let the various ideal extensions, forwards and backwards, include at least one common event, so that each of these selves regards that event as a part of his own life.

Then, *with reference to the ideal common past and future in question, I say that these selves constitute a community.* This is henceforth to be our definition of a community. The present variety of the selves who are the members of the spiritual body so defined, is not hereby either annulled or slighted. The motives which determine each of them thus ideally to extend his own life, may vary from self to self in the most manifold fashion.

Our definition will enable us, despite all these varieties of the members, to understand in what sense any such community as we have defined exists, and is one.

Into this form, which, when thus summarily described, seems so abstract and empty, life can and does pour the rich contents and ideals which make the communities of our human world so full of dramatic variety and significance.

II

The *first* condition upon which the existence of a community, in our sense of the word, depends, is the power of an individual self to extend his life, in ideal fashion, so as to regard it as including past and future events which lie far away in time, and which he does not now personally remember. That this power exists, and that man has a self which is thus ideally extensible in time without any definable limit, we all know.

This power itself rests upon the principle that, however a man may come by his idea of himself, the self is no mere datum, but is in its essence a life which is interpreted, and which interprets itself, and which, apart from some sort of ideal interpretation, is a mere flight of ideas, or a meaningless flow of feelings, or a vision that sees nothing, or else a barren abstract conception. How deep the process of interpretation goes in determining the real nature of the self, we shall only later be able to estimate.

There is no doubt that what we usually call our personal memory does indeed give us assurances regarding our own past, so far as memory extends and is trustworthy. But our trust in our memories is itself an interpretation of their data. All of us regard as belonging, even to our recent past life, much that we cannot just now remember. And the future self shrinks and expands with our hopes and our energies. No one can merely, from without, set for us the limits of the life of the self, and say to us: "Thus far and no farther."

In my ideal extensions of the life of the self, I am indeed subject to some sort of control,—to what control we need not here attempt to formulate. I must be able to give myself some sort of reason, personal, or social, or moral, or religious, or metaphysical, for taking on or throwing off the burden, the joy, the grief, the guilt, the hope, the glory of past and of future deeds and experiences; but I must also myself personally share in this task of determining how much of the past and the future shall ideally enter into my life, and shall contribute to the value of that life.

And if I choose to say, "There is a sense in which *all* the tragedy and the attainment of an endless past and future of deeds and of fortunes enter into my own life," I say only what saints and sages of the most various creeds and experiences have found their several reasons for saying. The fact and the importance of such ideal extensions of the self must therefore be recognized. Here is the first basis for every clear idea of what constitutes a community.

The ideal extensions of the self may also include, as is well known, not only past and future events and deeds, but also physical things, whether now existent or not, and many other sorts of objects which are neither events nor deeds. The knight or the samurai regarded his sword as a part of himself. One's treasures and one's home, one's tools, and the things that one's hands have made, frequently come to be interpreted as part of the self. And any object in heaven or earth may be thus ideally appropriated by a given self. The ideal self of the Stoic or of the Mystic may, in various fashions, identify its will, or its very essence, with the whole universe. The Hindoo seer seeks to realize the words: "I am Brahm;" "That art thou."

In case such ideal extensions of the self are consciously bound up with deeds, or with other events, such as belong to the past or future life which the self regards as its own, our definition of the community warrants us in saying that many selves form one community when all are ideally extended so as to include the same object. But unless the ideal extensions of the self thus consciously involve past and future deeds and events that have to do with the objects in question, we shall not use these extensions to help us to define communities.

For our purposes, the community is a being that attempts to accomplish something in time and through the deeds of its members. These deeds belong to the life which each member regards as, in ideal, his own. It is in this way that both the real and the ideal Church are intended by the members to be communities in our sense. An analogous truth holds for such other communities as we shall need to consider. The concept of the community is thus, for our purposes, a practical conception. It involves the idea of deeds done, and ends sought or attained. Hence I shall define it in terms of members who themselves not only live in time, but conceive their own ideally extended personalities in terms of a time-process. In so far as these personalities possess a life that is for each of them his own, while it is, in some of its events, common to them all, they form a community.

Nothing important is lost, for our conception of the community, by this formal restriction, whereby common objects belong to a community only when these objects are bound up with the deeds of the community. For, when the warrior regards his sword as a part of himself, he does so because his sword is the instrument of his will, and because what he does with his sword belongs to his literal or ideal life. Even the mystic accomplishes his identification of the self and the world only through acts of renunciation or of inward triumph. And these acts are the goal of his life. Until he attains to them, they form part of his ideal future self. Whenever he fully accomplishes these crowning acts of identification, the separate self no longer exists. When knights or mystics form a community, in our sense, they therefore do so because they conceive of deeds done, in common, with their swords, or of mystical attainments that all of them win together.

Thus then, while no authoritative limit can be placed upon the ideal extensions of the self in time, those extensions of the self which need be considered for the purposes of our theory of the community are indeed extensions in time, past or future; or at all events involve such extensions in time.

Memory and hope constantly incite us to the extensions of the self which play so large a part in our daily life. Social motives of endlessly diverse sort move us to consider "far and forgot" as if to us it were near, when we view ourselves in the vaster perspectives of time. It is, in fact, the ideally extended self, and not, in general, the momentary self, whose life is worth living, whose sense outlasts our fleeting days, and whose destiny may be worthy of the interest of beings who are above the level of human individuals. The present self, the fleeting individual of to-day, is a mere gesticulation of a self. The genuine person lives in the far-off past and future as well as in the present. It is, then, the ideally extended self that is worthy to belong to a significant community.

III

The *second* condition upon which the existence of a community depends is the fact that there are in the social world a number of distinct selves capable of social communication, and, in general, engaged in communication.

The distinctness of the selves we have illustrated at length in our previous discussion. We need not here dwell upon the matter further, except to say, expressly, that a community does *not* become one, in the sense of my definition, by virtue of any reduction or melting of these various selves into a single merely present self, or into a mass of passing experience. That mystical phenomena may indeed form part of the life of a community, just as they may also form part of the life of an individual human being, I fully recognize.

About such mystical or quasi-mystical phenomena, occurring in their own community, the Corinthians consulted Paul. And Paul, whose implied theory of the community is one which my own definition closely follows, assured them in his reply that mystical phenomena are not essential to the existence of the community; and that it is on the whole better for the life of such a community as he was addressing, if the individual member, instead of losing himself "in a mystery," kept his own individuality, in order to contribute his own edifying gift to the common life. Wherein this common life consists we have yet further to see in what follows.

The *third* of the conditions for the existence of the community which my definition emphasizes consists in the fact that the ideally extended past and future selves of the members include at least some events which are, for all these selves, identical. This third condition is the one which furnishes both the most exact, the most widely variable, and the most important of the motives which warrant us in calling a community a real unit. The Pauline metaphor of the body and the members finds, in this third condition, its most significant basis,—a basis capable of exact description.

IV

In addition to the instance which I cited at the last time, when I mentioned the New Zealanders and their legendary canoes, other and much more important illustrations may here serve to remind us how a single common past or future event may be the central means of uniting many selves in one spiritual community. For the Pauline churches the ideal memory of their Lord's death and resurrection, defined in terms of the faith which the missionary apostle delivered to them in his teaching, was, for each believer, an acknowledged occurrence in his own past. For each one was taught the faith, "In that one event my individual salvation was accomplished."

This faith has informed ever since the ideal memory upon which Christian tradition has most of all depended for the establishment and the preservation of its own community. If we speak in terms of social psychology, we are obliged, I think, to regard this belief as the product of the life of the earliest Christian community itself. But once established, and then transmitted from generation to generation, this same belief has been ceaselessly recreative of the communities of each succeeding age. And the various forms of the Christian Church,—its hierarchical institutions, its schisms, its reformations, its sects, its heresies, have been varied, differentiated, or divided, or otherwise transformed, according as the individual believers who made up any group of followers of Christian tradition have conceived, each his own personal life as including and as determined by that one

ideal event thus remembered, namely, his Lord's death and
resurrection.

Since the early Church was aware of this dependence of its
community upon its memory, it instinctively resisted every effort to deprive that memory of definiteness, to explain it away
as the Gnostic heresies did, or to transform it from a memory into
any sort of conscious allegory. The idealized memory, the back-
ward looking faith of an individual believer, must relate to
events that seem to him living and concrete. Hence the early
Church insisted upon the words, "Suffered under Pontius Pilate."
The religious instinct which thus insisted was true to its own
needs. A very definite event must be viewed by each believer as
part of the history of his own personal salvation. Otherwise the
community would lose its coherence.

Paul himself, despite his determination to know Christ, not
"after the flesh," but "after the Spirit," was unhesitating and un-
compromising with regard to so much of the ideal Christian
memory as he himself desired each believer to carry clearly in
mind. Only by such common memories could the community be
constituted. To be sure, the Apostle's Christology, on its more
metaphysical side, cared little for such more precise technical
formulations as later became historically important for the
Church that formulated its creeds. But the events which Paul regarded as essential to salvation must be, as he held, plainly set
down.

Since human memory is naturally sustained by commemora-
tive acts, Paul laid the greatest possible stress upon the Lord's
Supper, and made the proper ordering thereof an essential part of
his ideal as a teacher. In this act of commemoration, wherein each
member recalled the origin of his own salvation, the community
maintained its united life.

V

The early Church was, moreover, not only a community of
memory, but a community of hope. Since, if the community was to
exist, and to be vigorously alive, each believer must keep definite
his own personal hope, while the event for which all hoped must
be, for all, an identical event, something more was needed, in
Paul's account of the coming end of the world, than the more
dimly conceived common judgment had hitherto been in the

minds of the Corinthians to whom Paul wrote. And therefore the great chapter [2] on the resurrection emphasizes equally the common resurrection of all, and the very explicitly individual immortality of each man. Paul uses both the resurrection of Christ, and the doctrine of the spiritual body, to give the sharpest possible outlines to a picture which has ever since dominated not only the traditional Christian religious imagination, but the ideal of the united Church triumphant. . . .

In the expected resurrection, as Paul pictures it, the individual finds his own life, and the community its common triumph over all the world-old powers of death. And the hope is referred back again to the memory. Was not Christ raised? By this synthesis Paul solves his religious problem, and defines sharply the relation of the individual and the community.

And therefore, whenever, upon the familiar solemn occasions, this chapter is read, not only is individual sorrow bidden to transform itself into an unearthly hope; but even upon earth the living and conscious community of the faithful celebrates the present oneness of spirit in which it triumphs. And the death over which it triumphs is the death of the lonely individual, whom faith beholds raised to the imperishable life in the spirit. This life in the spirit is also the life of the community. For the individual is saved, according to Paul, only in and through and with the community and its Lord.

VI

Our present interest in these classic religious illustrations of the idea of the community is not directly due to their historical importance as parts of Christian tradition; but depends upon the help which they give us in seeing how a community, whether it be Christian or not, can really constitute a single entity, despite the multiplicity of its members. Our illustrations have brought before us the fact that hope and memory constitute, in communities, a basis for an unquestionable consciousness of unity, and that this common life in time does not annul the variety of the individual members at any one present moment.

We have still to see, however, the degree to which this consciousness of unity can find expression in an effectively united com-

[2] I Cor. 15—Editor's Note.

mon life which not only contains common events, but also possesses common deeds and can arouse a common love—a love
which passes the love wherewith individuals can love one another.

And here we reach that aspect of the conception of the community which is the most important, and also the most difficult
aspect.

VII

A great and essentially dramatic event, such as the imagined
resurrection of the bodies of all men,—an event which interests all,
and which fixes the attention by its miraculous apparition,—is well
adapted to illustrate the union of the one and the many in the
process of time. When Paul's genius seized upon this picture,—
when, to use the well-known later scholastic phraseology, the
spirits of men were thus "individuated by their bodies," even
while the event of the resurrection fixed the eye of faith upon
one final crisis through which all were to pass "in a moment, in
the twinkling of an eye,"—when the Apostle thus instructed the
faithful, a great lesson was also taught regarding the means
whereby the ideal of a community and the harmonious union of
the one and the many can be rendered brilliantly clear to the
imagination, and decisively fascinating to the will.

But the lives of communities cannot consist of miraculous
crises. A community, like an individual self, must learn to keep
the consciousness of its unity through the vicissitudes of an endlessly shifting and often dreary fortune. The monotony of insignificant events, the chaos of lesser conflicts, the friction and the
bickerings of the members, the individual failures and the mutual misunderstandings which make the members of a community
forget the common past and future,—all these things work
against the conscious unity of the life of a community. Memory
and hope are alike clouded by multitudes of such passing events.
The individual members cannot always recall the sense in which
they identify their own lives and selves with what has been, or
with what is yet to come.

And—hardest task of all—the members, if they are to conceive clearly of the common life, must somehow learn to bear in
mind not merely those grandly simple events which, like great
victories, or ancestral feats, or divine interferences, enter into
the life of the community from without, and thus make their
impression all at once.

No, the true common life of the community consists of deeds which are essentially of the nature of processes of coöperation. That is, the common life consists of deeds which many members perform together, as when the workmen in a factory labor side by side.

Now we all know that coöperation constantly occurs, and is necessary to every form and grade of society. We also know that commerce and industry and art and custom and language consist of vast complexes of coöperations. And in all such cases many men manage in combination to accomplish what no one man, and no multitude of men working separately, could conceivably bring to pass. But what we now need to see is the way in which such coöperations can become part, not only of the life, but of the consciousness of a community.

VIII

Every instance of a process of coöperation is an event, or a sequence of events. And our definition of a community requires that, if such coöperative activities are to be regarded as the deeds of a community, there must be individuals, each one of whom says: "That coöperation, in which many distinct individuals take part, and in which I also take part, is, or was, or will be, an event in my life." And many coöperating individuals must agree in saying this of the same process in which they all coöperate.

And all must extend such identifications of the self with these social activities far into the past, or into the future.

But it is notoriously hard—especially in our modern days of the dreary complexity of mechanical labor—for any individual man so to survey, and so to take interest in a vast coöperative activity that he says: "In my own ideally extended past and future that activity, its history, its future, its significance as an event or sequence of events, all have their ideally significant part. That activity, as the coöperation of many in one work, is also my life." To say such things and to think such thoughts grow daily harder for most of the coworkers of a modern social order.

Hence, as is now clear, the existence of a highly organized social life is by no means identical with the existence of what is, in our present and restricted sense, the life of a true community. On the contrary, and for the most obvious reasons, there is a strong mutual opposition between the social tendencies which secure coöperation on a vast scale, and the very conditions which so interest the individual in the common life of his community that it forms part of his own ideally extended life. We met with that opposition between the more or less mechanically coöperative social life,—the life of the social will on the one side, and the life of the true community on the other side,—when we were considering the Pauline doctrine of the law in an earlier lecture. In fact, it is the original sin of any highly developed civilization that it breeds coöperation at the expense of a loss of interest in the community.

The failure to see the reason why this opposition between the tendency to coöperation and the spirit of the community exists; the failure to sound to the depths the original sin of man the social animal, and of the natural social order which he creates;—such failure, I repeat, lies at the basis of countless misinterpretations, both of our modern social problems, and of the nature of a true community, and of the conditions which make possible any wider philosophical generalizations of the idea of the community.

IX

Men do not form a community, in our present restricted sense of that word, merely in so far as the men coöperate. They form a community, in our present limited sense, when they not only coöperate, but accompany this coöperation with that ideal extension of the lives of individuals whereby each coöperating member says: "This activity which we perform together, this work of ours, its past, its future, its sequence, its order, its sense,—all these enter into my life, and are the life of my own self writ large."

Now coöperation results from conditions which a social psychology such as that of Wundt or of Tarde may analyze. Imitation and rivalry, greed and ingenuity, business and pleasure, war and industry, may all combine to make men so coöperate that very large groups of them behave, to an external observer, as if they were units. In the broader sense of the term "community," all social groups that behave as if they were units are regarded as communities. And we ourselves called all such groups communities in our earlier lectures before we came to our new definition.

But we have now been led to a narrower application of the term "community." It is an application to which we have restricted the term simply because of our special purpose in this inquiry. Using this restricted definition of the term "community," we see that groups which coöperate may be very far from constituting communities in our narrower sense. We also see how, in general, a group whose coöperative activities are very highly complex will require a correspondingly long period of time to acquire that sort of tradition and of common expectation which is needed to constitute a community in our sense,—that is, a community conscious of its own life.

Owing to the psychological conditions upon which social coöperation depends, such coöperation can very far outstrip, in the complexity of its processes, the power of any individual man's wit to understand its intricacies. In modern times, when social coöperation both uses and is so largely dominated by the industrial arts, the physical conditions of coöperative social life have combined with the psychological conditions to make any thorough understanding of the coöperative processes upon which we all depend simply hopeless for the individual, except within some narrow range. Experts become well acquainted with aspects of these forms of coöperation which their own callings involve. Less expert workers understand a less range of the coöperative processes in which they take part. Most individuals, in most of their work, have to coöperate as the cogs coöperate in the wheels of a mechanism. They work together; but few or none of them know how they coöperate, or what they must do.

But the true community, in our present restricted sense of the word, depends for its genuine common life upon such coöperative activities that the individuals who participate in these common activities understand enough to be able, first, to direct their own deeds of coöperation; secondly, to observe the deeds of their individual fellow workers, and thirdly, to know that, without just this combination, this order, this interaction of the coworking selves, just this deed could not be accomplished by the community. So, for instance, a chorus or an orchestra carries on its coöperative activities. In these cases coöperation is a conscious art. If hereupon these coöperative deeds, thus understood by the individual coworker, are viewed by him as linked, through an extended history with past and future deeds of the community, and if he then identifies his own life with this common life, and if his fellow members agree in this identification, then indeed the community both has a common life, and is aware of the fact. For then the individual coworker not only says: "This past and future fortune of the community belongs to my life;" but also declares: "This past and future deed of coöperation belongs to my life." "This, which none of us could have done alone,—this, which all of us together could not have accomplished unless we were ordered and linked in precisely this way,—this we together accomplished, or shall yet accomplish; and this deed of all of us belongs to my life."

A community thus constituted is essentially a community of those who are artists in some form of coöperation, and whose art constitutes, for each artist, his own ideally extended life. But the life of an artist depends upon his love for his art.

The community is made possible by the fact that each member includes in his own ideally extended life the deeds of coöperation which the members accomplish. When these deeds are hopelessly complex, how shall the individual member be able to regard them as genuinely belonging to his own ideally extended life? He can no longer understand them in any detail. He takes part in them, willingly or unwillingly. He does so because he is social, and because he must. He works in his factory, or has his share, whether greedily or honestly, in the world's commercial activities. And his coöperations may be skilful; and this fact also he may know. But his skill is largely due to external training, not to inner expansion of the ideals of the self. And the more complex the social order grows, the more all this coöperation must tend to appear to the individual as a mere process of nature, and not as his own work,—as a mechanism and not as an ideal extension of himself,—unless indeed love supplies what individual wit can no longer accomplish.

X

If a social order, however complex it may be, actually wins and keeps the love of its members; so that,—however little they are able to understand the details of their present coöperative activities,—they still—with all their whole hearts and their minds and their souls, and their strength—desire, each for himself, that such coöperations should go on; and if each member, looking back to the past, rejoices in the ancestors and the heroes who have made the present life of this social group possible;

and if he sees in these deeds of former generations the source
and support of his present love; and if each member also looks
forward with equal love to the future,—then indeed love furnishes that basis for the consciousness of the community which
intelligence, without love, in a highly complex social realm, can
no longer furnish. Such love—such loyalty—depends not upon
losing sight of the variety of the callings of individuals, but
upon seeing in the successful coöperation of all the members
precisely that event which the individual member most eagerly
loves as his own fulfilment.

When love of the community, nourished by common memories, and common hope, both exists and expresses itself in
devoted individual lives, it can constantly tend, despite the
complexity of the present social order, to keep the consciousness
of the community alive. And when this takes place, the identification of the loyal individual self with the life of the community will tend, both in ideal and in feeling, to identify each
self not only with the distant past and future of the community,
but with the present activities of the whole social body.

Thus, for instance, when the complexities of business life,
and the dreariness of the factory, have, to our minds, deprived
our present social coöperations of all or of most of their common significance, the great communal or national festivity, bringing to memory the great events of past and future, not only
makes us, for the moment, feel and think as a community with
reference to those great past and future events, but in its turn,
as a present event, reacts upon next day's ordinary labors. The
festivity says to us: "We are one because of our common past
and future, because of the national heroes and victories and
hopes, and because we love all these common memories and
hopes." Our next day's mood, consequent upon the festivity,
bids us say: "Since we are thus possessed of this beloved common past and future, let this consciousness lead each of us even
to-day to extend his ideal self so as to include the daily work
of all his fellows, and to view his fellow members' life as his
own."

Thus memory and hope tend to react upon the present self,
which finds the brotherhood of present labor more significant,
and the ideal identification of the present self with the self of
the neighbor easier, because the ideal extension of the self into
past and future has preceded.

And so, first, each of us learns to say: "This beloved past

and future life, by virtue of the ideal extension, is my own life."
Then, finding that our fellows have and love this past and future in common with us, we learn further to say: "In this respect we are all one loving and beloved community." Then we
take a further step and say: "Since we are all members of this
community, therefore, despite our differences, and our mutual
sunderings of inner life, each of us can, and will, ideally extend his present self so as to include the present life and deeds
of his fellow."

So it is that, in the ideal church, each member not only looks
backwards to the same history of salvation as does his fellow,
but is even thereby led to an ideal identification of his present
self with that of his fellow member that would not otherwise
be possible. Thus, then, common memory and common hope,
the central possessions of the community, tend, when enlivened
by love, to mould the consciousness of the present, and to link
each member to his community by ideal ties which belong to
the moment as well as to the stream of past and future life.

X I

Love, when it exists and triumphs over the complexities which
obscure and confuse the common life, thus completes the consciousness of the community, in the forms which that consciousness can assume under human conditions. Such love, however,
must be one that has the common deeds of the community as
its primary object. No one understands either the nature of the
loyal life, or the place of love in the constitution of the life of
a real community, who conceives such love as merely a longing
for the mystical blending of the selves or for their mutual interpenetration, and for that only. Love says to the individual: "So
extend yourself, in ideal, that you aim, with all your heart and
your soul and your mind and your strength, at *that* life of perfectly definite deeds which never can come to pass unless all the
members, despite their variety and their natural narrowness,
are in perfect coöperation. Let this life be your art and also the
art of all your fellow members. Let your community be as a
chorus, and not as a company who forget themselves in a common trance."

Nevertheless, as Paul showed in the great chapter, such love
of the self for the community can be and will be not without

its own mystical element. For since we human beings are as narrow in our individual consciousness as we are, we cannot ideally extend ourselves through clearly understanding the complicated social activities in which the community is to take part. Therefore our ideal extensions of the self, when we love the community, and long to realize its life with intimacy, must needs take the form of *acting as if we could survey,* in some single unity of insight, that wealth and variety and connection which, as a fact, we cannot make present to our momentary view. Since true love is an emotion, and since emotions are present affections of the self, love, in longing for its own increase, and for its own fulfilment, inevitably longs to find what it loves as a fact of experience, and to be in the immediate presence of its beloved. Therefore, the love of a community (a love which, as we now see, is devoted to desiring the realization of an overwhelmingly vast variety and unity of coöperations), is, as an emotion, discontent with all the present sundering of the selves, and with all the present problems and mysteries of the social order. Such love, then, restless with the narrowness of our momentary view of our common life, desires this common life to be an immediate presence for all of us. Such an immediate presence of all the community to all the members would be indeed, if it could wholly and simply take place, a mere blending of the selves,—an interpenetration in which the individuals vanished, and in which, for that very reason, the real community would also be lost.

Love,—the love of Paul's great chapter,—the loyalty which stands at the centre of the Christian consciousness,—is, as an emotion, a longing for such a mystical blending of the selves. This longing is present in Paul's account. It is in so far not the whole of charity. It is simply the mystical aspect of the love for the community.

But the Pauline charity is not merely an emotion. It is an interpretation. The ideal extension of the self gets a full and concrete meaning only by being actively expressed in the new deeds of each individual life. Unless each man knows how distinct he is from the whole community and from every member of it, he cannot render to the community what love demands,—namely, the devoted work. Love may be mystical, and work should be directed by clearly outlined intelligence; but the loyal spirit depends upon this union of a longing for unity with a will which needs its own expression in works of loyal art.

XII

The doctrine of the two levels of human existence; the nature of a real community; the sense in which there can be, in individual human beings, despite their narrowness, their variety, and their sundered present lives, a genuine consciousness of the life of a community whereof they are members:—these matters we have now, within our limits, interpreted. The time-process, and the ideal extensions of the self in this time-process, lie at the basis of the whole theory of the community. The union and the contrast of the one and the many in the community, and the relation of the mystical element in our consciousness of the community to the active interpretation of the loyal life, these things have also been reviewed. Incidentally, so to speak, we have suggested further reasons why loyalty, whether in its distinctively Christian forms, or in any others, is a saving principle whenever it appears in an individual human life. For in the love of a community the individual obtains, for his ideally extended self, precisely the unity, the wealth, and the harmony of plan which his sundered natural existence never supplies.

Yet it must be not merely admitted, but emphasized, that all such analyses of the sort of life and of interpretation upon which communities and the loyalty of their members depend, does not and cannot explain the origin of loyalty, the true sources of grace, and the way in which communities of high level come into existence.

On the contrary, all the foregoing account of what a community is shows how the true spirit of loyalty, and the highest level of the consciousness of a human community, is at once so precious, and so difficult to create.

The individual man naturally, but capriciously, loves both himself and his fellow-man, according as passion, pity, memory, and hope move him. Social training tends to sharpen the contrasts between the self and the fellow-man; and higher cultivation, under these conditions of complicated social coöperation which we have just pointed out, indeed makes a man highly conscious that he depends upon his community, but also renders him equally conscious that, as an individual, he is much beset by the complexities of the social will, and does not always love his community, or any community. Neither the origin nor the essence of loyalty is explained by man's tendencies to love his individual fellow-man.

It is true that, within the limits of his power to understand his social order, the conditions which make a man conscious of his community also imply that the man should in some respects identify his life with that. But I may well know that the history, the future, the whole meaning of my community are bound up with my own life; and yet it is not necessary that on that account I should wholeheartedly love my own life. I may be a pessimist. Or I may be simply discontented. I may desire to escape from the life that I have. And I may be aware that my fellows, for the most part, also long to escape.

That the community is above my own individual level I shall readily recognize, since the community is indeed vastly more skilful and incomparably more powerful than I can ever become. But what is thus above me I need not on that account be ready wholly to love. To be sure, that man is indeed a sad victim of a misunderstood life who is himself able to be clearly aware of his community, to identify its history and its future, at least in part, with his own ideally extended life, and who is yet *wholly* unable ever to love the life which is thus linked with his own. Yet there remains the fate which Paul so emphasized, and which has determined the whole history of the Christian consciousness: Knowledge of the community is not love of the community. Love, when it comes, comes as from above.

Especially is this true of the love of the ideal community of all mankind. I can be genuinely in love with the community only in case I have somehow fallen in love with the universe. The problem of love is human. The solution of the problem, if it comes at all, will be, in its meaning, superhuman, and divine, if there be anything divine.

What our definition of the community enables us to add to our former views of the meaning of loyalty is simply this: If the universe proves to be, in any sense, of the nature of a community, then love for this community, and for God, will not mean merely love for losing the self, or for losing the many selves, in any interpenetration of selves. If one can find that all humanity, in the sense of our definition, constitutes a real community, or that the world itself is, in any genuine way, of the nature of a community such as we have defined; and *if* hereupon we can come to love this real community,—then the one and the many, the body and the members, our beloved and ourselves, will be joined in a life in which we shall be both preserved as individuals, and yet united to that which we love.

XIII

Plainly a metaphysical study of the question whether the universe is a community will be as powerless as the foregoing analysis of the real nature of human communities to explain the origin of love, or to make any one fall in love with the universe. Yet something has been gained by our analysis of the problem which, from this point onwards, determines our metaphysical inquiry. If our results are in any way positive, they may enable us to view the problem of Christianity, that is, the problem of the religion of loyalty, in a larger perspective than that which human history, when considered alone, determines. The favorite methods of approaching the metaphysical problems of theology end by leaving the individual alone with God, in a realm which seems, to many minds, a realm of merely concepts, of intellectual abstractions, of barren theories. The ways which are just now in favor in the philosophy of religion seem to end in leaving the individual equally alone with his intuitions, his lurid experiences of sudden conversion, or his ineffable mysteries of saintly peace.

May we not hope to gain by a method which follows the plan now outlined? This method, first, encourages a man to interpret his own individual self in terms of the largest ideal extension of that self in time which his reasonable will can acknowledge as worthy of the aims of his life. Secondly, this method bids a man consider what right he has to interpret the life from which he springs, in the midst of which he now lives, as a life that in any universal sense coöperates with his own and ideally expresses its own meaning so as to meet with his own, and to have a history identical with his own. Thirdly, this method directs us to inquire how far, in the social order to which we unquestionably belong, there are features such as warrant us in hoping that, in the world's community, our highest love may yet find its warrant and its fulfilment.

Whatever the fortunes of the quest may be, we have now defined its plan, and have shown its perfectly definite relation to the historical problem of Christianity.

21 ❧ THE DOCTRINE OF SIGNS [1]

The Christian doctrine of life is dominated by the ideal of the Universal Community. Such was the thesis defended in the first part of this series of lectures. The real world itself is, in its wholeness, a Community. This was the metaphysical result in which our study of the World of Interpretation, at the last time, culminated.

I

Herewith the two assertions to which our study of the Problem of Christianity leads, are before you. Our concluding lectures must make explicit the relations between these two assertions. Hereby each of them will be interpreted in the light of the other.

Metaphysical theory and religious experience are always contrasting realms of inquiry and of insight. Therefore the task of our three concluding lectures constitutes a typical exercise in the process of interpretation. We have to compare results which have been reached by widely different methods. We have to mediate between them. The method of interpretation is always the comparative method. To compare and to interpret are two names for the same fundamental cognitive process.

The fitting order for such an enterprise is determined by the subject-matter. Since the metaphysical thesis with which our last lecture closed is very general, it will prove to be, indeed, a worthless abstraction, unless we illustrate its application to various special problems of life as well as of philosophy. What I can hope, within the limits of our brief remaining time, to make clearer, is what I may call the ground plan of the World of Interpretation.

[1] Josiah Royce, *The Problem of Christianity* (New York: The Macmillan Company, 1913), Vol. II, Lecture XIV, pp. 279–302, 305–307, 309–314, 323–325.—Editor's note.

The universe, if my thesis is right, is a realm which is through and through dominated by social categories. Time, for instance, expresses a system of essentially social relations. The present interprets the past to the future. At each moment of time the results of the whole world's history up to that moment are, so to speak, summed up and passed over to the future for its new deeds of creation and of interpretation. I state this principle here in a simply dogmatic form, and merely as an example of what I have in mind when I say that the system of metaphysics which is needed to define the constitution of this world of interpretation must be the generalized theory of an ideal society. Not the Self, not the Logos, not the One, and not the Many, but the Community will be the ruling category of such a philosophy.

I must attempt, then, within our brief remaining time, to make this general metaphysical theory less abstract and more articulate. I must contrast our theory with others. I must make more explicit its relation to the Christian ideas. And then I must, in conclusion, survey what we have won, and summarize the outcome.

II

Let me begin by a few purely technical formulations. Charles Peirce, in the discussions which we have now so freely used, introduced into logic the term "Sign." He used that term as the name for an object to which somebody gives or should give an interpretation. I have not here to deal, at any length, with Peirce's development of his theory of Signs. His doctrine was, as you will recall, not at first stated as the basis for a metaphysical system, but simply as a part of a logical theory of the categories. My own metaphysical use of Peirce's doctrine of signs, in my account of the World of Interpretation at the last time, is largely independent of Peirce's philosophy. For the moment it is enough to say that, according to Peirce, just as percepts have, for their appropriate objects, individually existent Things; and just as concepts possess, for their sole objects, Universals,—so interpretations have, as the objects which they interpret, Signs. In its most abstract definition, therefore, a Sign, according to Peirce, is something that determines an interpretation. A sign may also be called an expression of a mind; and, in our ordinary social intercourse, it actually is such an expression. Or again, one may say that a

sign is, in its essence, either a mind or a quasi-mind,—an object
that fulfils the functions of a mind.

Thus, a word, a clock-face, a weather-vane, or a gesture, is a
sign. Our reason for calling it such is twofold. It expresses a
mind, and it calls for an interpretation through some other mind,
which shall act as mediator between the sign, or between the
maker of the sign, and some one to whom the sign is to be read.

Since an interpretation of a sign is, in its turn, the expression
of the interpreter's mind, it constitutes a new sign, which again
calls for interpretation; and so on without end; unless the process
is arbitrarily interrupted. So much can be asserted as a purely logical
thesis, quite apart from metaphysics. A sign, then, is an object
whose being consists in the fact that the sign calls for an
interpretation.

The process of interpretation, as it occurs in our ordinary social
life, sufficiently illustrates the meaning of Peirce's new term.
Peirce insists that the signs, viewed simply from a logical point
of view, constitute a new and fundamentally important category. He sets this category as a "third," side by side with the
classic categories of the "universals" which form the "first" category, and the "individuals," which, in Peirce's logic, form the
"second" category.

Peirce, as I have said, is not responsible for the metaphysical
theory about the world of interpretation with which our last
lecture closed. But his terminology enables us to summarize that
theory by stating our own metaphysical thesis thus: "The universe
consists of real Signs and of their interpretation."

In the order of real time the events of the world are signs.
They are followed by interpreters, or by acts of interpretation
which our own experience constantly exemplifies. For we live, as
selves, by interpreting the events and the meaning of our experience. History consists of such interpretations.

These acts of interpretation are, in their turn, expressed, in
the order of time, by new signs. The sequence of these signs and
interpretations constitutes the history of the universe. Whatever
our experience exemplifies, our metaphysical doctrine of signs
generalizes, and applies to the world at large.

The world's experience is, from this point of view, not merely
a flux. For, as Bergson rightly asserts, the world of any present
moment of time is a summary of the results of all past experience.
This view of Bergson's, however, is no mere intuition, but is itself
an interpretation. Our own metaphysical thesis states in terms

of interpretation what Bergson states as if it were a result of simple intuition.

Since any idea, and especially any antithesis or contrast of ideas, is, according to our metaphysical thesis, a sign which in the world finds its real interpretation, our metaphysical theory may be called a "doctrine of signs."

The title which I have given to this lecture serves to direct attention, through the use of a purely technical term, to the main issue. This issue is the one presented by the thesis that the very being of the universe consists in a process whereby the world is interpreted,—not indeed in its wholeness, at any one moment of time, but in and through an infinite series of acts of interpretation. This infinite series constitutes the temporal order of the world with all its complexities. The temporal order is an order of purposes and of deeds, simply because it is of the essence of every rational deed to be an effort to interpret a past life to a future life; while every act of interpretation aims to introduce unity into life, by mediating between mutually contrasting or estranged ideas, minds, and purposes. If we consider the temporal world in its wholeness, it constitutes in itself an infinitely complex Sign. This sign is, as a whole, interpreted to an experience which itself includes a synoptic survey of the whole of time. Such is a mere sketch of our doctrine of the world of interpretation.

III

I may aid towards a further understanding of our metaphysical thesis by using, at this point, an illustration.

When you observe, at a crossing of roads, a sign-post, you will never discover what the real sign-post is, either by continuing to perceive it, or by merely conceiving its structure or its relations to any perceived objects, or to any merely abstract laws in heaven or in earth. Nor can you learn what the sign-post is by any process of watching in the course of your individual experience the "workings" of any ideas that it suggests to you as this individual man. You can understand what the sign-post is only if you learn to read it. For its very being as a sign-post consists in its nature as a guide, needing interpretation, and pointing the way. To know the real sign-post, you must then learn to interpret it to a possible hearer to whom you address your interpretation. This being to whom you address your interpretation must be a self distinct from your individual self. If, then, the sign-post is a sign-post at all, there are beings in the world that are neither individual objects of perception nor yet beings such that they are mere universals, —the proper objects for conception.

If the sign-post is a real sign-post, there is in the world a community constituted of at least three distinct minds. There is, first, the mind whose intention to point out the way is expressed in the construction of this sign-post. There is the mind to which the sign-post actually points out the way. But the sign-post does not effectively point out the way to anybody unless, either by the aid of his own individual memory, or of somebody who helps him to read the sign, he learns what the sign means. There must then be a third mind which interprets the sign-post to the inquiring wayfarer. The wayfarer, if he knows how to read, may be his own interpreter. But there remain the three distinct mental functions. There is the function of the mind whose purpose the sign expresses; there is the mind which is guided by the interpretation of the sign; and there is the function of the interpreter to whom the reading of the sign is due. All these minds or functions must be real and distinct and must form one real community, if indeed the sign-post is a real sign-post at all.

This illustration may help us to grasp what the first thesis of our metaphysical doctrine means. Our experience, as it comes to us, is a realm of Signs. That is, the facts of experience resemble sign-posts. You can never exhaustively find out what they are by resorting either to perception or to conception. Nor can you define experience merely in terms of the sort of knowledge which pragmatism emphasizes. No "working" of any single idea can show what a real fact of experience is. For a fact of experience, as you actually view that fact, is first an event belonging to an order of time,—an event preceded by an infinite series of facts whose meaning it summarizes, and leading to an infinite series of coming events, into whose meaning it is yet to enter. But the past and future of our real experience are objects neither of pure perception nor of pure conception. Nor can you, at any present moment, verify any present idea of yours about any past event. Nor can you define past and future in terms of the present workings of any ideas. Past time and future time are known solely through interpretations. Past time we regard as real, because we view our memories as signs which need and possess their interpretations. Our expectations are interpreted to our future selves by our present deeds. Therefore we regard our expectations as signs of a future.

Therefore, to a being who merely perceived and conceived, or who lived wholly in the present workings of his ideas, past time and future time would be as meaningless as the sign-post would be to the wayfarer who could not read, and who found nobody to interpret to him its meaning. If the past and future are realities, then they constitute a life which belongs to some real community, whose ideas of past and of future are really interpreted.

Now our doctrine of the world of interpretation extends to all reality the presuppositions which we use in all our dealings with past and future time. Our memories are signs of the past; our expectations are signs of the future. Past and future are real in so far as these signs have their real interpretation. Our metaphysical thesis generalizes the rules which constantly guide our daily interpretations of life. All contrasts of ideas, all varieties of experience, all the problems which finite experience possesses, are signs. The real world contains (so our thesis asserts) the interpreter of these signs, and the very being of the world consists in the truth of the interpretation which, in the whole realm of experience, these signs obtain.

Let us turn back from these technical formulations and from these illustrations, and come again closer to the real life for which they are intended to stand.

I V

Despite my frequent mention of differences, there is one respect in which I am in full agreement with the spirit of pragmatism, as James defined it. Any metaphysical thesis, if it has a meaning at all, is the expression of an attitude of the will of the one who asserts this thesis.

In a remarkable recent book, entitled: "Die Philosophie des Als Ob," Vaihinger has given his own formulation to a view which he originally reached independently of the influence of pragmatism. It is the view that a philosophy is, in its essence, a resolution to treat the real world as if that world possessed certain characters, and as if our experience enabled us to verify these characters. This resolution is, in its essence, an active attitude of the will. Therefore Voluntarism must form an essential part of every philosophy which justly interprets our metaphysical interests. For our metaphysical interests are indeed interests in directing our will, in defining our attitude towards the universe, in making articulate and practical our ideals and our resolutions. So far, I say, Vaihinger and the pragmatists are right.

I do not believe, however, that our voluntarism must remain a *mere* pragmatism. I have long defended a philosophy, both of human life and of the universe, which I have preferred to call an "Absolute Voluntarism." I developed such a philosophy, partly under the influence of James, but long before recent pragmatism was in question. In its most general form, this philosophy to which I myself adhere, asserts that, while every metaphysical theory is the expression of an attitude of the will, there is one, and but one, general and decisive attitude of the will which is the right attitude, when we stand in presence of the universe, and when we undertake to choose how we propose to bear ourselves towards the world. Any philosophy is inevitably a doctrine which counsels us to bear ourselves towards our world *as if* our experience were such and such. But I do not believe that the "Philosophy of the 'As if' " is, as Vaihinger asserts, merely a system of more or less convenient fictions. For if there are absolute standards for the will (and, in my own opinion, there are such standards), then the world of the will is no world of fictions. If there is one, and but one, right attitude of the will towards the universe, this attitude, when once assumed, is essentially creative of its own realm of deeds. Its so-called fictions are, therefore, not mere fictions, for they constitute a real life. Its so-called successes are no merely transient successes. For if there is any true success at all, every such success, however petty it seems, has a world-wide meaning. The realm of true success is not merely a world of change. For deeds once done are irrevocable; and every deed echoes throughout the universe. The past is unchanging. The expression of the will constitutes itself an actual life. The creative activity of the will is therefore no mere play with figments. It has the reality of a realm of deeds. And every deed has a value that extends throughout the world of the will. Each act is to be judged in the light of the principle: "Inasmuch as ye have done it unto the least of these."

I do not wish here to dwell upon the general features which I have repeatedly ascribed to this world of the will, where every fact is the expression of an individual decision, and is therefore an absolute fact. I do not intend to repeat even the outlines of my former statements, both of this absolute voluntarism and of my own type of idealism. I have too often told that tale. So far as possible, I wish, in the present exposition, to speak as if all my former words were unspoken.

As a fact, I still hold by all the essential features of these former attempts to state the case for idealism. But at present I am dealing with the World of Interpretation, and with the metaphysics of the Community. This I believe to be simply a new mode of approach to the very problems which I have formerly discussed.

My present interest lies in applying the spirit of my absolute voluntarism to the new problems which our empirical study of the Christian ideas, and our metaphysical theory of interpretation, have presented for our scrutiny.

With this, then, as the end now in view, let me try to tell you what attitude of will, what practical bearing towards the universe, what resolution, what plan of life, should characterize, in my opinion, any one who undertakes to view the world in the light of that doctrine concerning the nature and the business of interpretation, which, at the last time, I sketched.

This essentially social universe, this community which we have now declared to be real, and to be, in fact, the sole and supreme reality,—the Absolute,—what does it call upon a reasonable being to do? What kind of salvation does it offer to him? What interest does it possess for his will? If he accepts such a view of things, how should he bear himself towards the problem of life? To what ideas of his own does such a view offer success? How can he bring such a view into closer relations with ordinary human experience?

V

James declared that the typical pragmatist is a man of an essentially dramatic temper of mind. I now have to point out that the believer in our world of interpretation also centres his interests about a genuinely dramatic undertaking.

I have already said that the world of interpretation includes an infinite series of acts of interpretation. I have shown, in an earlier lecture, that every act of interpretation involves novelty. The believer in this doctrine of signs, the one to whom every problem, every antithesis, every expression of mind, every tragedy of life, is a sign calling for interpretation, and in whose belief the world contains its own interpreter, both contemplates and shares in a world drama. But the attitude of will which befits one who holds this doctrine of signs can only be rightly understood in case we first distinguish three very general attitudes of the will with which, in certain of their special forms, we have now become well acquainted. Our will is always dramatic in its expressions. It passes from deed to deed. Its world is a world of sequences and of enterprises. But when it surveys this world, and when it summarizes the spirit of its undertakings, the will may assume any one of three distinct modes of appreciating both itself and its realm of actual or of possible deeds.

VI

The first of these modes, the first of the attitudes of the will to which I here direct your attention, is that to which Schopenhauer gave the name, "The Affirmation of the Will to Live." This phrase of Schopenhauer is intended by its author to be extremely general, and to apply to active dispositions which are exemplified by all sorts and conditions of men. Whatever the natural man seeks, he intends, says Schopenhauer, to live if he can. And when the natural man affirms this will to live, he may have in mind any one of countless different, or even conflicting, motives and purposes.

He may be seeking pleasure, wealth, power, praise, material possessions, or manifold spiritual goods. He may call it righteousness or food, that he desires. It may be the destruction of his enemies or the prosperity of his friends that he has in mind when he sets out towards his goal. He may be of any calling that you please. He may be a worldling or a recluse; a beggar or a king; an outcast or the centre of an admiring company. In brief, his special purposes may vary as you will. The ideas, the "leadings," which, in the pragmatic sense, he desires to have succeed, may vary from man to man and from life to life, throughout the whole range of our social and individual objects of desire.

But, in any case, if, in Schopenhauer's sense, such a man affirms the will to live, he essentially desires to be himself, whoever he may be, and to win his aims, whatever the special aims be to which he commits himself. This desire for self-assertion, then, is present in all the Protean shapes of the affirmation of the will to live, and vivifies them.

While one affirms the will to live, he therefore gives himself over to the great game of life. As an individual man he has his friends and his enemies; his triumphs and defeats; his joys and his sorrows of pain and grief. But what happens to him does not, in so far, touch the heart and core of his will. He may shout with triumph, or cry aloud in his woe; he may pray to his gods for help, or may curse his fate in what he calls his despair; but withal, he means to continue his pursuit of the objects of desire. He may repent of his sins; but not of being himself. He may, in his hatred of ill-fortune, resort even to suicide. But such suicide is merely a revolt against disaster. It only affirms in its own passionate way the longing for some life which is not indeed the present life of the rebel who seeks suicide, but which, in all his condemnation of his own deeds or of his own misadventures, he still longs to live, if only death and the universe will yet permit him to express himself.

VII

Schopenhauer usually emphasizes the essentially selfish nature of this will to live, as it inspires the individual man. Yet Schopenhauer fully recognizes that we are all social beings, and that the will to live can keep us eagerly busy in and with the world of our fellows. Only, as Schopenhauer rightly interprets this affirmation of the will to live, the recognition of his fellow-men which the victim of this will to live constantly makes, is based, so to speak, upon the natural solipsism of the individual will.

And here we come to the very root, the inmost meaning, of this first of the three attitudes of the will which we are here considering.

One who thus, in Schopenhauer's sense, affirms the will to live, may cheerfully and sincerely acknowledge that other men exist, and he may be a good member of society. But he tends to found this acknowledgment of his fellow-man, and of the social will, upon what most philosophers regard as an argument from analogy. A man may, by reason of such analogy, extend the realm to which his will to live applies its interests. The early and purely natural forms of family loyalty and of clan loyalty depend upon such practical expansions of the self. But, as we saw when we studied the Pauline doctrine of original sin, the will to live constantly meets its opponent in the wills of other individuals. And then its primal solipsism revives; and it hates its fellows. And even when such a will recognizes that an organized social will is in some sense a reality, it finds this social will either as a foreign fact, or as a mystery.

In brief, all the social facts seem to a man in whom Schopenhauer's will to live finds its natural affirmation, external and in general problematic,—known only through analogy and doubtfully. I will my own life; and observe my own life. My dealings with you seem, from this point of view, to be due to motives external to this will of mine. . . .

VIII

In strong contrast to the affirmation of the will to live, Schopenhauer placed that attitude which he defined as the resignation,—the denial of the will to live. Here we have to deal with a tendency too well known to all students of the history of the spiritual life to need, in this place, extended portrayal, and too simple in its fascinating contrast with our natural life to require minute analysis. This is the attitude of the will which Southern Buddhism taught as the sole and sufficient way of salvation. In the form of saintly resignation the same ideal has received countless Christian expressions. Repeatedly this form of self-denial has been supposed to constitute the essence of Christianity. Repeatedly the expounders and defenders of the Christian doctrine of life have been obliged to insist that the Christian form of salvation does *not* consist in this simple abandonment of the will to live. I will not here repeat the tale which the greatest work of Christianity throughout the ages has so freely illustrated. Resignation alone does not save. To abandon his will to live does not by itself enable the individual to win the true goal of life. Let us, for the moment, simply accept this fact.

But since we are here interested in the metaphysical relations of these attitudes of the will, let us mention, in passing, that the resignation of the will to live is an attitude to which there correspond appropriate forms of metaphysical opinion. Here, again, the connections are well known, and need not here be dwelt upon. It is enough to say that whoever abandons the will to live, ceases, of course, to be interested in those "workings" of ideas which pragmatism regards as bringing us into empirical and momentary touch with the real. To such a resigned will, there remain only the cognitive processes of pure conception and of pure perception to consider. On the whole, in the history of thought those for whom salvation consists in the denial of the will to live have resorted to the metaphysics of pure perception, and have been mystics. . . .

I X

But there is indeed a third attitude of the will. It is not Schopenhauer's attitude of the affirmation of the will to live. It is also not the other attitude which Schopenhauer believed to be the sole and sufficient salvation of the will. And this third attitude of the will possesses its appropriate metaphysics.

As for what this attitude of the will is,—when we consider, not its doctrine of the universe, but its doctrine of life,—we are already well acquainted with it, because our entire discussion of the Christian ideas was devoted to making us familiar with its moral and its religious meaning. In returning, at this point, to the mention of this attitude of the will, I do so because we now are ready to understand the relation between this type of will, and the metaphysical doctrine of which I believe it to be the fitting accompaniment. Whoever has learned to understand the meaning of this third way in which the will can bear itself towards its world, will therefore be better prepared to grasp the foundations upon which the metaphysics of interpretation rests. The human value of this practical attitude does not by itself fully reveal the grounds of the technical theory which is here in question. But the intimate relations between theory and life are nowhere more pronounced than in this case, where reason and sentiment, action and expression, throw light, each upon the other, as is hardly anywhere else the case.

The attitude of the will which Paul found to be saving in its power, just as, to his mind, it was also divine in its origin, was the attitude of Loyalty. Now loyalty, when considered from within, and with respect to its deepest spirit, is not the affirmation of the will to live of which Schopenhauer spoke. And loyalty is also not the denial of the will to live. It is a positive devotion of the Self to its cause,—a devotion as vigorous, as self-asserting, as articulate, as strenuous, as Paul's life and counsels always remained. The apostle himself was no resigned person. His sacrifices for his cause were constant, and were eloquently portrayed in his own burning words. They included the giving of whatever he possessed. But they never included the negation of the will, the plucking out of the root of all desire, in which Gotama Buddha found salvation. Paul died at his conversion; but only in order that henceforth the life of the spirit should live in him and through him.

X

Now this third attitude of the will, as we found in dealing with the whole Christian doctrine of life, has in any case its disposition to imagine, and also practically to acknowledge as real, a spiritual realm,—an universal and divine community. Christian theology, in its traditional forms, was a natural outcome of the effort to define the world wherein the loyal will can find both its expression and its opportunity. We have not now to consider the religious aspect of this third attitude of the will. But we are now fully prepared to state its relation to the metaphysical problems. All the threads are in our hands. We have only to weave them into a single knot.

As a reasonable being, when once I have come to realize the meaning of my dealings both with life and with the world, the first practical principle, as well as the first theoretical presupposition of my philosophy must be this: Whatever my purposes or my ideas,—whatever will to live incites mé to create and to believe, whatever reverses of fortune drive me back upon my own poor powers, whatever problems baffle me, through their complexity and my ignorance, one truth stands out clear: Practically I cannot be saved alone; theoretically speaking, I cannot find or even define the truth in terms of my individual experience, without taking account of my relation to the community of those who know. This community, then, is real whatever is real. And in that community my life in interpreted. When viewed as if I were alone, I, the individual, am not only doomed to failure, but I am lost in folly. The "workings" of my ideas are events whose significance I cannot even remotely estimate in terms of their momentary existence, or in terms of my individual successes. My life means nothing, either theoretically or practically, unless I am a member of a community. I win no success worth having, unless it is also the success of the community to which I essentially and by virtue of my real relations to the whole universe, belong. My deeds are not done at all, unless they are indeed done for all time, and are irrevocable. The particular fortunes upon which James lays so much stress are not even particular, unless they consist of individual events which either occur or do not occur. Each of these real events has therefore a being which lasts to the end of time, and a value which concerns the whole universe.

Such, I say, is the principle, at once theoretical and practical, upon which my philosophy must depend. This principle does not itself depend upon the momentary success of any individual idea. For it is a principle in terms of which we are able to define whatever real life there is, while, unless this principle itself holds true, there is no real life or real world in which we can find success.

.   .   .   .   .

XIV

. . . We have no ground whatever for believing that there is any real world except the ground furnished by our experience, and by the fact that, in addition to our perceptions and our conceptions, we have problems upon our hands which need interpretation. Our fundamental postulate is: *The world is the interpretation of the problems which it presents.* If you deny this principle, you do so only by presenting, as Bergson does, some other interpretation as the true one. But thus you simply reaffirm the principle that the world has an interpreter.

Using this principle, in your ordinary social life, you postulate your fellow-man as the interpreter of the ideas which he awakens in your mind, and which are not your own ideas. The same principle, applied to our social experience of the physical world, determines our ordinary interpretations of nature and guides our natural science. For, as we have seen, the physical world is an object known to the community, and through interpretation. The same principle, applied to our memories and to our expectations, gives us our view of the world of time, with all its infinite wealth of successive acts of interpretation.

In all these special instances, the application of this principle defines for us some form or grade of community, and teaches us wherein lies the true nature, the form, the real unity, and the essential life of this community.

Our Doctrine of Signs extends to the whole world the same fundamental principle. The World is the Community. The world contains its own interpreter. Its processes are infinite in their temporal varieties. But their interpreter, the spirit of this universal community,—never absorbing varieties or permitting them to blend,—compares and, through a real life, interprets them all.

The attitude of will which this principle expresses, is neither that of the affirmation nor that of the denial of what Schopenhauer meant by the will to live. It is the attitude which first expresses itself by saying "Alone I am lost, and am worse than nothing. I need a counsellor, I need my community. Interpret me. Let me join in this interpretation. Let there be the community. This alone is life. This alone is salvation. This alone is real." This is at once an attitude of the will and an assertion whose denial refutes itself. For if there is no interpreter, there is no interpretation. And if there is no interpretation, there is no world whatever.

In its daily form as the principle of our social common sense, this attitude of the will inspires whatever is reasonable about our worldly business and our scientific inquiry. For all such business and inquiry are in and for and of the community, or else are vanity.

In its highest form, this attitude of the will was the one which Paul knew as Charity, and as the life in and through the spirit of the Community.

Such, then, is the relation of the Christian will to the real world.

22 ❧ WORDS OF PROFESSOR ROYCE AT THE WALTON HOTEL AT PHILADELPHIA, DECEMBER 29, 1915 [1]

I was born in 1855 in California. My native town was a mining town in the Sierra Nevada,—a place five or six years older than myself. My earliest recollections include a very frequent wonder as to what my elders meant when they said that this was a new community. I frequently looked at the vestiges left by the former diggings of miners, saw that many pine logs were rotten, and that a miner's grave was to be found in a lonely place not far from my own house. Plainly men had lived and died thereabouts. I dimly reflected that this sort of life had apparently been going on ever since men dwelt in that land. The logs and the grave looked old. The sunsets were beautiful. The wide prospects when one looked across the Sacramento Valley were impressive, and had long interested the people of whose love for my country I heard much. What was there then in this place that ought to be called new, or for that matter, crude? I wondered, and gradually came to feel that part of my life's business was to find out what all this wonder meant. My earliest teachers in philosophy were my mother, whose private school, held for some years in our own

[1] After the dinner at the Walton Hotel, Professor Royce, in acknowledgment of the kindness of his friends, made a brief statement, largely autobiographical in its character. The following is a summary of this statement, and is founded upon some notes which friends present amongst the guests have kindly supplied, to aid the speaker to remind his friends of the spirit of what he tried to express.

[Josiah Royce, *The Hope of the Great Community* (New York: The Mac-Macmillan Company, 1916), Chap. VI, pp. 122–136. The chapter is reprinted in its entirety.—Editor's note.]

house, I attended, and my sisters, who were all older than myself, and one of whom taught me to read. In my home I heard the Bible very frequently read, and very greatly enjoyed my mother's reading of Bible stories, although, so far as I remember, I was very generally dissatisfied with the requirements of observance of Sundays, which stand out somewhat prominently in my memory. Our home training in these respects was not, as I now think, at all excessively strict. But without being aware of the fact, I was a born nonconformist. The Bible stories fascinated me. The observance of Sunday aroused from an early time a certain more or less passive resistance, which was stubborn, although seldom, I think, openly rebellious.

The earliest connected story that I independently read was the Apocalypse, from a large print New Testament, which I found on the table in our living room. The Apocalypse did not tend to teach me early to acquire very clear ideas. On the other hand, I did early receive a great deal of training in dialectics, from the sister nearest to me in age. She was three years my senior. She was very patiently persistent in showing me the truth. I was nearly as persistent in maintaining my own views. Since she was patient, I believe that we seldom quarrelled in any violent way. But on occasion, as I remember, our dear mother used, when the wrangling grew too philosophical, to set me the task of keeping still for an hour. The training was needed, but it was never wholly effective in suppressing for any great length of time the dialectical insistence.

I was not a very active boy. I had no physical skill or agility. I was timid and ineffective, but seem to have been, on the whole, prevailingly cheerful, and not extremely irritable, although I was certainly more or less given to petty mischief, in so far as my sisters did not succeed in keeping me under their kindly watch.

Since I grew during the time of the civil war, heard a good deal about it from people near me, but saw nothing of the consequences of the war through any closer inspection, I remained as vague about this matter as about most other life problems,— vague but often enthusiastic. My earliest great patriotic experience came at the end of the civil war, when the news of the assassination of Lincoln reached us. Thenceforth, as I believe, I had a country as well as a religious interest. Both of these were ineffective interests, except in so far as they were attached to the already mentioned enthusiasms, and were clarified and directed by the influence of my mother and sisters. Of boys outside the household I so far knew comparatively little, but had a considerable tendency, as I remember, to preach down to what I supposed to be the level of these other boys,—a predisposition which did not prepare me for social success in the place in which I was destined to pass the next stage of my development, namely San Francisco.

When we went to live in San Francisco, I for the first time saw, first San Francisco Bay, and then the Ocean itself, which fascinated me, but which for a long time taught me little.

About June, 1866, I began to attend a large Grammar School in San Francisco. I was one of about a thousand boys. The ways of training were new to me. My comrades very generally found me disagreeably striking in my appearance, by reason of the fact that I was redheaded, freckled, countrified, quaint, and unable to play boys' games. The boys in question gave me my first introduction to the "majesty of the community." The introduction was impressively disciplinary and persistent. On the whole it seemed to me "not joyous but grievous." In the end it probably proved to be for my good. Many years later, in a lecture contained in the first volume of my *Problem of Christianity,* I summarized what I remember of the lesson of the training which my schoolmates very frequently gave me, in what I there have to say about the meaning which lies behind the Pauline doctrine of original sin, as set forth in the seventh chapter of the Epistle to the Romans.

Yet my mates were not wholly unkind, and I remember lifelong friendships which I formed in that Grammar School, and which I still can enjoy whenever I meet certain of my dear California friends.

In the year 1871, I began to attend the University of California, where I received my first degree in 1875.

The principal philosophical influences of my undergraduate years were: 1. The really very great and deep effect produced upon me by the teaching of Professor Joseph LeConte,—himself a former pupil of Agassiz, a geologist, a comparatively early defender and exponent of the Darwinian theory, and a great light in the firmament of the University of California of those days; 2. The personal influence of Edward Rowland Sill, who was my teacher in English, during the last two years of my undergraduate life; 3. The literary influence of John Stuart Mill and of Herbert Spencer, both of whom I read during those years. There was, at that time, no regular undergraduate course in philosophy at the University of California.

After graduation I studied in Germany, and later at the Johns Hopkins University, still later returning a while to the University of California from 1878 to 1882. Since 1882 I have been working at Harvard. In Germany I heard Lotze at Göttingen, and was for a while strongly under his influence. The reading of Schopenhauer was another strong influence during my life as a student in Germany. I long paid a great deal of attention to the philosophy of Kant. But during the years before 1890, I never supposed myself to be very strongly under the influence of Hegel, nor yet of Green, nor of either of the Cairds. I should confess to the charge of having been, during my German period of study, a good deal under the influence of the Romantic School, whose philosophy of poetry I read and expounded with a good deal of diligence. But I early cherished a strong interest in logic, and long desired to get a fair knowledge of mathematics.

When I review this whole process, I strongly feel that my deepest motives and problems have centred about the Idea of the Community, although this idea has only come gradually to my clear consciousness. This was what I was intensely feeling, in the days when my sisters and I looked across the Sacramento Valley, and wondered about the great world beyond our mountains. This was what I failed to understand when my mates taught me those instructive lessons in San Francisco. This was that which I tried to understand when I went to Germany. I have been unpractical,—always socially ineffective as regards genuine "team play," ignorant of politics, an ineffective member of committees, and a poor helper of concrete social enterprises. Meanwhile I have always been, as in my childhood, a good deal of a nonconformist, and disposed to a certain rebellion. An English cousin of mine not long since told me that, according to a family tradition current in his community, a common ancestor of ours was one of the guards who stood about the scaffold of Charles the First. I can easily mention the Monarch in modern Europe, in the guard about whose scaffold I should most cheerfully stand, if he had any scaffold. So much of the spirit that opposes the community I have and have always had in me, simply, elementally, deeply. Over against this natural ineffectiveness in serving the community, and over against this rebellion, there has always stood the interest which has taught me what I nowadays try to express by teaching that we are saved through the community.

The resulting doctrine of life and of the nature of truth and of reality which I have tried to work out, to connect with logical and metaphysical issues, and to teach to my classes, now seems to me not so much romanticism, as a fondness for defining, for articulating, and for expounding the perfectly real, concrete, and literal life of what we idealists call the "spirit," in a sense which is indeed Pauline, but not merely mystical, superindividual; not merely romantic, difficult to understand, but perfectly capable of exact and logical statement.

The best concrete instance of the life of a community with which I have had the privilege to become well acquainted has been furnished to me by my own Seminary, one whose meetings you have so kindly and graciously permitted me to attend as leader, on this to me so precious occasion.

. . . But why should you give so kind an attention to me at a moment when the deepest, the most vital, and the most practical interest of the whole community of mankind are indeed imperilled, when the spirit of mankind is overwhelmed with a cruel and undeserved sorrow, when the enemies of mankind often seem as if they were about to triumph?

Let me simply say in closing, how deeply the crisis of this moment impresses me, and how keenly I feel the bitterness of being unable to do anything for the Great Community except to thank you for your great kindness, and to hope that we and the Community shall see better times together. Certainly unless the enemies of mankind are duly rebuked by the results of this war, I, for one, do not wish to survive the crisis. Let me then venture, as I close, to quote to you certain words of the poet Swinburne. You will find them in his *Songs before Sunrise*. Let the poet and prophet speak. He voices the spirit of that for which, in my poor way, I have always in my weakness been working.

A WATCH IN THE NIGHT

By A. C. Swinburne

Watchman, what of the night?—
   Storm and thunder and rain,
   Lights that waver and wane,
Leaving the watchfires unlit.
Only the balefires are bright,
   And the flash of the lamps now and then
From a palace where spoilers sit,
   Trampling the children of men.

Prophet, what of the night?—
   I stand by the verge of the sea,
   Banished, uncomforted, free,
Hearing the noise of the waves

And sudden flashes that smite
   Some man's tyrannous head,
Thundering, heard among graves
   That hide the hosts of his dead.

Mourners, what of the night?—
   All night through without sleep
   We weep, and we weep, and we weep.
Who shall give us our sons?
Beaks of raven and kite,
   Mouths of wolf and of hound,
Give us them back whom the guns
   Shot for you dead on the ground.

Dead men, what of the night?—
   Cannon and scaffold and sword,
   Horror of gibbet and cord,
Mowed us as sheaves for the grave,
Mowed us down for the right.
   We do not grudge or repent.
Freely to freedom we gave
   Pledges, till life should be spent.

Statesman, what of the night?—
   The night will last me my time.
   The gold on a crown or a crime
Looks well enough yet by the lamps.
Have we not fingers to write,
   Lips to swear at a need?
Then, when danger decamps,
   Bury the word with the deed.

Exile, what of the night?—
   The tides and the hours run out,
   The seasons of death and of doubt,
The night-watches bitter and sore.
In the quicksands leftward and right
   My feet sink down under me;
But I know the scents of the shore
   And the broad blown breaths of the sea.

Captives, what of the night?—
   It rains outside overhead
   Always, a rain that is red,

And our faces are soiled with the rain.
Here in the season's despite
   Day-time and night-time are one,
Till the curse of the kings and the chain
   Break, and their toils be undone.

Princes, what of the night?—
   Night with pestilent breath
   Feeds us, children of death,
Clothes us close with her gloom.
Rapine and famine and fright
   Crouch at our feet and are fed.
Earth where we pass is a tomb,
   Life where we triumph is dead.

Martyrs, what of the night?—
   Nay, is it night with you yet?
   We, for our part, we forget
What night was, if it were.
The loud red mouths of the fight
   Are silent and shut where we are.
In our eyes the tempestuous air
   Shines as the face of a star.

Europe, what of the night?—
   Ask of heaven, and the sea,
   And my babes on the bosom of me,
Nations of mine, but ungrown:
There is one who shall surely requite
   All that endure or that err:
She can answer alone:
   Ask not of me, but of her.

Liberty, what of the night?—
   I feel not the red rains fall.
   Hear not the tempest at all,
Nor thunder in heaven any more.
All the distance is white
   With the soundless feet of the sun.
Night, with the woes that it wore,
   Night is over and done.

May the light soon dawn. May the word of the poet and
prophet soon come true. This is my closing greeting to you.

A Chronology of Josiah Royce's Life

1855	Born in Grass Valley, California, on November 20
1866	Royce family moves to San Francisco
1871	Enters the University of California at Berkeley
1875	Graduates with B.A. degree from the University of California
1875–1876	Studies philosophy in Germany at Leipzig and Göttingen
1876–1878	Completes a Ph.D. at Johns Hopkins University
1878	Returns to Berkeley to teach in the English Department at the University of California
1880	Marries Katharine Head
1882	Joins the Harvard University faculty as Instructor in Philosophy
1885	Publication of *The Religious Aspect of Philosophy*
	Appointed Assistant Professor of Philosophy at Harvard
1892	Publication of *The Spirit of Modern Philosophy*
	Appointed Professor of the History of Philosophy at Harvard
1898	Publication of *Studies of Good and Evil*
1899–1900	Delivers the Gifford Lectures at the University of Aberdeen
	Gifford Lectures published in 1899 and 1901 as *The World and the Individual*
1906	Lectures at Johns Hopkins University
1908	Publication of *The Philosophy of Loyalty*
1911	Delivers the Bross Lectures at Lake Forest College in Illinois
1912	Publication of the Bross Lectures as *The Sources of Religious Insight*
1913	Lectures at Manchester College, Oxford
	Publication of *The Problem of Christianity*
1914	Appointed Alford Professor of Natural Religion, Moral Philosophy, and Civil Polity at Harvard
1916	Dies at Cambridge, Massachusetts, on September 14
	Publication of *The Hope of the Great Community*

SELECTED
BIBLIOGRAPHY

I. Josiah Royce's Major Works
(listed in order of publication)

Primer of Logical Analysis for the Use of Composition Students. San Francisco: A. L. Bancroft, 1881.

The Religious Aspect of Philosophy. Boston: Houghton Mifflin Company, 1885.

California from the Conquest in 1846 to the Second Vigilance Committee in San Francisco (1856): A Study of American Character. Boston: Houghton Mifflin Company, 1886.

The Feud of Oakfield Creek: A Novel of California Life. Boston: Houghton Mifflin Company, 1887.

The Spirit of Modern Philosophy. Boston: Houghton Mifflin Company, 1892.

The Conception of God, with "Comments" by S. E. Mezes, J. Le Conte, and G. H. Howison. Berkeley: Philosophical Union, 1895. Second Edition, including "Supplementary Essay" by Royce. New York: The Macmillan Company, 1897.

Studies of Good and Evil. New York: D. Appleton and Company, 1898.

The World and the Individual. 2 vols. New York: The Macmillan Company, 1899, 1901.

The Conception of Immortality. Boston: Houghton Mifflin Company, 1900.

Outlines of Psychology. New York: The Macmillan Company, 1903.

Herbert Spencer: An Estimate and a Review. New York: Fox, Duffield, 1904.

The Philosophy of Loyalty. New York: The Macmillan Company, 1908.

Race Questions, Provincialism, and Other American Problems. New York: The Macmillan Company, 1908.

William James and Other Essays on the Philosophy of Life. New York: The Macmillan Company, 1911.

The Sources of Religious Insight. New York: Charles Scribner's Sons, 1912.

The Problem of Christianity. 2 vols. New York: The Macmillan Company, 1913.

War and Insurance. New York: The Macmillan Company, 1914.

The Hope of the Great Community. New York: The Macmillan Company, 1916.

Lectures on Modern Idealism, ed. by J. Loewenberg. New Haven: Yale University Press, 1919.

Fugitive Essays, ed. by J. Loewenberg. Cambridge: Harvard University Press, 1920.

Royce's Logical Essays, ed. by Daniel S. Robinson. Dubuque: William C. Brown Company, 1951.

Josiah Royce's Seminar, 1913–1914: As Recorded in the Notebooks of Harry T. Costello, ed. by Grover Smith, with an essay on Royce's philosophy by Richard Hocking. New Brunswick: Rutgers University Press, 1963.

The Letters of Josiah Royce, ed. by John Clendenning. Chicago: The University of Chicago Press, 1970.

II. Recent Roycean Bibliographies

DEVAUX, ANDRÉ-A. "Bibliographie des traductions d'ouvrages de Royce et des études sur l'oeuvre de Royce." *Revue Internationale de Philosophie* 21 (1967): 159–182.

HUMBACH, KARK-THEO. "Bibliographie des Schriften von und über Royce." *Das Verhältnis von Einzelperson und Gemeinschaft nach Josiah Royce.* Heidelberg: Carl Winter Universitatsverlag, 1962: 181–206.

OPPENHEIM, FRANK M. "Bibliography of the Published Works of Josiah Royce." *Revue Internationale de Philosophie* 21 (1967): 138–158.

SKRUPSKELIS, IGNAS. "Annotated Bibliography of the Published Works of Josiah Royce." *The Basic Writings of Josiah Royce.* 2 vols. Edited by John J. McDermott. Chicago: University of Chicago Press, 1969. II:1167–1226.

III. Some Recent Books in English on the Life and Thought of Josiah Royce

BURANELLI, VINCENT. *Josiah Royce.* New York: Twayne Publishers, 1964.

COTTON, J. HARRY. *Royce on the Human Self.* Cambridge: Harvard University Press, 1954.

FUSS, PETER. *The Moral Philosophy of Josiah Royce.* Cambridge: Harvard University Press, 1965.

JARVIS, EDWARD A. *The Conception of God in the Later Royce.* The Hague: Martinus Nijhoff, 1975.

KUKLICK, BRUCE. *Josiah Royce—An Intellectual Biography.* Indianapolis: Bobbs-Merrill Co., 1972.

————. *The Rise of American Philosophy — Cambridge, Massachusetts, 1890–1930.* New Haven: Yale University Press.

MAHOWALD, MARY BRIODY. *An Idealistic Pragmatist — The Development of the Pragmatic Element in the Philosophy of Josiah Royce.* The Hague: Martinus Nijhoff, 1972.

MARCEL, GABRIEL. *Royce's Metaphysics.* Chicago: Henry Regnery Company, 1956.

MCDERMOTT, JOHN J., ed. *The Basic Writings of Josiah Royce.* 2 vols., including an annotated bibliography of the publications of Josiah Royce, prepared by Ignas K. Skrupskelis. Chicago: The University of Chicago Press, 1969.

OPPENHEIM, FRANK M. *Royce's Voyage Down Under: A Journey of the Mind.* Lexington: University Press of Kentucky, 1980.

POWELL, THOMAS F. *Josiah Royce.* New York: Washington Square Press, 1967.

ROBINSON, DANIEL SOMMER. *Royce and Hocking — American Idealists.* Boston: Christopher Publishing House, 1968.

ROTH, ROBERT J. *American Religious Philosophy.* New York: Harcourt Brace & World, 1967.

SINGH, BHAGWAN B. *The Self and the World in the Philosophy of Josiah Royce.* Springfield, Illinois: Charles C. Thomas, 1973.

SKINNER, JOHN E. *The Logocentric Predicament — An Essay on the Problem of Error in the Philosophy of Josiah Royce.* Philadelphia: University of Pennsylvania Press, 1965.

SMITH, JOHN E. *Royce's Social Infinite: The Community of Interpretation.* New York: Liberal Arts Press, 1950.

————. *The Spirit of American Philosophy.* New York: Oxford University Press, 1963.

————. *Themes in American Philosophy: Purpose, Experience, and Community.* New York: Harper Torchbooks, 1970. See also Smith's Introduction to Royce's *The Problem of Christianity.* Chicago: The University of Chicago Press, 1968.

STARR, KEVIN. *Americans and the California Dream 1850–1914.* New York: Oxford University Press, 1973.

STRATON, GEORGE D. *Theistic Faith for Our Time: An Introduction to the Process Philosophies of Royce and Whitehead.* Lanham, Maryland: University Press of America, 1978.

STROH, GUY W. *American Philosophy from Edwards to Dewey.* Princeton: D. Van Nostrand Company, Inc., 1968.

WHITTEMORE, ROBERT C. *Makers of the American Mind.* New York: Apollo Editions, 1964.

IV. Of particular interest to students of Josiah Royce are three special issues devoted to Roycean studies:

The Philosophical Review 25 (May, 1916)
The Journal of Philosophy 53 (April, 1956)
Revue Internationale de Philosophie 79–80 (1967)

INDEX